March 14   Linen for D[...]
          2 Squares of Glass
          5 Doz: of Iron Pegs   5 .. -
          5 Doz of Hooks   5 ..
          1½ Doz of Hold-fasts
          Iron rod for the frocks to hang on
          2,000 of Wall Nails
          Nails (of various sizes)
          2 pails.
          3 Scrubbing brushes
                        WHB -
19th   2 Putty Knives
          Whiting, Yellow ochre, & Glue; for
          the School Room, & Kitchen)
          2 Deals.
          2 lbs of Paint for the Music board
                                    WHB

The Real Lady Byron

The Real
Lady Byron

Joan Pierson

ROBERT HALE · LONDON

Photoset in Ehrhardt by
Derek Doyle & Associates, Mold, Clwyd.
Printed in Great Britain by
St Edmundsbury Press Ltd, Bury St Edmunds, Suffolk.
Bound by WBC Bookbinders Ltd, Bridgend, Glamorgan.

Contents

'Few are they who look to
the inside of things …
They are very different
from what they seem.
Truth comes in the last,
and very late,
limping along on the arm
of Time.'

Baltasar Gracián

List of Illustrations

Between pages 128 and 129

PICTURE CREDITS

Ferens Art Gallery, Hull City Museums and Art Galleries: 1.
National Portrait Gallery: 2, 13. The Rt Hon. the Earl of Lytton: 3,
4, 6, 12. Sotheby's: 5. British Library: 7. Guildhall Library, London:
8. The Royal Collection, St James's Palace: 9. East Sussex County
Library: 10. The Murray Collection: 11.

Acknowledgements

Other than the poet himself, there could be no happier choice for me than for Lord Byron's great-great-great-grandson to write a foreword in a book so closely concerned with his forebears. I would like to thank the Earl of Lytton most sincerely for agreeing to do this, and the Countess of Lytton for her interest and the trouble she has taken in obtaining the photographs of Seaham Hall and the cast of Lady Byron's hand.

The most significant of the sources of information I have consulted are the Lovelace Byron Papers at the Bodleian Library, Oxford, and my appreciation for permission to study them is due to their owner, the Earl of Lytton. I would like to thank Mary Clapinson, Keeper of Western Manuscripts, and other members of the staff at the Bodleian for always being ready to help.

I am indebted to the British Library and the Dr Williams Library. In particular I wish to thank Miss Gooding, the Local Historian Librarian of the Ealing Public Library, Adrian Henstock, the Principal Archivist of Nottingham Record Office, and Pamela Wood, the Keeper responsible for Newstead Abbey.

I should like to give special thanks to Peggy and Desmond Aldridge, who have been most helpful in many ways. Peggy's knowledge of Ockham, the Kings, the Lovelaces and all things relating to Byron was and continues to be impressive and of great interest.

I should also like to record my appreciation and thanks to: Gwen Beaumont, Anne Fleming, Beatrice Hanss, David Herbert, the late Lady Mander, Michael Rees and Derek Wise for giving me interesting and little known material. It would be difficult to name all the many people who have sent me items of Byronic interest from varied sources through the years. I am most grateful to everyone.

Lastly I must thank my typist, Michael, whose invaluable help and shrewd advice has in so many ways been indispensable. He was and amazingly still is my husband.

Foreword

by the Earl of Lytton
the great-great-great-grandson of Lord and Lady Byron

It can never be easy for a third party to comprehend fully the relationship between two people and the task is made more difficult by the passage of time, particularly when one has to rely on written evidence only. On the one hand Lord Byron's brilliant letters and poetry need no introduction but on the other, Lady Byron's papers and manuscript letters which on her own admission are often written in a tortuous style, are far less well known.

Whilst Lady Byron sought the advice of eminent lawyers to safeguard with great competence her and her child's interests following separation from her husband, Lord Byron's advisers gave the impression of being a good deal less careful; however, he himself possessed the most powerful weapon of all in the form of his sharp wit and pen. He used both to ridicule his wife's family and succeeded in conveying a picture of Lady Byron as cold and 'mathematical' at the same time as praising her for being 'truth itself'.

Joan Pierson has not allowed Lord Byron's literary brilliance to colour her research and in so doing dispels the impression of Lady Byron's coldness to reveal a woman of intelligence, sensitivity and loyalty. She goes on to demonstrate Lady Byron's wide-ranging interests in poetry, education and medicine as well as her competent running of the Noel Estates; furthermore, from the many contacts she made and the correspondence, it is apparent that she acquired considerable knowledge in many widely diverse subjects and was keenly interest in politics both at home and worldwide.

This book demonstrates that Lady Byron clearly strove to live according to the high moral standards in which she believed, no easy task either for her or for her circle of acquaintances having easy task either for her or for her circle of acquaintances having regard to the lax moral standards of contemporary fashionable society. It becomes clear that whilst she did not suffer fools gladly, she was generous with her considerabale wealth and lavished her affection on those around her whom she loved and cared for.

As to the brief marriage of Lord and Lady Byron, there is a refreshing impartiality in Joan Pierson's narrative. Far from seeking to find fault with either party so long after the event, she sets out to demonstrate compellingly that Byron's wonderful romantic poetry, so full of love and fun and understanding of complex emotions, was not an accurate reflection of his domestic behaviour, especially in a person of such changeable temperament at a time of intense personal and financial strain. By the same token no attempt is made to judge Lady Byron by reference to the letters written to family lawyers at the time when contemporaries describe her as looking and sounding like a shadow of her former self and convulsed in grief.

Whilst Lady Byron's literary style never acquired the 'facility of expression' to which Lord Byron exhorted her in their early correspondence, she is seen to have remained loyal and constant, characteristics which he obviously admired. Byron may have loved the company of less serious women but she was the only one whom he 'esteemed' sufficiently to have married.

Joan Pierson quotes extensively to give us a much fuller picture of Lady Byron than hitherto, not only during her undoubtedly tumultuous relationship with the poet but also long after his death. Much of the correspondence which has been passed down through my family, owes its continued existence to the diligence and foresight of successive women and I warmly welcome this long-overdue attempt to put the records straight. Joan Pierson is to be commended on the balanced manner in which she handles the emotionally charged circumstances surrounding the relationship of Lord and Lady Byron and for taking the standpoint that neither can necessarily be regarded as a reliable witness to all the facts; in doing so, she succeeds in shedding much-needed light on the largely eclipsed life of a very remarkable woman.

The Earl of Lytton
Newbuildings Place
14 May 1992

Preface

She was gentle, artless; approachable as a little child; with ready outflowing sympathy for the cares and sorrows and interests of all who approached her; with a naïve and gentle playfulness, that adorned, without hiding, the breadth and strength of her mind; and, above all, with a clear, divining, moral discrimination; yet with a mercifulness that made allowance for every weakness, and pitied every sin.

There was so much of Christ in her, that to have seen her seemed to be to have drawn near to heaven.

These words were written about Lady Byron in 1870 by Harriet Beecher Stowe, who is considered to have been one of the most important and distinguished women of the nineteenth century.

After reading many biographies of Lord Byron I began to examine what seemed to be the mandatory portrayal of Lady Byron. I found her difficult to imagine, for most people have some redeeming features, but she apparently had none. I searched long and diligently for a book that would give a more unprejudiced account of her part in circumstances which culminated in tragedy and great suffering. I supposed there must be sources of information unknown, perhaps unavailable, to me which would explain why she was so relentlessly maligned. I questioned Byron scholars but their answers were evasive and unconvincing, and they were reticent as to how they could be so sure the portrayal was just.

Perhaps it would be useful to refer to examples of the kind of treatment that Lady Byron is given in biographies of Byron, so that judgement may be made as to why a reappraisal is needed.

Among the few books not hostile to her is *Astarte* by Ralph Lovelace, the grandson of Lord and Lady Byron. *Astarte* was published in a limited edition in 1905, and with additions in 1921. But like other books that are unprejudiced, it is belittled if noticed at all, and is not easily obtainable. Ethel Colburn Mayne wrote *The Life of Lady Byron* which was published in 1929, and according to Doris Langley Moore, she had permission to consult the Lovelace Papers on condition she did justice to Lady Byron, but this justice is not immediately apparent.

The only other biography of Lady Byron is *Lord Byron's Wife* by Malcolm Elwin, published in 1962, which finishes when Lady Byron left her husband after one year of marriage. In this book four pages in the index are filled with animadversions of its subject such as: self-absorption, self-deception, self-esteem, self-justification, self-pity, smugness, spoilt child – to take a few from the 'S' section alone, but she was also 'humourless', 'egotistical', 'jealous', 'complacent' etc. With these and many other such undesirable attributes it is surprising that she attracted so many acceptable suitors, and interested the celebrated Lord Byron enough to propose to her not only once, but twice.

It is not clear how these assessments, which depend only on the author's perception of motives, can be made so positively, for it is not easy for most people to always be perfectly sure of their own reasons for their actions. How then can it be assumed with such certainty what the thoughts, intentions and feelings were of someone who was esteemed by many distinguished men and women in her lifetime. Biographies can be seductive and self-perpetuating, the truth coloured by the writer's personal bias, and what began as perhaps a disapproving remark is repeated and expanded in following accounts until it becomes established fact. A character is thus created that is distinct, memorable and hateful, but it may be false. If every harsh word written about Lady Byron be omitted or replaced by a kind one, by what criteria could this be proved less accurate? Lord Byron, it must be remembered, in speaking of his wife called her 'Truth Itself', and praised her to the end of his life, telling Lady Blessington in 1823 that he was sorry for his bitterness to her in his poetry. He said it was meant to 'spite and vex' her for not responding to his overtures after their separation. It might be thought that he would consider himself fortunate to have escaped from the displeasing person generally represented.

There must be an explanation for reputable biographers to have appeared to form a cabal for the purpose of verbally assassinating Lady Byron.

Firstly, during the last century, partly due to the prevailing change in public opinion on morality, Byron's poetry lost its general appeal and reached its nadir by the turn of the century. Efforts were made to restore him to his previous exalted status by those who had always recognized and adored his genius. Certain aspects of his life were suppressed, his letters edited before being considered for publication and strangers allied themselves in a vehement campaign against Lady Byron.

Secondly, Byron has always attracted from his supporters an extraordinary and enduring loyalty. Doris Langley Moore, his favoured biographer, owned that she fell in love with Byron when she was sixteen, and her allegiance to him was crowned by being married over his tomb in Hucknall Torkard church. A different sort of loyalty concerns Lady Seaford, a distant relative of Byron, who in recalling her meetings with him in 1823 at Genoa to her friend Lady Waldegrave, omitted an episode that Byron had confided to her during their conversation about the separation. Lady Waldegrave evidently questioned her about this and she replied: 'I did not *forget* to mention Lord B's threat of shooting Lady B but I never *told* his owning this threat as I did not like to add a stone towards hurting his memory.' This was in 1870 when she was eighty-two years old and nearly blind, but all who are familiar with Byron will understand her reticence, even forty-six years after his death.

Doris Langley Moore's love for Byron endured and perhaps was the inspiration for her biography of his daughter *Ada Countess of Lovelace* which is used as an effective vehicle for constant disparagement of Lady Byron. She is mocked: 'Different ills beset her all the way. One day it was a kidney inflammation, another the third finger of her right hand felt stiff and she supposed it would get worse.' She is ridiculed: 'There [Wiesbaden] she was obliged to contemplate the horrors of gambling. She composed an unsigned circular entreating visitors to desist from this vice ...', but the fact that it was the number of suicides due to gambling debts that shocked Lady Byron into attempting to check this tragic toll is omitted.

Omission in quoted extracts from letters is a favourite tactic skilfully employed by Doris Langley Moore, thus changing their meaning. For instance she writes that Lord Byron's grandson, Ralph Lovelace, had been so much afraid of his grandmother that he recalled in a letter written forty years later that he had never dared to speak to her fully and frankly of anything (he desired to become a Roman Catholic) but omits to say that the letter continued: '... She really did understand my state of mind in religion and humoured me a good deal, for she had personally a very friendly feeling to Catholics and the bitterest contempt for No Popery, being above all a Christian'. Lady Byron is accused of refusing to give a reference for her maid through pique but what is omitted is that stolen goods were found in the maid's trunk when it was searched by the bailiffs.

Her friends are dismissed as 'sycophantic bores because first rate people usually had independent pastimes and were not likely to place themselves at her beck and call'. Even her death could not be unalloyed for it is stated that 'the cause of her death was given as 'ossification of the lungs' ... Nowadays ossification – otherwise petrifaction – is a disease unrecognized'. According to her death certificate Lady Byron died of pleurisy and bronchitis. Doris Langley Moore, with reason, was well satisfied with the portrait of Lady Byron that she achieved in her biography of Ada. 'I cannot think anything would astonish her more than that she now seems to deserve a harsher verdict than the betrayed and subjected Augusta', she wrote, and she did not think that Lady Byron's reputation was likely to emerge from the shade cast over it.

My purpose has not been to give a verdict, but to provide what does not seem to exist, a different interpretation to many aspects of Lady Byron's life than that generally accepted, and the following pages comprise the kind of book for which I searched in vain. Byron told his wife that had she accepted his first proposal, he would have written no more poetry. Like Byron, she must have regretted her refusal, but should not posterity be grateful?

Lady Byron's spirit is doubtless resigned to the criticism she has continually endured, but Lord Byron's unruly spirit could be in turmoil at some of the misinterpretations that have been made through loyalty to him. He had told his friend Thomas Moore, to whom he had given his memoirs: '... and above *all, contradict* anything if I have *mis*-stated: for my first object is the truth, even at my expense'.

1   *Annabella Milbanke*

On 14 May 1824 the news became known in England that the poet Lord Byron was dead. Jane Welsh wrote to her future husband Thomas Carlyle that, 'If they had said the sun or the moon was gone out of the heavens, it could not have struck me with the idea of a more awful and dreary blank in the creation than the words: Byron is dead.' In a far continent, a girl of thirteen called Harriet Beecher, devastated by the calamity, ran to a lonely hillside to pray for him. As the news spread a profound feeling of universal loss prevailed throughout the civilized world, encompassing the mighty and learned, as well as common men and woman of all ages. Edward Bulwer summarized this widespread reaction in the words: 'So much of us died with him, that the notion of his death had something of the unnatural, of the impossible.'

In view of his previous disgrace and exile it is not easy at first to understand the swift change in public mood. Neither is it easy to visualize him since many of his contemporaries who knew him well have testified that his portraits do not do him justice, and are very little like him. Coleridge said of Byron: 'So beautiful a countenance I scarcely ever saw … his eyes the open portals of the sun – …'. Jane Porter, famous for writing historical romances, wrote of his voice: 'I was not aware of his being in the room, or even that he had been invited, when I was arrested … by the Sounds of the most melodious Speaking Voice I had ever heard. …' His supreme mastery of words and his flair in expressing deep emotions simply, had the effect of making others relate to them, feeling they were their own. His remarkable fascination and magnetism had attracted all kinds of people to him and was never surpassed. Goethe said: 'The like would never come again.' It seemed unbelievable and terrible that a being of such legendary fame could be extinguished without warning and the world continue. However many accounts of Byron's last hours are read, it never ceases to be moving. Perhaps Edward Bulwer's words are fitting, and we weep, as they wept then, for ourselves.

Among those who grieved was one the world forgot, a small, serious-minded woman who Byron had said would always appear a lady even to her personal maid. He called her Bell but she was given the names Anne Isabella by her parents, which were soon shortened to Annabella.

She was probably the only girl who met Lord Byron in that heady year of 1812 when he first became famous, who would have turned down his proposal of marriage. The waltz had just been introduced and, in spite of disapproval by some people, was the rage of the season. Byron did not favour it because he was lame and unable to join in, but it was at Caroline Lamb's morning waltzing party on 25 March that he first saw Annabella Milbanke. She was repelled by him, rather than attracted as everyone else seemed to be, for there was a show-off quality about his manner, and 'the poetry I had admired & even loved, lost its charm under the personality of its Author', she later wrote. She declined an invitation to be introduced to him, as well as the offer of his carriage, which he made on overhearing there was a difficulty with her own.

The next time she saw him was at a party given by Lady Cowper and this time she was introduced because she had been told that Byron attributed his 'personal defect', for he was very conscious of his lameness, to her evident lack of enthusiasm to meet him. However his first words to her were: 'I wonder to see *you* where there is not one who dares to look into himself,' and these words at once excited her interest for Annabella was prone to introspection herself, and would be only too ready to look into Byron if he would allow her to. She later wrote in her narrative of this period: 'Wherever I met him the character of his communication with me was that of a confiding intuition (This is very difficult to express – as if he had said "I know we think alike of all this").' In 1813 she overheard him say at a supper party: 'Thank God I have not a friend in the World.' Her silent response was 'you *have*'. She did not question his solitary state but 'vowed in secret to be a devoted friend to this lone being'.

In later years he described his first impressions of her. She was slender and small. 'Exquisitely finished ... her figure perfect for her height.' By comparison he said that her cousin by marriage, Caroline Lamb, had scarcely any personal attractions and her figure, though 'genteel', was too thin to be good. He continued: 'There was something piquant and what we term pretty in Miss Milbanke. Her features were small and feminine, though not regular. She had the fairest skin imaginable, there was a simplicity, a retired modesty about her which was very characteristic, and formed a happy contrast to the cold artificial formality and studied stiffness, which is called fashion.' She had an aura of purity which he had not met with before, and when she spoke, she was direct and unaffected in her manner. He listened and noticed the quality of truth in what she said. He knew that he interested her but she did not favour or flatter him like others she observed, 'who were absurdly courting him, and trying to *deserve* the lash of his satire'.

Annabella wrote often and at some length to her mother making many comments about him; in her journal she noted that he was very handsome and 'Lord Byron is without exception of young or old more agreeable in conversation than any person I ever knew.'

Annabella was born on 17 May 1792. Since the house the Milbankes were rebuilding at Seaham would not be finished in time, her birth took place at Elemore Hall near Durham, the home of their friends George Baker and his wife Isabella. They named her Anne, after her royal godmother the Duchess of Cumberland, and Isabella after Mrs Baker. Her parents, in spite of many hopes and subsequent disappointments, had waited fifteen years and nine months before their first and only child was born. Her mother Judith, born in 1751, was the eldest daughter of Sir Edward Noel of Kirkby Mallory Hall in Leicestershire, who had become the first Viscount Wentworth in 1762. Judith had one older brother, Thomas Noel, and two younger sisters, Elizabeth and Sophia. Their mother died in 1761 when Judith was ten and Mary Noel, an unmarried sister of her father, brought up the four children as if they were her own. She was very fond of them all but Judith was her best-beloved, her 'First Darling'. Annabella's father, Ralph Milbanke, was the eldest son of Sir Ralph Milbanke, the sixth Baronet of Halnaby Hall in Yorkshire. Ralph and Judith were married at Kirkby Mallory in 1777, and it is very obvious from the many letters Judith wrote to her aunt Mary Noel, that they were a devoted couple, and that it was, an unusual event for those days, a very happy marriage.

Ten years before Annabella was born, Judith's sister, Sophia Curzon, died and immediately Sophy, one of her two children, who was then three years old, was taken home by Judith and Ralph and became in every way their treasured little daughter. In Judith's letters to Mary Noel there were always enthusiastic accounts of Sophy's accomplishments and charms, for she always enjoyed having the child near her '... she has a little playfellow in the house with her ... they are now with me and making such a noise I scarcely know what I am writing ...'. When the Milbankes visited Scarborough 'we must travel by easy stages for fear of over fatiguing my sweet little companion' Sophy was taken to the Rooms to see the dancing, and was properly impressed by 'Uckle Mils' performance and he repeated her 'bon mots' to his friends as if he were her father. She had other qualities too, for Judith reported to her aunt that 'the first field of Wheat she saw Sophy said what nice Grass it was, which proves her to be a Person of Observation'. Her brother Nathaniel was looked after by his grandparents Lord and Lady Scarsdale and he and other children were always welcome at the Milbankes' home. Judith liked children and when she had her own baby it did not lessen her devotion to Sophy.

From 1798 Mary Anne Clermont looked after Annabella as her nursemaid, and later as her governess and became devoted to her charge. She was an educated young woman, and had entered the Milbanke household as Judith's maid in 1789, her address then being Princes Street, Cavendish Square, London. Although unmarried she was known by the courtesy title of Mrs Clermont and she became a close friend and confidante of the family.

The Milbankes lived in the relatively modest house at Seaham in preference to the large Hall at Halnaby inherited by Ralph on his father's death in 1798, which was also too expensive for them to have maintained throughout the year. However they visited Halnaby regularly, and entertained many guests of diverse description, including Sarah Siddons who became a regular correspondent, and the delicate Mary Montgomery, whose parents were dead and through her long and frequent visits became Annabella's oldest, if not dearest friend.

Annabella was brought up to be concerned for others, and to appreciate her own comfortable and happy life. Her parents set her a good example and in later years her recollections of this period describe the personal association she was taught to have with workers and tenants:

If in a small village, you cannot go out of the gates without seeing the children of a few Families playing on the Green, till they become 'familiar faces', you need not be *taught* to care for their well-being. A heart must be hard indeed that could be indifferent to little Jenny's having the Scarlet Fever, or to Johnny's having lost his mother. ... Among the many interests that engaged the zealous good offices of my parents, I never saw any preferred to the comfort of the labouring poor. It then seemed to me as a mere matter of course that the best horse should be sent many miles for the best Doctor, to attend on Rustics who are usually consigned to the Parish Medical Officer – that the finest claret should be taken out of the cellar to be applied to the exhausted Patients in the Tenants house. I did not think that property could be possessed by any other tenure than that of being at the service of those in need. It was all so simple! Yet my mother put a spirit into it – she did not leave it to servants. She saw that the execution was as good as the Intention.

Judith was very up-to-date in medical knowledge and tried to persuade the villagers to have their babies inoculated, as she herself had done with her own child. Her zeal had led to a little difficulty with Lady Curzon, Nathaniel's grandmother, who had resented Judith's well-meant attempt to pass on first-hand information and experience and nor did she have much success with the villagers. She took a lively interest in all matters concerning their tenants and tried to help them with their domestic problems, including those regarding virtue. When any of her servants became pregnant Judith would investigate the matter; seducers were encouraged to regularize the relationship, in which case the couple would be helped in every way possible. Annabella continues in her description of life at Seaham: 'The moral standard by which they were judged was very indulgent. A girl's first false step was, in some cases, considered as a claim to greater instead of less kindness: 'we must make the best of what can't be undone' was the spirit in which transgressors were treated. ...'

Judith's mind was informed on many and various subjects, and the liberalism of her views was advanced for her period. She was at the same time entertaining, and her letters are interesting in their vivid description of her and her husband's successful social life. She was a good shot and played whist with skill, liking to play for high stakes. She never forgot the care her aunt had given them all when they were children and wrote often to her, always careful to see that she did not want for anything. Judith was with her aunt

when she died in 1802 and was very upset at her death. She was a
great help to her husband in his political career for he had become
a Whig MP in 1790 and remained so until 1812. Sir Ralph
Milbanke was a bluff, good-natured, jolly man, conscientious in his
Parliamentary duties and later became involved in trying to
improve the prevailing unhealthy sanitary conditions for the poor
and gave strong support to William Wilberforce in Parliament, for
his work in reform and the abolition of slavery. To be associated
with the welfare of the oppressed at that time needed courage and
determination.

Annabella was a serious and intelligent child who enjoyed
learning. She could read before she was five and the range of her
reading was formidable even at an early age. She was particularly
good at mathematics and had the advantage of studying astronomy
and mathematics under the distinguished reformer and scientific
writer William Frend of Jesus College, Cambridge, whom her
parents had known for many years. He was noted for his
unorthodox views and distaste for dogma and through their many
discussions on such matters as education and social reform, the
idea of freedom of thought had been instilled in Annabella from an
early age. She was duly instructed in all the skills and
accomplishments thought proper for a young lady to learn prior to
being launched into society, which mysteriously included the art of
making shoes. William Frend calculated it cost three or four times
as much to make your own shoes as to buy them from the most
expensive shoemakers.

There was always plenty for Annabella to do, such as drawing,
book collecting and writing poetry. She was very fond of riding,
and while on her horse many feats of heroism and deeds of courage
were performed in her imagination. A magazine was compiled by
her with much enthusiasm, which contained an advertisement for
'Messrs Milbanke and Clermonts' superior style of cutting shoes
for ladies of fashion.' She wrote numerous letters, not always in her
native tongue it would appear, since her uncle, Lord Wentworth,
wrote to Judith: 'Tell Annabella that altho' she is such a proficient
in Latin & French, some good plain English in a letter to an
Affectionate Uncle will be most acceptable.' There must have been
reform for a year later he wrote: 'Annabella's letters are capital
ones indeed, & I wish you would unknown to her send me a list of
such Books as she will most like.'

There were many visitors, particularly from friends who had

children, and Judith much preferred to stay with people when Annabella had also been invited. In the evenings there would be amateur dramatics, card games such as cribbage, or chess and musical recitals when her father played the violin and her mother the piano. She was certainly not a lonely 'only child' and was never brought down from nursery quarters to be exhibited in the requisite short visit to the drawing-room, as was customary in that period. It is unlikely that she was greatly spoilt since Judith, although always deeply grateful for her 'blessing' that she had ceased to hope for, had too positive an outlook to over-indulge her child.

Her dancing master said that since he had started to teach dancing 'he never saw such a first lesson' and she soon became an accomplished and graceful dancer who enjoyed social occasions. However, underneath the sophisticated veneer her nature was shy and she lacked confidence; these characteristics she was never to lose, and although they were masked they were sometimes mistaken for arrogance or priggishness. When Annabella was seven the whole family went to London and Hoppner painted a charming picture of her, a serious little girl gracefully dancing in a pretty dress.

Annabella was desolate when Sophy left them to get married in 1800. The misery of her loss was 'insupportable' but she was too diffident to express it, afraid that no one would understand and she would be rebuffed, so these feelings were kept hidden. In 1801 Judith had anxiously left Annabella with Aunt Mary Noel in London for a short spell, but Judith's concern was unnecessary, and Annabella flourished. Several of Mary Noel's friends had been to visit her '... but really to see my dear Companion; she was in high Spirits & shewed off in her best manner & sent them all away enchanted'.

Sometimes Annabella accompanied her parents on their political expeditions. When Judith, an enthusiastic Whig, addressed a political meeting in 1803, Annabella, then aged eleven, was present to comment, appraise and record; although encouraging in her judgement of her mother's performance she established her own independence in thought: '... as it is I remain an impartial Tory'.

One of her interests was the poet Joseph Blackett, who had been a cobbler. The Milbankes encouraged him in his writing and provided him with a cottage in Seaham under their 'benevolent protection and patronage'. Annabella had shown him some of her verses and she was very impressed with his, thinking they compared favourably with Burns' poetry. He died in 1810 at the age of twenty-three. He had given Annabella a copy of some of his poems, and the following extract from a letter to her mother indicates that the Milbankes' kindness was appreciated.

> November 23rd, 1809
> Your Ladyship's generous zeal in contributing so largely to my happiness and welfare has been such as to render me incapable of thanking you as I ought, yet believe me Madam, the many liberal kindnesses you have shown me, the hospitalities I have received from Sir Ralph, and the friendly countenance of the truly amiable Miss Milbanke shall ever be remembered with grateful respect. They are indelibly stampt on my heart. ...

Byron, however, wrote of him scornfully in *English Bards and Scotch Reviewers* which had been published earlier in the year:

> *When some brisk youth, the tenant of a stall,*
> *Employs a pen less pointed than his awl,*
> *Leaves his snug shop, forsakes his store of shoes,*
> *St. Crispin quits and cobbles for the Muse,*
> *Heavens! how the vulgar stare! how crowds applaud!*
> *How ladies read, and Literati laud!*

A case of injured pride perhaps, for no crowds had yet applauded Byron.

Sir Ralph Milbanke had been a Member of Parliament for the county of Durham since 1790, and it was customary for the family to go to London every year. Annabella reached the age of seventeen with no desire to do the London season, but in March 1810 she went with her mother for the purpose of, as one biographer describes, 'Placing herself as decently as possible on the marriage market'. If this indeed was the object, he neglected to add that she was extraordinarily successful, in spite of the unattractive qualities he gives her, such as egoism, pedantry, pomposity, preference of mixing with social inferiors so that she could condescend to them, and many others. She must have had compensating attractions, for she was to have many suitors.

One of these was George Eden, who proposed in 1811 and was often seen with her at parties. He would seem to have been a very suitable candidate for her hand since their families knew each other well. He was then twenty-six, a practising barrister and a Member of Parliament. Three years later he succeeded to his father's title of Lord Auckland, and he proceeded to enjoy a brilliant career during which he became First Lord of the Admiralty and a Governor General of India. However Annabella was not in love with him and in his reply to her refusal he wrote: 'I dreamt a dream of happiness and presumptuously attempted to realize it ... I will try to forget it all. Be a friend to my mother and to my sisters. I have taught them to love you and they need not unlearn it ...'.

Annabella had previously stayed at Eden Farm, the Aucklands' home near Beckenham, and after Lady Auckland learned of the refusal of her son she wrote to Annabella:

From the time of your visit we had certainly blinded ourselves. And the conversation we had had together during that short stay had convinced us that the family that might obtain you would possess a great blessing. As to our own beloved Georgie's sentiments, he has spoken for himself, whether he has the strength of mind to accept of that friendship so kindly offered ... His affectionate kindness to us all endears him so much to his family, that there is no sacrifice we would not make to save him one pang ... As to Lord Auckland and myself we so warmly admire what you have permitted us to know of a character so far beyond what any of your years possess that it will be a real grief to us should our intercourse cease here. ...

She continues by saying how much they hope Annabella will visit them again at some future time. It is plain that the whole family regretted that she would not become one of them, and George Eden never married.

Another admirer that year was Lord Seaforth's son William Frederick Mackenzie. 'I like Mr Mackenzie particularly and danced with him the only country dance ... the waltzing was most prevalent ...', she wrote to her mother. In her Auto-description she said of the year 1811:

I met with one or two who, like myself, did not appear absorbed in the present scene and who interested me in a degree. I had a wish to find amongst men the character I had often imagined – but I found only parts of it. One gave proofs of worth, but had no sympathy for high aspirations – another seemed full of affection towards his family, and yet he valued the world.

Annabella was nineteen when she came again to London in 1812 after some discord at home which had been traumatic both to her parents and herself. Although she admired and respected her mother, she had often found her very trying. Annabella was by no means immune from the feelings of irritation, guilt and friction that so often exist between mother and daughter. Moreover she had a very quick temper which she had only partly learned to suppress. There had been times when she had wanted to be in London with Mary Montgomery, her friend of long standing, who it was thought had not long to live; but she knew her parents missed her when she was away and wished her to remain with them in Seaham where her father too was ill. On this occasion there had been a particularly acrimonious discussion and Annabella wrote a letter to her mother the next morning, 9 February:

> I express myself in writing ... because I want to *collect* my sentiments in order to make them known to you & my father.
>   I am perfectly aware of the great effort you make in sacrificing to me not only your wish for my presence, but your fears for my absence. I regard it as an extraordinary proof of *disinterested* affection, and hope that the remembrance of it will prevent me from ever again indulging my irritable humours at the expense of your feelings ... I cannot express how calm & contented my mind has become since your kindness last night.

Was this indulging in an 'orgasm of self-justification' as it has been called by her biographer, or was it simply a girl of nineteen trying to clear her own mind as to where her duties and priorities should lie, and to let her parents understand that she did not want to seem selfish or uncaring towards them. These conflicts of conscience and guilt relating to parents are timeless and are known to most people.

Annabella had an affinity with her father and did not feel she was under scrutiny as she did with her mother, so that she was more relaxed with him. In a letter to her old friend Hugh, Mary Montgomery's brother, it is somewhat surprising to read: '... When my Dad and I get tipsy together, our toast is always "Friends far away" ...'. She looked forward to receiving his 'pot hooks' as she called his letters and was not bored by his stories. She was amused at his little jokes about fleas and lice, and in return told him about the ladies at the Lord Mayor's Ball who gathered up their skirts before being seated: 'Till I was acquainted with this custom I thought the action had rather a suspicious appearance.'

After peace was restored Annabella departed from Seaham on 21 February and conscientiously wrote to her parents on each of the four days travelling to London, where she stayed with their old family friends Lord and Lady Gosford. Judith fretted about her and Annabella wrote reassuringly: 'If I should die, Aird [her maid] will instantly inform you, and I have bequeathed her fifteen new pens for the purpose.'

Mary Gosford was seven years older than Annabella but they became and remained very close friends, Mary being the 'M.G.' in Annabella's correspondence. This time Annabella had acquired enough self-confidence to enjoy herself. She went to concerts, sometimes with her aunt, Sir Ralph Milbanke's only sister Lady Melbourne, but she was slow to appreciate music: 'I most firmly believe that I have no love of music.' However, she loved dancing and often recorded after a ball that she had 'stayed till Sunrise'. Her father had to give up his parliamentary duties and curtail social events because of his ill-health and it was rumoured that he was ruined and had lost much of his property by funding elections in twenty-two years of 'Whiggery'.

She went with Mrs George Lamb, Lady Melbourne's daughter-in-law, to hear Thomas Campbell's first lecture in a series on poetry at the Royal Institution, and in June attended the last one. 'Lord Byron sat before me at this lecture and when Campbell introduced the mention of Religion, he writhed himself into the strangest positions, perhaps embarrassed by the consciousness that many eyes were fixed on him.' He had already seen some poems Annabella had written and shown to Caroline Lamb, who without Annabella's knowledge had passed them to Byron. Caroline was related to Annabella by marriage, being the wife of William Lamb (later Lord Melbourne), the eldest son of Lady Melbourne, Annabella's aunt. Byron's opinion was favourable.

My Dear Lady Caroline,
    I have read over the few poems of Miss Milbanke with attention. They display fancy, feeling, & a little practice would very soon

induce facility of expression. – Though I have an abhorrence of
Blank verse, I like the lines on Dermondy so much that I wish they
were in rhyme. – The lines in the cave at Seaham have a turn of
thought which I cannot sufficiently commend & here I am at least
candid as my own opinions differ upon such subjects. – The first
stanza is very good indeed & the others with a few slight alterations
might be rendered equally excellent. ... She certainly is a very
extraordinary girl, who would imagine so much strength & variety of
thought under that placid countenance?

He goes on to say that a friend of his, fifty years old and an
author, was more enthusiastic even than him and thought her
verses were beautiful. It was characteristic of Byron to be kind and
encouraging when he was asked for his opinion of the work of
amateur poets, but here his optimism seems misplaced for she was
rarely to achieve the 'facility of expression' to which he alluded.

Annabella was painted by Hayter for a miniature to give to her
parents. He was just becoming known and although not much
older than she was, he was able to sense her shyness and
self-consciousness, and decided she should pose with her long
brown hair loose around her shoulders to give an air of informality.
She wrote woefully to her friend Lady Gosford that he had never
seen her countenance 'because it is under the depressing influence
of shyness'.

She had many eligible suitors that year. Amongst them was
Augustus Foster, the son of the Duchess of Devonshire by her first
husband; Lord Jocelyn, Treasurer of the Household to the Prince
Regent; General Pakenham, Lord Longford's eldest son; William
Bankes, a friend of Byron's at Cambridge, who had called so often
that she had 'some idea of returning his cards to him, for his own
pocket's sake'; Frederick Douglas, the only son and heir of Lord
Glenbervie; and the diplomat Stratford Canning who, his
biographer wrote, became deeply depressed following Annabella's
refusal.

However, eclipsing all others by far was the most interesting
man she had ever met, to whom she dreamed of becoming a
faithful friend; the brilliant and disturbing Lord Byron.

2   Lord Byron

The childhood of George Gordon Byron was very different from the comfortable and secure environment that surrounded Annabelle Milbanke and helps to explain the turbulence and instability of his nature.

His mother was of royal descent, from a daughter of James I of Scotland and the Earl of Huntly, and was the only child and heiress of George Gordon of Gight. After their marriage Captain Byron proceeded to get through her fortune with as much speed as he had that of his first wife. While married to the Marquis of Carmarthen, heir to the Duchy of Leeds, Lady Carmarthen had met the handsome John Byron, with whom she soon fell in love, and deserted her husband and children to elope with him. When a divorce was granted, she and John Byron were married. Their union lasted five years, ending in her death after giving birth to their daughter Augusta.

Captain Byron thereupon returned to England with many debts and in the elegant town of Bath met and married Miss Catherine Gordon in 1785. She was just twenty years old, had inherited the fiery Gordon temperament, but loved John Byron to distraction and could refuse him nothing. After two years they returned to France to escape from creditors and were joined in Paris by Catherine's stepdaughter Augusta, now aged three and a half. Soon after Augusta became dangerously ill, and Catherine, in advanced pregnancy, nursed the child devotedly, while her husband dallied with his fashionable friends. In later years Catherine reminded Augusta of this time: 'I still recollect with a degree of horror the many *sleepless* nights and days of *agony*, I have passed by your bedside drowned in tears, while you lay insensible and at the gates of death.'

When the child was better Mrs Byron left her husband in France, and returned to England with Augusta who was handed over to her grandmother Lady Holderness.

Byron was born in Holles Street, London, on 22 January 1788. His mother knew few people in England and arrangements were made for her confinement by her solicitor's wife. The baby was born with a deformed right foot, the cause of which has been a matter for controversy ever since, despite immediate attention from John Hunter, the famous surgeon who specialized in malformities of the Achilles tendon.

As soon as she could she went with her child to Aberdeen, where she could live more cheaply and be among her own people. Captain Byron joined his wife and attempted to get even more money from her. Gight Castle had been sold, and just enough money was secured from the sale to give Mrs Byron an annual income of £150 – later reduced to £135 to pay off urgent debts. They quarrelled constantly and at one time Captain Byron lived at one end of a street, while Mrs Byron lived at the other. He soon returned to France, there being no more money to extract from his wife. His debts soared, he was embroiled in scandal and he reached the lowest depths of degradation before he died when Byron was three years old. His death might seem to have been a good thing for Mrs Byron but she had loved him and was deeply upset.

Byron, from an early age, was difficult and rebellious. While he was living in Aberdeen his father told the nurse he would like to have his son to stay for a little while. Mrs Byron demurred, but the nurse advised her to agree, since she was sure he would not wish to repeat the visit. And so it was – the child being returned very promptly the next morning. On another occasion he had a childish tantrum and ripped his clothes from top to bottom. At his infant school he often fought the other children. He constantly fell out with his nurse and among the souvenirs of his life in Aberdeen was an old china saucer out of which he had bitten a large piece. Yet at other times he could be gentle, affectionate and companionable, and he did well at school. His reading before he left Aberdeen Grammar School was prodigious: 'I could never bear to read any Poetry whatever without disgust and reluctance,' he recalled later, and one of the first books that gave him pleasure was Knolles's *Turkish History* – 'I believe it had much influence on my subsequent wishes to visit the Levant, and gave perhaps, the oriental colouring which is observed in my poetry.'

At the age of ten, following the death of his great uncle, he became the sixth Lord Byron and inherited Newstead Abbey in Nottinghamshire, the home of his Byron ancestors. Unfortunately it had been allowed to deteriorate, and the income from rents in no way equalled the amount that had to be spent repairing the neglected farm buildings and priory. In August 1798 Mrs Byron, having sold her few possessions, left Scotland with her son, to inspect the derelict property and start a new life in England. It was at this time that a friend of Mrs Byron's from Aberdeenshire recommended John Hanson of Chancery Lane to her, and as her solicitor he proceeded to handle her affairs and those of her son. Thus started the association which was to last through many vicissitudes for the rest of their lives.

Hanson induced Byron's kinsman, the Earl of Carlisle, to act as Byron's guardian to which he reluctantly consented. It was decided that Byron was not receiving proper treatment for his deformed foot in Nottingham, and he should go to London to see the famous Dr Baillie. Mrs Byron, in spite of her poverty, had always obtained what was considered the best advice and treatment available. This was often protracted and painful, and mostly useless. It was also decided he should attend, as a boarder, a small school in Dulwich run by Dr Glennie.

Mrs Byron is generally depicted as being hotheaded and given to upsetting people, and in particular at this time she found Lord Carlisle, Dr Glennie and Mr Hanson especially difficult to deal with. Perhaps she refused to meekly acquiesce in all the tiresome plans these gentlemen proposed. Lord Carlisle always had as little to do with Byron as possible, and in 1809 Byron's request to be introduced by him to the House of Lords was churlishly ignored. Mr Hanson was to prove dilatory to the point of negligence. It is largely due to Dr Glennie that the derogatory picture of Mrs Byron is given through the years in so many biographies, for when Thomas Moore, the poet and Byron's great friend, was asked to write Byron's biography six years after his death, he wrote to Dr Glennie for his recollections of his famous pupil. Dr Glennie replied:

He was playful, good humoured and beloved by his companions. His reading in history and poetry was far beyond the usual standard for his age, and in my study he found many books open to him, both to please his taste and gratify his curiosity; among others a set of our poets from Chaucer to Churchill, which I am most tempted to say he had more than once pursued from beginning to end. He showed at this age an intimate acquaintance with the historical parts of the Holy Scriptures, upon which he seemed delighted to converse with me, especially after our religious exercises of a Sunday evening ... Mrs Byron was a total stranger to English Society and English manners; with an exterior far from prepossessing, an understanding where nature had not been more bountiful, a mind almost wholly without cultivation, and the peculiarities of northern opinions, northern habits and northern accents, I trust I do no great prejudice to the memory of my countrywoman, if I say Mrs Byron was not a Madame de Lambert, endowed with powers to retrieve the fortune, and form the character and manners of a young nobleman, her son.

Mrs Byron had in fact achieved a great deal in restoring order to Newstead Abbey, in spite of her very limited resources, and she was far from being uncultivated. Wherever she visited, she attended plays and belonged to the circulating library. Byron wrote some of his most interesting letters to his mother when he was abroad, which quite surpassed the call of duty. In 1808 she told him he was like Rousseau, which was perceptive of her – not that he appreciated this: 'I do not know that I resemble Jean Jacques Rousseau. I have no ambition to be like so illustrious a madman'. Madame de Staël made the same comparison in 1813, and the *Edinburgh Review* referred to this affinity in 1818: 'There are two writers in modern literature whose extraordinary power over the minds of men, it may be truly said, has existed less in their works than in themselves – Rousseau and Lord Byron.' But Mrs Byron said it first.

A bed had been put in Dr Glennie's study for Byron to sleep in, and he was therefore a captive audience for the interminable discussions which Dr Glennie thought so beneficial to his pupil. To have read all that Dr Glennie maintained that he did, Byron must have spent much of his time at school in reading, which Mrs Byron presumably felt could have been used more profitably in other areas of education. In 1801 when he left the school after two years, he was found to be far below the usual standard for entry into Harrow school, which had been selected for him.

Newstead Abbey was let to a tenant called Lord Grey de Ruthyn in 1803. Mrs Byron moved to lodgings in Nottingham and in the

next year to a house called Burgage Manor at the top end of the
village green in Southwell. Here, in the summer holidays of 1804,
discord between mother and son reached distressing proportions.
Byron had become impossible to control. Even at Harrow he was
not amenable to any kind of discipline. He remembered himself as
he was at that time in the journal he wrote in 1813: 'I differed not
at all from other children, being neither tall nor short, dull nor
witty, of my age, but rather lively – except in my sullen moods and
then I was always a Devil.'

Many instances are given of Byron's unpredictable behaviour.
He caused so much trouble at Harrow during his last year 1804–5
that Dr Drury, the headmaster, did not want him to return, and
suggested that he went to a private tutor for his final preparation
for university. However, Dr Drury relented and Byron returned for
the next term, but it was to be a time of continuous violence and
insolence on his part. At the same time, in between these
outbursts, he would show the lovable side of his nature, and
indications of the charm, brilliance and wit that were later to
captivate London society.

His friendships at Harrow were tempestuous, and were mostly
with boys younger than himself. Among these were Lord Clare,
Lord Delawarr, the Duke of Dorset, John Wingfield, William
Harness and Edward Noel Long. In his notebooks written years
later he wrote: 'My school friends were with me *passions* (for I was
always violent) but I do not know that there is one that has endured
(to be sure some have been cut short by death) till now.' In *The Life
of Rev. William Harness* there is the following reference to Lord
Delawarr written not long after his death: 'I believe there was no
actual quarrel with Byron. It was simply a case of incompatibility.
The ardour of B. was more than D. could adequately meet.'

Girls too had inspired his passion, and he was unable to explain
the intensity of his feelings. His first love had been, before he was
eight years old, his distant cousin Mary Duff. In the journal that he
wrote in 1813 he recounted his early emotions:

> I have been thinking lately a good deal of Mary Duff. How very odd
> that I should have been so utterly, devotedly fond of that girl, at an
> age when I could neither feel passion, nor know the meaning of the
> word. And the effect! ... I remember, too, our walks, and the
> happiness of sitting by Mary, in the children's apartment at their

house not far from the Plain-Stones at Aberdeen, while her lesser
sister Helen played with her doll, and we sat gravely making love, in
our way. How the deuce did all this occur so early? Where could it
originate? I certainly had no sexual ideas for years afterwards; and
yet my misery, my love for that girl were so violent, that I sometimes
doubt if I have ever been really attached since. Be that as it may,
hearing of her marriage several years after was like a thunder-stroke
– it nearly choked me – to the horror of my mother and the
astonishment and almost incredulity of everybody ... and lately, I
know not why, the *recollection* (*not* the attachment) has recurred as
forcibly as ever.

Possibly this early love showed good judgement, for Mary Duff
became Mrs Mary Cockburn and was said to be 'extremely
beautiful, full of grace, extremely kind with some mixture of proud
serenity'.
    Another youthful love was for his cousin: 'My first dash into
poetry was as early as 1800. It was the ebullition of a passion for my
first cousin, Margaret Parker ... My passion had its usual effects
upon me – I could not sleep – I could not eat – I could not rest ...'.
    Even more serious was his love for his neighbour Mary
Chaworth when he was fifteen and she seventeen and already
bespoken to John Musters. Byron called her the Morning Star of
Annesley and was affected again by passionate and restless energy,
which caused him to miss a whole term from Harrow school.
    There was possibly another attachment while Byron was at
Harrow. He wrote to his mother telling her that he had been
troubled about a young woman who was a favourite of his friend
Curzon. Curzon died and after his death the young woman found
herself pregnant, and declared that Byron was the father. He
assured his mother that this was not the case, but believing that
Curzon was indeed the father, he wished the child should be
brought up with all possible care and entreated his mother to take
care of it. She answered with kindness and said she would willingly
receive the child as soon as it was born. However, the infant died
almost immediately. Thomas Moore, his friend and biographer,
says he was told this story by a person to whom Mrs Byron
communicated the circumstances. The poem 'To My Son', signed
'B. 1807' was written about two years later. Probably not many
mothers in Mrs Byron's circumstances would have reacted to this
request with such generosity.

During the time he was at Harrow Byron became acquainted with his half-sister Augusta. Understandably Lady Holderness had wanted nothing to do with the wife of the man who had seduced her only child, and Augusta became wholly estranged from her father's family. When Lady Holderness died in 1801, Mrs Byron sent a letter of condolence to Augusta and suggested the past was forgotten. She was to regret this friendly overture.

Thus started a casual acquaintance between Augusta and Byron, until she became his most frequent correspondent. He wrote telling her in terms of unreserved intimacy and passionate prejudice, all the shortcomings of his life in Southwell, and in particular of his troubles with his mother. Augusta was four years older than Byron, and already engaged to her cousin George Leigh. It might have been supposed that as an older half-sister she would try to pour oil on troubled waters, in view of the debt she owed Mrs Byron for her care when she was a child. Augusta, however, threw herself into fuelling the estrangements between mother and son, and even intrigued with Mr Hanson against Mrs Byron, who realized the disturbing influence Augusta was having on Byron, but was powerless to prevent it.

It seems unjust, in view of the evidence that no one could control Byron at this time, that Mrs Byron, who had to bear the responsibility and worry of her son alone, with very little money should be so often condemned as an unsatisfactory mother. One biographer wrote of her '... a woman of violent ungovernable temper, the most injudicious, most unliveable with of recorded mothers'. Moreover Moore says that Byron 'Notwithstanding the abuse which evidently more in sport than seriousness he lavishes in the course of these letters upon Southwell, he was in after years, taught to feel that the hours which he has passed in this place were far more happy than any he had known afterwards.' By October 1811 Byron was enthusiastically recommending it to his kinsman Robert Dallas as a very desirable place to live.

In October 1805, Byron entered Trinity College, Cambridge. Here he led the life style of most of the undergraduates of the time – drinking, socializing and making friends. He dressed flamboyantly, was obsessed with his appearance, and endured a strict diet in order to look pale, thin and interesting. He behaved eccentrically and kept a tame bear.

Among his friends at Cambridge were John Cam Hobhouse, Edward Noel Long, whom he had known at Harrow, Scrope

Berdmore Davies, Francis Hodgson, William Bankes and the brilliant Charles Skinner Matthews.

The friend who meant most of all however was John Edleston. He was a choir boy at Cambridge when Byron first met him and it was for Edleston, it is believed, that he wrote the emotional poems to 'Thyrza'. The letters he wrote to Miss Pigot vividly describe the affection that Byron felt. The Pigots were a family that lived opposite Mrs Byron at Southwell, and their house became a refuge for him. He once had a holiday in Harrogate with Elizabeth's brother John and he was friendly with all the family. Elizabeth, who was a few years older than Byron, became his particular confidante. She never married, and never forgot her friendship with the wild and lovable boy who was sixteen years old when she first knew him. They wrote frequently to each other when he was at Cambridge, and an insight into his life there and his character is revealed in his correspondence with her. In the following extracts he described his feelings for Edleston:

> June 30th, 1807
> ... On Monday I depart for London. I quit Cambridge with little regret because our set are vanished, and my musical protégé before mentioned has left the choir, and is stationed in a mercantile house of considerable eminence in the metropolis. You may have heard me observe he is exactly to an hour two years younger than myself. I found him grown considerably, and as you will suppose, very glad to see his former Patron. He is nearly my height, very thin, very fair complexion, dark eyes, and light locks. My opinion of his mind you already know; – I hope I shall never have occasion to change it. ...

> July 5th, 1807
> ... At this moment I write with a bottle of claret in my *head, tears* in my *eyes*, for I have just parted with my 'Cornelian', who spent the evening with me. As it was our last interview, I postponed my engagement to devote the hours of the *Sabbath* to friendship; – Edleston and I have separated for the present, and my mind is a chaos of hope and sorrow ... I rejoice to hear you are interested in my protégé; he has been my most constant associate since October, 1805, when I entered Trinity College. His *voice* first attracted my attention, his *countenance* fixed it and his *manners* attached me to him for ever. ... I certainly love him more than any human being and neither time nor distance have had the least effect of my (in general) changeable disposition ... In short we shall put Lady E Butler and Miss Ponsonby to the blush ... He certainly is perhaps more

attached to me than even I am in return. During the whole of my
residence at Cambridge we met every day, summer and winter,
without passing *one* tiresome moment and separated each time with
increasing reluctance. I hope you will one day see us together. He is
the only being I esteem, though I *like* many. ...

It is unlikely that Byron would have written in this frank, open
way to a young woman whose family were friendly with his mother,
if this had been an impure relationship. Leslie Marchand says this
friendship, like his other passions before Edleston, has the 'aura of
innocence'. It was simply that when he loved he loved to excess, as
he recalled in his journal of 12 January 1821: '*His* friendship,
[referring to Edward Noel Long] and a violent though *pure*, love
and passion – which held me at the same period – were the then
romance of the most romantic period of my life.' Furthermore after
Byron and Edleston had left Cambridge, the letters that passed
between them surely confirm Byron's role as a protector: '... At
present I must beg leave to repeat that it is only the favor (sic) of
your Lordship's *personal* influence and Patronage which I humbly
presumed in my last as well as now, – to request'. (Byron had
assumed he needed money.)

Before he set off on his travels in 1809, Byron had become very
insistent with Hanson that it was essential for him to go abroad,
and that the reason must remain a secret. Whilst he was away, he
was informed by Francis Hodgson, one of his Cambridge friends,
that Edleston had been accused of indecency. Byron had probably
become aware that his guiltless friendship and love for Edleston
was threatened, and to avoid a painful situation, he must leave
England. Just before he returned, Edleston died of consumption.

Whilst at Cambridge Byron got heavily into debt and thus into
the hands of moneylenders from which it became impossible to
extricate himself. His mother, with memories of his father's
appalling record, became increasingly anxious, and almost
certainly this worry contributed to her early and unexpected death.
Byron bought a carriage, employed menservants and kept horses.
He wrote pompously to his mother:

... I intend remaining in Town a month longer, when perhaps I
shall bring my horses and myself to your residence in that *execrable*
kennel. I hope you have engaged a man servant – else it will be
impossible for me to visit you, since my Servant must attend chiefly

to his horses, at the same time you must cut an indifferent figure with only maids in your habitation, I remain yours, Byron.

Mrs Byron was distracted and wrote to Hanson in 1806: '... he has behaved as ill as possible to me for years back, this bitter truth I can no longer conceal'. He came home. He was forgiven. She managed to raise a loan of £1,000 for him on the security of a large part of her little capital still left in Scotland.

In 1807 his first book of poems, *Hours of Idleness*, was published; followed by *English Bards and Scotch Reviewers*, which was a satire inspired by Pope's *Dunciad*. The second volume was a bitter and brilliant revenge for the malicious criticism that was given rather unnecessarily to *Hours of Idleness*. This was followed by a long poem in blank verse on Bosworth Field, which may have contained some reference to the family motto 'Crede Byron' but this was apparently never finished.

Byron had conceived the idea of 'collecting the pictures of my most intimate school-fellows' to take with him on the travels he was planning to make in 1809. He was somewhat disillusioned when one friend refused to sit because he thought he would have to pay for it so Byron delicately made it clear to him and to the other friends that it was to be at his own expense. Something of his idealized conception of friendship is reflected in the poem 'L'Amitié est l'Amour sans Ailes'.

> *... Seat of my youth! thy distant spire*
> *Recalls each scene of joy;*
> *My bosom glows with former fire, –*
> *In mind again a boy.*
> *Thy grove of elms, thy verdant hill,*
> *Thy every path delights me still,*
> *Each flower a double fragrance flings;*
> *Again, as once, in converse gay,*
> *Each dear associate seems to say,*
> *'Friendship is Love without his wings!'*
> Dec 29th, 1806

The strong sentiment for friendship was doubtless born in him, for the Byron family acquired their motto through loyalty to a friend. In an old history of Bosworth Field by W.H. Hutton, FASS, is an account of the origin of 'Crede Byron'. Sir John Byron and Sir Jervis Clifton were friends. Both lived in Nottinghamshire.

Byron was for Henry VII, Clifton was for Richard III. They exchanged oaths that should either be killed in action the other would do his best for the family. Seeing Clifton receive a blow which felled him, Byron rushed to the rescue saying 'Stay, my dear Clifton, stay.' But it was too late, for Clifton was dead. After much difficulty Sir John managed to obtain a grant which he passed on to Clifton's children. Henry VII was impressed by such loyalty and stamped this act of good faith to a friend by giving to Byron the motto 'Crede Byron'.

He set off on his travels with Hobhouse in 1809, and the day before there was an incident that rankled for many years, for Byron did not easily forgive or forget what he considered to be an insult. His kinsman by marriage, Robert Dallas, called to see him and found him bursting with indignation:

'Will you believe it?' he said, 'I have just met up with –, and asked him to come and sit an hour with me: he excused himself and what do you think was his excuse? He was engaged with his mother and some ladies to shopping! And he knows I set out tomorrow, to be absent for years, perhaps never to return! – Friendship!'

Among Byron's attendants accompanying him because 'like myself he seems a friendless animal' was Robert Rushton, a page from Newstead. Byron wrote to Mr Rushton from Gibraltar during the first part of his travels:

I have sent Robert home with Mr Murray [Joe Murray, his old retainer at Newstead], because the country which I am now about to travel through is in a state which renders it unsafe, particularly for one so young. I allow you to deduct five and twenty pounds for his education for three years provided I do not return before that time, and I desire he may be considered as in my service, let every care be taken of him and let him be sent to school; in case of my death I have provided enough in my will to render him independent. – He has behaved extremely well, and has travelled a great deal for the time of his absence. – Deduct the expense of his education from your rent.

Byron also wrote to his mother: 'Pray show the lad kindness as he is my great favourite,' as well as to Hanson about his arrangement for Rushton's education.

The following year, in a letter to his mother on 28 June Byron wrote:

> It is my opinion that Mr Bowman [the son of a tenant] ought to marry Miss Rushton, our first duty is not to do evil, but alas! that is impossible, our next is to repair it, if in our power, the girl is his equal, if she were his inferior a sum of money and provision for the child would be some, though a poor compensation, as it is, he should marry. I will have no gay deceivers on my Estate, and I shall not allow my tenants a privilege I do not permit myself, viz – *that* of debauching each other's daughters. ... Pray, take some notice of Robert, who will miss his master, poor boy, he was very unwilling to return. – I trust you are well and happy, it will be a pleasure to hear from you. ...

After he returned to England it was necessary to write to Rushton reprimanding him for his erring behaviour. Byron's letter of 21 January 1812 told Rushton he was to be civil to the maids, and reminded him of his own previous care and good opinion of him. A postscript was added: 'I wish you to attend to your arithmetic, to occupy yourself in surveying, measuring, and making yourself acquainted with every particular relative to the *land* of Newstead, and you will *write* to me *one letter every week*, that I may know how you go on.' Byron was twenty-four at this time, and his evident concern for the workers of his estate suggest that he showed the makings of a leader or statesman of uncommon intelligence and high-mindedness.

He was away two years, but at the end of one year he became tired of Hobhouse's company and they separated, Hobhouse returning to England in August 1810. On his way back to England Byron returned to Athens and stayed in a Capuchin monastery at the foot of the Acropolis and wrote the poems 'Hints from Horace' and 'The Curse of Minerva'.

While there he met and became friendly with various interesting foreigners and English people, amongst whom was Lady Hester Stanhope, and he agreeably took part in the social life of the town. He told Hobhouse that 'We had balls, dinners, and amours without number. ... I had a number of Greek and Turkish women and I believe the rest of the English were equally lucky for we were all clapped'. He wrote notes for his poem 'Childe Harold' of a serious nature concerning the divided state of the Greeks and their country, their reaction to tyranny, and the effect on them of abuse by foreigners. He also studied Italian and Modern Greek, and in the evening there were receptions for local and visiting dignitaries. He placed a curse on Lord Elgin and, rather unfairly, on his seed, though Byron had not been averse to scraping some crumbling stones from St Luke's tomb in Thebes, nor would he be in later years to removing stones from places like Juliet's tomb in Verona or carving his name on prime antiquities.

The monastery had a school for six boys, and Byron organized boxing contests between the Catholic and the Orthodox boys and the Father rejoiced to see the Catholics win. There were great 'scamperings and eating fruit and pelting and playing and I am at school again ...'. Even the convent washerwomen joined in the fun – sticking laundry pins into poor Fletcher, Byron's valet from Newstead. 'We have nothing but riots from morn to night ... I am vastly happy and childish ...', wrote Byron to Hobhouse in a letter, dated 23 August, reminiscent of his poem 'I would I were a careless child' in *Hours of Idleness*. He continued: 'However it is too good to last. I am going to make a second tour of Attica with Lusieri who is a new ally of mine, and Nicolo goes with me at his own most pressing solicitation.'

Nicolo Giraud was at that time Byron's favourite boy and became his protégé and a sort of major-domo on their travels. Byron arranged for a priest to give him extra tuition, and he later attended a school. His mother sent grateful messages to Byron for his interest. Through Giraud, who was a brother-in-law of Lusieri, the well-known Neapolitan painter employed by Lord Elgin, Byron met interesting Danish and German people who were cultured and well-informed.

According to André Maurois Byron asked one of the friars, Father Paul of Ivrea, if he might live in a cell: 'He said that he was no atheist, and asked the father for a crucifix, which he kissed with tears.' Religion, like everything else in which he was immediately engaged, was a powerful emotion for Byron. When Byron said no one knew what he was up to in the monastery, it was possibly very different from what some of his friends thought.

While away he had written many long and interesting letters to his mother, and she kept him informed of the topics of the day and items of news, which impressed her son: 'You seem to be a mighty reader of magazines: where do you pick up all this intelligence, quotations, &c. &c?' He never saw her alive again for when he

arrived in England on 17 July 1811 he wrote to her saying he would
be delayed in London for a few days on business, but on 31 July he
received news that she was ill and started off to Newstead
immediately. The next day, while he was still on the way, he was
told she had died. He was devastated by his loss and unhappily
remembered Gray's words that 'we can only have one mother'.
There would be no one now to go to with his troubles, no one who
would always forgive. No one to compare him with Rousseau, or be
angry if his poems weren't appreciated. All night he sat beside her
bed. Mrs Byron's maid tried to comfort him, but amid his sobs she
heard him lament, 'Oh, Mrs By, I had but one friend in the world
and she is gone.' Byron had been savagely attacked in the previous
March issues of *The Scourge*. The abuse included that '... he was
the illegitimate descendant of a murderer ... and a son of a
profligate father and a mother whose days and nights are spent in
the delirium of drunkenness'. He wrote to Hanson 'I will have no
stain on the memory of my mother; with a very large portion of
foibles and irritability, she was without a *vice* (and in these days that
is much) ...'. He had contemplated suing over the libel, but
Hanson persuaded him that it would be unwise.

After he left Trinity College Byron corresponded with and sent
messages to the dazzling Charles Skinner Matthews, the friend
whom he had met at Cambridge and who was known to be
homosexual. These messages, written in Greek, are very explicit
and boastful, of the kind some men make to show their adroitness
and success in captivating fantasies, suggesting they could be
private and teasing lewd jokes, all the more enjoyable when they
were conveyed through Hobhouse, who was 'so crabbed and
disagreeable' and took them very seriously.

Byron was very upset when he learned that Matthews had
drowned in the weeds of the Cam two days after his mother's
death. He admired Matthews more than anyone he had known, for
his intelligence, knowledge and wit, and always spoke of him with
profound esteem. He added a note to the end of the first canto in
'Childe Harold':

> ... I should have ventured a verse to the memory of the late Charles
> Skinner Matthews, Fellow of Downing College, Cambridge, were
> he not above all praise of mine. His powers of mind, shown in the
> attainment of greater honours against the ablest candidates than
> those of any graduate on record at Cambridge, have sufficiently
> established his fame on the spot where it was acquired.

Byron told Dallas, who questioned such enthusiasm, that: 'To him all the men I ever knew were pigmies. He was an intellectual giant,' and that 'For me I did not love quite so much as I honoured him.' He did not envy Matthews's 'infinite superiority' he said, but stood in awe of it. In 1820 Byron wrote to John Murray the publisher, who had consulted him regarding a proposed memoir: 'Matthews and I, meeting in London and elsewhere became great cronies. He was not good tempered – nor am I – but with a little tact his temper was manageable, and I thought him so superior a man that I was willing to sacrifice something to his humours, which were often, at the same time, amusing and provoking.' It is apparent his admiration for his friend had not waned through the years.

Robert Dallas had written to Byron when *Hours of Idleness* was published. He wrote poetry and novels himself, and was able and willing to be helpful with matters connected with publishing. More than this, he was a valuable and discerning critic, so that when Byron returned from his travels and they met, Dallas was given the two poems 'Hints from Horace' and 'The Curse of Minerva'. He took them away, read them with disappointment, and returning the next day, tactfully asked if anything else had been written. Byron reluctantly took some papers from a trunk, saying one other person had seen them, but had rather disparaged them and he was sure Dallas would do so too. The one other has never been identified, for the chief suspect, Hobhouse, denied that it was him. The papers were a collection of verse called 'Childe Harold's Pilgrimage' and were based on the wanderings and adventures experienced during the two years away. Dallas was enraptured and could not put it down, and told Byron he would stake his life on its success. Though still doubtful, Byron gave the poem to him and through Dallas began his long association with John Murray. Early in March 1812 he wrote the celebrated words: 'I awoke one morning and found myself famous.'

He also found that everyone wanted to meet him. Women from all walks of life read his poems and fell in love with him. He was incredibly handsome with his pale face and curling dark hair, and there was something of mystery, sadness, and scorn in his expression. His lameness, the cause to him of so much mental and physical suffering, merely served to enhance his attraction. His reputation as a poet soared and spread, and his dazzling personality shone above others. His fame spread to Europe and America where he received even greater adulation and he was generally acknowledged as the most acclaimed poet of the time.

1812 was also the year of love affairs which included one with the foolish and passionate Caroline Lamb; the year in which began his inimitable friendship with the powerful and sophisticated Lady Melbourne, who was then sixty-two years old; the year of his maiden speech in the House of Lords; but more momentous than any of these, it was the year he first proposed to Anne Isabella Milbanke.

3   Courtship

Annabella continued to meet Byron socially and at Lady Gosford's assembly on 13 April they discussed the poet Blackett. That night she wrote to her mother: 'I have met with much evidence of his goodness. You know how easily the noblest heart may be perverted by unkindness – perhaps the most easily a *noble* heart because it is more susceptible to ungenerous indignities.'

Five days later she attended a party given by Caroline Lamb when Lord Byron and Samuel Rogers were among the guests. During the conversation the question was posed 'Must a poet have felt in order to make his readers feel?' Byron asserted that was not true. She gave a dinner party herself at her parent's home in Portland Place and included in the sixteen people she invited were Lord and Lady Gosford, her uncle Lord Wentworth, Mr and Mrs George Lamb, Major Dickens and her other great friend Mary Montgomery, who was always referred to as 'MM'. It was her ill-health that caused the trouble at Seaham before Annabella came to London, but 'MM' was tougher than she seemed and was to outlive many of her friends, including Annabella.

Even in her letters to her mother and in her journal Annabella tended to write in a 'strangulated' style as Anna Jameson, her friend of later years, described it, which has made it credible for biographers to give an image of a cold and self-absorbed woman, that differs widely from contemporary reports of those who knew her. It was her evident sincerity, a certain innocent charm, a genuine interest in others, including those of a very different background, that made people like her, for even her critics admit that she was liked. It does not seem credible that she always preferred to be with 'inferiors' so that she could be condescending

43

towards them when, as has been seen, she attracted many socially desirable suitors who had the additional advantage of being financially secure. Like Byron, she believed it prudent to marry someone from a similar social background as herself, solvency being a prerequisite since she had a horror of debts. She also said she would not wish to marry into a family in which there was a history of insanity.

Annabella became aware of the relationship between Caroline Lamb and Byron and it did not occur to her that his obvious interest in herself was anything other than friendly. It *had* occurred to Caroline however, and she firmly informed Byron that Annabella was engaged to George Eden, who was frequently seen with her at dances. Caroline also warned Annabella, both verbally and by letter, that it would be unwise for her to have anything to do with Byron. In her letter of 22 May 1812 she wrote: 'I have faild (sic) in keeping my promise with you for you must be aware that when great duties are forgotten lesser ones are seldom remembered. Besides I once more repeat the advice I ventured to hint to you – shun friendships with those whose practice ill accords with your Principles ...'. Her counsel continued on these lines at length, but the only reaction it seems to have prompted from Annabella were the words 'A letter from Lady Caroline Lamb to me – 1812 – very remarkable' written on the cover.

Judith was getting more and more alarmed at the long enthusiastic letters coming from her usually steady and calm daughter. At first Byron seemed in every way so very unsuitable for Annabella. She confided her fears to her sister-in-law Lady Melbourne who could say nothing to reassure her. She decided that she and Ralph must come to London immediately, and on arrival in May they rented a house in Richmond, Surrey. Meanwhile Caroline Lamb kept Byron up to date with information she had learned from her mother-in-law Lady Melbourne, probably by secretly reading her letters, of the concern felt by Lady Milbanke over her daughter's increasing friendship with Byron. This was an insult and he there and then decided that he did not like Annabella's mother.

The love affair between Byron and Lady Caroline Lamb had been passionate and violent. However, Caroline behaved with great indiscretion and Byron soon tired of her eccentric behaviour, but found it very difficult to be rid of her. It all caused great distress to her husband William Lamb, later Lord Melbourne, and

to her mother Lady Bessborough. At last Caroline was persuaded
to go with her family to their home in Ireland. Lady Melbourne
wrote to Byron reproaching him for all the sorrow he had caused
through this affair. She was sad for her son William Lamb, and
anxious for his political career, which was likely to suffer from a
long stay in Ireland.

Byron's reply was unexpected. Dated 13 September 1812 he
wrote a very long letter in which was the following information:

> ... now my dear Ly. M. you are all out as to my real sentiments. I
> was, am, and shall be I fear attached to another, one to whom I have
> never said much, but I have never lost sight of and the whole of this
> interlude has been the result of circumstances which it may be too
> late to regret ... there was, and is one whom I wished to marry, had
> not this affair intervened, or had not some occurrences rather
> discouraged me ... As I have said so much I may as well say all – the
> woman I mean is Miss Milbanke – I know nothing of her fortune
> and I am told that her father is ruined, but my own will, when my
> Rochdale arrangements are closed, be sufficient for both ... But I
> know little of her, and have not the most distant reason to suppose
> that I am at all a favourite in that quarter, but I never saw a woman
> whom I liked, esteemed and could love so much – but that chance is
> gone, and I had better not think of her.

This was evidently not a sudden impulse, nor was he apparently
attracted to Annabella because he thought she was an heiress, as
has been supposed. On 19 September he wrote again to Lady
Melbourne:

> Miss M. I admire, and as I said in my last could love if she would let
> me, still I cannot believe what you say, that she is not engaged to E.
> [Eden]. I have been assured of the contrary by such good authority.
> Aunts are not to be trusted on such subjects. M.M. ... is a clever
> woman, an Amiable Woman, and of high blood, for I have still a few
> Norman and Scotch inherited prejudices on that score. Whatever
> you may think, I assure you I have a very domestick turn, and should
> wish to be married to a woman I could love and esteem and in
> whom I could place the greatest confidence. Such is M.M. – she
> always reminds me of 'Emma' in the Modern Griselda and whom
> ever I may marry, that is the woman I should wish to marry.

One ominous remark was that his only objection to the desired
engagement would be to his 'Mamma', as he called Annabella's
mother, from whom he had 'already by instinct imbibed a mortal

aversion'. But on the other hand he would be happy to call Lady Melbourne 'Aunt'. He wrote again to Lady Melbourne on 28 September:

> I have always openly professed my admiration of yr ... niece and have ever been anxious to cultivate her acquaintance but C[aroline] told me she was engaged to E[den] so did several others. Mrs [George] L[amb], *her* great friend, talked in the same strain and was moreover certain that E. would make the best husband in the world. Under these circumstances I withdrew, and wished not to hazard my Heart, with a Woman I was so extremely inclined to love but at the same time sure could be nothing to me. The case is now different – and upon hearing from a friend of hers that they are coming here. I have put off my journey to Rochdale – and sent my Agent to settle some Business of importance without me. If you should have any means of introducing me to their society pray do. I have trusted you with my secret and am entirely in your power. I do not care about her fortune, and should be happy if the floating capital of which I am now Master, could by some arrangements turn out to be advantageous to both. Does Miss M. waltz? – it is an odd question – but a very essential point with me. I wish I had any hopes that it should be possible for me to make myself agreeable to her, but my fears predominate, – and will I am sure give me a very awkward appearance. I wish you would undertake to say a few words for me – could you not say that I wish to propose, but I have great doubts of her.
>
> Excuse my asking this favour but you have always been so kind to me that I trust to your being my friend in this case. Everything rests with M.M. herself for my earnest wish is to devote my whole life to her.

Although these are well-known letters, quotations are given at length from them to support the assumption that Byron can only have married Annabella because he thought he could love her. He longed for the stable home that he had never had and for which he yearned, for the rewards of passion had been transient and unsatisfying and it does not seem in character for him to pretend an affection he did not, *at that time*, feel. It is more believable that he was carried away himself at times by his own mastery of words, so that to write of love was to be in love, but he could not write without the stimulus of feeling. If he were attracted to Annabella on account of the possibility that she was an heiress, which many people believe, apparently because they cannot see what other attributes she had for him, he would have done better to find someone with more reliable financial resources and for him at that time there would have been no lack of choice.

These revelations in the above extracts came as a complete surprise to Lady Melbourne. As the sister of Annabella's father Sir Ralph Milbanke, she certainly had not looked on his only child as a prospective wife for her friend Byron. She decided the best way of dealing with the situation would be to ask Annabella what qualities she desired in a husband. It was quite usual for young ladies to write 'characters' in their common-place books, and Annabella set to work with a will, and gave a serious and perhaps a little pompous testimony of what she expected of her husband, and added a bit about her own character '... I am never sulky, but my spirits are easily depressed, particularly by seeing anybody unhappy ...'.

Lady Melbourne wrote a long and very astute letter calculated to puncture Annabella's self-esteem by telling her that she never would find a husband while she required such exacting qualities, and she should take off 'the stilts on which you are mounted'. Her warning had the hoped-for effect. Annabella responded amiably and ended up 'After so full an explanation you will perhaps take off my *stilts* and allow that I am only on *tiptoe*. I quite agree with what you say ... Most Affectionately, Yours, A.I.M.' It is a pity Lady Melbourne's spirit could not always have been with Annabella when she put pen to paper.

Annabella was soon informed that the husband her aunt referred to was Lord Byron, and that he wished to marry her. Before she wrote back to Lady Melbourne she tried to sort out her mixed feelings of surprise, pleasure, fear, doubts on his method of proposing, and general bewilderment by writing a Character of Byron. Some of it is perceptive: 'The passions have been his guide since childhood, and have exercised a tyrannical power over his very superior intellect ...'. She quotes from one of his juvenile poems: 'I love the virtues I cannot claim.'

A few days later she gave her reply to Lady Melbourne:

I do not give my answer without the serious deliberation which is due to the honourable and disinterested nature of Lord Byron's sentiments. I am convinced that he considers my happiness not less than his own in the wishes which he has expressed to you and I think of them with the sincerest gratitude ...

... I should be totally unworthy of Lord Byron's esteem if I were not to speak the truth without equivocation. Believing that he never will be the object of that strong affection which would make me happy in domestic life I should wrong him by any measure that might, even indirectly, confirm his present impressions. From my limited observations of his conduct, I was predisposed to believe your strong testimony in his favour, and I willingly attribute it more to the defect of my own feelings than of his character that I am not inclined to return his attachment. After this statement which I make with real sorrow from the idea of its giving pain, I must leave our future intercourse to his judgement. I can have no reason for withdrawing from an acquaintance that does me honour and is capable of imparting so much rational pleasure, except the fear of involuntarily deceiving him.

... The general delicacy of his whole conduct towards me, particularly when he acted from the false information of my engagement to another person, is one of many proofs that his principles of honour deserve my entire reliance. I assure him of my perfect silence on this subject.

Richmond. October 12th, 1812.

Her style was a little stilted as usual and her meaning sometimes obscure, but her concern for Byron's feelings are clear. How easy it would have been to let it get spread around in the fashionable world, that the distinguished and celebrated Lord Byron had been turned down by the quiet 'Blue' Annabella Milbanke. The delicacy with which she refused the offers of her suitors, often remaining on friendly terms, was characteristic of her consideration for the sensitivities of people with whom she came in contact. She had obviously given great thought to her reply – trying to keep all channels of communication open, so that she might yet be his friend. Surprisingly she recalled in her narrative that her mother had regretted her reply: '– she said, as was natural with her feelings towards me, that he was one of the few who could appreciate me –'.

However, no sooner had she despatched her reply to Lady Melbourne than reaction set in. Life lost its lustre. No longer did she stay out at parties and dance until dawn. She wondered if she had been too precipitate; ought she perhaps to have 'looked-in' to the matter with more care; had she now renounced not only the love, but all chance of a friendship that she so dearly desired from the most fascinating and interesting person that she had ever met?

To 'M.G.', her close friend Mary Gosford to whom she revealed the innermost secrets of her heart, she confessed that the reasons she could not accept Byron's offer were: firstly that he had this theory of her perfection 'which could not be fulfilled by the trial' and therefore must end in disappointment for him, and secondly the self-confessed irreligious nature of his principles, 'but you know that I regard the latter too strongly to sacrifice it to the love of Man'. She ends up with a very wise observation for a girl only twenty years old: 'I think matrimonial unhappiness is often the consequence of one or both the persons having believed that they should be too easily contented.'

After all these doubts she began to hear noble reports of Byron, the most important to her being that he '... never suffers the slightest hint in disrespect to Religion to pass at his table'. She had seen what Lady Melbourne thought suitable to show her of the correspondence from Byron relating his feelings towards her; he was shown the Character she had written on him, which he thought 'indulgent ... in some points very exact' and they went their separate ways.

The Milbankes returned to Seaham, and Annabella spent the following months in an agitated and restless state of mind. In her journal were such entries as 'At home dead' and 'Wearied with want of tranquillity and found no pleasure.' Sometimes she did not bother to write in it at all. Later in her life she wrote of this period '... my state was that of high excitement ... I studiously endeavoured ... to alter the character of my feelings and fancied I had succeeded; ... I felt that I had been uncharitable ...'.

In the following summer of 1813 she met Byron again, by which time she had worked herself up into a high state of nerves, and was extremely agitated on seeing him, when she gave him her hand for the first time. She wrote in her narrative that he turned pale as he pressed it: 'Again that Evening I found his eyes fixed upon me, tho' many heads were between us, with an expression of mild intensity, which came from the best & deepest part of his Nature. It was *the Poet*, never before revealed to me. – Every meeting that season called forth sympathy from my heart, but not love – far from it.' Soon after this she saw Byron's half sister Augusta sitting with him on a sofa at Lady Glenbervie's. Annabella was favourably impressed by his 'gentler qualities' and his playful affectionate manner towards Augusta. Perhaps she pictured herself happily laughing and talking in Augusta's place beside him.

Annabella and her parents decided to leave London earlier than they had intended. She wrote in her narrative that her health had suffered and she wished to be quiet, adding 'It was not to *his* Image that my thoughts turned the most.' Before they departed she wrote to her aunt and included a message for Byron, possibly because she was afraid he would forget her, to the effect that she would always be glad to hear that he was happy however long his planned visit abroad might be. Byron, in his reply to Lady Melbourne, sent his best acknowledgements to Miss Milbanke in a postscript, and asked Lady Melbourne to 'Say what is proper' to her. Lady Melbourne took the opportunity to send the kind of message that she knew would most appeal to Annabella. She was anxious for Caroline's attention to be diverted from the vacillating Byron finally and for ever, and for him to marry Annabella seemed an excellent solution, enhanced by the fact that he could then call her aunt. It is impossible not to suppose that Lady Melbourne deliberately encouraged Byron and Annabella with this object in view.

Annabella wrote accounts of her life from time to time which she variously called 'Auto-description', 'Narrative' or simply a 'Statement'. She felt there should exist a record of events, especially those concerning Byron, as she had perceived them so that they could be understood from her point of view and could be used in a proposed memoir of her life. They were undated, unfinished, not consecutive and often written on small pieces of paper, but in their main substance agreement was complete, even when many years had elapsed between the writing of them.

In one narrative she tells of her dilemma when she received the message from Byron.

He was known to be on the point of departure for the East, & as he had said 'for ever' – & *under these circumstances* he wished through her [Lady Melbourne] to send me a last message, telling me I did not know what it would have been to him to believe I felt an interest in his welfare – This affected me with the most painful sense of responsibility – Ought I to let him go without an expression of my real kind feeling? Would it not be mistaken if transmitted to him? – After much consideration I thought I could prevent any misconception by writing myself, which my Mother sanctioned, ... To *him* I confided that which no one else knew, & which must effectually prevent the misinterpretation of my *friendly* sentiments. It was left to him to accept or reject them.

Mrs Gally Knight, the mother of Byron's friend – Henry Gally Knight, a writer of Greek and Oriental verses, lived near Newstead. Annabella heard from her that Byron had relieved the pecuniary difficulties of his brother-in-law Colonel Leigh, was kind to his old dependants, and was living a retired life at Newstead with his sister, thus contradicting, it appeared, the rumours of his dissipated life. From Lady Melbourne she heard of a 'rare instance of high Principle' he had shown to a woman who had thrown herself at his feet. It is not therefore surprising that Annabella's earlier, critical view of Byron was now changing to an idealized vision of a man about whom she knew little except through his wonderful poetry which deeply affected her.

She was oblivious to Caroline Lamb's advice, 'shun friendships with those whose practice ill accords with your Principles', and she disregarded the family friend Dr Fenwick, who warned her that Lady Melbourne, whom she now cultivated, 'Can deceive, & has been in the habit of deceiving'. Sadly she reflected in later life: 'I was clear sighted ... but I was to become blind.'

4   The Engagement

Annabella's first letter to Byron was very long.

> August 22nd, 1813
>
> I have received from Lady Melbourne an assurance of the satisfaction you feel in being remembered with interest by me. Let me then more fully explain this interest, with the hope that the consciousness of possessing a friend whom neither Time or Absence can estrange may impart some soothing feelings to your retrospective views. You have remarked the serenity of my countenance, but mine is not the serenity of one who is a stranger to care, nor are the prospects of my future untroubled. It is my nature to feel long, deeply, and secretly, and the strongest affections of my heart are without hope. I disclose to you what I conceal even from those who have most claim to my confidence, because it will be the surest basis of that unreserved friendship which I wish to establish between us – because you will not reject my admonitions ... when you know that I *can* suffer as you have suffered ...

She told him that she understood his sufferings; that he was either flattered or persecuted by admirers and did not have true friends; that she was conscious of his sense of moral rectitude, and she offered him guidance from her own experience to direct his thoughts towards 'an object which will permanently occupy your feelings & exercise your reason'. It is written in Annabella's most ponderous and tortuous style, giving rise to the charge of priggishness. It is a little unexpected therefore that Byron's reply was immediate.

Dated 25 August, it too was long and he said he was honoured by her letter; that his proposal had been '... the first direct or indirect approach ever made on my part to a permanent union with any woman & in all probability it will be the last ...'; that he felt a kind of pride in her rejection '... for it reminds me that I once thought myself worthy of the affection of almost the only one of your sex I ever truly respected ...'; he was surprised that she had loved someone and that it had not been returned; he did not feel he could trust himself in friendship with her, since he doubted that he could help loving her. The reference to it being his first and last proposal was apposite since, apart from a half-hearted approach he allowed Augusta to make on his behalf to her friend Lady Charlotte Leveson-Gower, Annabella was the only woman to whom he proposed marriage.

When he wrote this letter he was planning to go abroad in the very near future, so there seemed to be a finality about it which must have disappointed Annabella. It occurred to her on reflection that through her zeal in attempting to point the way to 'soothing feelings', she had perhaps been too earnest and had only succeeded in sounding pompous, and the strategy of revealing her unrequited love so that he would not be deceived into thinking she would accept him, by the friendship she was hoping to promote, had miscarried.

Chastened and briefly she replied:

> I will trouble you no more – only this to express – what I cannot withhold – my heartfelt thanks for your most kind, most indulgent answer. Nothing in your letter can displease me – the recollection of my own may. I ought more to have respected your sorrows, and I cannot forgive myself for having intruded on them from the impulse of an ill-judged kindness. That I may not encrease (sic) the error – farewell. I will not regret the friendship which you deem impossible, for the loss is *mine*, as the comfort would have been *mine*.
> God Bless You.

But it was not the end of the correspondence, and he did not go abroad as the plague had broken out in the East. It was Byron who encouraged its continuance by his long and immediate reply. He said that he had been presumptuous; that Annabella had not encouraged him; that Lady Melbourne had only tried to save him from a personal repulse; and that during the last winter he and William Bankes had consoled each other in tears and laughter in their both joining the corps of her rejected suitors. He ended by writing:

... If you regret a single expression in your late 2 letters, they shall be destroyed or returned. Do not imagine that I mistake your kindness – or hope for more, I am too proud of the portion of regard you have bestowed upon me to hazard the loss of it by vain attempt to engage your affection. I am willing to obey you – and if you will mark out the limits of our future correspondence and intercourse they shall not be infringed. Believe me with the most profound respect.

Every gratefully yours

P.S. I perceive I *begin* my letter by saying 'I do not wish to draw you into a correspondence' and end by almost soliciting it. Admirably consistent! but it is human nature and you will forgive it – if not you can punish.

Even those sympathetic to Annabella have to concede that her letters seem today very long, ponderous, usually without humour and, worst of all perhaps, rather boring. But the surprising reaction from Byron was to invariably reply immediately, often on the same day, whatever his activities and wherever he was. He was still highly sought after, had several clandestine affairs in progress, and was always fearful of a new flare-up from Caroline Lamb, which at the same time he seemed to encourage. There was no social or moral reason to continue writing to Annabella, and there can be only one conclusion – he wanted to; he liked exchanging ideas with a woman he found well-read and intelligent, and who interested him.

The second surprising feature is that Byron, acknowledged as one of the world's best letter writers, comes near to rivalling Annabella in the verbosity of his letters to her. Even when it is recalled that letters which seem prim and lengthy and even embarrassing to us now, may not have seemed so in another age where different values and tastes prevailed, it is still to be wished that wings had been lent to Annabella's words. It may have been her analytical brain which made her record her sentiments and ideas in an orderly and uninspiring manner, but she seemed to touch a chord in Byron which had hitherto been dormant. Her tender concern for him, and her utter sincerity, shine through every word. He trusted her implicitly, and there is a side of him revealed in his letters to her, which did not appear in any others, or even in his journals. If his letters to her are read consecutively and then his *Collected Letters* are referred to, there is a noticeable difference in his manner of writing. His letters generally are scintillating, interesting and succinct, but they are as if polished for posterity, or to be read aloud, and his latest exploits laughed over. He enjoyed writing to Lady Melbourne, and his letters to her invariably have a somewhat mocking strain running through them, as have hers to him. To Annabella he wrote from his heart, and with no trace of self-consciousness. He responded to questions about religion, poetry and many other subjects seriously, and wished to know her views. His was a complex, chameleonic personality, and it was as if she kindled a flame in the good side of his nature, as tragically later she was to bring forth the worst. He seemed happy not to feel the need for wit, jest, merry quip, or learned Greek quotation and to be able to diverge from his customary and sophisticated style of writing, as he did at times in his poetry. She was conscious of the inner turmoil that was ever present, and she hoped in some way, inspired by her deeply-held faith, to be an influence in bringing him a measure of peace. There was an ingrained spiritual side to Byron, seldom revealed, and he esteemed purity in a woman. Perhaps this was the reason Annabella attracted him, for he had met few virtuous women.

They continued to write fairly regularly, but Byron had distractions during these months which he concealed from Annabella. She asked him in one letter if he didn't laugh '... when you feel, because you are too proud to accept sympathy?' He replied on 26 September:

> To the charge of Pride – I suspect I must plead guilty – because when a boy & a very young one it was the constant reproach of schoolfellows, tutors ... It was however originally defensive – for at that time my hand like Ishmael's was against every one's and every one's against mine ... I now come to Religion ... I was bred in Scotland among Calvinists in the first part of my life – which gave me a dislike to that persuasion – since that period I have visited the most bigoted and credulous of countries – Spain – Greece – Turkey – as a spectacle the Catholic is more fascinating than the Greek or ye Moslem – but the *last* is the only believer who practices the precepts of his Prophet to the last chapter of his Creed – my opinions are quite undecided ...
>
> Goodnight – I have sent you a long prose – I hope your answer will be equal in length – I am sure it will be more amusing – you write remarkably well – which you won't like to hear – so I shall say no more about it ...

In October 1813 Annabella read 'The Giaour' and wrote to Lady Melbourne describing her reaction to it: '... the description of Love almost makes me in love ... I consider his acquaintance so desirable that I would incur the risk of being called a Flirt for the sake of enjoying it'. She had not heard from Byron for some weeks, so bravely wrote to him again in her usual fractured style about religion, revelation and reason. She had little confidence in the reception it would receive for she ended '... I am not exacting an answer. I only request to be informed when my communications become unacceptable'.

On 10 November he wrote again and asked her if she would accept a copy of 'The Bride of Abydos'; he sympathized with her over her friend Mary Montgomery's departure abroad for '... I believe the friendship of good women more sincere than that of men'; he said he had '... heard a rumour of another added to your list of unacceptables [Stratford Canning] – and I am sorry for him – as I know he has talent – & his pedigree ensures wit and good humour'. He also mentioned that his little cousin Eliza Byron '... the prettiest little blackeyed girl of Paradise – & but 7 years old ...' would be coming up to Stockton and would Annabella see her. It was a letter into which almost anything or nothing could be read. She must have smiled wryly at his remark about another suitor, for she was beginning to realize that now for her there could ony be 'unacceptables'. Ever since the unexpected communication from Lady Melbourne that Byron wanted to marry her, Annabella had had her normal equilibrium upset. If the approach had come through someone else, like Mary Gosford for instance, instead of the fashionable Lady Melbourne with whom neither she nor her parents had much affinity, she might have believed that he truly meant it and reacted in a different way.

As it was she had had to provide a reason to turn down his proposal which would not wound his pride or check their friendship. She realized that, unfortunately for her, Byron had put her on a higher plane because of her 'Purity', and by telling him of her own fictitious unrequited love she had hoped that by their shared experience she would come off her pedestal. Her religion meant more to her than life itself and she felt deeply that, for some reason that she did not as yet understand, in this she had been blessed. It was spiritually conferred for a purpose, rather than earned, for virtue alone could not ensure absolute belief. All her life she was dismayed that some people were inclined to put a halo

round her, but there was little she could do about it – she could not
spit on the Cross just to show she was not especially good or 'pi'.
Her friends knew and accepted her as she was, but with Byron,
closer acquaintance with her she suspected, could destroy the
glimmer of his desire for spiritual insight that he had allowed to be
revealed to her. All these thoughts made her very emotionally
confused and she decided to write them all down to Mary Gosford
before she replied to Byron's letter:

> ... I do not always succeed when I wish to be enjouée. It is not my
> proper character ... Everyone of my friends has a different
> influence on my humour. M.M. makes me romantic; you make me
> thoughtful; H.M. lighthearted (with a few exceptions); Joanna
> humble; By – religious; Miss Raine reasonable; ... you will be
> surprised at the product of my piety; but surely the survey of
> Heaven-born genius without Heavenly grace must make a Christian
> clasp the blessing with greater reverence than love. ... Should it
> ever happen that he & I offer up a heartfelt worship together – I
> mean in a sacred spot *my* worship will then be almost worthy of the
> Spirit to whom it ascends. ... It is not the poet – it is the immortal
> soul lost or saved; now I have written and thought till my tears
> flow ...

After writing to Mary Gosford she regained her composure and
expressed herself with unusual clarity in a friendly letter to Byron:

> Pray let me have your new composition – I have received more
> pleasure from your poetry than from all the Q.E.D.'s in Euclid ...
> People of methodized feelings are to me very disagreeable, being
> myself so *un*demonstrative as to prefer, if not always to approve,
> these generous spirits 'who are pleased they know not *why* & care
> not *wherefore*'. I hope I have not appeared to assume either
> mathematical or any other superiority ... Perhaps I have
> occasionally forgotten the humility which should have regulated my
> opinions ... but could you read my thoughts – and I hoped you
> could – you would know that my general feeling is very different. I
> never meant to engage you in religious controversy – you will
> remember that I owned myself not qualified for converting – I
> would only persuade you to take the means of convincing
> yourself ...
> P.S. I shall like very much to be the playfellow of your little
> cousin if I can contrive it ... we will gladly send for her, if she may
> have leave to spend some holidays here.

On 29 November Byron wrote one of his longest letters to her: 'No one can *as*sume or *pre*sume less than you do ... My only reason for avoiding the discussion of *sacred* topics – was the sense of my own ignorance & the fear of saying something that might displease – but I *have listened* & will listen to you with not merely patience but pleasure. ...' He had just started to keep a journal and wrote in it on 30 November his reaction to this letter. 'A very pretty letter from Annabella ... she is a very superior woman ... and yet, very kind, generous, and gentle, with very little pretension. ...'

Annabella had a severe illness towards the end of 1813. She had heard that Byron had left England, though he had not written to tell her, but it was some relief not to hear any rumours that he had made plans to marry. She was uncertain of her own feelings. She had known when she first learned of his interest in her that she could not marry a practising infidel, which she had been told that he was, but now it seemed that he almost wanted to believe in a religion. She remembered the strange way he had looked at her on the occasion they had met in London, and with misgivings as to her ability, it occurred to her that perhaps she had been predestined to be a sort of compass to point Byron towards the road he was seeking.

However, first of all she had to overcome the problem of how best to regain 'Truth' – as she put it – revealing to Byron that she had not lost her heart irretrievably to someone else, or if she had it was now redeemed, and implant in his mind the idea of proposing again to her, alone and not through a third person. Then she heard that he had not gone abroad after all, but had left London for a visit to Newstead Abbey. While she waited anxiously for a letter from him, she consulted with Mary Gosford and turned over in her mind phrases giving an acceptable explanation for the apparent change in her attachment. That she had loved another may not have been totally false for she had certainly favoured Major Dickens, one of the guests at her dinner party who she often met in the spring of 1813, 'but pray do not let Judy fancy that I am in love with him – whatever I *may be*', she had told her father, but Major Dickens sailed away to the East Indies leaving no evidence of his intentions, and it was not, according to her narrative, to Byron's image that her thoughts had turned the most after the 1812 season.

The year of 1814 came and it was still not any easier for Annabella to analyse the relationship between herself and Byron. His letters seemed so sincere, warm, and candid, and he said things about her which made her nearly sure that he felt the same feelings for her as when he had proposed. Yet, there had been one or two unexplained gaps in the correspondence, and from time to time vague and sinister allusions which she could not understand – like the one in the letter dated 10 November 1813: 'You won't take *fright* when we meet will you? – imagine that I am about to add to your thousand and one pretendants? – I have taken exquisite care to prevent the possibility of that ...' and the one on 19 February 1814: '... I am at present a little feverish – I mean mentally – and as usual on the brink of something or other which will probably crush me at last, & cut our correspondence short with everything else. Till then I must take as much of it as I can get ...'. Curbing her curiosity in her reply, Annabella wrote: '... if the cause of these attacks of anguish ought to be secret, I will not seek to divine them – but if the secrecy be only *self-imposed* cannot my prayer dissolve it?' She received no reply to her question.

The ever present problem of removing the belief that she was unattainable became a little easier in February by Byron writing about his youthful but very deep love for Mary Chaworth, who had lived on a neighbouring estate to Newstead, had married unhappily and had recently written to him asking him to see her. On 3 March his letter was even more helpful. In a P.S. he added: 'I was told today that you had refused me 'a *second* time' so that you see I am supposed to be the most permanent of your plagues & persevering of Suitors. ...' Annabella wrote back a very long letter full of complexities in which she hid the message she longed for him to divine – that she would warmly welcome being proposed to again. Byron remarked in his diary: 'A letter from Bella ... I shall be in love with her again if I don't take care', and on 15 March he replied: '... you do not know how much I wish to see you – for there are so many things *said* in a moment, but tedious upon the tablets. ... there are several opinions of yours I want to request, & though I have two or three able & I believe very sincere *male* friends, there is something preferable to me in ye delicacy of a woman's perceptions ...'.

Annabella now felt the only way out of the confusion that her life had become for her, would be if Byron was persuaded to visit Seaham as had been tentatively suggested previously when he was planning to visit Scotland. On 13 April she cautiously asked 'am I mistaken in imagining that you are disposed to visit us?' and intimated that her father would invite him 'if you will give us a reason to hope it will be accepted. Perhaps these are idle speculations, and then think of them no more'.

Byron replied on 20 April. Annabella was encouraged by his saying that he would avail himself of an invitation if made, but as she read on she was dismayed to read of his plans to travel. Not only was 'Italy my magnet' but he would 'fix no precise period for my return'. He went on to say that he was utterly confounded and baffled by the fall of Bonaparte and the restoration of the Bourbons – 'the triumph of tameness over talent'.

Annabella answered that she was glad she did not wish in vain to see him and added: 'I promise you that neither on this or any future occasion will I make any sacrifice for your sake ... will you adopt the same principles towards me?' She was anxious that he should feel under no obligation to make his visit if his feelings about it had changed.

She eagerly awaited a reply but it did not come. She wrote again explaining that they were going to Halnaby for a week – and that they still hoped to see him. Even this did not elicit an answer and when she could bear it no longer she wrote in June:

> Pray write to me – for I have been rendered uneasy by your long silence, and you cannot wish to make me so. Though my conjectures as to the cause – which has much and anxiously occupied my thoughts – have been various, they have never assumed any motive on your part but the best. On mine I do not feel equally confident. I have perhaps been too careless of forms, and expressions, having expressed & omitted so injudiciously that it might be impossible to understand my meaning ...

There is little sign here, of the self-esteem or complacency that is so often associated with her. At last, on 21 June he replied and she was still not sure of his motives. She did not know if the delay was due to indifference on his part, or whether the excuse he gave was true, that he was awaiting her return to Seaham before fixing a time for his visit. He still prevaricated: 'I shall await your answer and your convenience before I pretend to name any period when I can hope to see you.' It would not be surprising if Annabella had had a strong urge to abandon Byron and his friendship and look for someone less tiresome but she did not even consider this and answered his letter immediately:

I am made very happy by your letter and the certainty which it affords of your intention to visit us ... The formality and coldness which are, I know sometimes observable in my manners as well as in my writing have a source that is painful to myself – therefore pray do not allow me to seem what to you I can never mean to appear. After each time that I met you last year in London, I was vexed by the idea of having been repulsively cold towards you. It would have remained a source of great regret had not the means of removing so false an impression (did you receive it) been in my power.

Byron wrote to Lady Melbourne, telling her of Caroline Lamb's renewed onslaught on him: '... you talked to me – about keeping her out – it is impossible – she comes at all times – at any time – & the moment the door is open in she walks – I can't throw her out of the window ...' but he did not confide this to Annabella. Neither did he mention to her another matter, which was causing him disquiet.

Annabella waited with mounting tension for a reply to her last letter, but it did not come and she could wait no longer: 'If I am in any respect mysterious to you, if you desire any explanation of the past or present ... believe that I shall give it most willingly.'

Byron made two attempts to reply on 1 August as he had had difficulty in understanding her: '... I have read your letter once more – and it appears to me that I must have said something which makes you apprehend a misunderstanding on my part of your sentiments – my memory is still retentive enough not to require the repetition that you are attached to another'.

On 6 August Annabella made one more effort to regain truth, ending with: 'The reasons which led me to believe the character of one person suited to my own, have disappeared with opportunities of fuller investigation ... nothing could now induce me to marry him. You are therefore mistaken if you deem *this* the cause or any part of the cause, why I am not *even more* affectionately yours ...'.

Byron was aware some kind of movement was needed if they were ever to get out of the impasse, so on 10 August he wrote plainly that:

I will answer your question as openly as I can. – I did – do – and always shall love you – and as this feeling is not exactly an act of will – I know no remedy – it would be a very hard case – if a woman were obliged to account for her repugnance – you would probably like me if you could – and as you cannot. ...

Perhaps because she felt instinctively that it was unwise to commit herself until she had seen him again, and his visit to Seaham seemed further away than ever, she did not grasp his affirmations as firmly as it might have been supposed. Her shyness always made her diffident in taking it for granted that he would want to reply to her letters and in this case there was justification for her doubts. She ended her letter: '... I will only request you to use or discontinue my intercourse, now and always, as it may be found to give pleasure or pain ...'.

Byron sounded cross when he replied on 16 August: 'Very well – now we can talk of something else', but as if to make amends he inquired after her health, and commented on the weather.

In her reply Annabella began by hoping that the correspondence was not disagreeable: '... I shall now try to make a better use of it than late, since I infer from your silence that my dream of seeing you soon is to end ...'. She asked him to tell her more about himself – she admitted she found a fashionable life a slavery which she had only endured because her mother thought it advantageous for her – but she had realized it was pride in mortals to be offended at what God beholds and suffers, so she would concentrate on the loveliness of human character. She told him that she had read 'Lara': 'In the last *Edinburgh Review* I find an opinion which I had formed before it prevailed as it does at present – that Shakespeare alone possessed the same power as you have shown, of diving into the great deep of the human heart.'

They had returned to the safe and comforting realm of literature, and Byron sent her a long list of uplifting books to read. In her reply she offered to copy out a special passage from an unpublished work by Porson, and ended by asking, 'Pray write soon. I have no right to ask it – but I *do* ask it ...'. On 7 September Byron replied that he knew all about Porson and his intoxication 'to brutality – I hate to think of it ...'. He referred to their 'apparent inconsistencies' with which each one accused the other, and then pointed out that *her* religious preference for the contemplative life was 'the very essence of the Epicurean philosophy'.

Annabella responded by referring to the consistency theme: 'The "apparition" of my consistency ought not to be "formidable" to you, since like other apparitions, it may owe its effect chiefly to the imagination of the spectator, and might vanish with the light of day,' and then defended Porson from Byron's charge of drunkenness, since according to her friend Elizabeth Raine: 'Not withstanding their great intimacy, it is a fact that to her he never appeared in that disgraceful state.'

At the same time as she wrote the above letter she wrote to Hugh Montgomery, including in it some verses her father had impulsively composed when she boasted she could walk blindfold to the gate of the field behind their house, and instead had plunged into the horse-pond.

> Five miles a man did walk to fame
> Blindfold, a mighty prank!
> Says one, I'd nearly do the same
> And that was Miss Milbanke.
>
> Away she went as bold as brass
> And gaily held her course;
> Nimbly avoiding Jacky Ass
> And also the pond horse.
>
> But Dr Southey by her side
> Did stand her much in stead,
> Like Pallas when she once did ride
> At Troy with Diomed

There were no such light-hearted frivolities in her letters to Byron.

Before Byron received her letter his new proposal, written on 9 September was on the way to her. 'Are the "objections" to which you alluded insuperable? ... It is not without a struggle that I address you once more on this subject. Yet I am not very consistent ...'.

Consistent or not Annabella understood his meaning, and wrote back the same day, but this time there were no convoluted sentences and she wrote at last unreservedly from her heart, surrendering herself to him totally. There was no idea of reforming him, she was unaware of any need.

I have your second letter – and am almost too agitated to write – but you will understand. It would be absurd to suppress anything – I am and have long been pledged to myself to make your happiness my first object in life. If I *can* make you happy, I have no other consideration. I will *trust* to you for all I should look up to – all I can love. The fear of not realizing your expectations is the only one I now feel. Convince me – it is all I wish – that my affection may supply what is wanting in my character to form your happiness. This is a moment of joy which I have too much despaired of ever experiencing – I *dared* not believe it possible. ...

Byron wrote back on 18 September 1814:

Your letter has given me a new existence – it was unexpected – I need not say welcome ... – I have ever regarded you as one of the first of human beings – not merely from my own observation but that of others – as one of whom it was as difficult *not* to love – as scarcely possible to deserve ... – I wish to answer your letter immediately – but am at present scarcely collected enough to do it rationally – I was upon the point of leaving England without hope without fear – almost without feeling ... from the moment I became acquainted my attachment has been increasing ... permit me to assure you how faithfully I shall ever be. ...

They had become engaged.

When she was thirty-nine she wrote 'I offered my existence to him. The reply was gratifying beyond words to describe – it made me feel inspired with the purest happiness.'

The next day, 19 September, Byron told her how emotional he had been when her letter came, and how much he wished to see her. The following day he wrote again:

There is one point on which – though you have not lately pressed it – I am sure you feel anxious on my behalf – and to this will I speak, I mean – Religion. ... I will read what books you please – hear what arguments you please – and in leaving the choice to your judgement – let it be a proof that my confidence in your understanding & your virtues is equal. ...

In later years she wrote of this period:

I cannot speak of his letters otherwise than as most honourable to him. Their sincerity has been proved by circumstances which were afterwards made known to me. He did not attempt to deceive me in any way, neither by a false exhibition of his own sentiments, nor by pretending to agree with mine – I valued highly the privilege of communicating with such a mind.

It was always deeply painful for Annabella to recall this precious part of her life.

5   Marriage

The engagement at first proceeded quite favourably. Byron wrote two or three letters to every one of Annabella's and continued in the same warm manner as before. Her rather pedantic way of writing softened so that her letters became more interesting and sometimes amusing. But Byron's longed-for visit to Seaham was delayed again and again. His financial affairs were not straightforward, and he had many debts. Newstead Abbey had been put up for auction in 1812 but did not reach the required figure and was withdrawn. Thomas Claughton had been wanting to buy it for many months but did not complete the purchase although he had made a deposit. Matters had reached the stage where the transaction had to be concluded one way or another and Byron had told his solicitor, John Hanson, that 'This place I fully intend to dispose of – unless a wife – a legacy or a lottery ticket (and I have put in for neither) induced me to retain it: – so if you hear of any personage inclined to purchase ...'. Byron did not then know he would shortly be engaged to be married, and it is therefore evident that Newstead was not sold, as has been represented, expressly in order to provide a marriage settlement for Annabella, but for other reasons.

On 18 September 1814 Byron wrote to Hanson telling him of his engagement: '... let me see you soon for obvious reasons – to discuss the state of my affairs – & the expediency of retaining or selling Newstead or Rochdale – also what settlements it will be proper for me to make – with various other details which will arise at our meeting ...'. Hanson was more than usually dilatory because he was very involved with his son-in-law, Lord Portsmouth, whose brother had taken out a commission of lunacy to try and annul his marriage to Hanson's eldest daughter.

Over and over again Byron wrote to Hanson urging him to make arrangements for a visit to Seaham. 22 October: 'when I tell you that your delay if prolonged will probably make a serious difference ... I presume you will think that Mr Viney & his mines can perhaps condescend to let you go ...'. [Hanson had gone to Ilfracombe to see a client.] 24 October: 'It is now *five Weeks* since I announced to you Miss M's resolutions & mine & since that time little or nothing has been done ...'. Then he heard that Hanson was ill and wanted to send his son Charles in his place. 25 October:

> Your illness is more than unfortunate – at least to me – had you but proceeded as at first intended you would probably have preserved your own health & saved me much misery. – It is useless to send Charles ... what to say to them I know not – after the delays already – they will merely look upon your illness as a new excuse – in short – this marriage will be broken off – & if so – whether intentional or accidental – I can't help it – but by God – I can never look upon anyone again as my friend who has even been the innocent cause of destroying my happiness.

Due to the delays, his annoyance with Hanson, and concern over the kind of reception he would now receive, Byron lost his momentum and his sense of purpose. He wrote to Lady Melbourne: 'I feel very odd about *it*, not *her*; it is nothing but shyness and a hatred of strangers which I could never conquer.' At last however, he was ready to start on his visit at the end of October, but he interrupted his journey to stay with Augusta at Six Mile Bottom, and it was five days before he arrived at Seaham.

Meanwhile Annabella was growing more and more uneasy. She was not helped by having to contend with the impatience and disquiet of her parents. Lord Wentworth, Judith's brother, from whom Annabella would eventually inherit, was staying at Seaham with the hope and expectation of meeting Byron, but had to leave before he arrived. Letters of congratulation which she received seemed to dwell on the *hope* that she might be happy rather than on any confidence that she would be and she felt compelled to put on a brave face that she was far from feeling, out of loyalty to Byron, and to bolster her own pride. 'There are abominable stories in circulation concerning me – we don't care for all the attempts to make us appear wrong and ridiculous,' she wrote to Mary Gosford.

Her feelings of anxiety and dread increased as her mother fussed around, but as usual sympathy for her is tempered by her stiff mode of expression, even to her closest friends, which was made worse by strain and tension.

When Byron at last joined them everyone was charmed by his personal magnetism. He listened amiably to Sir Ralph's long stories, got on well with Judith, was nice to their solicitor's little boy, and was in every way on his best behaviour – except with Annabella when they were alone, and then he was 'strange, moody, and unaccountable' so that she thought he could not love her. She consulted her mother and her very old, experienced, friend and tutor Dr Fenwick, and they both urged her to regard his behaviour as due to 'highly wrought feelings & irritating circumstances'. She remained uneasy, thinking she must save him from a fate he seemed to dread so much, and in her narrative she describes her attempt to free Byron from his commitment:

> One evening, when alone with him, I asked him gently & affectionately to *trust* me, – to tell me openly whether there was not some reason which made him look forward to our Marriage with altered feelings, – that I should never seek to know what that reason was, my only wish being to act as his true friend & to take upon myself the rupture of the Engagement. – He became quite livid whilst I was saying these words, staggered, & fell back upon the Sofa fainting – Minutes must have elapsed before he could recover himself he murmured indistinct words of anger & reproach – 'you don't know what you've done' – I implored pardon at his feet, but he remained inflexible, petrified. I could not put any other construction on such a frenzy of despair, than that he thought I had meant to break with him – so I determined never to renew that train of feeling in his mind. But from that time he lost the confiding manner he had had towards me, & continued to refer to the Past as involving some fearful mysteries. – ... I *could* have broken the Bond before, but not now that the question was 'shall he *suffer* alone or not' – Little did I dream that I was to aggravate those sufferings, & form the bitterest drop in his lap.

It must have been a disheartening ordeal for Annabella. Already tense with nervous anticipation before he came, as she had not seen Byron for over a year; probably anxious that her parents would show themselves to advantage; perplexed by his strange behaviour and odd references to his half-sister Augusta; and most

difficult of all having to control her feelings in response to his
passionate embraces, for she was inexperienced in these matters
and surprised by her own reactions. He talked often of Augusta
with tenderness and affection and told Annabella she reminded
him of Augusta when she was playful. He told her too, 'if you had
married me two years ago, you would have spared me what I can
never get over'. She asked him what he meant but he did not tell
her. He discovered that 'her passions are stronger than we
supposed', as he informed his confidante Lady Melbourne, and
this presented problems of its own.

Characteristic of those who indulge in, or are afflicted by silent
gloomy moods, Byron acted as if he were unaware of them, and of
the distress they caused Annabella. There does not seem to exist
any restorative that will remedy this unfortunate affliction. If
questioned, however gently, for an explanation none will be given;
there will be no admission there is anything amiss to account for
the dejected, sulky demeanour. It is difficult to be cheerful and
playful with someone in the grip of sullenness and silence, and
Byron reacted typically in feeling himself a martyr when Annabella
was understandably quiet.

Byron wrote to Lady Melbourne three times while he was at
Seaham. In the first letter, written on 4 November he said: 'I have
been here these two days ... your brother pleases me much – to be
sure his stories are long – but I believe he has told most of them –
and he is to my mind the perfect gentleman ... but I fear she won't
govern me – & if she don't it will not do at all – but perhaps she
may mend of that fault ...'. Apart from finding Annabella 'silent'
and not liking Lady Milbanke, though he did not know why – all
seemed so far satisfactory. It was a pity that Lady Melbourne did
not show that letter to Annabella in view of its reference to being
governed.

The second letter was written on 6 November:

Annabella and I go on extremely well – we have been much together
and if such details were not insipid to a third person it would not be
difficult to prove that we appear much attached – and I hope
permanently so ... Our lawyers are in a fair train of concluding their
parchment passports to matrimony – and I am happy to say – in the
most amicable way without disputes – demurs – or more delays –
when quite done – which may be in a fortnight – we are to marry
quietly – and to set off by ourselves to Halnaby for *the* Moon. ... I

think we all *improve* to suit very well – I endeavour to conform to their habits which is not difficult – and I could hope that I am not a troublesome inmate – *they* are very kind and A., of course, still kinder – I hope she will be happy – I am sure she can make and keep me so if she likes – I wrote to you a day or two ago – and hope to sign myself soon – not more affectionately but more entirely.

But by 13 November, when he wrote again to Lady Melbourne, the situation had deteriorated and it seems apparent that Annabella was at the end of her tether:

Do you know I have great doubts – if this will be a marriage now. – her disposition is the very reverse of *our* imaginings ... for my part I have lately had recourse to the eloquence of *action* ... and find it succeeds very well, and makes her very quiet; which gives me some hopes of the efficacy of the 'calming process' so renowned in 'our philosophy' ... She is like a child in that respect, and quite caressable into kindness and good humour; though I don't think her temper bad at any time, but very *self* tormenting and anxious and romantic. ...

What with his ardour and his gloom and his constant reproaches for not marrying him before, Annabella took to her bed when she could, but it was at her instigation Byron left Seaham on 16 November and on the same day he wrote from Boroughbridge:

My heart – we are thus far separated, but after all one mile is as bad as a thousand – which is a great consolation to one who must travel six hundred before he meets you again. If it will give you any satisfaction, I am as comfortless as a pilgrim with peas in his shoes, and as cold as Charity, Chastity or any other virtue – I expect to reach Newstead tomorrow and Augusta the day after. Present to our parents as much of my love as you like to part with, and dispose of the rest as you please.

Annabella wrote to him on the same day as he left and on each of the two following days:

... the Elders are not in very good humour with me as accessory to your departure, which they regret for their own sake at least.
  Are you quite sure that I love you? Why did you doubt it? It is *your* only trespass. As for *my* trespasses I must not think of them – I wish

we were married, and then I could do my best and not quarrel with myself for a thousand things that you would not mind. ...

My own dearest, there is not a moment when I would not give my foolish head to see you ... Dad and Mam are quite disconsolate without you. You made yourself agreeable here with so much success that amongst all who have seen you there is not a difference of opinion as to *your* perfection – I am in 'dim eclipse'. Even Billy Hoar told his wife you were fascinating. Your interest in his boy must have formed a great part of the charm – lest you should be too vain I tell you so ... – Will you take me to your heart? My home 'till Death do us part' – and don't turn me out of doors in revenge as you threatened.

My own Byron – I must say goodnight before I go to rest ... I certainly was not myself during your stay ... *Myself* is by no means the grave didactic, deplorable person that I have appeared to you. I am only sage under some visitation of anxiety ... Those who have seen me *quite* as a domestic animal have had more reason to complain of my nonsense than my sense. It has however always been a long time before I could recover my natural temperament with a new inmate. ...

According to Shakespeare: 'There is a time in the affairs of men, which, taken at the flood, leads on to fortune; Omitted, all the voyage of their life is bound in shallows and in miseries.' Such a tide in Annabella's life was Byron's first visit to Seaham. After he left she was miserably aware of the dismal impression she must have given him when she had most wanted to captivate and radiate confidence, good sense, gaiety and wit. At this crucial meeting with him, so long anticipated, freed from the artificial confines of society, she had imagined they would get to know each other more fully. Had she seized the initiative by establishing some kind of dominance, however small or unimportant – reminding him for instance that her heritage was older than his might have helped, for Byron respected rank and informed Hanson: 'I believe Lady B's title by heritage is older than mine (though that is ancient)'; had she developed a formula for dealing with his moods; had she demanded an explanation for his strange words concerning an awful fate which had befallen him due to her refusal, her future life could well have been different.

Instead, because she was shy and immature, unsure of herself and even more so of him, nervous and tense, she allowed herself to adopt a position of weakness from which she never recovered. At that time the scales of fortune were tipped in her favour, for since she had offered to release him on friendly terms, she had nothing to lose, and it was Byron who was overcome with apparent distress when she suggested breaking off the engagement. A 'temporary' delay for financial reasons, or until the sale of Newstead Abbey was complete would have made an acceptable excuse for postponing or cancelling the marriage. After she was married it was too late. She was entrenched in a subordinate role that she herself had accepted and it became too perilous to change.

From Six Mile Bottom Byron wrote in a P.S.: 'I don't ask you to consider this as a letter, but merely a memorandum that I am thinking of you now – and loving you ever – my wife. A, sends her hundred loves and regrets very much her absence from S.' (Augusta had been invited to stay at Seaham.)

On 20 November Annabella wrote to him: 'I hope for a line from you today – I want it very much – not so much as yourself; yet I still think ... that just now we are better apart ... I have nothing to tell you, and only wish you knew – I will leave you to guess what –.'

They wrote to each other often and were expecting to meet and marry in a week or two, for Byron had requested a very quiet wedding. But there were further complications when Claughton made an offer for Newstead well below the price that had been agreed. Byron would not accept this and on 8 December wrote to Annabella explaining the situation and adding that he would 'leave it to you and yours to determine how far this may – will – or ought to cause any further delay in our marriage.'

Annabella replied to him on 10 December. Her letter is plainly sincere and sensible and, had her suggestions been acted on, the course of their lives again could have been different, but she was only twenty-two, there was no one to advise her and she was powerless to implement them.

Byron, my own, there shall not be any delay to our marriage on account of these circumstances if you are sure you can reconcile yourself to the privations necessarily attendant on so limited an income. I can be as happy with little as with much, provided that little be not exceeded and debt incurred. Of debt I have so great a horror that I should cheerfully make any exertions to avoid it. You are not perhaps aware of the small establishment which our present means can support, yet I think it may be rendered perfectly comfortable (which to me is luxury) if we live for comfort, not for *style* – if we do not sacrifice to the absurd pride of *keeping up our situation* ... As far as I know your taste, I don't think the present restrictions to our expenditure would interfere with your happiness. We can only keep one carriage and one house – if it be within a day's journey from London we may in a great degree unite the advantages of Town and Country, we may receive that quiet kind of society which I think we both prefer ... I love retirement – how much more shall I love it with the person who is dearest to me and the few associates whom he may select or approve ... I shall never desire beyond what your fortune can supply. If your opinions differ, tell me – you know I *will* look to you as the guide ...

My father and mother express and feel the greatest desire to see me yours. If Hanson should not fulfil within the promised ten days, I shall begin to think he means to keep you for another Miss Hanson. ...

Byron replied on 14 December:

Dearest – I waited an entire day and night in the hope or rather intention of sending thee a most heroic answer – but it won't do – the truth is my Love – you have made me vain enough to believe that you would marry me if I had not a 'denier' – and I am very sure I would *you* – if you *were* never to have one ... The Sale of Nd would have liquidated all my debts and left us an immediate surplus sufficient for most of our present exigencies and even wishes – as it is 'I am cabined – cribbed' – at least for the present – I should not have cared for the limitation of income – so much as the *debts* – they have however lessened during the last year – and might perhaps have been done away – were it not that there were others whom – it was in some instances my duty – and in others my inclination – to assist – but even this would not have signified – had my purchaser kept to his bargain – though poor devil – I can't blame him – since his forfeiture is heavy enough ... but love me and regard me as from my heart of hearts truly thine – B.

Annabella's anxiety was increased by Byron's silence regarding her letter of 10 December, and by the delays. These, plus the fact that his letters seemed less than ardent, and he had not given her a gift such as a ring, caused her secretly many misgivings. Neither was the situation helped by being 'scolded every day for your absence, besides feeling it most myself' and she decided to write to him frankly:

> December 16th
> ... We have gone on too long with the magnanimity that might keep us at a distance for ever; and if you won't, I must take the responsibility of speaking plain – only – don't let me marry you against your will. If assured that I shall not, I desire with all my heart to give myself to you. We can have Halnaby as long as we like; therefore do not precipitately determine our future residence – at least not till we have met. When will you come down? Your absence is as unwelcome as possible to everybody.

Not only did Byron's letters fail to reassure her but on 18 December he added that Lord Portsmouth's 'lunatic business' was coming off shortly and he might have to be present to give evidence.

In her letter of 20 December she said bluntly:

> ... I have one request to make for *myself*. If you conceive or feel there is *any* cause which can render you dissatisfied, or less satisfied, with your intended return next week, that you will prefer it to all I have said in favour of that measure. Your letters leave something for conjecture. We shall have many things to ask and hear. But it is useless to think of them before, so I will try and go to sleep.
> P.S. Why should I not own to some conjectures which, if the mere workings of imagination, I am not too proud to submit to censure – if not, it is for *my* good they should be confirmed. I will then ask – are you less confident than you were in the happiness of our marriage? *You will never deceive me* – to that promise I trust – entirely and exclusively.

On 21 December she apologized for her apparent lack of confidence and summarized her only doubt: 'If we do not marry under circumstances that might afterwards cause you to wish it had been delayed, I care little what they are ... I shall accede to whatever is thought best ...', but she did not receive the response she had desired from Byron:

> ... I do not see any good purpose to which questions of this kind are to lead – nor can they be answered otherwise than by time and events. You can still decide upon your own wishes and conduct

before we meet, and apprize me of the result at our interview. Only make sure of your sentiments – mine are – yours ever.

On the next day, 23 December:

If we meet let it be to marry. Had I remained at S. it had probably been over by this time. With regard to us being under the same roof and *not* married – I think past experience has shown us the awkwardness of that situation. I can conceive nothing above purgatory more uncomfortable.

If a postponement is determined upon it had better have been decided at a distance. I shall however set out tomorrow, but stop one day at Newmarket. ...

Annabella must have been overwrought with her own misgivings, her mother's constant railing against Byron, and her father's threats to cancel the marriage. At last Byron and Hobhouse, the friend with whom he had shared so many adventures at Cambridge and during their travels abroad before he became famous, arrived at Seaham at eight o'clock in the evening of 31 December. They were shown to their rooms, and later came down to the library. Annabella heard Byron leave his room and ran to meet him. She threw her arms around his neck and burst into tears. However according to Hobhouse they had a jolly evening and he noted that 'The young lady is most attractive'. The next evening he wrote 'We had not quite so jolly a dinner as yesterday' but he added 'Byron loves her personally when present, as it is easy for those used to such indications to observe'. On their wedding day Hobhouse declared in his diary that Annabella had made a very favourable impression on him.

At eleven o'clock on 2 January 1815, Byron and Annabella were married in the drawing-room at Seaham. Byron was excessively agitated and Annabella had a sudden premonition of disaster but 'I had made up my mind & entered calmly upon a life which promised anything but Sunshine'. By this time she had little choice. Did they ever hear the song – the epithalamium that Sir Ralph had composed for the occasion with so much care and concern? Was the cake that Lady Milbanke had given such special attention to appreciated? In the evening the bride's parents, Hobhouse, and a few friends met for 'a sort of a wedding dinner' – as Hobhouse called it – in Sunderland.

After the ceremony Byron and Annabella set off for Halnaby, alone at last. Byron was silent and morose, and then engaged in 'a wild sort of singing'. When they arrived at Durham joy-bells rang out, for Sir Ralph had been a very popular Member of Parliament for Durham and the family were well known. People had gathered to see the bridal carriage. Inside Byron broke his silence and angrily told her, 'It must come to a separation! You should have married me when I first proposed.' And later: 'I wonder how much longer I shall be able to keep up the part I have been playing!' He told her he detested her mother, how discontented he was with the settlements and her small fortune – how he had longed to break the engagement. In between these ravings he laughed and expressed every feeling of tenderness' – so that she wondered with increasing misery if it was all supposed to be some kind of joke, or whether it was due to him being overwrought, as she knew herself to be.

At last they reached Halnaby. The servants and tenants had assembled to greet the newly-married couple. The bridegroom did not hand her out of the carriage but walked away. Harriet Martineau was later told by the butler, who greeted them, that the bride got out 'with the face and attitude of despair. She came up the steps with a countenance and frame agonized and listless … He longed to offer his arm to the young, lonely, creature'. In her narrative Annabella described how the snow fell heavily after they arrived, increasing the sense of desolation. She felt Byron's aim was to make her feel helplessly in the power of a vindictive tyrant determined to intimidate her by every means he could devise. 'Then for the first time in my life I knew what it was to be alone with God.'

During the unhappy night Byron cried out 'I am surely in Hell!' It was the next morning when they met in the library that 'perhaps the deadliest chill fell on my heart', Annabella recalled. 'He met me repellently and uttered words of blighting irony: 'It is too late now. It is done and cannot be undone'. I told him I did not repent, and tried to inspire a hope which was almost extinguished in my own heart.'

The same morning Byron received a letter from his half-sister Augusta. It began: 'Dearest, first and best of human beings …'. It went on to describe her feelings at the time he was being married, 'As the sea trembles when the earth quakes.' He read this and the opening words to Annabella. He asked her what she thought of them. The effect on him was 'a kind of fierce and exulting transport'.

Byron and Annabella were now set on a course which would have the relentless inevitability of a Greek tragedy.

6   The First Year

The three weeks of 'the Moon', as Byron called it, were remembered with horror by Annabella for the rest of her life. Byron told her he had not loved her, but had married her out of revenge for her first refusal of him. He talked of suicide, murder, incest, and always came the theme 'If you had married me two years ago, you would have saved me from what I can never get over.' In his raging he told her many instances of his vices, some of which she was convinced must have been untrue.

One day he attacked her with a dagger but she remained calm, and he put the dagger down and said: 'If anything could make me believe in heaven it is the expression of your countenance at this moment.' She said many years later: 'Even now I feel that the remembrance of bitterness may wear out, but the remembrance of those few softer moments will to the end remain.' She copied for him some of the poems he wrote while they were at Halnaby in her neat handwriting; they read books together and discussed them; they gave each other pet names – Pippin for her, because of her round face, Duck for him. However she always spent a lot of time by herself, as her presence seemed to irritate him.

In spite of the end of all her hopes and aspirations for their marriage and the anguish that it caused her, it was the intensity of his sufferings that absorbed her feelings so that she almost forgot her own. Sometimes she was able to comfort him a little, as when he worried about his health and 'I would feel his pulse gravely, and then laugh away his fears.' One night he roamed the gallery armed with dagger and pistol, and came to her exhausted and haggard. 'Seeking to allay his misery' – she moved her head until it rested on his breast. He said: 'You should have a softer pillow than my heart.' She replied: ' "I wonder which will break first, yours or mine?" – the only words of despair he ever heard me utter.' She had some small successes for she was able to make him speak to her of his 'little foot' on which he had always been painfully silent. She wrote in her narrative:

> In looking over these pages to see how far they would give to a stranger the true colour of our life at Halnaby. – I find that I have not spoken of the morbidly tenacious feeling he had as to his lameness. There was a connection in his Imagination between that, & his predestination to Evil, or his being an exiled Angel. – These ideas were not suggested to his mind by chance circumstances, but appeared to be deeply rooted there. – There was a bitter feeling towards his Mother in regard to his Foot – I could not understand why, & I did not like to ask questions. ...

From Halnaby, Byron wrote to Lady Melbourne, John Murray, Hanson, Hobhouse and others, and always spoke of Lady Byron in the most natural and cheerful manner, and nothing of the trauma suffered can be guessed from the correspondence. Every day brought letters from Augusta, most being addressed to Annabella. She replied cheerfully in 'Those half-jests in which misery is so fertile' she recalled, but Augusta could guess some of the perplexities Annabella was experiencing. Byron wrote to Augusta sometimes, but he burnt what letters he wrote, and seemed ashamed if they were mentioned. It seems curious in view of the frequent references Byron made of his love for Augusta, that Annabella seemed to encourage her letters and in one letter asks: 'Augusta – will you be my *only* friend?' It reveals the depth of her despair, that this highly regarded and proud girl was reduced, like someone drowning, to seize the only straw she could find – the friendship and support of a woman she had not met but who was beloved by her husband. However, she dreamed of gaining a sister, who would return her affection and thus set the seal on her union with the Byron family. Since Sophy had left home many years ago she had often wished there had been someone close to her that she could talk to. How agreeable it would be, if Byron's loving sister could be hers as well.

There was no one else to confide in, and desperately she asked Augusta to join them at Halnaby. She had heard so often that no one could make him happy but Augusta, that she must have imbued this half-sister with mystic powers, some of which she hoped she herself might acquire, and so learn how to make Byron happy. Perhaps the thought came too, that if she saw Augusta and Byron together, she would see that they were quite a normal half-brother and sister who were fond of each other, and the suspicions that had begun to prey on her mind through Byron's words could be banished and she would be light-hearted again. But Augusta was not able to come, and Byron told Annabella he would make a new will in favour of Augusta, as well as saying he had two natural children and another wife. Annabella thought he seemed disappointed she was not 'mortified' and only laughed at his tales of woe, which she could not take seriously. One day he told her he could no longer endure to be parted from Augusta, and he proposed that she should stay at Halnaby with Mrs Clermont while he visited Augusta, but she insisted that she would accompany him and the plan was dropped.

After three weeks they returned to Seaham and he seemed more kind. It was here that Byron first spoke to her of Thyrza. Although he spoke with emotion of his deep love, and the sorrow he had felt at Thyrza's death, he did not say that Thyrza was not a woman, as Annabella had supposed. He told her then that he loved her – better even than Thyrza – but now he was not able to feel as he had once, when he had felt such a state of excitement before the hour of meeting, that had it continued it must have destroyed him. It was these reflections that led him to compose at midnight, after drinking brandy and water, the verses which he sent to Moore on 2 March 1815 while they were still at Seaham, telling him they were inspired by the death of his school-friend the Duke of Dorset.

There's not a joy the world can give like that it takes away,
When the glow of early thought declines in feeling's dull decay;
'Tis not on youth's smooth cheek the blush alone which fades so fast,
But the tender bloom of heart is gone, ere youth itself be past.

Then the few whose spirits float above the wreck of happiness
Are driven o'er the shoals of guilt or ocean of excess:
The magnet of their course is gone, or only points in vain
The shore to which their shiver'd sail shall never stretch again.

Then the mortal coldness of the soul like death itself comes down;
It cannot feel for others' woes, it dare not dream its own;

That heavy chill has frozen o'er the fountain of our tears,
And though the eye may sparkle still, 'tis where the ice appears.

Though wit may flash from fluent lips, and mirth distract the breast,
Through midnight hours that yield no more their former hope of
    rest;
'Tis but as ivy-leaves around the ruin'd turret wreath,
All green and wildly fresh without, but worn and grey beneath.

Oh could I feel as I have felt. – or be what I have been,
Or weep as I could once have wept, o'er many a vanished scene;
As springs in deserts found seem sweet, all brackish though they be,
So midst the wither'd waste of life, those tears would flow to me.

A year later, during the separation proceedings, he reminded
Moore of these verses '... as being the truest, though the most
melancholy, I ever wrote'. The words reveal that a terrible kind of
spiritual transmutation was taking place and in his despair he
blamed Annabella. Had she responded to his first overture, he
believed, she could have warded off the evil which lurked round
him but now he was doomed, it must be forever, and she should be
punished.

Annabella ended the narrative in which she described this
period of her life with the words: 'If I have been faithful, the
Reader will feel that the insight thus gained into his inner being,
must, whether he was supposed sound in mind or not, have excited
the most intense Commiseration. It would have been a cold heart
indeed which could have left such suffering to itself, to work out
the moral suicide he believed inevitable.'

It is possible that this first experience of ordinary family life at
Seaham might not have been unpleasing to Byron. They played
games in the evening and walked and jumped by the sea where he
was happiest. He listened to Sir Ralph's speeches, and tolerated
his renderings on the violin. Augusta's letters continued to arrive
almost daily and were peppered with comments such as: 'Only
think of B. playing draughts! I never should have suspected him.';
'He has now so many occupations – walking, dining, playing
draughts with Mamma ... but I am vain enough to think he does
not forget Gus.'; 'Here comes *Medora* ...'; 'Your ramble scramble
tumble-cum-jumble must have been delightful.'

Byron's mercurial spirit only needed such persistent little shafts
of mockery to change the loving home atmosphere from being

agreeable to seeming boring and humdrum, as he described in a letter to Moore. Byron continued to make sinister allusions to his half-sister, and Annabella later wrote: 'I *would not* entertain those suspicions, it was odious to believe that my thoughts might sully a relationship so dear and sacred.'

One night Byron sat up late writing and put some water on the fire to quell it, which caused some gas to form and nearly suffocate him. Annabella revived him, and while semiconscious he imagined he was on the way to hell and declared he would defy his Maker to the end. Later he softened and said: 'I have tried everything – I will try virtue, I think. Perhaps I shall go to Heaven holding by the hem of your garment.'

On 9 March they left Seaham to visit Augusta on their way to London. At their last stop Byron said: 'You married me to make me happy didn't you? Well then you do make me happy.' She said later: 'He spoke with passionate affection. I was silent, and he did not see but felt the tears of joy which rose from my heart. Then again he seemed to pity me for some impending, inevitable misery.'

The two women seemed to like each other immediately. That night Byron said to Annabella: 'Now I have *her* you will find I can do without you – in all ways,' and she was forced to think again about the suspicions that had been sown at Halnaby. One evening Annabella said she would like to have Byron painted when he was looking at Medora, Augusta's youngest child, who was then eleven months old. 'The tenderness of his expression I thought quite lovely' she afterwards recorded. A night or two later he told her in front of Augusta that Medora was his child, but she thought he must be joking. Byron's conduct was intolerable, and at nine o'clock at night he would tell Annabella to go to bed, saying, 'We don't want you.' She later recorded: 'What I suffered during our stay at S. M. B. was indescribable.'

Throughout the nightmare fortnight Augusta was as kind to Annabella as possible, for she seemed afraid of Byron, and embarrassed by his churlish behaviour and his vulgar way of speaking. He showed signs of passion for Augusta to which she submitted with apparent confusion, although she always wore her gold brooch containing their hair and engraved with three crosses, the symbol of their love which seemed to encourage him. Byron had ordered one for each of them from a London jeweller, and they were received two or three days after he and Annabella had arrived at Augusta's home. Annabella later wrote:

I could not go to my restless bed till the time of leaving A, and I trembled as I heard his terrible step. He swore at Fletcher as he was undressing with a degree of rage that seemed to threaten his life, and every night he came into my room in the same mood, except once or twice, when I heard the sound of freezing professions – more intolerable than his uncontrolled abhorrence.

They left Six Mile Bottom on 28 March 1815, and proceeded to London to take up residence at 13 Piccadilly Terrace. Lady Melbourne had rented it for them but it was large and expensive and quite the opposite to the modest home that Annabella had wished for in view of their straitened financial situation. During the first ten days after leaving Six Mile Bottom Byron was more friendly to Annabella than she had ever known him to be. She was called to her dying uncle's bedside soon after their arrival in London and Byron wrote her a note asking her to come home. 'Dearest – Now your mother is come I won't have you worried any longer – more particularly in your present situation [Annabella was now pregnant] which is rendered very precarious by what you have already gone through. Pray – come home – ever thine B.'

Then Augusta arrived. She had come to London because she had been appointed a woman of the bedchamber to Queen Charlotte, but since this position secured rooms for her in St James's Palace it seems incredible that she not only came, but stayed until Annabella firmly asked her to leave over two months later. Annabella said afterwards that her willingness to come had suggested innocence, and if she had not allowed her, she would have had to have given a reason; a false excuse would have been seen through and overruled. If she had spoken of the true reason for not wishing her to come, which at that time was a suspicion that some criminal act had taken place once in the past between Augusta and Byron, this would have angered Byron and perhaps closed for ever any hopes for their united welfare. Also there was the possibility that all that he was saying might have been a figment of his disordered imagination, or that he was using it to be cruel to her, as he had done with other imputations that she could not believe. He had told her once '... not to mind my words, and then we may get along very well'.

The uncertainty was overwhelming, for in front of people he would be everything that she could wish for. George Ticknor, the American diarist and traveller, who paid several calls on the Byrons at Piccadilly Terrace wrote:

She [Lady Byron] is pretty, not beautiful for the prevalent expression of her countenance is that of ingenuousness. ... She was dressed to go and drive, and after stopping a few moments, went to her carriage. Lord Byron's manner to her was affectionate: he followed her to the door and shook hands with her, as if he were not to see her for a month.

A few days later he met her again:

She did not seem so pretty to me as she did the other day, but what she may have lost in regular beauty she made up in variety and expression of countenance. She is diffident – she is very young ... but is obviously possessed of talent, and did not talk at all for display. For the quarter of an hour during which I was with her, she talked upon a considerable variety of subjects – America, of which she seemed to know considerable, of France and Greece, with something of her husband's visit there – and spoke of all with a justness and a light good-humour that would have struck me even in one of whom I had heard nothing.

Soon after this meeting Ticknor had a seat in Byron's box at Drury Lane:

There was nobody there ... but Lord and Lady Byron, and her father and mother ... Lord Byron was pleasant, and Lady Byron more interesting than I have yet seen her ... Lady Milbanke, Lady Byron's mother, is a good natured old lady, – a little fashionable, however, I fear – and her husband, a plain, respectable Englishman who loves politics ... I think I have received more kindness from Lord Byron than from any person in England on whom I had not the regular claim of a letter of introduction.

Ticknor's was not the only record of Byron's apparent devotion to his wife. William Harness remarked that at parties '... he would be seen hanging over the back of her chair, scarcely talking to anybody else, eagerly introducing his friends to her ...'. Murray was favourably impressed, it being his opinion that 'She is a most delightful creature, and possesses excellent temper and a most inordinate share of good sense.' Indeed those who saw them together thought that they were happy.

Byron at first had been cool to Augusta on her arrival at Piccadilly Terrace but soon his old familiarity towards her reasserted itself, and his treatment of Annabella was generally that of hatred and loathing. She related: 'There were moments when I could have plunged a dagger in her heart, but she never saw them ... I resisted suspicion to the utmost ... I was almost mad – and to prevent myself indulging the passion of revenge. I was obliged to substitute another – that of romantic forgiveness.'

After the separation Annabella wrote to Augusta in July 1816 reminding her of this time:

> You will remember some things by which I intimated that I knew more than you thought, and I almost offered myself to your confidence ... As you do not, and never have attempted to, deceive me about *previous facts* of which my conviction is unalterable – I rely more on your simple assertion of 'never wronged me' intentionally – *I believe it implicitly* ... Dearest Augusta, you will think, perhaps justly, that I erred in encouraging you myself – but my situation was most extraordinary. I could not till a late period bear to admit things to myself ... and you were the kindest friend and comforter ... Let the past be *understood* now, to be buried in future.

As at Six Mile Bottom, Byron told Annabella to go to bed early. Augusta would sit up to try and keep him from drinking brandy, which had a bad effect on him. Annabella, pregnant, and unable to get to sleep, could hear them laughing and talking to each other as they came up the stairs at a late hour.

> When Augusta left at Annabella's request, things seemed better for a time, and she wrote: ... he would converse familiarly ... there was a sort of conventional language of nonsense between us, relieving his fears of *sermons* and *sentiments*. He would give play to his imagination and suddenly deliver the deepest reflections, then shrink from them into frolic and levity. The transitions had all the grace of genius, and formed its greatest charm for me. They were as the foam that might float on the waters of bitterness.

In August Byron visited Augusta for a few days to try to sort out the deeds of the house which the Leighs were planning to sell, and when he came back the situation deteriorated badly but Annabella kept her distress to herself. In a letter to her mother she describes how the parrot made another attack on her toe:

... but without either injuring or alarming me. However when I mentioned the circumstances to B., thinking it would amuse him, he left the room and informed me when he came back that he had thrown Parrot and cage out of the window down the Airy (I don't know how to spell it), and I feared I had been too well revenged. But the Bird came down quite safe and did not lay in a trance like Satan but called out 'Johnny'!

They seemed to have been accident-prone for Byron had written to Annabella while he had been staying with Augusta that a mousetrap had been left in his room and as a consequence he had nearly lost a toe.

On 1 November Annabella wrote some reflections on Byron's character. She continued with her theme in a letter to Augusta:

His misfortune is an habitual *passion for Excitement* ... It is the Ennui of a monotonous existence that drives the best hearted people of this description ... to seem to act from bad motives, when in fact they are only flying from internal suffering by any external stimulus. The love of tormenting arises chiefly from this source. ... As for seeking a cure in worldly dissipation, it is added to the evil. ... At the same time I would have his mind diverted from itself by every possible means ... if I find that the disease is making a progress I will court Lady M[elbourne]'s society for him, or anything in the world to arrest its *fatal* course. ... with such apprehensions, will you wonder if I am sometimes almost heart-broken before my time? My dear A., do give me every opinion of *yours on this*, & don't mistrust your own judgement. ...

Annabella's analysis seems to have a fair degree of accuracy when the many accounts of Byron flaunting himself are considered – biting a saucer when a small child; his exploits at Cambridge with a tame bear; his bizarre clothes; and later going into exile in an expensive replica of Napoleon's carriage even though the rent for Piccadilly Terrace remained unpaid. Goethe commented that if Byron had invented the separation drama he could not have chosen a more suitable subject for his creative ability. Emilio Castelar, the Spanish statesman, asserted that Byron never gained a heart without afflicting it, or himself. Peace and quiet he desired, Byron said, but action and sensation were what he sought.

On 9 November Annabella wrote again to Augusta:

Everything is explained by a bailiff sleeping last night in the house. ... God knows what I suffered yesterday, & am suffering from B's distractions, which is of the *very worst* kind. He leaves the house, telling me he will at once abandon himself to every sort of desperation, speaks to me only to upbraid me with having married him when he wished not, and says he is therefore acquitted of all principle towards me, and I must consider myself *only* to be answerable for the vicious courses to which his despair will drive him. ... Things never were so serious – I don't mean the circumstances, for they must mend, but his feelings. ... Don't be unhappy about *me* – and perhaps you will see less cause than I do to be so about *him*. ...

P.S. I have waited till the last in hopes of some change, but all is exorable pride and hardness. O Augusta, will it ever change for me?

Next day:

He does not think I know the circumstances of our unwelcome guest. I wish George B or some manfriend of common-sense were in the way to laugh B out of his excessive horrors on this subject, which he seems to regard as if no mortal had ever experience anything so shocking; and *we* can do less, because he thinks that women don't enter into those sublime grievances.

After Post

I must tell you that you are 'Augusta' again to B. – for you were 'Mrs Leigh' during the paroxysm, & I expected you would soon be 'The Honourable'. I ought to have laughed at this; but I took it as another misery, fancying that *I* was in some way the cause of such an alteration. And now for my peace and comfort, dearest A. let me express my earnest desire that whatever you may see or hear towards me, you will never think it an act of friendship for me to risk B's displeasure. I suspect you of any *disinterested folly* of this kind. But in the first place, under any circumstances, I should be more *grieved* if he & you were to differ; and in the second (which may have more weight with you) I don't think it could do *me* any good to have *my part taken*. So remember.

I am afraid *this* bailiff is a sad brute, & will proceed to very great inconvenience. I have written to my Mother on the subject, who if she can, will certainly send me some money – but my father has been as nearly in Gaol as possible.

A common criticism of Annabella is that she was not sympathetic to Byron's financial worries, but letters show she was very actively employed in desperately trying to arrange loans and consulting everybody she could think of who might help. Her father had tried to raise money for them by selling farms on the Seaham estate, but it was a bad time to sell and it seemed that payment would not be forthcoming before the execution for the sale of Byron's books and other objects. 'Do you know of any means by which a week might be gained?' Annabella anxiously asked her mother. She continued, 'I should very much lament the seizure of his books. ... When B – has any hope of avoiding the last extremity, he is quite a different man – for he feels it dreadfully. ... I care very much to see him in an agony.' Judith explained that many people were in a similar predicament: '... unavoidable and heavy losses from Bankruptcies of those who rented collieries and also the recent failures of the Durham and Sunderland Banks have swept away *many thousands*'. It must have been especially bitter for Annabella, having disclosed to him before they were married her own horror of debt and urgently advised him that they should live modestly, to find that Lady Melbourne had arranged for them to live in the Duchess of Devonshire's expensive house in Piccadilly Terrace, when there was no money to pay the rent.

Augusta had been asked to return, but before she arrived on 15 November Annabella had written to her:

> Don't be afraid for my carcase – it will do very well. Of the rest I scarcely know what to think – I have many fears ... My heart aches – it has been severely tried – but I won't say more on paper – You will do good, I think, – if any can be done –
> My dearest A. – I feel all your kindness –.

Annabella wrote in a letter to her father: 'I suppose my mam will choose to come and fidget while I squall ...'. Judith, her mother, came to stay at Mivart's Hotel, but she was ill when she arrived, became worse, and had to take to her bed with asthma, erysipelas and fever before Annabella's confinement. Although Annabella's parents knew only of the financial problems, it is likely her mother at least could sense that something was very wrong. At this time Byron was working as a sort of actor-manager at Drury Lane and boasted of his many mistresses to annoy both Augusta and Annabella. Creditors were pressing hard for payment, and bailiffs were again installed in the house.

In spite of her own sufferings, it was far worse for Annabella to see Byron in such mental agony. He said to her once: 'I have been too bad ever to be good ... if I had known you since I was five years old, I might have been happy.' When she tried to persuade him that the past could be redeemed, he said she could not know what was oppressing his conscience, and yet he often seemed to want to confide in her. Another day she told him she believed he would love her yet, and still came the old refrain: 'It is too late now. If you had taken me two years ago ... but it is my destiny to ruin all I come near.'

He had long felt he was under a fatal curse, manifested by the malevolent stigma of his deformity. Perhaps he was. His grandfather, Admiral Byron, was known as Foul Weather Jack because he always encountered such appalling weather, beyond that of normal chance. When he had been a young midshipman, sailors from his ship were involved in an incident with some Indians who had previously been friendly, until their women were interfered with during the night, and they became very angry. It was said they evoked a frightful curse on the future amours of those who had engaged in the escapade, which could have included the young, good-looking Byron. Certainly his son – Byron's father – could not be said to have had a very satisfactory life, and Byron, while being notorious for his love affairs, never had one that did not bring unhappiness in one form or another to those he loved.

Annabella was forced to believe that not only was she not bringing him the peace she had hoped, but she was actually harmful in the sense that she seemed to greatly provoke and irritate him. His behaviour was getting more erratic, to the point when it was wondered if he were sane. She had tried everything she could think of, and had willingly submitted to the humiliation of asking Augusta to return. There was one last hope – that the birth of their baby would change the haunted look on his face to the gentle expression that she had only seen when watching him look at Medora, and so bring peace to the troubled household.

One night coming home late from a party he found Augusta and Annabella waiting up for him. Looking at his wife he appeared suddenly to be overcome with remorse and flung himself at her feet saying he was a monster – she could never forgive him – he had lost her forever. Annabella, deeply touched, said: 'Byron all is forgotten; never, never shall you hear of it more!' He got to his feet, and folding his arms, burst into laughter. 'What do you mean?' Annabella asked. 'Only a philosophical experiment, that's all. I wished to ascertain the value of your resolutions, ...' was Byron's reply.

On 9 December Annabella's labour pains began, and she went to see Byron in the library, but came away convulsed with grief for he had asked her if she intended to go on living with him. The next day at one o'clock in the afternoon a baby girl was born, and the names given were Augusta Ada. It was even more dreadful than could have been imagined. Beforehand Byron told Annabella he hoped that she and the baby would die during the birth. During her labour he was knocking furniture and soda-water bottles about in the room beneath her. Afterwards he sent her a message to say that her mother had died, and entered the room saying, 'The child *was* born dead wasn't it?'

Throughout this period and through the confinement, Augusta showed great kindness and was of such comfort to Annabella that she never forgot it. The baby did nothing to bring the parents closer together and Byron's condition worsened. He was drinking large quantities of brandy, taking laudanum, threatening suicide, and when he did visit Annabella he left her in floods of tears. Augusta had previously taken the precaution of imploring his cousin George Byron and Mrs Clermont to stay in the house because it was feared that he might mortally injure Annabella or himself. Mrs Clermont had not only been a governess to Annabella, but from long employment with the family, had become a staunch friend and reliable counsellor. The servants, including Byron's valet Fletcher, were so alarmed that without being instructed they had arranged to protect their mistress at night by taking it in turns to be on guard outside Byron's room.

Annabella and Augusta were increasingly anxious about Byron's behaviour, and were more and more afraid that he might be mentally deranged. Augusta confided their fears to Byron's aunt, Sophia Byron, who often visited Piccadilly Terrace and was convinced that insanity must be the cause. She therefore earnestly advised that they should consult Dr Baillie, who had attended Byron when he was a boy concerning his foot. He suggested a temporary absence of his wife 'as an experiment'. Annabella also asked Le Mann, who was her own doctor, for his opinion. He considered that lunacy rather than depravity must account for Byron's behaviour, for he had been told by an acquaintance from the theatre where Byron was actor-manager that his odd conduct there was well known. Neither doctor, however, could make a statement without seeing Byron, and both women feared his rages too much to risk discussing their concern with him. Annabella then went to see Mr Hanson to tell him of their fears and to report what the doctors had said, including Dr Baillie's recommendation. She asked him if he would try and persuade Byron to join her at Kirkby, and if this was not possible, she assured him she would come back at a moment's notice if it was necessary or desirable. She told Mrs Clermont: 'If he is insane I will do everything possible to alleviate his disease.'

Judith, now Lady Noel through the conditions of the will of her brother, the recently deceased Lord Wentworth, had inherited the Kirkby Mallory estate from him. She wrote to Byron on 28 December warmly inviting him, his wife and child to Kirkby Mallory Hall, adding: 'I trust *you* would not think yourself under any constraint but to do exactly what you like.' On the same day she wrote a very kind letter to Annabella, welcoming them to stay as long as they wished, and repeating her assurance that Byron would be under no pressure to conform to a meal routine and could always do just as he pleased.

However, on 6 January, less than four weeks after her child was born Byron wrote a note to Annabella which Augusta was asked to deliver. It read:

> When you are disposed to leave London, it would be convenient that a day should be fixed – and (if possible) not a very remote one for the purpose. Of my opinion upon that subject you are sufficiently in possession – and of the circumstances which have led to it – as also to my plans – or rather intentions – for the future. As Lady Noel has asked you to Kirkby, there you can be for the present – unless you prefer Seaham. As the dismissal of the present establishment is of such importance to me, the sooner you can fix on the day the better – though of course your convenience and inclination shall be first consulted.
>
> The child will of course accompany you – there is a more easy and safer carriage than the chariot (unless you prefer it) which I mentioned before – on that you can do as you please.

When Annabella receive this note, she burst into tears and said through her sobs: 'I expected it, but I can't help feeling this – to think that I have lived to be hated by my husband.' The next day she sent a reply through Augusta. 'I shall obey your wishes, and fix the earliest day that circumstances will admit for leaving London.' She had intended to stay until after Le Mann's visit, which had been arranged for 15 January, but on the 13th there was such a frightening scene that George Byron said that he would not allow her to stay any longer in the house without informing her parents of the situation, about which they were still ignorant. Annabella then realized it was considered her life was in danger and arranged to leave on 15 January.

The night before she left she went into the room where Byron and Augusta were sitting together and, offering her hand, said: 'Byron, I have come to say goodbye.' He got up and stood in front of the fire with his hands behind his back. 'When shall we three meet again?' he asked. 'In heaven I hope,' she answered. They were never to see each other again.

She wrote afterwards of the last night she spent at Piccadilly Terrace:

I fell into a sound sleep on the last night, as I believe is often the case in such cases of deep sorrow. Next morning I woke exhausted. I went downstairs – the carriage was at the door. I passed his room. There was a large mat on which his Newfoundland dog used to lie. For a moment I was tempted to throw myself on it, and wait at all hazards, but it was only a moment – and I passed on. That was our parting.

That night Byron and Augusta went with George Byron, and Byron's friend Scrope Davies, to the theatre.

7 The Separation

Dr Baillie had advised that during his wife's absence 'as an experiment' she should avoid all but mild and soothing topics in her correspondence with Byron and accordingly Annabella sent him two light-hearted notes. These were later used as evidence that her parents had coerced her into the separation which she had never before contemplated. The first letter was written at Woburn on the way to Kirkby Mallory on 15 January 1816. It was mild and playful in tone, telling him the child was well, and he was to remember medical injunctions, ending: 'Ada's love to you with mine. Pip.'

The next day she wrote from Kirkby Mallory in the same light, humorous manner (which she was far from feeling), hoping that Byron might feel persuaded to join her:

> Dearest Duck, – We got here quite well last night, and were ushered into the kitchen instead of the drawing-room, by a mistake that might have been agreeable enough to hungry people. Of this and other incidents Dad wants to write you a jocose account, and both he and Mam long to have the family party completed. Such … ! and such a *sitting* room or *sulking* room all to yourself. If I were not always looking about for B., I should be a great deal better already for country air. *Miss* finds her provisions increased, and fattens thereon. It is a good thing she can't understand all the flattery bestowed upon her, 'Little Angel'. Love to the good Goose, and everybody's love to you both from hence.
>
> Ever thy most loving
>
> Pippin … Pip … ip

The 'Goose' in the letter was Augusta's nickname. Although

advised against it, she had insisted on staying with Byron because she feared Byron would do away with himself, and this worry may have influenced her husband in not insisting on her return. Her presence was a great comfort to Annabella, for she wrote every day giving long bulletins on Byron's condition, and all that was going on in what Annabella still considered her home.

Meanwhile Annabella clung to the theory that Byron was suffering from temporary insanity which could be diagnosed and treated, encouraged by Augusta's letters that seemed always to foster the idea of 'malady'. Her parents were shocked and distressed by her appearance, but were unaware of the cause, and they were all still hoping that Byron would soon join them. By 18 January Annabella had heard that Le Mann was treating him for his liver but there was no reference to his mental condition. Byron's cousin George and his aunt Sophia had convinced her that should she be persuaded to return she would never leave his house alive.

Matters were brought to a head at Kirkby by a letter from her friend Selina Doyle, to whom Annabella had written on 15 January, and who was partly aware of the situation at Piccadilly Terrace. Apparently her mother, being also a friend of Selina, had inquired for news, and had been given the letter to read. Seeing the words 'outrages' and 'ill-treatment' Judith at last elicited an anguished account of the treatment Annabella had had from Byron since the beginning of their marriage. She immediately decided to go to London for legal advice from the renowned lawyer Sir Samuel Romilly, and took with her a statement from Annabella. On Romilly's advice she saw Dr Stephen Lushington, a distinguished barrister and civil legal adviser, with whom she was most impressed as being 'Gentlemanlike, clear-headed and clever.' Lushington at once took a hard line and advised that Byron must not go to Kirkby Mallory, neither should Annabella see or write to him, for otherwise he could apply for restoration of conjugal rights giving him custody of Ada, which might well be granted. Further, he agreed with Sir Samuel that a letter should be sent from Sir Ralph to Byron requesting a quiet separation. Annabella wrote to Mrs Clermont urging her to persuade her mother to forbear every harsh measure that was not necessary for her safety and justification: '... it will break my heart if she takes up the case with bitterness against him'.

Sir Ralph duly wrote on 28 January the letter drafted by Lushington:

Very recently circumstances have come to my knowledge which convince me that with your opinions it cannot tend to your happiness to continue to live with Lady Byron, and I am yet more forcibly convinced that her return to you after her dismissal from your house and the treatment she experienced whilst in it is not consistent either with her comfort or, I regret to add, personal safety. ...

The letter arrived on 29 January, but Augusta, who had been warned of its arrival, intercepted it, and returned it unopened. She wrote to Annabella explaining:

For once in my life I have ventured to act according to my own judgement – not without 10,000 fears I assure you. But I do it for the best and I do hope at least it will not be productive of evil, as I only wish a few days delay and that you would hear all I have to say before you send the enclosed.

There followed a long and flustered effort to warn Annabella of the possible dire effect on Byron of the letter, and of the fact that Byron had been to see Lady Melbourne at her, Lady Melbourne's, request, and had returned suitably admonished for his past behaviour to Annabella.

Lady Noel was very angry at Augusta's presumption in returning Sir Ralph's letter and immediately wrote to her saying that her 'barbarous and hard hearted brother' had broken the heart that was devoted to him. She was almost incoherent in her rage and distress but Annabella restrained her from posting the letter and Judith wrote to Mrs Clermont instead. Annabella had also written to Mrs Clermont and in a postscript added; 'I am so sure that a little *time* could do a great deal – and relieve me from that responsibility which I have suffered so much with a view to avoid – that it would be a pity if after all I incurred it without absolute necessity. Urge this against any immediate measure.'

Sir Ralph took the precaution of taking the letter the second time to Byron and delivering it by hand. Byron was amazed and shocked. He asked Augusta to write to his wife and ask her if the request for a separation was by her wish. The answer came at once. 'You are desired by your brother to ask if my father has acted with my concurrence in proposing a separation. He has.' Annabella went on to recall Byron's avowed and insurmountable aversion to the married state and that all her attempts to contribute towards his happiness were wholly useless and most unwelcome to him.

It was too late for salvage attempts and the leading characters thrashed around for a while as if in a kind of time warp, in which they had, without knowing what they were doing, become entrapped and entrenched. The letters from which the following extracts are taken describe incomparably the final phases of the doomed marriage for which Annabella had had such high hopes.

Byron replied to Sir Ralph on 2 February stating that he had not dismissed Lady Byron – that she had left by medical advice – they had parted in harmony – against his inclination, which was to later accompany her. It was true that a temporary residence with her parents had been decided on because of his pecuniary situation, and that Lady Byron 'who is Truth itself' would vouch for the truth of his statement. He had been distressed by worry and ill-health which had made him irritable and at times violent. He continued:

> And now Sir – not for your satisfaction, for I owe you none – but for my own, and in justice to Lady Byron, it is my duty to say that there is no part of her conduct, character, temper, talents, or dispostion, which could in my opinion have been changed for the better ... She has ever appeared to me as one of the most amiable of beings – and nearer to Perfection than I have conceived could belong to Humanity in its present existence ... there are parts of your letter, which – I must be permitted to say – arrogate a right which you do not possess. For the present at least, your daughter is my wife; – she is the mother of my child – and till I have her express sanction of your proceedings, I shall take leave to doubt the propriety of your interference. ...

He wrote to Annabella on 3 February:

> I have received a letter from your father proposing a separation between us – to which I cannot give an answer without being acquainted with your own thoughts and wishes ... To conclude – I shall eventually abide by your decision – but I request you most earnestly to weigh well the probable consequences, – to pause before you pronounce. ... Whatever may occur, it is but justice to you to say that you are exempt from all fault whatever – and that neither now nor at any time have I the slightest imputation of any description to charge upon you.

Byron wrote two days later, for Annabella had not yet given him an answer:

Dearest Bell – No answer from you yet – perhaps it is as well – but
do recollect – that all is at stake – the present – the future – and
even the colouring of the past. The whole of my errors – or what
harsher name you chose to give them – you know – but I loved you –
and will not part from you without your *own* most express and
expressed refusal to return to or receive me. Only say the word – that
you are still mine in your heart – and 'Kate! – I will buckler thee
against a million.

Mrs Clermont wrote to Judith telling her that Colonel Doyle,
Selina's brother, was most anxious that Annabella should not be
'pressed to pursue the course *legally* – if she is not quite certain of
having sufficient strength to persevere in it … he is doubtful
whether self reproach for having carried it into effect might not kill
her before her reason had recovered sufficient power to sustain
her': the alternative being a negotiation 'which might leave it more
open to reconciliation at a future period'. But Annabella was past
wishing 'O that I were in London, if in the coal-hole,' as she had
written to Augusta, and past the worst of her derangement when
her maid Mrs Fletcher reported to her husband, Byron's valet, that
'… she was rolling on the floor in a paroxysm of grief at having
promised to separate from Lord Byron'.

Now that the worst had happened and she was removed from
the dread of some unknown but terrible event and the atmosphere
of threatened and past evil that had enveloped her ever since she
was married, she began to feel positive relief. But she was always
aware of the very real possibility that her child could be taken away.
At times, when she remembered Byron's gentler moments, and his
own genuine mental torment, her longing for him and her grief
were extreme so that her conversation was almost incoherent. 'I
never must see him again – I shall wish otherwise when I am less
sure – but let me be preserved from it by every means,' she wrote to
Mrs Clermont. She knew that it would be impossible for her to
meet him as he had requested, and not respond to his overtures,
which could be just another 'philosophical experiment'. She knew
too that she was helpless against his matchless command of words,
as instanced in his letter to her father, where behind the façade of
apparent candour for his misdeeds and tribute to her perfection,
lay an expanse of fallacy and omission, so that even her dismissal
was rendered as 'parting in harmony'.

She replied to Byron on 7 February:

If I had not written to Mrs Leigh what I deemed a sufficient answer to the contents of your first letter, I should not have deferred the still more painful task of addressing yourself. Your second letter, received yesterday seems to require from me this exertion. I am surprised at the manner in which that letter was delivered to me, since my correspondence, as well as my determination, is free. [He had addressed the letter to Annabella's maid with the instruction to deliver it with her own hands to Lady Byron.] I have indeed placed myself under the protection of my parents, but I act on my own conviction – independently – as they do theirs. You know what I have suffered, and would have sacrificed to avoid this extremity – and the strong proofs of duty and attachment I have given by a persevering endurance of the most trying inflictions. After seriously and dispassionately reviewing the misery that I have experienced almost without interval from the day of my marriage, I have finally determined on the measure of a Separation – which my father was authorized to communicate to you – and to carry into effect.

It is unhappily your disposition to consider what you *have* as worthless – what you have *lost* as invaluable. But remember that you declared yourself *most miserable* when I was yours.

Every expression of feeling, sincerely as it might be made, would here be misplaced.

A I Byron

Next day, on receiving her letter, he wrote:

All I can say seems useless – and all I could say might be no less unavailing – yet I still cling to the wreck of my hopes, before they sink for ever. Were you then never happy with me? – did you never at any time express yourself so? – have no marks of affection – of the warmest and most reciprocal attachment passed between us? – or did in fact hardly a day go down without some such on one side and generally on both? – do not mistake me.

I have not denied my state of mind, but you know its causes – and were these deviations from calmness never followed by acknowledgement and repentance? – was not the last more particularly so? – and had I not – had we not – the days before and on the day when we parted, every reason to believe that we loved each other – that we were to meet again – were not your letters kind? – had I not acknowledged to you all my faults and follies – and assured you that some had not and would not be repeated? – I do not require these questions to be answered to me, but to your own heart ...

Will you see me? ... I will say and do nothing to agitate either – it
is torture to correspond thus ...
You say it is my disposition to deem what I *have worthless* did I
deem *you* so? – did I ever so express myself to you – or of you to
others? – you are much changed within these twenty days or you
would never have thus poisoned your own better feelings – and
trampled on mine.

At the same time she had a letter from Augusta who had not
written for six days:

My silence will not have been misinterpreted by *you* but all I could
have said within ye few days would only have added to what I know
you are suffering. You have better advisers than I can be, tho none
more anxious for yr peace and happiness. I *am on the spot* however
and feel it a duty to say that I am apprehensive of the most serious
consequences from the manner in which *he* has taken this *sad*
business to his heart. He writes today to ask you to see him – *pause*
ere you refuse *for God's sake*. Heaven direct and bless you! my
dearest Sis. ...

Annabella realized that the letter she had sent Byron on arriving
at Kirkby could be misconstrued, and on 13 February she wrote a
lucid and sincere letter to Byron, explaining her actions:

On reconsidering your last letter to me, and your second to my
father, I find some allusions which I will not leave to be answered by
others, because the explanation may be less disagreeable to you
from myself.
My letters of Jany 15th and 16th. It can be fully and clearly
proved that I left your house under the persuasion of your having a
complaint of so dangerous a nature that any agitation might bring
on a fatal crisis. My entreaties, before I quitted you, that you would
take medical advice – repeated in my letter of Jan. 15th – must
convince you of such an impression on my mind. My absence, if it
had not been rendered necessary by other causes, was *medically*
recommended on that ground, as removing an object of irritation. I
should have acted inconsistently with my unchanged affection for
you, or indeed with the common principles of humanity, by arguing
my wrongs at that moment. From subsequent accounts, I found that
those particular apprehensions which I and others had entertained
were groundless. Till they were ascertained to be so, it was my wish
and intention to induce you to come to this place, where, at every

hazard, I would have devoted myself to the alleviations of *your* sufferings, and should not then have reminded you of *my own*, as believing you, from physical causes, not to be *accountable* for them. My parents, under the same impression communicated by me, felt the kindest anxiety to promote my wishes and your recovery, by receiving you here ...

I have consistently fulfilled my duty as your wife. It was too dear to be abandoned till it became hopeless – Now my resolution cannot be changed.

It is not difficult to understand why Byron affected to or really did believe that the separation was due to her parents' influence, for he had disliked her mother since Caroline Lamb had reported to him Lady Milbanke's lack of enthusiasm for him as a suitor for her daughter. But it is strange that those who know the circumstances which had existed at 13 Piccadilly Terrace, and know that Annabella had been advised to leave by *his* relatives and doctors, and ordered to leave by Byron, should also take this view. Had she stayed or returned and Byron had blown his brains out or fatally injured her, they would have said that her pride and self-esteem would not allow public admission of the failure of their marriage, even though she and others of the household had known and were alarmed that these acts had been threatened.

Hobhouse and Hodgson wrote to Annabella. Hobhouse was clumsy in expression but had genuinely thought she was mistaken in leaving Byron. However, when both Augusta and George Byron told him of 'great tyranny and menaces, furies, neglects, and even real injuries' that had been inflicted on her, even though Augusta had told him that she had heard Byron crying in his room, he wrote in his diary 'I found it difficult to account for his deceiving me. ... and I now thought it my duty to tell him I had changed my opinion – Alas, what a ruin!'

On 22 February Annabella, being unable to bear the suspense, joined her father in London. She remained firm in her decision, but her grief was overwhelming. During her stay she met Augusta two or three times and Augusta reported to Hodgson:

... I never can describe Lady Byron's appearance to you but by comparing it to what I should imagine a being of another world. She is positively reduced to a skeleton, pale as ashes, a deep hollow tone of voice and a *calm* in her manner quite supernatural. She received *me* kindly, but that really appeared the only *surviving* feeling – all else was *death-like* calm. I can never forget it, never!

Annabella's own account of her feelings at this time was written many years later:

> I felt appalled at the desert which seemed spread before me. At first indeed I felt relief from breathing an atmosphere of innocence – but it was not for long. There was a burning world within which made the external one cold – I had given up all that was congenial with youth – The imagination of what *might have been* was all that remained ... In this state I had a singular degree of insensibility to the *real* – The touch of every hand seemed cold. I could look on tears without sympathy – and I returned kindness heartlessly & mechanically.

Annabella's dominant reason for going to London was her anxiety that if the separation was insisted upon, Byron would hand over the care of their child to Augusta, if not immediately, at some future date. This fear was justified for Byron had already spoken of it, and indeed continued to speak of it when he was many miles away. She suspected that in view of the revenge he now seemed to crave because of her first refusal of him, he would feel very much more bitter after the separation. She was afraid that with his persuasive and beguiling manner, plus the fact it could be said that she had deserted him, he would be able to convince a court of his paternal rights to his child. She was not being unnecessarily anxious for Henry Brougham, the distinguished advocate, was consulted by Wharton & Ford the family attorneys, and replied that '... if upon the return to the writ the tender age of the child were set forth, the father could only obtain possession of it by offering to take back the mother – but if that offer were made, Mr B apprehends, that Lady B could not retain possession of the child from the father'.

Lushington saw Annabella on the day she arrived in London and had a long conversation with her, during which she told him of circumstances that she had not divulged to her parents. Lushington then told her that in his opinion a reconciliation was impossible, and should she consider it 'he would not, either professionally or otherwise, take any part towards effecting it'. He must have warned her that should she return to Byron with knowledge or suspicions of a relationship between him and Augusta, it would have been to condone incest – a crime then considered worse than murder.

Meanwhile the rumours concerning Byron and his half-sister which had been prevalent before his marriage were again spreading rapidly. Annabella was determined to protect Augusta as much as possible by letting her intimate relationship with her be widely known. She loved her still, and remembered with gratitude Augusta's kindness, especially towards the end of her pregnancy. She very much wished to avoid disclosing matters to the world which would harm Byron and which she felt were private and should remain so, not only out of consideration for her child and Augusta, whom she did not wish to hurt, but also in the hope she would always retain, that there could some day be a reconciliation. Apart from this, Augusta would be the only source of regular and reliable news concerning Byron. Lushington, who did not approve of Annabella's wish to protect Augusta, insisted on drawing up a document giving her reasons for continuing to show friendship with Mrs Leigh, thus making provision that Lady Byron's conduct now would not be prejudicial to her, if a charge later had to be made.

Byron wrote the famous verses 'Fare Thee Well' and sent a copy to his wife with a short letter written on 20 March:

Dear Bell
    I send you the first thing I ever attempted to compose upon you – and, it may be, the last I shall compose at all. This may look at the present moment like an affectation – but it is not so ...

> Fare thee well! and if for ever
> Still for ever, fare *thee well*;
> Even though unforgiving, never
> 'Gainst thee shall my heart rebel.
>
> Would that breast were bared before thee
> Where thy head so oft hath lain,
> While that placid sleep came o'er thee
> Which thou ne'er canst know again:
>
> Though my many faults defaced me,
> Could no other arm be found,
> Than the one which once embraced me,
> To inflict a cureless wound?

> All my faults per chance thou knowest –
> All my madness – none can know;
> All my hope – where'er thou goest –
> Wither – yet with *thee* they go.
>
> Fare thee well! thus disunited –
> Torn from every nearer tie –
> Seared in heart – and lone – and blighted –
> More than this I scarce can die.

Annabella wrote to her mother: 'I had a copy of verses from his Lordship yesterday – very tender – and so he talks of me to Everyone.' Perhaps Byron here overacted, for these verses are generally considered banal and those attacking Mrs Clermont in *The Sketch*, which he wrote at the same time, are indeed unworthy of him. Murray was commissioned to print them for private distribution, but apparently by mistake they were both published by *The Champion* on 14 April and quickly followed by other journals – adding to the prevailing deep disapproval of Byron. Caro George (so called to distinguish her from the other Caroline Lamb, her husband's sister-in-law, who was known as Caro William) wrote to Annabella:

> I am desired by the publisher of these verses to send them to you, and to tell you that as he is obliged to publish them, he does not like that they should be seen by you without some apology from him. He says he could not as Ld. B's bookseller refuse to publish them, but hopes you will believe that he did so with pain & reluctance. ...

In his book *The Life of Lord Byron* Moore wrote that he had at first agreed with the opinion of many that the 'Fare Thee Well' verses were 'mere showy effusion of sentiment, as difficult for real feeling to have produced as it was easy for fancy and art ... the taste that prompted or sanctioned their publication appeared to me even still more questionable'. However, when he later read in Byron's *Memoranda* his own account of how they were written one night, when memories came flooding back and he was overcome with emotion, Moore change his mind. He was convinced of their sincerity, believing that there had been no intention of general publication, and that an injustice had been done to Byron by thinking the feelings expressed were feigned.

Byron had also written the verses 'Stanzas to Augusta', which he requested Murray not to circulate, from which the following three verses are taken:

> When Fortune changed – and Love fled far,
> And Hatred's shafts flew thick and fast,
> Thou wert the solitary star
> Which rose and set not to the last.
>
> Thou stood'st, as stands a lovely tree
> That still unbroke, though gently bent,
> Still waves with fond fidelity
> Its boughs above a monument.
>
> The winds might rend – the skies might pour.
> But there thou wert – and still wouldst be
> Devoted in the stormiest hour
> To shed thy weeping leaves o'er me.

On 9 April Byron and Augusta attended a party given by Lady Jersey. They were warmly received by their hostess, but Byron was shocked to see some of their acquaintances, amongst whom was Mrs George Lamb, deliberately cut Augusta, and the men turned their backs and walked away, plainly showing their disapproval of him they had so recently courted. This experience seemed to shake Byron into a decision, and he gave up the fight, agreed to sign the deed of separation and made arrangements to leave England.

The supreme irony was the last letter that he wrote to Annabella before he sailed from Dover on 25 April. He reproached her, then instructed her in words showing his complete confidence that they would be obeyed, to be kind to the woman of whom Annabella later wrote: 'I see what was, what might have been, had there been one person less amongst the living when I married.'

April 14th, 1816

'More last words' – not many – and such as you will attend to – answer I do not expect – nor does it import – but you will hear me. ... I have just parted from Augusta – almost the last being you have left me to part with – and the only unshattered tie of my existence – wherever I may go – and I am going far – you and I can never meet again in this world – nor in the next – let this content or atone. If any accident occurs to me, be kind to her, – if she is then nothing – to her children.

Some time ago – I informed you that with the knowledge that any

child of ours was already provided for by other and better means – I
had made my will in favour of her and her children – as prior to my
marriage: – this was not done in prejudice to you for we had not
then differed ...

... She is gone – I need hardly add that of this request she knows
nothing – your late compliances have not been so extensive, as to
render this an encroachment: – I repeat it – (for deep resentments
have but half recollections) that you once did promise me thus
much – do not forget it – nor deem it cancelled – it was not a vow ...

There were no parting words of regret or sorrow, nor of hope,
for his wife.

The letter was delivered to Mrs Fletcher, who told Hobhouse
that on receiving it, Annabella said, 'I shall answer this' – but on
her way to do so she met Mrs Clermont, and her letter stayed
unwritten.

8   Augusta and the Separation Mystery

Between Byron's first proposal to Annabella in 1812 and his second in September 1814 it is evident that something searing and irreparable had occurred. Throughout their honeymoon and many times afterwards she was haunted by his words that she should have married him when he had first proposed. To understand what lay behind these words it is necessary to return to 1813.

According to Plato, in the beginning Man was created whole, a smooth round man, complete in himself, but he was misguided enough to give himself airs and laugh at the immortal gods. Zeus therefore cut his creation in half and cast the halves down into the world, where they wander to and fro, each seeking, while life should last, its other half, each yearning to be rejoined. Hence said Plato 'The Desire and the Pursuit of the whole is called Love'.

Perhaps this concept of love was akin to Byron's love for Augusta, which he supposed was returned. They were brought up apart, and had seen very little of each other. The correspondence that was started when Byron was at Harrow, lapsed while he was at Cambridge due to a petty disagreement between them. Augusta had married a cousin, Colonel George Leigh in 1807, and they lived at Six Mile Bottom near Cambridge. Colonel Leigh was an equerry to the Prince of Wales and was given an appointment attached to the prince's stud at Newmarket, though later he lost the patronage of his royal employer. Augusta and Byron were later reconciled and their correspondence was resumed.

In June 1813 Augusta came to stay in London and saw Byron more or less continuously until the end of August. They were inseparable, and they went to many social events together. Augusta was an agreeable companion of the kind who, while not being academic and knowing very little in depth about anything, could yet make intelligent remarks on topical subjects, and be pleasing and amusing to those of an intellectual turn of mind. They laughed a lot when they were together and were never bored when they were alone with each other.

Their affection developed easily and naturally, so as to be almost unnoticed, into passion, – a passion so sublime that when they realized the reality of what had happened they were horrified, but could not retreat. They discussed going abroad together, for life apart seemed unthinkable. Then Augusta remembered her three children and the plans were shelved. When she returned to Six Mile Bottom at the end of August she was pregnant. On 22 August 1813, Byron wrote to his friend Thomas Moore: '… I am at this moment in a far more serious – and entirely new – scrape than any of the last twelve months – and that is saying a great deal. * * It is unlucky we can neither live with nor without these women'. The asterisks suggest he gave Moore additional confidences.

Byron intimated to Lady Melbourne the relationship between himself and Augusta, and of their plans to go abroad. Lady Melbourne was alarmed and shocked. She wrote at once telling him that he was on the brink of a precipice: 'If you do not retreat you are lost for ever – it is a crime for which there is no salvation in this world, whatever there may be in the next.' She rebuked him for 'the cruelty of depriving of all future peace and happiness to a woman who had hitherto, whether deservedly or not, maintained a good reputation'. Her emphatic words and warning of ruin for them both must have shaken Byron. She was a woman of the world and all her children were believed to have different fathers, so that if anyone could have convinced him that his relationship with Augusta must cease, it would have been Lady Melbourne whom he loved, trusted, and valued as a friend. Byron replied:

> August 31st, 1813
> My dear Lady Melbourne – your kind letter is unanswerable – no one but yourself would have taken the trouble – no one but me would have been in a situation to require it. – I am still in town so that it has as yet had all the effect you wish …
> Ever my dear Ly. M.   yrs B.

Byron frequently visited Augusta at Six Mile Bottom. The tree under which it is said he used to sit and write and play with the children has now been cut down, leaving just bumps in the ground.

The house is now a hotel, and a photograph of what is said to be Byron's tree is displayed there while in the hall is a small framed account of a past resident's famous brother, who brought his wife here '… and the marriage ended when Annabella went to the court and tried to have Byron certified insane'.

Later that year Augusta sent him a lock of her hair tied with white silk and wrapped in a piece of paper on which she had written: *'Partager tous vos sentimens, ne voir que par vos yeux, n'agir que par vos conseils, ne vivre que pour vous; voila mes voeux, mes projets, et le seul destin qui peut me rendre heureuse.'* (To share all your feelings, to see only through your eyes, to act only on your advice, to live only by you; these are my desires, my plans and the only destiny that can make me happy.) Byron added to her words *'La chevelure* of the *one* whom I most *loved.* +.' A cross was the sign always used between them in their letters to denote love and passion.

The following quotations from letters to Lady Melbourne reveal that Byron was aware of the seriousness of the situation, but could not turn back. He knew that if he and Augusta did decide to go abroad, for Lady Melbourne to continue to be known as his friend would be to implicate her in his disgrace, and with charm and delicacy he let her know he would terminate their correspondence.

> – I leave town tomorrow for a few days – come what may – and as I am sure you would get the better of my resolution – I shall not venture to encounter you. – If nothing very particular occurs you will allow me to write as usual – if there does – you will probably hear *of* but not *from* me (of course) again – Adieu – whatever I am – whatever and wherever I may be – believe me most truly yours obliged & faithful B.
>
> [Sept. 8th, 1813]

> You say 'write to me at all events' depend upon it I will – till the moment comes (if it does arrive) when I feel that you ought not to acknowledge me as a correspondent – in that case a sense of what is due to yourself – and a very grateful remembrance of all you have done to save one not worth preserving – will of course close our correspondence and acquaintance at once – the sincerest and only proof I could then afford of the value I set upon your friendship –.
>
> [Sept. 9th, 1813]

> … – the kind of feeling which has lately absorbed me has a mixture of the *terrible* which renders all other – even passion (*pour les autres*) insipid to, a degree – in short one of its effects has been like the

108 · THE REAL LADY BYRON ·

habit of Mithridates who by using himself gradually to poison of the
strongest kind at last rendered all others ineffectual when he sought
them to remedy for all evils and a release from existence. ...

[Jan. 11th, 1814]

– I do not see how you could well have said less – and that I am not
angry may be proved by my saying a word more on ye subject. – You
are quite mistaken however as to *her* – and it must be from some
misrepresentation of mine that you throw the blame so completely on
the side least deserving and least able to bear it ... – the intentions of
both were very different and for some time adhered to – and when *not*
it was entirely my own – in short I know no name for my own conduct.
– Pray do not speak too harshly of her to me – the cause of all. ...

[Jan. 13th, 1814]

I am not 'forbidden' by ... [Augusta] though it is very odd that like
everyone – she seemed more assured (and not very well pleased) of
your influence than of any other – but – I suppose being pretty certain
of her own power – always said 'do as you please – and go where you
like' ... You will easily suppose – that – twined as she is around my
heart in every possible manner – dearest and deepest in my hope and
my memory – still I am not easy – it is this – if anything – my own – in
short I cannot write about it. ... – It is the misery of my situation – to
see it as *you* see it, – to *feel* it as I feel it – on *her* account – and that of
others – as for myself – it is of much less – and may soon be of no
consequence – But – I will drop ye subject. ...

[Fy. 21st. 1814]

As the year of 1813 progressed into 1814 he could think of
nothing else but his obsessive love for Augusta and the sin that they
were committing. He was like an alcoholic unable to resist the
poison he knows will lead to shame, disgust, and certain ruin.
Never discreet, he began to talk openly about incest, and at times
he feared he would lose his reason. His sole relief was in writing
and he wrote in quick succession some additions to 'The Giaour',
'The Bride of Abydos', 'The Corsair' and 'Lara' and all reflect his
gloomy thoughts and inner conflict in some degree. 'The Bride of
Abydos' was published by Murray in December 1813 and had for
its theme incestuous love. It contains the lines:

Thrice happy I ne'er to feel nor fear the force
Of absence, shame, pride, hate, revenge, remorse!
And, oh! that pang where more than madness lies!
The worm that will not sleep – and never dies;

Thought of the gloomy day and ghastly night,
That dreads the darkness, and yet loathes the light,
That winds around, and tears the quivering heart,
Ah! Wherefore not consume it – and depart!

In 'The Corsair' he took for his motto Tasso's words from *Jerusalem Delivered*: 'Within him his thoughts cannot sleep.'

His friends were concerned, and on one occasion when they had left Byron after they had been to the theatre, Hobhouse and Kinnaird 'made mutual confessions of frightful suspicions'. Byron was heading for what might be termed today a severe nervous breakdown, but at that time not to be raving mad was to be sane. Murray also had noticed and remarked on his state of tension during his visits to Albemarle Street, telling Augusta that Byron was in a 'complete frenzy' during the time he was writing 'The Corsair'. The severe nervous strain from which it is apparent that Byron was suffering both before and at the time of his marriage, must have been responsible for or contributed very largely to its inevitable disaster. The following extracts from his journal which he began on 14 November 1813, and continued until 19 April reveal his mental turmoil:

Nov. 17th, 1813 ... I must see my agent tonight. I wonder when that Newstead business will be finished. It cost me more than words to part with it – and to *have* parted with it! What matters it what I do? or what becomes of me? ... I wish I could settle to reading again – my life is monotonous, and yet desultory. I take up books, and fling them down again. I began a comedy and burnt it because the scene ran into *reality*; – a novel, for the same reason. In rhyme, I can keep more away from facts; but the thought always run through, through ... yes, yes through. I have had a letter from Lady Melbourne – the best friend I ever had in my life, and the cleverest of women ... I wonder what the devil is the matter with me! I can do nothing, and – fortunately there is nothing to do ... Oh my head – how it aches? – the horrors of indigestion! ... My head! I believe it was given to me to ache with.

Nov. 23rd ... I awoke from a dream! well! And have not others dreamed? Such a dream! – but she did not overtake me. I wish the dead would rest however. Ugh! How my blood chilled – and I could not wake – and – and – heigho! ... Since I rose I've been in considerable bodily pain also; but it is gone. ... Past events have unnerved me; and all I can now do is to make life an amusement, and look on, while others play.

Nov. 24th. I am tremendously in arrear with my letters, – except to **, and to her my thoughts over power me, – my words never compass them.

December 6th. Campbell last night seemed a little nettled at something or other – I know not what ... Lord Holland brought out of the other room a vessel of some composition similar to that which is used in Catholic Churches, and, seeing us, he exclaimed, 'Here is some incense for you'. Campbell answered – 'carry it to Lord Byron, he is used to it.'

Dec. 12th ... I have sent an excuse to Madame de Stael. I do not feel sociable enough for dinner today; – and I will not go to Sheridan's on Wednesday; Not that I do not admire and prefer his unequalled conversation; but – that 'but' must only be intelligible to thoughts I cannot write.

Feb. 18th, 1814 ... Began a letter which I threw into the fire. Redde [sic] – but to little purpose. Did not visit Hobhouse as I promised and ought. No matter, the loss is mine. Smoked cigars.

Feb. 27th. Here I am alone instead of dining at Lord H's where I was asked, but not inclined to go any where. Hobhouse says I am growing a 'loup garou' – a solitary hobgoblin ... Heigho! I would I were in my island! – I am not well; and yet I look in good health. At times I fear, 'I am not in my perfect mind.' – and yet my heart and head have stood many a crash and what should ail them now? They prey upon themselves, and I am sick – sick.

March 6th. ... Asked to Lady Keith's tomorrow evening – I think I will go; but it is the first party invitation I have accepted this season.

March 22nd. Last night, party at Lansdowne House. Tonight party at Lady Charlotte Greville's – deplorable waste of time, and something of temper. Nothing imparted – nothing acquired – talking without ideas – if anything like *thought* in my mind, it was not on the subjects on which we were gabbling. Heigho! – and in this way half London pass what is called life. Tomorrow there is Lady Heathcote's – shall I go? Yes – to punish myself for not having a pursuit.

March 28th. This night got into my new apartments, rented of Lord Althorpe, on a lease of seven years. Spacious, and room for my books and sabres. – – – The last few days, or whole week, have been very abstemious, regular in exercise, and yet very *un*well ... Augusta wants me to make it up with Carlisle I have refused *every*body else, but I can't deny her anything. ...

In January 1814 Augusta went to Newstead, intending to stay only a few days, but they became snowbound, and they were forced to have three weeks there alone – three weeks of perfect happiness, contentment, and laughter. They wished it would last for ever.

On 15 April Augusta's baby was born and named Elizabeth Medora. Byron was with Augusta a week before her confinement and returned to see her soon afterwards. There had been gossip about them for some time, but now virulent rumours were spreading rapidly. A nephew of Augusta's at Eton was asked if it was his aunt who was portrayed in 'The Bride of Abydos', but Augusta seemed to be oblivious to what was being said.

On 25 April Byron wrote to Lady Melbourne referring to the birth of the baby, and to a medieval belief that a child born as a result of incest would be an ape:

My dear Ly. Me ... Oh! but it is 'worth while' – I cannot tell you why – and it is *not* an 'Ape' and if it is – that must be my fault – however I will positively reform – you must however allow – that it is utterly impossible I can ever be half as well liked elsewhere – and I have been all my life trying to make someone love me – and never got the sort that I preferred before. – But positively she and I will grow good – and all that – and so we are *now* and shall be these three weeks and more too. ...

Extracts from Byron's letters to Lady Melbourne clearly reveal the relationship that existed between him and Augusta, which until recently has been widely denied or challenged.

– *You* – or rather I have done *my* A much injustice ... but really and truly as I hope mercy and happiness for her, by that God who made me for my own misery, and not much for the good of others – *she* was not to blame, one thousandth part in comparison. She was not aware of her own peril till it was too late, and I can only account for her subsequent 'abandon' by an observation which I think is not unjust – that women are much more *attached* than men, if they are to be treated with any thing like fairness or tenderness. ...

[April 30th, 1814]

... You *have* done everything in your power – and more than any other person breathing would have done for *me* – to make me act rationally – but there is an old saying – 'whom the Gods wish to destroy – they first madden'. I am as mad as Caroline Lamb on a different topic and in a different way – for I never break out into scenes – but am not a whit more in my senses. ...

[June 10th, 1814]

On 4 May 1814 Byron wrote to his friend Thomas Moore: 'Thou hast asked me for a song, and I enclose you an experiment which has cost me something more than trouble, and is, therefore, less likely to be worth your taking in your proposed setting ...'. He enclosed the following verses which he had written for Augusta and in the same week he gave Augusta £3,000 towards payment of her husband's debts.

I speak not, I trace not, I breathe not thy name –
There is Grief in the sound, there is Guilt in the fame –
But the tear which now burns on my cheek may impart
The deep thoughts that dwell in that Silence of heart.

Too brief for our passion, too long for our peace,
Was that hour – can its hope, can its memory cease?
We repent, we adjure, we will break from our chain –
We must part, we must fly to – unite it again!

Oh! thine be the Gladness, and mine be the Guilt –
Forgive me, adored one – forsake, if thou wilt –
But the heart which is thine shall expire undebased
And man shall not break it whatever thou mayst.

And stern to the haughty, but humble to thee,
This soul in its bitterest moment shall be –
And our days seem as swift, and our moments more sweet
With thee at my side, than the world at my feet.

One sigh of thy sorrow, one look of thy love
Shall turn me or fix, shall reward or reprove –
And the heartless may wonder at all I resign
Thy lip shall reply – not to them – but to mine.

In July Byron took Augusta and her children to Hastings for three weeks, where they were visited by his Cambridge friend Hodgson, and his cousin George Anson Byron. Lady Melbourne's correspondence with Byron had perforce ceased. They returned to London on 11 August, and on 20 August Newstead returned to his possession through the default of Claughton to raise the required money. On the following day he and Augusta and her children proceeded to Newstead. They spent the summer weeks happily swimming and fishing, and in Augusta's words a 'state of glorious uncertainty'.

It had been decided that Byron should marry as soon as possible to stem the escalating rumours. Augusta did not approve of his choice of Annabella Milbanke, whom he had chosen himself when he had the world of women at his feet, and to whom he had proposed when he was a free agent in 1812, well before there had been any illicit involvement with Augusta. Through Augusta's influence he apathetically consented to her making an overture on his behalf to her friend Lady Charlotte Leveson-Gower, who seemed confused and rambling in her response. Byron told Lady Melbourne he 'made + write a kind but satisfactory answer, taking it *all* on herself and getting the other out of it completely'. Augusta decided in favour of expediency, and allowed him to send the letter he then wrote proposing for the second time to Annabella.

Her answer came accepting his proposal. It was time for Byron and Augusta to leave Newstead. On the day before their departure they carved their names in the bark of an elm tree behind the old abbey with the date 20th September 1814. Augusta had been away from her home in Six Mile Bottom for almost three months. Byron wrote to Lady Melbourne telling her of Annabella's acceptance and asking, 'May I hope for your consent too? ... In course of time I mean to reform most thoroughly ... I will endeavour to make your niece happy ...'.

It was in this state of severe strain, mental disturbance and emotional and passionate subjection to Augusta that he had made the visit to Seaham in the beginning of November, and married Annabella in the following January.

No marriage estrangement can have generated more interest and speculation than that of Lord and Lady Byron. It is strange that biographers of Byron, who differ widely in their approach to some aspects of his life, unite in the single belief that Annabella, by her unforgiving and disagreeable nature was to blame for it, but there is not one among them who will say what she could or should have done in the very difficult circumstances. Certainly she would never have given up her role as Byron's wife except as a very last recourse, for to break her solemn vows of matrimony was not only a grave sin in the eyes of God but a humiliating and public admission of failure. Nor was desertion by a wife approved of by society or the law since women were deemed to have no rights.

Had Byron's first proposal in 1812 been more orthodox, or had Annabella been a different type of girl with a more worldly approach to religion, she might have accepted his offer then, and his affair with Augusta not have happened. It was for this, it seemed, that Byron could not forgive her – that she could have saved him from the guilt that tormented him to the point of madness and she had not done so. It was characteristic of Byron not to forgive or forget what he considered a rebuff. Yet it *was* her virtue, simplicity, and deeply-held faith that had singled her out from all others when they first met, and that was the kind of woman he thought he wanted. Were the qualities that Byron told Lady Melbourne he desired in a wife computerized, the result would strongly resemble Annabella Milbanke. Why then were these qualities not enough to save a marriage where neither husband nor wife desired to marry again, and each constantly dreamed that they some day might be reunited?

It could be supposed that Lady Melbourne, aware of the rumours circulating, knowing the truth of Byron's obsessive love for Augusta and that a child had been born as a consequence, should have tried to persuade him to tell Annabella what had happened, or to have given her some kind of warning herself. She was not only Annabella's aunt, but had often chaperoned her and it had been through her that Byron had made his first proposal. Moreover it was her opinion that Augusta was 'a wicked woman' who had encouraged Byron and should not have allowed the relationship to develop. But Lady Melbourne's loyalty to him prevailed – she had had her own reasons for encouraging the marriage – and Annabella remained unenlightened.

Lady Melbourne however had tried to give Annabella good advice, kindled perhaps by Byron's letter to her from Seaham before they were married in which he has written the ominous words '... I fear she won't govern me ...'. She wrote to Annabella while they were at Halnaby stressing the merit of patience and telling her a parable about a young bride she knew who had been urgently warned that in her approach to her husband she must 'Subdue him at first, for if she gave way to him she would find it impossible to live with him – he was of such a Sulky bad Temper.' Lady Melbourne tried to hammer the point home by continuing at some length on '… what Ly Asgill says is ye real test of a Woman's Cleverness – that is managing her Husband …'. [Jan. 16th 1815]

If only Annabella had perceived the message, and refused to go up to bed when bidden, and given Byron's face a resounding slap when he had laughed at the fond forgiveness given after his 'confessions', it might have helped to concentrate his mind a little. But her religion had taught her to submit and that to allow her pride to be foremost was a sin, and at the same time it must be recognized that hindsight allows judgements to be made without knowing the realities at the time, and without having to face the consequences. Byron was never far away from loaded pistols and a dagger, which he frequently threatened to use and he was often under the influence of brandy or laudanum, which had a bad effect on him. Furthermore she was always aware that his suffering seemed to be greater even than her own. Her response to the feelings of anger and jealousy she felt, was to focus all the mental force she could summon on a 'principle of forgiveness'. But she failed to govern or influence him, and her submissiveness exasperated him beyond control.

It is quite possible that Annabella would still have married Byron had she known what was distressing him, so great was her love and her belief that all sins, where there was repentance, could be redeemed. The bitter confusion, bewilderment and self-doubt, plus the ever-present consciousness of some impending or past doom, that she endured during the whole of the first year of her marriage would have been diminished or eliminated. With foresight Annabella would not have allowed Augusta to stay with them, and from the beginning of the relationship could have played the cards that fate had dealt her from strength rather than weakness. She would have thought again before asking Augusta to be her friend, for this was to prove a critical misjudgment, and she might then have acquired control of the situation, and learned to 'govern Byron'.

It has been thought that the reason for the separation was due to complete incompatibility. When it is considered how many matters there were in which Byron and Annabella were like-minded, it would seem they were more compatible than many contented married couples.

Literature was a common love and interest. Both Byron and

Annabella were exceptionally well-read and informed, and both liked discussing issues and matters of interest arising from their reading. This kind of discourse, that they had enjoyed in their letters before they were married, and the talk at John Murray's gatherings in Albemarle Street were what Byron was to miss most when he was in exile. Lady Blessington later recalled in her book *Conversations With Lord Byron* that: 'He observed on the pleasure he felt in meeting people with whom he could go over old subjects of interest, whether on persons or literature, and he said that nothing cemented friendship or companionship so strongly as having read the same books and known the same people.' Perhaps he was thinking of Annabella. Another time he told Lady Blessington:

> When a man chooses a friend in a woman, he looks to her powers of conversation, her mental qualities and agreeability; and as these win his regard the more they are known, love often takes the place of friendship, and certainly the foundation on which he builds is likely to be lasting; and in this case I admit that affection, or, as you more prettily call it, tender friendship, may last for ever.

In the much quoted letter of 16 January 1816 from Kirkby Mallory she refers to the room that had been specially set aside for his use, and her mother's assurance that he need not conform to any schedule, so that it is unlikely that he would be denied this consideration in his own home. Besides which, Annabella had always recognized his genius and encouraged him by reporting any reviews and acclaim she had heard about his poems to him and humbly adding her own. In a letter to Byron in 1814 she had written:

> Your ode to Buonaparte was read in company I have just left. It was not thought perfectly lyrical – of this I cannot judge, but it appeared to me like a spontaneous effusion ... I was amazed indeed when his 'magic of the mind' melted into air. I rejoice in the hope of peace, yet could not join in the triumphant exultation over his fall – a very serious, if not melancholy contemplation. ...

His friends, by contrast, often tried to suppress his work – 'I tried to break to him that he should write less and not think the world cared so very much about his writing,' Hobhouse wrote in his journal – and Byron was even advised by his friends not to publish his most famous poem 'Don Juan'.

In politics Byron and Annabella held positive and similar views, and were both sympathetic to Napoleon. Byron gave three speeches in the House of Lords, all of which were concerned with reform. Annabella's father had worked hard for better conditions for the poor and for the abolition of slavery. Today the importance of what was achieved by people like Byron and the Milbankes is sometimes underrated, it being thought that with their background they could know little of the problems of the underprivileged; but the underprivileged had hardly any means themselves of making their voices heard due to their lack of education and it was in this field that both Byron and Annabella had each recognized the urgent need for action and to which each had made some contribution before they met, and each continued to do so. Byron had long admired Napoleon for his legal and economic reforms in France, and was devastated by his forced abdication in 1814. He wrote to his cousin Robert Wilmot on 1 April 1815:

> Dear Wilmot –
> With great pleasure ... Bell called to claim cousinage with Mrs W. & you today but missed. As I have not seen you since that happy event [Napoleon's escape from Elba] I beg leave to congratulate you upon the resurrection of Bonaparte.
> ever yrs
> Byron.

In the following letter, written to a friend in Paris long after Byron's death, will be seen the kind of political views held by Lady Byron which seem to be compatible with those of Byron. She is referring to events in France:

> Esher. March 2 '48.
> Dear Mr Colman –
>   I knew that you would not stand aloof in the scenes of trouble & danger, but if need were, that 'you would do the service of a younger man' .... Of the permanency of the Republic I doubt on two grounds chiefly –
> 1.   The millions do not appear capable of Universal Suffrage yet, – even tho' their moral character be so much improved, as well as many of their objects. They would still judge the Govt. according to

Supplies of food, & success in undertakings flattering to the
National Vanity –
2. That commercial confidence cannot easily be re-established –
    … I still believe in a form of Cooperation arising from a Voluntary
partnership of Masters & Men, as the future antidote to the evils of
such Competition as has made more victims in every decade of the
Century than 'Plague Pestilence & Famine'.
    … Stability & Universal consent must depend on the
harmonizing of the Old & the New – Is there one Man equal to that
task? on any Council in the Country?
                                    Ever your friend
                                    A.I. Noel Byron.

Throughout his life Byron gave much thought and discussion to
theology and had many talks with Annabella on the subject. It is
likely these had added to his feelings of anger and resentment
during their year of marriage. His state of near mental breakdown
before their marriage was made worse by her calm patience and
unshakeable faith. He felt goaded into attempts to make it crumble
because she failed to convince him by reasoning and could not
teach him how to believe. 'Oh point to me the path of truth!' he
had written in an early poem. She believed goodness was
immutable. How could it be, he asked, when what was right in one
country was criminal in another. He said: 'I like the Albanians
much; they are not all Turks, some tribes are Christians. But their
religion makes little difference in their manner or conduct.'
    In 1870 Dr Lushington told Henry Allen Bathurst, Annabella's
only surviving trustee, that the real cause of the separation was
Byron's brutally indecent conduct and language, which he
described as 'most foul and gross'. Even though this was more than
half a century after Annabella had confided in him, Lushington
spoke with great emotion. It is certain that although his conduct
was strictly correct, there was never any chance of reconciliation
while he remained Lady Byron's legal representative and friend. In
this role he assumed proprietary powers and was uncooperative
even with Byron's grandchildren in their quest for truth.
    Annabella is depicted as having a cold and unresponsive nature.
However when Byron was desperately trying to persuade her to
return to him, and unlikely to remind her of unpleasing matters he
referred pointedly to 'marks of affection – of the warmest & most
reciprocal attachment', and after Annabella's visit to Newstead

Abbey she wrote one of her best poems inspired by similar sentiments.

Caroline Lamb, who had all her life shown signs of nervous mental instability had been unable to accept that her love affair with Byron was over for him in 1812 and 1813. In March 1816 she requested an interview with Lady Byron which was arranged at Mrs George Lamb's house, during which she said that Byron had talked to her late one night in 1814 of his homosexual practices and of boys he had corrupted as well as of his incestuous love for Augusta. She had, shortly before this visit, written to Byron imploring him not to publish the verses he had written to Augusta: 'Believe one who would perhaps die to save you ...'. If he did say these things it could well have been to deter Caroline, and in this he was successful for she never bothered him again with her visits and her mental condition rapidly deteriorated. No reference to Byron and homosexuality was apparently ever made by Annabella who merely wrote down Caroline Lamb's information and gave it to Lushington, with no indication that might suggest she had been previously enlightened.

It was Shelley, the friend whose noble virtues and worth Byron constantly extolled, who did most damage to Byron's reputation by his letter to Thomas Love Peacock in 1818 which was subsequently published:

> He [Byron] associated with wretches who seem almost to have lost the gait and the physiognomy of man, and do not scruple to avow practices which are not only not named, but I believe seldom even conceived in England ... No, I do not doubt, and for his sake I ought to hope, that his present career must end soon in some violent circumstance.

Byron's grandson Ralph Lovelace declared in his book *Astarte:* 'Trustworthy contemporary information from Venice, dating from the first half of the nineteenth century, disposes completely of the most repulsive abominations. There was no foundation for the crass and egregious suggestion of Shelley ...'.

Byron's friend Hobhouse pencilled in his copy of Moore's *Life of Byron* copious remarks such as Moore 'had not the remotest guess at the real reason which induced Lord B. at that time to prefer having no Englishman immediately or constantly near him' and 'M. knows nothing, or will tell nothing, of the principal cause and motive of these boyish friendships.' Hobhouse had learned from Moore's book that Byron had got very bored with him in Greece and was glad when they separated. Hobhouse's copy with his comments was bought from a bookseller by Harold Nicolson who showed it to Peter Quennell and in Quennell's book *Byron: The Years of Fame* (published 1935), Byron was for the first time publicly described as bisexual. Later came *Lord Byron's Marriage* (published 1957) by G. Wilson Knight who agreed with Quennell's conclusions and accused Annabella and Augusta with having a homosexual relationship for good measure. Contemporary opinion is that Byron was bisexual, yet when a prominent Byron scholar was asked for the names of those with whom Byron could be linked in this way he could give only four names, three of which, John Edleston, Robert Rushton and Nicolo Giraud, have been referred to in Chapter 2 and the fourth, Loukas, belonged to the last period of his life.

While Byron waited in Cephalonia, prior to crossing to the mainland of Greece, he was kind to a family called Chalandritsanos. Their good-looking son Loukas, who was fifteen years old, hearing of this, returned from Crete and asked to join him and so became Byron's page and accompanied him to Missolonghi. Loukas inspired in Byron a deep emotional possessive love that he had experienced before, starting with Mary Duff when he was seven, and was a kind of antidote to all the frustration and trials that had become his life. Loukas inspired the last poem Byron was to write, from which the following verses are taken:

> I watched thee when the fever glazed thine eyes,
> Yielding my couch and stretched me on the ground,
> When overworn with watching, ne'er to rise
> From thence if thou an early grave hadst found.

> The earthquake came, and rocked the quivering wall,
> And men and nature reeled as if with wine.
> Whom did I seek around the tottering hall?
> For Thee. Whose safety first provide for? Thine.

> Thus much and more; and yet thou lov'st me not,
> And never wilt! Love dwells not in our will.
> Nor can I blame thee, though it be my lot
> To strongly, wrongly, vainly love thee still.

Byron had also given up his bed to Fletcher and others when

they were ill and this was typical of the solicitous way he treated his servants.

John Murray III delayed publication of this poem until 1887, but Hobhouse had taken the precaution of adding a comment: 'A note attached to the verses by Lord Byron states they were addressed to no one in particular and were a mere poetical scherzo.' His deductions are clear but they may be mistaken, and Leslie Marchand's concept that Byron visualized in Loukas something of the ideal and innocent love that he had had for Edleston may be nearer the truth. Perhaps Thomas Mann was expressing the same kind of emotion that some people occasionally experience in the presence of an aesthetically pleasing youth: 'His face revealed the noblest moment of Greek culture – the expression of time, or the birth of pure and godlike serenity. The sight of this living figure conjured up past theologies ... it was like a primaeval legend handed down from the beginning of time, of the birth of form of the origin of the gods ...'. However, Byron, who had once held so much glamour and charisma for men and women alike, found no response of any kind from his indifferent page.

Annabella had been afraid when Byron first proposed to her that she 'could not be fulfilled by the trial' but she hoped that once he perceived she was as others, fallible, she would come down off the pedestal on which he had placed her, and so her love for him prevailed.

The crucial reason for the breakdown of the marriage Byron did not confront, but a glance at two letters reveals what cannot be ignored. 'My dearest Augusta – I always loved you better than any earthly existence, and I always shall unless I go mad –.' [19 August 1820] and his letter to Annabella four months later 'As to Augusta – ... Her life and mine – & yours & mine were two things perfectly distinct from each other – when one ceased the other began ...'. Had that been true there might have been hope.

Annabella recognized that Byron's love for Augusta was no ordinary love that might burn itself out as others had, and she had seen the anguish that remorse and guilt had caused. This was why she could not return to him while it lasted, whatever sacrifice she might have been prepared to make.

She knew that he could never have loved her as he had loved Augusta, but she would have settled for less. She would have settled for the friendship she had offered him when they first met. The pity was, for Byron it had not been enough.

9   The Salvation of Augusta

No reason was given publicly for the separation and the rumours about Byron and Augusta were intensified. Augusta became increasingly distraught and the stress led to deep depression. She was pitifully frightened of losing her social position and fearful of the resulting stigma that would rebound on her children and relations.

In February 1816, Annabella detected signs of duplicity in Augusta's letters, which made her wonder if Augusta's conduct towards her had always been honest. Augusta now seemed almost hostile to the idea that Annabella should have custody of her baby and certainly she would have benefited financially if it were placed in her care. Annabella had no wish to injure Augusta, whom she still loved in spite of the awareness that she had been deceived by her. She was ready to make any sacrifice but one. In the event of any attempt to take her child away she would make known to the Lord Chancellor facts which must have invalidated Augusta as guardian. Annabella was therefore persuaded that she must limit her association with Augusta, who was pregnant, and because of this she did not wish to create distress by communications which could be upsetting until after the child was born. She hoped too, that it might be unnecessary and wrote to Lushington on 10 March:

> From different causes I am convinced that Mrs Leigh would give me the most secure promise in writing that could be required, never to accept the care of the Child whilst I lived without my consent. Would not this obviate all difficulties and prevent the cruel necessity of stigmatizing her either directly or indirectly? I could obtain this promise without Lord B's knowledge.

Lushington replied that night: 'I have just received your letter respecting Mrs Leigh, but cannot acquiesce in your expedient at present ... I am fully aware of the very disagreeable predicament in which you are placed ... but I do think that it would be extremely improper to renew any intercourse with Mrs L ...'. Annabella realized it was unwise at this time to disregard the advice of so distinguished a lawyer, but she did not like severing her connection with Augusta for whom she felt pity. 'I never was, nor can be so *mercilessly* virtuous, as to admit *no* excuse for even the worst of errors' she wrote to Mrs George Lamb on 1 April.

Augusta discussed her problems with her intimate friend the Hon. Mrs George Villiers whom she had known since childhood. Mrs Villiers, a well-liked and respected woman, had met Lady Byron when Augusta was staying at Piccadilly Terrace, and had formed an unfavourable opinion of her. Nevertheless she wrote to Lady Byron in February asking her, in view of the current reports, if she would make 'known to your friends in general these sentiments of confidence, esteem and affection' she was sure that she felt for Augusta.

Annabella replied that none of the many rumours were sanctioned by her, and her friends had ever heard only of the gratitude and affection which she had for Augusta. She added that it would not be right to disclose the details of the differences between herself and Lord Byron. The two women arranged to meet in April 1816. Mrs Villiers then learned some of the circumstances leading up to the separation, and this caused her to totally change her previous opinion of Annabella's conduct and she asked forgiveness for former reproaches.

Annabella returned to Kirkby and wrote to Mrs Villiers on 27 April:

> Since you so kindly approve my conduct from the *partial* knowledge of its real grounds which one conversation could afford, I can feel no doubt that if more fully explained *you* would *enter* into those motives which the world would call romantic or insane ... you will admit that whilst imputations are countenanced directly against my friends, and obliquely against me, I *have* stepped beyond the bounds of mere justice and it is only painful to me that I am *not able* to do more.

She wrote again to Mrs Villiers concerning Augusta on 29 April from Kirkby:

I feel some reluctance to call her attention at this moment [just before the birth of Frederick Leigh] ... she has certainly of late pursued a line of conduct very detrimental to me, countenancing the accusation of 'unforgiving', when she knows *all* the forgiveness has been on my side, and all the revenge on his – and whilst giving me to the world in general the unmeaning praise of 'perfection' which never creates sympathy, representing him with all the interest of repentant error, and blighted affection – perfectly incompatible with what she herself acknowledged of his *conduct* – ever since we parted.

All this hurts me I confess – not so much for the injury it can do me in the opinion of others, as for the injury it does her in mine – I had rather she had openly attacked me – but I say this *only* to her friend – who will defend her if it be possible.

The *facts* in contemporary accounts of the separation and the subsequent relationship between Annabella and Augusta seem to have been overlooked and a legend created, sometimes near saintly, about Augusta, and in doing so Lady Byron has become the victim of malignant, unkind and unproven accusations.

Lady Melbourne, known for her shrewdness and perception, expressed the view that Augusta was clever and very wicked. Certainly a case can be made for this view by recalling the early letters encouraging Byron to react against his mother and the readiness with which she left her young family to enjoy the bright lights of fame with Byron while her husband complained of worries and inexcusable neglect. She must have needed an extended wardrobe for the many parties she attended in London, thereby adding to the financial problems for which her husband is always blamed. She forgot, in her liaison with Byron, her responsibilities as a mother, wife and older half-sister. There were the frequent letters with their sly nuances when Byron and Annabella were on their honeymoon, starting on the first day with one expressing sentiments surely deliberately designed to agitate Byron. She was indiscreet or intentionally mischievous in allowing the pair to visit Six Mile Bottom when she knew her husband would be away and her Aunt Sophia, who had been expected, was not coming. She knew Byron's passionate inclinations towards her and her own weakness, yet she constantly wore the special gold brooch engraved with their sign for love, thus encouraging his suggestive and degrading remarks.

Many would consider it unnecessary for Augusta to have come

to Piccadilly Terrace a week after Byron and his newly-wed wife had left Six Mile Bottom with all its unhappiness for Annabella while they were there. It was wrongly represented by Augusta to Mrs Villiers as Annabella's *'urgent requests to her'*, so that being misled, Mrs Villiers had advised that she should go. Augusta's new appointment with Queen Charlotte entitled her to accommodation in Flag Court, St James's Palace. She knew what a person of habit Byron was. It could be she determined that he would have no chance to settle into what she guessed would be a well-ordered home where all his foibles and idiosyncrasies would be devotedly attended to, and there is no indication that she ever firmly attempted to release Byron from his obsessional love for her.

Augusta seems to have had a stronger will than that with which she is generally credited. She chose *her* friend, Lady Charlotte Leveson-Gower, for Byron to marry and only after her rejection of him was he allowed to send his proposal to Annabella who had attracted his interest before his relationship with Augusta had begun. Again, when Byron had left England and was reluctantly having an affair with Claire Clairmont, he felt constrained to explain to Augusta on 8 September 1816: '... as to all these 'mistresses' Lord help me I have had but one. Now don't scold, but what could I do? ... now dearest – I do most truly tell thee – that I could not help this – that I did all I could to prevent it – and have at last put an end to it ...'. It would seem he was required to be faithful to Augusta more than three months after he had left England.

Other instances of her determination on occasion are, her returning Sir Ralph's important letter concerning Annabella's decision not to return to Piccadilly Terrace without consulting Byron and, later in 1826 allowing her daughter Georgiana, just over seventeen years old, to marry Henry Trevanion, with disastrous results, notwithstanding the fact that neither father would give permission.

However, the reasons for her conduct can only be surmised. Certainly she could not have *made* Byron love her, and love her as few women have ever been loved. Annabella loved her too and from the moment they first met there seemed to be a bond between them, perhaps because at times certain aspects of Augusta reminded her poignantly of Byron:

> *She was like me in lineaments: her eyes*
> *Her hair, her features, all to the very tone*

Even of her voice, they said were like to mine:
But softened all, and tempered into beauty:

Manfred

On 3 June 1816, after the birth of Frederick, Annabella wrote to
Augusta telling her that she would have to limit her friendship:

> ... I should more deeply lament this ... if your feelings towards me
> could give me the power of doing you any good – but you have not
> disguised your resentment against those who have befriended me
> ... can I then longer believe those professions of affection, and for
> exclusive zeal for *my* welfare, which I have been most reluctant to
> mistrust?

Annabella wrote to Mrs Villiers on 16 June from Lowestoft
where she went to stay for a time after the separation, and told her
it was very bitter to write in altered terms to one she had not ceased
to love. She continued: '... do you not consider it mutually
advisable that I should write to her occasionally without adverting
further to this subject? – I do not expect that her affections will ever
be *detached* from him, but I trust they will be purified by reflection
and sorrow'.

Thus started a correspondence in which letters flew backwards
and forwards between Annabella and Mrs Villiers and Annabella
and Augusta. Sometimes they make uncomfortable reading, but
they were not written for other people to read. Lady Byron did not
keep copies of these letters as is sometimes stated. Her grandson
Ralph Lovelace wrote in *Lady Noel Byron and the Leighs* (1887), that
Lady Byron's letters to Mrs Villiers were 'carefully preserved by
her, and her heirs, and restored by them to Lady Byron's family in
1869'. This correspondence has been universally condemned and
criticized by biographers, the following quotations being
representative of their views:

> There is no point in Annabella's behaviour which has met and
> meets with more condemnation than what is variously called her
> *gloating over the incest* in these letters and the *spiritual blackmail*
> which she and Mrs Villiers held over Augusta. (Ethel Colburn
> Mayne in *The Life of Lady Byron*.)

> The intercourse was resumed as soon appeared, for the purpose of
> securing from Augusta an admission of guilt. While Byron lived,
> Annabella compelled Augusta to show her his letters to her though

it was soon apparent that Byron had no intention of disturbing her custody of the child. (Malcolm Elwin in *Lord Byron's Wife*.)

It is to be observed that Byron had made 'an admission of guilt' to more than one person and had often been indiscreet at places like Holland House as well as in his poems, and it was his constant references to incest which had first started the rumours concerning himself and Augusta which were prevalent before he was married, and which gave the necessary stimulus to his second proposal to Annabella. The motives of others cannot be accurately known, but what this correspondence achieved for Augusta should be recognized before judgement is made on the woman who initiated it.

On 31 August Annabella started a two-week stay in London, and during this time she saw Augusta, who was still living at St James's Palace, almost every day. After one meeting Annabella thought Augusta seemed rather subdued and this upset her, making her wonder if she had been insensitive to Augusta's feelings. It seems this was not so for Augusta replied to her enquiries:

> I am so sorry for your bad night – and for your *idea* of my *uncomfortableness* – which is however quite a *fancy of your own* – but I dare say I *looked* something or other which made you fancy. Pray have a good night & write me a 2d post note to say when I am likely to see you again, & tell me you are no longer sorry. I assure you I only feel & felt pleasure and comfort in seeing you & c,. *All* at least I am now capable of feeling.

During this stay in London Annabella reported to Mrs Villiers that 'She has shown me of her own accord *his* letters to her – having only suppressed them because of the bitterness towards me – they are *absolute love-letters*, and she wants to know how she can stop them ...'.

Augusta continued to regularly show Annabella Byron's letters. Conceivably this was Augusta's opportunity to gloat, for they could give only sadness to Annabella, there being no word of affection or appreciation for her, no regret for her pain, only beautiful words of love for his sister; however it could be that Augusta genuinely wanted forgiveness and advice, and did not consider that showing these letters to Annabella was a betrayal of Byron.

It is difficult to understand how it can be thought that Augusta was 'compelled' to show Annabella these letters, Annabella would not have known of their existence if she had not been informed of them. Augusta lived in a palace and need not have seen Lady Byron at all had she not wished it. If Augusta feared that revelations would be made or that the friendship with Annabella, which was so vital to her re-establishment in society, would cease if she did not appear to be responsive to counsel and suitably penitent, she surely could have asked Byron to write letters occasionally that were appropriate for Lady Byron and others to see. There is no reason to suppose that Augusta was not sincere when she expressed her desire for repentance and that she chose to show Byron's letters to Annabella in order to receive advice on how best to reply to them.

Annabella advised Augusta to continue to write to Byron since it would be hurtful to him if she ceased, but to refrain from making signs and suggestions of love in the way that he did to her. When it seemed that he was returning to England she thought it prudent for Augusta not to see him, but counselled that if she did she should always avoid seeing him alone. Did Annabella advise this because she was jealous of Augusta as alleged, or was it simply practical commonsense which Augusta clearly lacked? She did not ever reproach or condemn Byron or Augusta for their love but she knew from her own experience of Byron's magnetism that for them to meet alone would render useless everything to which she had aspired for them both. Her advice was practical and kind and was to continue for three years with emphasis on the need for Augusta to think and act with judgement:

> I feel sure that the gentler expedient will appear to you the best. We must act consistently with *our own* opinions, not with those even of the person we most esteem – if we would secure the peace of retrospect – Endeavour to clear your ideas as to what your relative duties require, act according to the best conclusions you can form, and then rest in the feeling that 'duties are ours – events are Gods'. ...
>
> [27 June 1819]

André Maurois is more pragmatic than other biographers about the correspondence between Annabella and Augusta following the separation:

Anne Isabella Milbanke, aged about 8 years, by John Hoppner

Ada, Countess of Lovelace,
when a child, by Count D'Orsay

Ralph Milbanke, Lord
Wentworth, Ada's younger son

Ada, Countess of Lovelace, aged about 20

Kirkby Mallory Hall, Leics., the ancestral home of the Noels since *c.* 1622. Judith Noel, Lady Byron's mother, was born there and succeeded to the estate in 1815. The Hall was Ada's home for her first six years, and was demolished in 1953

Seaham Hall, Lady Byron's home. This picture was recently found with other drawings in an old scrap-book. It is thought to have been drawn by Lady Byron when a young girl and signed Seaham (*bottom left-hand corner*) by her. It is now a private nursing home

Lady Byron's drawing-room at Fordhook,
her home for almost ten years

Ealing Grove School, which Lady Byron established in 1833

Marble bust by Bertel Thorwaldsen of Lord Byron,
who sat for it in Rome during May 1817

The Reverend Frederick Robertson, one of Lady Byron's close friends and a brilliant preacher and thinker

John Murray's drawing-room at 50 Albemarle Street, *c.* 1815. *From left to right:* Isaac Disraeli, John Murray, Sir John Barrow, George Canning (*by fireplace*), William Gifford, Sir Walter Scott, Lord Byron

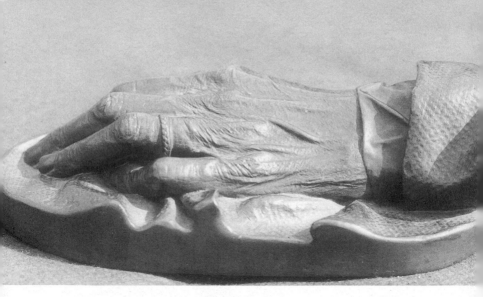

Lady Byron's hand, sculpted by Thomas Woolner RA.
This photograph was taken by the Earl of Lytton of the original cast

The Anti-Slavery Society Convention was held in the Great Room of the Freemasons' Tavern in June 1840. Lady Byron is in the second row, third from the right. The freed slave, John Beckford, delegate from Jamaica, is centre front. The artist was B.R. Haydon, and his intention was to represent the concluding moments of Thomas Clarkson's emotive speech

... Mrs Villiers, a woman of high character, was at once stupefied and deeply interested. Augusta had always spoken to her of the separation and the current reports in a tone of such outraged innocence that she had difficulty at first in believing Lady Byron's account. But once convinced, she was furious. Forgiveness might have been possible, she said, for a sorry and penitent Augusta, but this frivolous pride in wrong doing was intolerable. ... Mrs Villiers was at one with Lady Byron in believing that Augusta must be led back from pride to penitence. Mrs Leigh seems to think it quite natural that friendly relations between herself and her sister-in-law should continue for the world to see.

Augusta had at first reluctantly and then with more enthusiasm, wanted to be absolved from her guilt, and she gratefully accepted Annabella's hand to lead her out of the darkness that was enveloping her. In her way she was quite religious, and was very fond of giving bibles for presents. She had given Byron one on the day that they parted which he kept safely through all his vicissitudes and it was on his table beside him when he died.

Annabella and Mrs Villiers analysed and discussed the most effective and least hurtful way to achieve Augusta's redemption. This must have been the single object of the correspondence, because if that is not believed the whole exercise is incomprehensible. Mrs Villiers always remained loyal to Augusta and vindicated her whenever she could, even when in years to come there were grave differences between Augusta and Annabella. If their only concern was to reduce Augusta to a state of grovelling humiliation and shame after receiving her confessions, this could have been soon achieved and they would have lost interest, there being little left to gloat over. If Annabella felt anger and jealousy, and yearned for revenge, it would be easy to understand but it would have been very much more rewarding for her in that case to have retired to the country and left Augusta to her fate, which is exactly what all her friends and legal advisers had advised her to do. Her revenge would have been public and complete, her conduct unassailable.

Annabella knew very well that there were those who would condemn her quixotic conduct and she later wrote:

I feel I am liable to the censure of some for having continued to address her in terms of affection. My answer is that to support her in the recovered path of innocence and to save her children was my

first object, that I conceived she was to be governed by feelings of
kindness – that I had 1000 times received the consolation of her
devoted attention – that we had suffered together – and for each
other – all this has made her dear to me, and for her sake I believe it
right that I should treat her as if it were so, at the risk of being
deemed too lax a moralist by those with whom – 'Every fault a tear
can claim Except an erring sister's shame'. ... She was quoting
Byron's words from 'The Giaour'.

Could she have foreseen the unscrupulous use made of these
letters by her traducers many years later to establish Augusta's
innocence, it is certain that she would not have been deflected
from her purpose.

Augusta did not at first see the magnitude of her offence, nor did
she seem aware of having been the cause of so much suffering for
Annabella. She freely admitted her relationship with Byron but
maintained her innocence after he was married, although she
acknowledged that it might have been wrong to go to 13 Piccadilly
Terrace. She entreated Annabella 'in the most humble and
affecting way' to point out how she could atone for the past.
Annabella became convinced it was more self-deception than
duplicity that had caused Augusta to be unsympathetic towards
her, and she now felt 'I never would forsake her'. She continued in
a long letter to Mrs Villiers from Lowestoft on 8 July 1816:

Your feelings are most friendly towards her, but should her pride of
self-delusion at any future moment excite your displeasure, I now
ask you to forgive her *for my sake* ... It is to you I am indebted for the
particular suggestion, by following which, an effect so gratifying to
me has been produced. ... Mr W[Wilmot] expressed some thoughts
of rebuking her for the unfavourable impressions she might have
given or encouraged respecting me – but unless such errors were
renewed (which I now think quite impossible), it is certainly
desirable not to create irritation by making *me* in any way an
occasion of reproach – it would interfere with my present views –
and how much better to influence by gratitude than by fear – My
heart is full, and I hope you can read it better than I can write.

Because Annabella was emotional and deeply religious she
adopted a romantic idea of self-sacrifice, for she believed that this
life was but a preparation for immortality and existence hereafter.
She put her faith into practice, which is so unusual that when it is

encountered it is often unrecognized, and unworthy motives attributed. She tried to explain her ideas to Mrs Villiers – of Augusta redeemed and, with her faith strengthened, able to generate in Byron an exorcism from his demons, so that the role she had once believed would be hers, could be undertaken by Augusta:

> It is impossible to have given up the heart devotedly and on principle without feeling for the being who has possessed it under every circumstance – and I – who believe that Heaven is always open cannot yet part with the hope that his thoughts may at last turn towards it – unavailing as any such change would be to me personally.

Augusta at the time was most grateful for she had reached the lowest depths of despair. There seems no reason to doubt her sincerity in the love and gratitude she expressed to Annabella, who was realistically aware it could not endure. In the following letter of 23 July is a typical example of her appreciation:

> … you are so kind and good to me I would not have you think that I feel it one bit less than I really do – & it is impossible you *can* know *how* much that is – but I *know* you will make allowances.
> Your last letter my dearest A was such a comfort to me – ye greatest I can at present receive – since I think from it you *do* 'understand me as well as any human being can another'.
> … Georgy's love *and she is going to write* to you immediately.
> Ever my dearest A –
> Most Affect^ly & gratefully

It is unlikely that Byron's reflections concerning talking to her through a grating would have raised Augusta's spirits nearly as effectively as Annabella's positive assistance in reinstating her in society:

> Had you been a Nun – and I a Monk – that we might have talked through a grate instead of across the sea – no matter – my voice and my heart are ever thine.
> [17 Sept 1816]

Annabella discovered that doing good to Augusta was very therapeutic. The correspondence gave her something to think about other than her own unhappiness, and brought her a measure of peace and comfort through being able to befriend Augusta, her only link with Byron. Also the discovery at last of the full truth about what had happened in the past in itself had a calming effect. She found that Augusta's spirits were not as completely crushed by the correspondence as its traducers believe. For example on 18 July 1816 Mrs Villiers described to Annabella how she had been with Augusta the evening before. It was the first meeting the two had had since Augusta knew that her friend was aware of her guilt, and Mrs Villiers had felt most uneasy, assuming it would be embarrassing for both of them. But the whole of their conversation 'turned on Gauzes and Sattins ... I thought her looking quite stout and well & perfectly cool and easy, having apparently nothing on her mind ...', which Mrs Villiers thought was a little improper for a true penitent.

The main purpose of the correspondence was achieved. Augusta was able to keep her home, her husband and children, her position at court, and her standing in society, due to the known friendship between her and Annabella. The following extract from a letter written by Percy Bysshe Shelley to Byron reflects the prevailing change in public opinion as a direct result of Annabella's behaviour:

> Sunday Sept. 29th 1816.   Bath.
> I saw Kinnaird, and had a long talk with him. He informed me that Lady Byron was now in perfect health ... and that she was living with your sister. I felt much pleasure at this intelligence. I consider the latter part of it as affording a decisive contradiction to the only important calumny that ever was advanced against you. On this ground at least, it will become the world hereafter to be silent. [Lady Byron did not ever live with Augusta.]

Byron was always ready to sacrifice everything for Augusta and in many ways it was in her interest to join him abroad as he pressed her to do, in view of her financial and other problems. Lady Byron's friends, particularly her mother, Lushington and Doyle still hoped that this would happen. She could then have obtained a divorce; she was still young and attractive, or could have been if she had ceased grieving over Byron; she was now an heiress; the name

Byron imparted to her a considerable aura of interest; some of her suitors from 1812, such as George Eden, were still around and unattached.

But as her grandson, Lord Lovelace, relates in *Astarte*: 'She dreamed of miracles of Augusta purified from sin', and perhaps above all Annabella was motivated by the words, *his* words, 'Be kind to Augusta.' She could have had the world at her feet after the separation, and of this she must have been aware but she ignored it. Could this really have been in order to gloat over Augusta's misery, or was it not more the case that she had made by this 'infamous correspondence' an act of supreme altruistic magnanimity?

10 The Aftermath – Annabella

During the months following the separation Annabella became very ill through her misery and distress and her mother feared for her reason. In June 1816 it was decided she should have a complete change of scene by visiting Lowestoft, taking with her Ada, who was now a chubby, good-tempered baby of six months. On the way they stayed two days at Worlingham Hall, the family home of the Sparrows, Lady Gosford's family. Her great friend 'M.G.' had also experienced matrimonial tribulations and found her husband impossible to live with because, through his sister, Lady Olivia Sparrow, he had become engrossed with the Evangelicals. Annabella had taken a small establishment next door to Mary Gosford in Lowestoft near the sea, and gradually the health and spirits of both women improved.

However the girl who had danced until dawn, received proposals and mixed in the most fashionable, cultured and intellectual society, now, as her grandson declared later in his book *Astarte*: 'fell among Methodists, Quaker philanthropists, Unitarians, educationalists, reformers, Co-operators and other destructives of the pleasures of this world'.

She became friendly with the rector of Pakefield church not far from Lowestoft, and helped him in the parish. He was the Revd Francis Cunningham, and through him she became on visiting terms with his brother, the Revd John William Cunningham, vicar of Harrow since 1811. John Cunningham was well known for his book *The Velvet Cushion* and other works, and was a prominent member of the famous Clapham Sect, so called because many influential evangelists such as William Wilberforce lived in Clapham. Possibly to find out more about this movement

Annabella stayed with the Cunninghams in Lowestoft and later visited the Harrow Cunninghams with whom she became friendly. She returned to Kirkby Mallory restored in health but was often emotionally upset through continually hearing news of Byron. She heard that he was ostracized in Geneva where there was a large English population and that he wanted a reconciliation. She was always apprehensive lest Ada should be taken from her, for it was not as clear to Lady Byron as it is to some modern biographers that Byron had no intention of disturbing her custody of Ada; it had been threatened before she had even left Piccadilly Terrace, and he told many people he could claim his daughter at any time. It remained an ever-present threat and evidence of Byron's hopes and intentions are plainly stated in his letters to Augusta and Hanson his solicitor, as the following extracts from his letters show.

In September he told Augusta that 'your having seen my daughter is to me a great satisfaction; it is as if I had seen her myself. Next to you – dearest – she is nearly all I have to look forward to with hope & pleasure in this world'. On 1 October, he again refers to Ada: '... and although it is a very deep privation to me to be withdrawn from the contemplation and company of my little girl ...'. He goes on to protest against 'my daughter' being taken abroad by Lady Byron, as Byron had heard was rumoured. He wrote to Hanson from Venice on 25 March 1817: 'I request you to get me best advice how to proceed in chancery – because I am determined to *reclaim* the child to myself – as the natural guardian ... how and in what manner to assume the care and personal charge of my daughter. – I will return directly if necessary.' Byron was incensed to hear that Annabella had been legally advised to make their child a ward of court and on 10 May 1817 he wrote in a letter to Augusta: 'Give me but a *fair share* of my daughter – the half – my natural right and authority and I am content: – otherwise I come to England and "law and claw before they get it" ...'. There can be no doubt that Byron would have found comfort in those lonely years of exile in the thought that Augusta – a Byron – was the legal guardian of his only legitimate child, for she had become emotionally quite important to him: *Ada! sole daughter of my house and heart.* He continued to refer to the matter, warning Murray on 4 December 1819 that if 'Don Juan' was pronounced indecent or blasphemous 'I lose all right in my daughter's *guardianship* and *education* ...'. It was a pity he had shown so little interest or affection when the baby was under his roof, his often quoted remark being 'Oh, what an implement of torture have I received in thee!', made when he first looked at the child.

He was shocked and sorry to hear that Annabella was very unwell and was inspired to write the verses 'Lines on hearing that Lady Byron was ill.

> *And thou wert sad – yet I was not with thee;*
> *And thou wert sick, and yet I was not near;*
> *Methought that joy and health alone could be*
> *Where I was not – and pain and sorrow here!*

Byron had just heard that the attempt for a reconciliation made by his friend and neighbour Madame de Staël had been unsuccessful and as the poem developed, the sentiments towards his wife became progressively more hostile and resentful. He wrote to Mme de Staël on 24 August 1816, declaring that he sincerely desired a reunion:

> To say that I am merely sorry to hear of Lady B[yron]'s illness is to say nothing – but she herself has deprived me of the right to say more – The separation may have been *my fault* – but it was *her* choice – I tried all means to prevent – and would do as much & more to end it, – a word would do so – but it does not rest with me to pronounce it, – You asked me if I thought that Lady B[yron] was attached to me –, to that I can only answer that I love her, – I am utterly unable to add a word more upon the subject and if I were to say ten thousand they could only come to the same conclusion – and be as unavailing as sincere.

Three days later on the 27th Byron wrote to Augusta ending with a cross, their symbol of love:

> Your confidential letter is safe and all the others. This one has cut me to the heart because I have made you uneasy. ... do not be uneasy – and do not 'hate yourself' if you hate either let it be *me* – but do not – it would kill me; we are the last persons in the world – who ought – or could cease to love one another.

It is difficult not to believe that Byron genuinely meant every word he wrote. It was characteristic of him to state opinions and more especially emotions one day, that were at variance with those he would maintain with conviction on another, not because he was insincere, but because his feelings fluctuated wildly according to his mood of the moment. These two letters so close together in time, so apparently sincere in expression and so wide apart in meaning, embody the dichotomy that had from the beginning characterized the relationship between Byron and Annabella, and Byron and Augusta. Byron, usually so perceptive of the frailties of human nature, never made any attempt, or was unable, to come to terms with the division in his own character – his guilty adherence to what was wrong and his inner yearning for what was right.

Annabella replied to Mme de Staël's approach that 'Lord Byron is well aware that my determination *ought not* to be changed' but because her friendship with Augusta was well known other attempts for a reunion were made, and these too were doomed to fail. Annabella found these communications disturbing, for dearly as she longed to resume her role as Byron's wife, she was unhappily aware that she had been totally rejected, and her presence caused him increasing ill humour, convincing her that whatever the reason was, until this altered, she not only could do him no good, but her return could have dangerous consequences. This was the view of the medical advisers, as well as Byron's Aunt Sophia, George Byron, and Mrs Clermont, who had all been aware of the serious circumstances.

Byron's letters to Augusta became fewer as he received such confusing replies from her, and he could not understand her singular lack of enthusiasm when he said that he was thinking of visiting England. He referred to this when he wrote to her on 28 October 1816:

> All I know is – that no human power short of destruction – shall prevent me from seeing you when – where & how – I may please – according to time and circumstance: that you are the only comfort … left me in prospect in existence, … but anything which is to divide us would drive me quite out of my senses; Miss Milbanke appears in all respects to have been formed for my destruction; …

Four days later on 1 November he wrote to 'Miss Milbanke':

> … I cannot (though I sometimes mention you myself) without great pain – hear from others upon any subject connected with you – since our separation – Do not mistake this feeling for resentment – I

bear you none. – I do not say that I have *not* deserved it – I do not say that you intended it – for it could not *be* in your nature – but I do not think a human being ever suffered a greater degree of mental torture than I have undergone since & during our separation: – if it has not destroyed my health with my peace – it is because I have a great capacity of suffering – ... you will not relieve me, you will not even believe me – but I loved you and love you most entirely; – things which you know – and things which you did not know – made me what I was – or rather appeared to you – and amongst others – a want of confidence – had I trusted you – as I had almost resolved soon after our marriage – all would have been better – perhaps well. ... Do not write to me – do not destroy whatever slender or remote hope I may still cling to – but believe me when I protest to you with the most sincere solemn truth to you and before God – that if there were a means of becoming reunited to you I would embrace it – and that I am very wretched. – Be assured also that I am past the sensation of resentment ...

> ever & most truly and affectionately yrs. B

No woman could receive this affecting letter from a man she loved and remain unmoved. Had Annabella not seen his letters to Augusta, she must have found it difficult to resist his plea, but she had seen them all.

When the third Canto of 'Childe Harold' was published in November 1816, Annabella was nettled that 'his allusions to me in "Childe Harold" are cruel and cold, but with such a semblance as to make *me* appear so, and to attract all sympathy to himself'. She did not mind so much the sentimental references to his loss of 'my daughter' – she too was writing verses with similar sentiments about Ada – 'Thou art not in a Father's arms' and 'Thou fatherless – who may'st not rest', but she was deeply hurt by the words:

> *Yet though dull Hate as duty should be taught,*
> *I know that thou wilt love me.*

She wrote to her friend Lady Anne Barnard:

> It is said that hatred of him will be taught as a lesson to his child. I might appeal to all who have ever heard me speak of him, and still more to my own heart, to witness that there has been no moment when I have remembered injury otherwise than affectionately and sorrowfully ... so long as I live, my chief struggle will probably be not to remember him too kindly.

Perhaps she smiled wryly at his confident 'I know that thou wilt love me' for she herself had had misgivings. 'Ada loves me as well as I wish and better than I expected, for I had a strange prepossession that she never would be fond of me' she confided to Mrs Villiers. Annabella told her mother of her distress because she felt relegated by Grimes, Ada's nurse, into second place and was used as a 'bug-bear' with the child who 'never saw me without beginning to cry'. In 1817 she therefore had the disagreeable task of dismissing the nurse who was devoted to Ada, as diplomatically as possible. Annabella listed some guidelines for the new nurse to follow:

The great thing is to be always calm and gentle, but steady and determined with the child – never allowing her to get the better when once she has been told that she is to do any thing. But consider how many occasions of dispute with her may be avoided, as they often may by not putting things in her way which are likely to give rise to them, and by attention on your part in general.

Be most careful always to speak the truth to her – never give a false reason to keep her quiet. If she ought not to know the real one, tell her only that it is for her good.

If she happens to be hurt by any thing don't call it *naughty*, as if it meant to hurt her – which is very foolish – but soothe her tenderly & reasonably. Your great endeavour should be to show a gentle, composed, & cheerful temper before her on every occasion.

She considered too, that those who cared for the young should have 'a happy spirit'. These precepts had influenced her own happy childhood, and she desired them to be practised in the schools that she founded, as well as by those responsible for looking after Ada, or any other child in her care.

After the separation Annabella found it difficult living at home – which was now Kirkby Mallory Hall in Leicestershire. 'It is essential to the comfort of all parties that my Mother and I should have separate establishments' she wrote to Mrs Villiers, adding that there had been no quarrel but 'a great difference in the lives we lead'. Therefore in April 1817 Annabella moved to a house at Frognal in Hampstead where she accepted invitations and returned hospitality. Lady Noel advised from a distance, and this was not always appreciated. One letter from her to Annabella begins: 'So my dear, you are very angry with me – but you must allow for the anxieties of love ...'. This letter arrived on

Annabella's twenty-fifth birthday and she burst into tears. However she wrote back full of remorse and was duly forgiven.

It was not long before Annabella heard that it was considered by some that she was too cheerful, and she was pleased that the misery and unhappiness she felt were not apparently obvious: 'I had much rather keep my flinty character.' She urged her mother to visit her but Lady Noel declined saying 'I might perchance see those than whom I would rather see the devil', for Augusta was among Annabella's guests. Not until March 1816 had Lady Noel learned the nature of the rumours surrounding Byron and Augusta, Annabella having withheld this knowledge from her parents. On 16 March Lady Noel had written to Sir Ralph: 'I *now* know what was the report to be so shocking – it was that the Brother and Sister *forgot they were so*.' Since then she had found it impossible to conceal her bitter blame and disgust of Byron and Augusta, and this and the constant reproaches for not having confided fully in her parents got on Annabella's nerves, and she found it difficult to be patient with them.

In the summer of 1817 Annabella decided to have a change of air by taking a holiday in the north to visit old friends and her beloved home in Seaham, now let to the daughter of the Bakers at whose house she had been born. She asked Sarah Carr, who later married Dr Lushington, to accompany her. 'She has no sorrow' and they were newly acquainted, which Annabella hoped would be beneficial in restoring her equilibrium. Unfortunately Sarah's delicate health proved unequal to the occasion, although Annabella's condition was greatly improved. It was the first time she had returned to Seaham since she had been there with Byron, and Sarah Carr's journal reveals that as they approached she was disconcerted by the overwhelming distress of her friend and her 'suffocating sobs'. Annabella's happiest memories were of Byron leaping on the rocks, and running by the shore. She wrote a poem in which she remembered the past and the present.

'On Seaham' – 1817

> Ada! Wilt thou by affection's law,
> My thoughts from the darken'd past withdraw –
> Teach me to live in that future day
> When those hands shall wipe these tears away
> Which flow, as I think on the craggy brow
> Where I stood ... that form is before me now!

That eye is beholding the waters roll,
It seems to give them a living soul;
That arm by mine is trembling prest,
I cherish the dream, he *shall* be blest!
O yet – tho' the phantom melt in air,
The heart's devotion may *not* despair!

Again must I break from the magic bond,
Which Memory fastens with links too fond?
Had I been happy I might have wept,
The resisting nerve of my soul had slept;
But I must not soften beneath the spell,
Nor pause o'er the spot where the vain tear fell!

During this expedition she crossed the border and visited Walter Scott at Abbotsford. He was a member of the coterie who had met regularly at John Murray's establishment in Albemarle Street. He and Byron respected and liked each other, in spite of Scott being indicted by Byron in *English Bards and Scotch Reviewers* of writing 'stale romance' for money. Walter Scott had written a favourable review in the *Quarterly Review* of the third Canto of 'Childe Harold' which had angered Annabella's parents and friends although she herself was resigned. She remained deeply hurt at Byron's words on 'dull hate' being taught their child and decided to send a message to Scott through a friend. On 6 March 1817 she wrote to Mrs Villiers: '... I have had a communication from Walter Scott as long as a marriage settlement, whereby he makes over to me his esteem and admiration in such as it becometh me not to repeat'. However he had gone on to praise Byron in such terms that Annabella felt 'Nothing short of taking Lord B. "for better or worse" would, I think cure Walter Scott.' After her visit she wrote to Mrs Villiers: 'Scott accompanied me along the Yarrow, Ettrick and Tweed. ... My curiosity was in many respects gratified ...'.

In a letter to his friend, the poet and playwright Joanna Baillie, Scott described her visit and remarked how very suitable Annabella had seemed for Byron:

Now, one would suppose Lady Byron, young, beautiful, with birth, and rank, and fortune, and taste, and high accomplishments, and admirable good sense, qualified to have made happy one whose talents are so high as Lord Byron's, and whose marked propensity it is to like those who are qualified to admire and understand his talents; and yet it has proved otherwise. ... I can safely say, my heart ached for her all the time we were together ... to me she was one of the most interesting creatures I had seen for a score of years. I am sure I should not have felt such strong kindness towards her had she been at the height of her fortune, and in the full enjoyment of all the brilliant prospects to which she seemed destined.

Like others he found he had liked Annabella very much more than he had expected to from the impression made by the gossip he had heard through Byron's friends and Byron's cold allusions to her in 'Childe Harold'.

When she arrived home in October she wrote in her diary: 'I feel as if in a desert – and do not like passing through the dark alone. ... Two months ago the reality of Solitude did not give me these sensations ...'. Later that month she recorded: 'A blight in the evening. Received from Dr. Lushington the copy of a paper written by Lord B. Date Venice, Aug 9th, 1817. I could not read it – heart heavy.' This was a statement on the separation in which Byron declared he had no idea what the charges against him were '... if their lips are sealed up, they are not sealed up by me ...'. Although he regretted writing it and his friends prevented it from being circulated widely or published, Annabella later heard about it from Augusta to whom it had been reported by Hobhouse.

The next year Annabella heard from Mrs George Lamb that Lady Melbourne had died on 6 April 1818. She was strangely affected. They had never had a close relationship, but memories of the beginning of her association with Byron came flooding back and she knew how saddened he would be by the news, especially if he had been aware of the pain and mental suffering Lady Melbourne had endured for the last months of her life. Mrs Lamb also told her: 'Hobhouse wrote yesterday a most disgusting letter, asking for Lord B's letters – really one of the most unfeeling I ever read, saying he was desired by Lord B. to apply the moment of Lady M's demise, and no expression of sorrow or kindness to the family. I always had the worst possible opinion of that man ...'. Annabella had always been of the opinion that Hobhouse had not only been a bad influence on Byron but was unsympathetic towards herself and that he was unperceptive and insensitive in his manner and conduct.

Soon after this people she knew, who included Hugh and Mary Montgomery, reported they had seen Byron in Venice and that he was fat and bloated. Her heart ached for him because she knew how this appearance would distress him. Impulsively she decided to go to Newstead and not disclose who she was. She made some notes afterwards at Mansfield on 22 May.

> Just come from Newstead. The sunshine, the blue lakes, the reappearing foliage of the remaining woods, the yellow gorse over the wild wastes gave a cheerful effect to the surrounding scenes. My feelings were altogether those of gratification. In becoming familiarized with the scene I seemed to contemplate the portrait of a friend. I entered the hall – and saw the Dog; ... I saw the old flags which he used to hang up on the 'Castle walls' on his birthday. The apartments which he inhabited were in every respect the same – he might have walked in. They looked not deserted. The Woman who had lived in his service regretted that the property was transferred. He should have lived there, particularly after he was married – but his Lady had never come there, and 'she, poor thing! is not likely to come there now,' compassionately & mysteriously. She said that he was 'very fond of Mrs L–, very loving to her indeed,' ... The parapets & steps where he sat – the leads where he walked. His room – where I was rooted having involuntarily returned ...

In spite of her sadness the visit seemed to comfort her. She was moved to write some verses:

> *I passed the portal, trod the twice-worn stone*
> *Where thou would'st meditative sit alone;*
> *I thanked the careless guide who left me free –*
> *She knew not how it touched each word of thee!*
>
> *Yet I remember when beside the bed*
> *Which pillowed last that too reposeless head,*
> *I stood – so undeserted look'd the scene*
> *As there at eve its habitants had been.*
> *Struck by that thought and rooted to the ground,*
> *Instinctively I listen'd, look'd around,*
> *Whilst banished passion rush'd to claim again*
> *Its throne, all vacant in my breast till then;*
> *And pardon'd be the wish, when thus deceiv'd,*
> *To perish, ere of hope again bereav'd!*

Just to hear her husband's name in this setting was gratifying, but even this innocent pleasure was to be distorted by the usual channels of relayed information to Byron, into a story that she had been questioning the housekeeper about his past.

The letters between Annabella and Augusta became less frequent since Augusta was reinstated in society and the ugly rumours about her and Byron were now rarely heard. Annabella had come to realize that she could never completely trust Augusta either in matters of common sense such as making unsuitable remarks in front of Ada about her father, or in her loyalty and integrity towards herself.

In May the fourth and last Canto of 'Childe Harold' was published and Murray sent Annabella an advance copy. She had always been among the most ardent admirers of Byron's work and owned that 'the new canto is beautiful indeed' but some of it was so emotive it affected her in spirit and in health:

> But I have lived, and have not lived in vain.
> My mind may lose its force, my blood its fire,
> And my frame perish even in conquering pain;
> But there is that within me which shall tire
> Torture and Time, and breathe when I expire;
> Something unearthly, which they deem not of,
> Like the remember'd tone of a mute lyre,
> Shall on their soften'd spirits sink, and move
> In hearts all rocky now the late remorse of love.

He seemed to be talking to her, and when she reached the verse beginning:

> And I have lost thee, Ocean! and my joy
> Of youthful sports was on thy breast to be
> Borne, like thy bubbles, onward from a boy
> I wanton'd with thy breakers – they to me

She returned in mind to Seaham with unbearable memories.

Later that year Annabella again visited Seaham and meditated on the past. 'The visions of earlier days reappear, without their power to deceive – no longer embodied in hope – I do not feel confident that I view myself with reference to my actual situation – but I shall do so – shall disperse those mists of error in which I have long been involved.' She reflected on the IVth Canto recently published: 'May not each of the children of passion feel that he understands so much more intimately than all the other multitude that to him the revelation is really private? So I have felt.' While she was there she was provoked into writing to John Cunningham, vicar of Harrow. This letter is indisputable testimony to the belief that not only did she never injure Byron's name herself but she would not countenance any disparagement of him from others even at the risk of losing a valued friend.

Seaham June 24th 1818

Dear Mr Cunningham,
Very recently in a company where two of my friends were present, a gentleman said that Lady Byron declared Lord Byron to be 'guilty of every crime but blasphemy' – and gave as his authority, Mrs Cunningham *to whom Lady Byron had said it* – If, as I have reason to believe Mrs John Cunningham were intended, I cannot for a moment admit the supposition that she would thus attribute to me a declaration which she never heard me utter. But I consider it justly to say to you, as well as otherwise incumbent on me, to name the circumstance, because it is the second of the kind which has come to my knowledge – Last year another gentleman affected upon your authority, as avowedly derived from me, though he mentioned that you had given some caution as to the use of it, that Lord Byron was guilty of offences too heinous for disclosure … it must have been a very mistaken inference from my conversation which could lead to the supposition that I intended in any measure to lend my authority to such other causes as may have been assigned by reports, certainly not originating with me, or my connections, and to which the expressions of these Gentlemen would be applied by the hearers – on the contrary, the uniform tenor of my wishes, and they were surely made known to you, though it might have seemed less necessary to enforce them, to one who professed every kind & charitable consideration for Lord Byron, has been that my friends should refrain from gratuitous accusation, even in connection with the leading facts of my personal experience, – & should merely refute such calumnies, and rectify such misconceptions, as decidedly reflected on my conduct and character. To find that this boundary has been exceeded must always give me great pain – Before I had the pleasure of becoming personally acquainted with you, I had known some proofs of your friendly interest in Lord Byron's welfare. The manner in which it had been shown particularly predisposed me to believe it sincere and valuable – and with a view to future contingencies (improbable indeed, but not hopeless!) I was happy to find that these dispositions still existed on your part – you expressed a willingness to 'make great sacrifices' in order to befriend Lord Byron on any possible occasion, and from the kindly & compassionate feeling with which you considered what I most deeply lamented I received a degree of consolation for which

I have always felt grateful – I should be truly concerned if any circumstances were to interfere with this impression, but I shall hope for some elucidation from your kindness which will remove my anxiety – and be assured [word illegible] that I have every disposition to remain with sincerly friendly regard

Yours – AN Byron

His reply was presumably acceptable to her for she continued to see him.

The next occasion for disquiet was the news from Augusta that Byron was writing the story of his life for publication. She wrote to Colonel Doyle:

The worst consequence, to my feeling, would be the opposition between my own views and those of some of my friends. I am sick, quite sick, of taking my part. I never did it but as an act of duty towards Ada, and the pains which on that principle I have taken ... have been the most laborious and vexatious of my life. May I not, on such an occasion as I now contemplate, let things take their course?

She tried to explain her diverse feelings in a scrapbook of 1818 headed *Reminiscences*:

In explaining the tenor of my own conduct, I do not attempt to maintain the defensibility of every part of it. At the time of my quitting, my mind was certainly possessed by passion; and was prevailed upon in his favour by what could not have been of any weight in the scale of reason. Of this he was probably aware, and made use of it accordingly. I clung to an hypothesis repeatedly overthrown – that there was some secret good at the bottom of his heart – though such motives were never evidenced; and such delusion will always be liable to return. It then embarrassed my conduct ... To wound him by a word was intolerable to me – perhaps I may never be able to perform the duty of making such a statement without experiencing afterwards all the pangs of Conscience. This was my weakness throughout; it is A's to a still greater degree – and I can feel for it.

Her insecurity is apparent. She must have written during the same period in similar vein to Mrs Clermont, who replied on 14 October:

You are by constitution timid & apprehensive, which leads you into difficulties in some cases & enhances your fears, *often* is the sole cause of them. I should say timidity is the sole cause of any errors their [sic] may have been in your conduct – do not be discouraged by feeling that you have acted as a fallible mortal nor think that failure of success has been in error. ...

Annabella receive a letter dated 21 June 1820 from Georgiana, Augusta's eldest child, hinting that they would like to see her more often. It reveals that as well as the correspondence, there had been social intercourse between the two women and their children, the purpose of which could hardly have been to punish Augusta:

My Dearest Aunt,
    I am sorry that you have been ill, poor dear Cat. I hope you are better now, take care of yourself now. I will tell you something. My poor little bird is dead, the cage gave way from the nail and down it fell, it was a goldfinch. I am sure Ada will be sorry for it bye the bye I saw a little girl so like Ada the other day. George Villiers went to Russia on Saturday. I am making some baby's caps. I have got a prize for work and for reading, the one for work is to be a book. Mama has given me a silver pencil case for reading. I long to see you and dear Ada and to be of your parties; the kittens send love and kisses. Goodbye I love you better and better your ever affectnt.
                               G.L.

During these years Byron had written long and interesting letters to Annabella, many of which had not been sent. In those that he had sent he reminded her, almost commanded her, that she should remember her promise made when they separated to 'be kind to my sister and her children'. He wrote to her on 25 October 1820 firstly dealing with their mutual financial matters which he thought would be affected by war and revolution in Italy and Austria, and then he expressed his delight with the prints he had been sent of Ada's picture:

... she is strikingly like yourself – I do not see much resemblance to me unless something in the bust I think. – There is a great deal of character in the head altogether – and very strongly marked for a Child of the age. ... And if in these '*kittle* times' any accidents should occur which may throw the settlement into your own hands – be kind to my Sister and her children – as I have all along entreated you – though apparently to no great purpose.

On 10 December, perhaps because it was Ada's birthday, Annabella replied:

When you first expressed the wish respecting Mrs Leigh which is repeated in your last letter of October 8th I determined to act consistently with it. If the assurance of that intention would conduce (as you state in a former letter, & as appears from your reiterated requests) to calm your mind, I will not withhold it. The past shall not prevent me from befriending Augusta Leigh & her children in any future circumstances which may call for my assistance. I promise to do so. She knows nothing of this.

That was Annabella's last letter to Byron.

Byron was grateful, though he felt that her style was 'a little harsh' and that she should have been more prompt with her reply, but she prudently did not write to him as her heart longed to, for she had been warned that for her own security and the interest of her child, every communication to Byron should be revised or dictated by legal advisers and that any words or proceedings which appeared like a renewal of former ties would invalidate the separation agreement. Ten days after he had written to Annabella he was writing of her to Augusta: 'The Lady Byron I suppose retains her old starched obstinacy – with a deeper dash of sternness from the dint of time, and the effort it has cost her to be "magnanimous", as they call her mischief-making.' Was he referring to the promise for which he had asked? Annabella could not know then how much trouble and pain this promise was to bring her, or what calumny would be heaped on her efforts to keep it, though perhaps she should have been warned by Byron's anxious and persistent requests and by her own knowledge of Augusta's ominous family problems. She had once observed that Augusta had a kind of 'Moral Idiotcy' [sic] from birth. By not severing her ties with Augusta after the separation, and by reaffirming this extraordinary – in the circumstances – promise to Byron which there was no logical or moral reason for her to make, she was surely herself showing lunacy of a kind beyond belief and devotion above price. It would rebound on her in a way that was unforeseen, ceaselessly prejudiced and very unjust.

On 28 January 1822 Lady Noel died at Kirkby after a long illness. Through the terms of Lord Wentworth's will Annabella and Byron were required to assume the name Noel – a clause not

irksome to Byron since his initials were now those of his hero
Napoleon. It is surprising to discover from his letters to Douglas
Kinnaird, his banker and business agent, not only how grasping
was Byron's attitude towards the spoils that he would now inherit
but how extensive his knowledge was on the complexities of estate
management: 'I have no objection to Sir Ralph occupying the
Mansion house during his lifetime – but the *option* of occupying it
after his demise – to *revert* to & remain with *me* ... in the event of
the estates rising in value I should have no objection to increasing
Lady B's allowance in proportion ...'.

Byron was annoyed to learn of Lady Noel's instructions in her
will that the portrait of him that she had possessed was not to be
shown to Ada until she was twenty-one, and then only with the
consent of her mother. Once again Byron was talking of consulting
Chancery about the education of Ada: 'I will *not* willingly have my
daughter prejudiced' to ensure she was not influenced against him,
and also to get a better deal for himself from the 'rascally' trustees
acting for Annabella.

Annabella was now mistress of Kirkby Mallory and the
Wentworth estates. Her yearly income had increased from £500 to
£4,000. In 1823 she began to hear reports of Byron's plans to go to
Greece, and then that he had departed to Cephalonia, one of the
Ionian islands off Greece. From there Augusta received a letter
from Byron, who had heard that Ada had been ill, commenting that
Ada's symptoms seemed similar to those he had experienced at the
same age. He suggested that she might be 'quite well – when she
arrives at womanhood ... You will excuse me touching on this topic
medically and *en passant* ... I need not say how anxious I am (at this
distance particularly) to hear of her welfare'. At the end of a long
letter he returned to Ada, expressing a strong wish to have an
account from his wife of Ada's disposition and character.

Annabella responded with alacrity and understanding, enclosing
a silhouette of Ada that she had specially commissioned.

Hastings
Dec 1, 1823

My Dear Augusta,
     I will now answer those passages from Lord Byron's letter of Oct
8th which requests information from me. ... She [Ada] is by no
means devoid of imagination – but it is at present chiefly exercised
in connection with her mechanical ingenuity – her self-invented

occupation being the manufacture of ships & boats – & whatever else may attract her attention.

Hitherto she has preferred prose to verse because she is puzzled by the poetical diction – She is particularly fond of reading ...

She is now in really good health ... There is great justice in Lord Byron's *medical* conjecture – but I am informed that the tendency to local congestion is not always relieved at *that period*, as the depletion may not be more than adequate to the increased supply of blood, – & for some other reasons –

I hope I have not omitted to notice any point specified by Lord B.

I am

yours affectionately

A.N.B.

She had included many details that would be of interest to any loving father. Byron was delighted when he received it at Missolonghi, and wrote to Augusta on 23 February 1824 telling her the news had been of great comfort

and I wanted some – having been recently unwell ... her [Lady Byron's] description of much of her disposition and tendencies very nearly resembles that of my *own* at a similar age – except that I was much more impetuous. – Her preference of *prose* (strange as it may now seem) *was* and indeed *is* mine – (for I hate *reading* verse – and always did) and I never invented anything but *boats* – *ships* and generally something relative to the ocean. ...

He asked Augusta to tell his wife that he had had a severe attack recently which he thought might be epilepsy, so that she would be warned to be vigilant on that account with Ada. He also mentioned that he was considering adopting a little girl called Hatagée whom he thought Lady Byron might allow to come to England to be a companion for Ada.

Their communications, although directed through Augusta, were warmer than at any time since they parted. It is possible that, now older and wiser and sadder, through their mutual concern and affection for Ada, they might have come together again, which hope neither had ever abandoned. Two months later however, Byron was dead. When he was dying he had tried desperately to leave his wife a message, but it could not be understood.

11   The Aftermath – Byron

The years since they separated had not been happy for Annabella but they were even less so for Byron. In the months following his self-imposed exile in April 1816, there had been much to induce the melancholia to which he had always been prone, enough even to cause him to contemplate suicide. Letters from his friends who had rallied round him at the time of the separation became fewer and his entertaining accounts of his activities to them often begin with a reproach: 'My Dear Hobhouse – I have written to you several times & merely wish to say that I have not had a line since we parted – from you in return ...'. Sometimes, even to Augusta he apologized '... I am so hurried and sleepy, but so anxious to send you even a few lines my dearest Augusta, that you will forgive me troubling you so often ...'. It is unexpected and moving to learn that the notorious poet of depraved and immoral repute had been shopping for trinkets just like ordinary virtuous tourists. He had chosen presents to send Augusta through one of his returning friends: 'seals – necklaces – balls – & – & I know not what – formed of Chrystals – Agates – and other stones – *all of & from Mont Blanc* bought & brought by me on & from the spot – expressly for you to divide among yourself and the children – including also your niece Ada ...'.

In June he had moved into the Villa Diodati by the lake at Geneva, near the ménage of the poet Shelley, Mary Godwin and Claire Clairmont. In August friends from England visited him and he temporarily became more cheerful. But he still felt keenly the humiliation of the separation and the ignominy of having been booed on the stage and in the streets of London, and was bitterly aware of the hostility towards him from the English colony in

Geneva, believed by him to be fostered by Lord Brougham. He had tired of Claire, who was still besotted with love for him and had become pregnant with his child. The Shelley household returned to England in August and in September his friends, except for Hobhouse, departed.

He told Augusta how wretched he was:

> ... the Separation – has broken my heart – I feel as if an Elephant had trodden on it – I am convinced I shall never get over it – but I try, – I had enough before I ever knew her and more than enough – but time & agitation had done something for me; but this last wreck has affected me very differently, – if it were *acutely* – it would not signify – but it is not that, – I breathe lead. – While the storm lasted & you were all pressing & comforting me with condemnation in Piccadilly – it was bad enough – & violent enough – but it is worse now. – I have neither strength nor spirits – nor inclination to carry me through anything which will clear my brain or lighten my heart.

Repeatedly Annabella said that his suffering had been worse than hers and these words reveal his torment that she neither caused nor could cure.

At the beginning of October Byron and Hobhouse started their travels through Italy, arriving in Venice on 10 November. Byron was planning a visit to England but was mystified and despondent to learn from Augusta that if he returned she would not renew their previous relationship. He became more cheerful when he had settled and told Murray that 'Venice pleases me as much as I expected ... it is one of those places that I know before I see them, and has always haunted me the most after the East ...'. He soon fell in love with Marianna Segati, the wife of a merchant in whose house he had taken rooms, and he studied the Armenian language daily on the peaceful and beautiful island of San Lazzaro in the lagoon. As a result of partaking in the nightly merrymaking of Carnival and finishing the dynamic dramatic poem 'Manfred' in the first few weeks of 1817, Byron became indisposed with exhaustion and ennui. After a time the Albrizzi and Benzoni salons were found to be a poor substitute for Holland House and the other great drawing-rooms of London, where all the interesting members of society gathered and had requested to be presented to him.

He wrote to Moore enclosing a short poem on 28 February:

You will, perhaps complain as much of the frequency of my letters now, as you were wont to do of their rarity. ... The mumming closed with a masked ball at the Fenice, where I went, as also to most of the ridottos, etc, etc; and, though I did not dissipate much upon the whole, yet I find 'the sword wearing out the scabbard', though I have just turned the corner of twenty-nine.

> So we'll go no more aroving
> So late into the night,
> Though the heart be still as loving,
> And the moon be still as bright.
>
> For the sword outwears the sheath,
> And the soul wears out the breast,
> And the heart must pause to breathe,
> And love itself have rest.
>
> Though the night was made for loving,
> And the day returns too soon,
> Yet we'll go no more a roving
> By the light of the moon.

He went to Rome in April, meeting Hobhouse, who being well-versed in the antiquities, made a welcome and knowledgeable guide, and was persuaded by him to sit for a bust by the famous sculptor Bertel Thorwaldsen. While in Rome Byron heard from Shelley that Claire Clairmont had given birth to their child, Allegra, on 13 January. Friends from England visited him in Venice on his return and Hobhouse stayed with him for the rest of the year during which they took part in the social round of events. Hobhouse departed for England in the early part of January 1818 and now that he was alone Byron was bitterly aware of his exile. He increasingly felt the loss of congenial company, which was underlined by the news of Lady Melbourne's death. He wrote to Murray on 23 April: 'The time is past in which I could feel for the dead – or I should feel for the death of Lady Melbourne the best & kindest female I ever knew – old or young – but "I have supped full of horrors" & events of this kind leave only a kind of numbness worse than pain ...'.

Claire, supported by Shelley, had agreed to give Byron full and sole custody of their child, so that Allegra would have the advantages of rank, money and fame, that Shelley and his followers always professed to consider worthless. Claire still hoped that the child might bring about a reunion with Byron, who was now bored and exasperated with her. Allegra and her nurse Elise arrived in Venice on 2 May. Byron was enchanted with his daughter but he informed Augusta that he found her 'much more like Lady Byron than her mother – so much as to stupefy the learned Fletcher and astonish me – she has very blue eyes – and that singular forehead – fair curly hair – and a devil of a Spirit – but that is Papa's'. Because his life became progressively more dissolute and there was much quarrelling between the all-male servants, he arranged for Allegra to be looked after by his friend Richard Hoppner, the British Consul in Venice, and his wife.

Life for Byron was now at a low ebb. He was disheartened not to know if his work was being published or what opinions were expressed about it; although he had heard that Newstead was sold in the previous December he did not know if the sale was progressing, or the state of his affairs at Rochdale; no literary gossip or scandal reached his ears and it seemed he was totally forgotten. On 3 June he wrote to Douglas Kinnaird: 'Though I wrote to you last week I will refresh your memory with the present letter …' and again five days later:

> As a much longer period has elapsed without my hearing at all from England – though I write repeatedly – I am under the necessity of troubling you (but too often) to apply to Hanson for any balance in his hands – and to Murray to make some payments … I hope you will not forget to fillip Hanson about that eternal Rochdale. P.S. – Pray write –.

On the same day he wrote to Hobhouse: 'Hearing nothing from you or anybody – makes me trouble you with five words – just to beg you to remind *Hanson – Kinnaird* & Murray … & to spur the others …'. He tried humour, writing as if he was his 'Vally de Sham' Fletcher:

> With great grief I inform you of the death of my late dear Master – my Lord – who died this morning at ten of the Clock of a rapid decline & slow fever – caused by anxiety – sea bathing – women & riding in the sun against my advice. – He is a dreadful loss to everybody, mostly to me – who have lost a master and a place. …

On 18 June he wrote to Murray:

> Business and the utter inexplicable silence of all my correspondents renders me impatient and troublesome ... *your* silence makes me doubt the success of C[ant]o 4th, ... When I tell you that I have not heard a word from England since very early in May – I have made the eulogium of my friends – or the persons who call themselves so – since I have written so often & in the greatest anxiety ... P.S. Tell Mr Hobhouse ... that I will never forgive him (or anybody) the atrocity of their late neglect – silence at a time when I wished particularly to hear (for every reason) from my friends.

Byron's misery was acute and as a kind of anodyne he feverishly threw himself into a life style of debauchery and self-indulgence. But he continued to write verse and in July he started the first Canto of 'Don Juan'.

After some irritating delays, Hanson and his son Newton finally arrived in November with papers concerning the sale of Newstead and other urgent financial matters, but bringing only one of the three packages Murray had prepared and that mostly containing insignificant objects and worst of all not one book. Byron's disappointment was immense and for a little while he was speechless with frustration and disappointment. Newton later described Byron as looking forty; his face had become pale, bloated, and sallow and he had grown very fat, matching the description which had already reached England and distressed Annabella. Byron wrote to Murray on 24 November 1818: 'Mr Hanson has been here a week and went five days ago; he brought nothing but his papers, some corn-rubbers, and a kaleidoscope; "For what we have received, the Lord make us thankful!" – for without his aid I shall not be so.' The letter also contains Byron's reaction to hearing of Sir Samuel Romilly's suicide because his dearly beloved wife had died:

> So Sir Samuel Romilly has cut his throat for the loss of his wife – Three years ago (nearly) when, after a long and general retainer, he deserted to Miss Milbanke, and did his best, or his worst, to destroy me, or make me destroy myself ... There would have been some excuse for such a fit at twenty-seven – but at sixty-four! Could not the dotard wait until his drivelling did it?

Byron had paid a retainer fee to Romilly, who was distinguished by his work in legal reform in Britain and Europe and extremely highly thought of by everyone. However, Romilly felt, when he was approached by Lady Noel, that Lady Byron had a right to a separation and advised her accordingly, and through him Lady Byron was referred to Lushington. Not only did Byron write with savage exultation to Murray, but he had written at length six days earlier to Annabella with even more vindictiveness, revealing the crazed passion and cruelty that could be aroused in his emotions by those whom he felt had slighted him. He never relinquished his intention of challenging Lord Brougham to a duel for slandering him and attempting to adversely influence Mme de Staël's reconciliation attempts; nor did he forgive Robert Southey, Poet Laureate, who commemorated Byron and those of 'diseased and depraved imaginations' who paid homage to him, as the Satanic School.

In the beginning of April 1819 Byron was introduced to Teresa Guiccioli, not yet twenty years old, whose husband was nearly forty years her senior. 'She is fair as Sunrise – and warm as Noon – we had but ten days to manage all our little matters ...' Byron wrote. Teresa remained his 'last attachment' only through her determination and because Byron, now thirty-one, had developed a sense of responsibility. He told Hobhouse: '... I will leave the country reluctantly indeed – but I will do it – for otherwise if I found a new liaison she would cut the figure of a woman *planted* – and I never will willingly hurt her self-love ...' and to Murray he wrote: '... I have been almost obliged to run away with a married woman. – But with some difficulty – & many internal struggles – I reconciled the lady with her lord ...'.

Byron and Augusta rarely wrote to each other in those days, Byron having become discouraged by Augusta's general lack of enthusiasm. Even now the memory of her could evoke in him tumultuous emotions, and he was overwhelmed by his longing. Six weeks after his affair with Teresa started he wrote Augusta the following letter:

Venice [Monday] May 17th 1819
My dearest Love – I have been negligent in not writing, but what can I say[.] Three years absence – & the total change of scene and habit make such a difference – that we have now nothing in common but our affections & our relationship. –

But I have never ceased nor can cease to feel for a moment that perfect & boundless attachment which bound & binds me to you – which renders me utterly incapable of *real* love for any other human being – what could they be to me after *you*? My own XXXX [Short word crossed out] we may have been very wrong – but I repent of nothing except that cursed marriage – & your refusing to continue to love me as you had loved me – I can neither forget nor *quite forgive* you for that precious piece of reformation. – but I can never be other than I have been – and whenever I love anything it is because it reminds me in some way or other of yourself – for instance I not long ago attached myself to a Venetian for no earthly reason (although a pretty woman) but because she was called XXXX [short word crossed out] and she often remarked (without knowing the reason) how fond I was of the name. – It is heart-breaking to think of our long Separation – and I am sure more than punishment enough for all our sins – Dante is more humane in his 'Hell' for he places his unfortunate lovers (Francesca of Rimini & Paolo whose case fell a good deal short of *ours* – though sufficiently naughty) in company – and though they suffer – it is at least together. – If ever I return to England – it will be to see you – and recollect that in all time – & place – and feelings – I have never ceased to be the same to you in heart – Circumstances may have ruffled my manner – & hardened my spirit – you may have seen me harsh & exasperated with all things around me; grieved & tortured with *your new resolution*, – & the soon after persecution of that infamous fiend who drove me from my Country & conspired against my life – by endeavouring to deprive me of all that could render it precious – but remember that even then *you* were the sole object that cost me a tear? and *what tears!* do you remember *our* parting? I have not spirits now to write to you upon other subjects – I am well in health – and have no cause of grief but the reflections that we are not together – When you write to me speak to me of yourself – & say that you love me – never mind common-place people & topics – which can be in no degree interesting – to me who see nothing in England but the country which holds *you* – or around it but the sea which divides us. – They say absence destroys weak passions – & confirms strong ones – Alas! *mine* for you is the union of all passions & of all affections – Has strengthened itself but will destroy me – I do not speak of *physical* destruction – for I have endured & can endure much – but of the annihilation of all thoughts feelings or hopes – which have not more or less a reference to you & to *our recollections* –

Ever dearest

[Signature erased]

He wrote again in July imploring Augusta to come to him; he would provide for her whole family, he would be little trouble to

her and give her no more of his company than she would like, or
should he go to her? It is sad to read his appeals.

A few weeks later Teresa and Byron visited the theatre in
Bologna. The play was Alfieri's *Mirra*, the theme of which was
incest. The next day, 12 August, Byron described to Murray the
effect it had had on him: '... the two last acts of which threw me
into convulsions ... the agony of reluctant tears – and the choking
shudder which I do not often undergo for fiction ...'.

He was ready to return to England while he made up his mind
where he would settle next. He wrote to Douglas Kinnaird on 16
November:

> I do not come to England for pleasure – but I know not where to go
> unless to America ... I return to England with a heavier heart than
> when I left it – with no prospects of pleasure or comfort – and
> indifferent to everything – but that which it is my duty to do – &
> which I could wish done with all proper speed. – I shall bring my
> little daughter Allegra with me – but I know not where to go – I have
> nobody to receive me – but my sister – and I must conform to my
> circumstances. ...

But Teresa was ill in Ravenna, and because she pleaded for him
to go to her, he postponed his departure and travelled in his
Napoleonic coach, arriving with Allegra at the Palazzo Guiccioli on
Christmas Eve 1819.

He was welcomed into the social life of Ravenna, and they
settled into a domesticated routine in 1820 which Teresa wanted
people to think was idyllic, but in reality Byron chafed at the
constraints of his role as *cavaliere servente*. He told Hobhouse that
he was: '... so nervous that I cry for nothing ... I feel it strongly that
a man should not consume his life at the side and on the bosom of
a woman and a stranger ...'. Through Teresa's father Count
Gamba, and her brother Pietro, Byron became involved in the
Carbonari, the most important of the many libertarian societies
formed in the rising revolt in Italy against the Austrians, and due to
these activities, the house began to resemble an arsenal.

At first Byron sometimes played with Allegra, and Teresa took
her out for drives in her carriage but Allegra was at a difficult age.
Her nurse Elise had earlier been dismissed and Allegra rapidly
became beyond the control of the servants, so that she was bitterly
resented by Teresa who had no children of her own. It was

therefore arranged that when Allegra was four she should go to a convent warmly recommended by Teresa's grandparents, at Bagnacavallo, twelve miles from Ravenna. On 1 March 1821 she entered the convent and, being younger than the other pupils, was put in the special care of Mother Vicar Suor Fedele. Byron sent his peer's robe with a message that part of it should be made into a frock for his daughter.

In July, due to the political situation, the Gambas, followed three months later somewhat reluctantly by Byron, left Ravenna and eventually arrived at the Casa Lanfranchi which Shelley had taken for them in Pisa. Here they joined the 'little nest of singing birds' as Mary Shelley called the circle of friends Shelley had gathered together, hoping 'to form for ourselves a society of our own class, as much as possible, in intellect or in feelings'. Byron continued to brood over England and Augusta, and repeated his invitation for her to join him with her children and her 'drone' of a husband. He also wrote to Lady Byron in a conciliatory manner, but like many letters he had written to her but had not sent, he showed it to friends and acquaintances, perhaps as an excuse to talk about her, for she was never long out of his thoughts.

Allegra died from a fever on 20 April 1822. She was five years and three months old, and although Byron had never visited her in the convent, he was disconsolate. He later told Lady Blessington that 'while she lived her existence never seemed necessary to my happiness; but no sooner did I lose her than it appeared to me as if I could not live without her'. Perhaps Annabella's words during the separation: 'It is unhappily your disposition to consider what you *have* as valueless – what you have lost as invaluable' returned to haunt him, for Byron was learning their truth the hard way, as others have done. Allegra had written to her father before he left Ravenna asking him to visit her 'as it is fair time' but this was interpreted by Byron as asking for 'paternal ginger-bread' and he paid no attention to her appeal. Instead of choosing a secluded position for her grave near the only place where she had had a degree of happiness, and where her distraught mother might visit and grieve, Byron decided to send her body to England, which he constantly said he hated, to be buried in the church he had attended when a pupil at Harrow school '*where* – though I never *was happy* – I was once less miserable as a boy'. He wrote to Murray on 22 April, telling him of Allegra's death and his wishes for her burial when the embalmed body reached England and asked '… would you have any objection to give the proper directions on its arrival'. He added a P.S.: '… you are aware that protestants are not allowed holy ground in Catholic countries'. An account of Allegra's burial is given at the end of this chapter.

The Gambas, with Teresa, moved to Genoa in October the same year, again for political reasons, and again Byron reluctantly followed. In the following year on 1 April he met the beautiful and accomplished Marguerite Blessington, her husband the Earl of Blessington and their friend Count D'Orsay who had arrived in Genoa the day before. Lady Blessington assiduously recorded the many talks she had with the illustrious Lord Byron, and made a clear-sighted appraisal of him. He in turn was delighted to once again meet sophisticated and cultured people from England, so that a rapport was quickly established between him and Lady Blessington and most days they rode together and lunched or dined with friends. Her accounts of her meetings with Byron bring vividly to life the impressions he made on her, from which she later wrote her book *Conversations With Lord Byron*. He told her: '… I sometimes believe myself mad, … I seem to have *two* states of existence, *one* purely contemplative … and the other *active* …' and he owned that he was 'everything by turns and nothing long I am such a strange mélange of good and evil'. Byron did not see how this strange dualism inherent in his character had manifested itself in relation to his marriage, and he continued to declare he had no idea why his wife had left him.

Lady Blessington observed that Byron at first impressed his listeners with his beautiful words and sentiments as his eyes filled with tears and his voice became tremulous, but it appeared inconsistent with the sarcastic remarks which followed. She thought he rather exulted in his feelings, talked for effect, and liked to excite astonishment '… and certainly destroys in the mind of his auditors, all confidence in his stability of character'.

One day when he was holding forth, as he often did in front of people he did not know, on his matrimonial misfortunes – as he called his separation from his wife, Lady Blessington and the others present considered his behaviour unworthy, and she wrote a few verses expressing their feelings:

> And canst thou bare thy breast to vulgar eyes?
> And canst thou show the wounds that rankle there?
> Methought in noble hearts that sorrow lies
> Too deep to suffer coarser minds to share.

The wounds inflicted by the hand we love,
(The hand that should have warded off each blow)
Are never heal'd as aching hearts can prove,
But *sacred* should the stream of sorrow flow.

If *friendship's* pity quells not real grief,
Can *public* pity soothe thy woes to sleep? –
No! Byron, spurn such vain, such weak relief,
And if thy tears must fall – in secret weep.

She passed these verses, written while he was sitting for his portrait, to Byron and it was obvious that his feelings were deeply hurt. However Lady Blessington formed the opinion that Lady Byron indeed continually occupied his thoughts and that he most sincerely desired a reconciliation with her.

One day he told her of a letter he had had from a man called John Shepherd, whose wife had watched Byron playing on the rocks at Hastings. After Mr Shepherd's wife died, he went through her secret papers which no one had seen during her lifetime and came across a prayer she had written for Lord Byron, and he enclosed it in his letter. Byron read it to Lady Blessington, and gave it to her to copy observing: 'Before I had read this prayer I never rightly understood the expression so often used, 'The beauty of Holiness'. This prayer and letter has done more to give me a good opinion of religion and its professors, than all the religious books I have read in my life …'. The reply he wrote to Mr Shepherd on 8 December 1821 from Pisa, was a long and interesting letter contending that

> … a man's creed does not depend on *himself*, – *who* can say I *will* believe – this – that – or the other? … I can assure you that all the fame which ever cheated Humanity into higher notions of its own importance – would never weigh in my mind against the pure and pious interest which a virtuous being may be pleased to take in my welfare. …

Byron had one last request to make from Lady Blessington before she and her party departed on 2 June. He knew that her friend Hugh Montgomery was at present visiting Genoa and that he was the brother of Mary Millicent, the M.M. to whom Annabella had been devoted for many years. Byron told Lady Blessington that he had no mementoes of his wife and that he particularly desired to obtain a copy of a miniature of her, the one that had been in the possession of the late Lady Noel. Hugh Montgomery had possibly been the fictional object of Annabella's unrequited love, in the excuse she had made for refusing Byron's first proposal. Hugh reported to her that Byron had talked 'kindly and nobly' of her, adding that he had been wearing Augusta's hair in a large brooch and a bracelet. When M.M. was told of Byron's request for the miniature, her comment was: 'I am disposed to believe all this tenderness is directed to the £3,500 a year which in case of a reconciliation would return to his possession', referring to Annabella's inheritance now divided between Byron and herself. The miniature was not delivered, possibly due to counsel from Annabella's friends.

Augusta had disappointed Byron by not taking advantage of the pressing invitations he still made to her, and in the previous October he had written: '... I would remove from Genoa to Nice to be near you – if you would like that – (but I should occupy a separate house) or just as you like ...' – a thought then occurred to him – the irony of which he would hardly have missed and he added 'You will be pleased to recollect that you would not be required to know any Italian acquaintance of mine – the Countess G[uiccioli] has a distinct quarter ...'.

However, now that the gossip about herself and Byron had stopped Augusta was not interested in leaving England and refuelling the rumours. She had always fostered the idea in herself and others that Byron was mad, which allowed her to maintain that whatever he proclaimed he had done, in his poems and to the world, were due to delusions induced by his 'malady'. Neither was she moved by his letters for she told Annabella: '... I do not believe any feelings expressed are by any means permanent – only occasioned by ye passing & present reflection & occupation of writing to the unfortunate Being to whom they are addressed'.

But Augusta was mistaken. Byron did mean what he said in his letters to her. He would have sacrificed his life for her and she was the only object to which he remained constant. He believed his love was returned, but Augusta's affections were not of the same calibre. She was busy with her unmanageable children, her social life, her distractions with voiles ribbons and laces. His ardour was too much, just as it had been for his school-friends at Harrow, and it had become an encumbrance. Had Augusta been able to love Byron as he loved her, no one could have made her behave disloyally towards him. The truth was that she was glad to have been saved, and relieved that she was separated by land and sea from temptation she knew she would be unable to resist. Augusta did not relish tying herself down in a foreign land with one man, particularly one from whom if all went wrong she had much to lose financially, and with recollections of Piccadilly, much to fear physically as well as mentally. Moreover Byron's suggestion that her husband and children came with her at his expense did not make the prospect any more attractive.

In May 1823 Byron heard that he had been elected a member of the London Greek Committee; in June he chartered a boat called the *Hercules* and in July, showing little sorrow at leaving Teresa, he left Italy for Greece. *I am ashes where once I was fire* he had written in a poem to Lady Blessington, but now the strands of fate were irrevocably weaving their course. He had told her that he had a presentiment he would die in Greece, he hoped in action, '... but as I have not been famous for my luck in life, most probably I shall not have more in the manner of my death, and that I may draw my last sigh, not on the field of glory, but on the bed of disease ...'. Within a year, on 19 April 1824, this prophecy was fulfilled.

In view of the situation at that time, it is likely that Byron died thinking his life in Greece had been a failure. However, the importance of the poet to the Greek cause is described by André Maurois in his book *Byron*. He explained that in 1826 Missolonghi was besieged for the second time and almost destroyed:

> If Europe at that moment had deserted the Greek cause, it would have foundered, ... everything depended on England. By the sacred axioms of the Foreign Office and the Duke of Wellington, Greece stood condemned. ... It is not too much to say that, without the support lent to the Greek cause by Byron's name and Byron's death, Canning would certainly not have been upheld by English public opinion.

This led to the battle of Navarino in 1827 in which the independence of Greece was assured by the fleets of England, Russia and France.

Allegra's Burial

Allegra had been of small importance during her short life but after death she became a cause célèbre, and her story is told in numerous biographies. While she lived she had been passed from stranger to stranger and received little affection, Mr Hoppner saying: 'She was by no means an amiable child nor was Mrs Hoppner or I particularly fond of her', and Byron had looked on her as a kind of investment: 'I must love something in my old age.' He had written again to Murray on 26 May 1822 telling him that Allegra's body was embarked on a ship bound for England, and expressing his wishes for the funeral to be very private. He specified an area where he intended Allegra should be buried by quoting the words on a slab near the door in Harrow church, on which he had looked down from his seat in the gallery. He wished a marble slab to be placed on the wall bearing the inscription:

In memory of
Allegra –
Daughter of G.G. Lord Byron –
who died at Bagnacavallo
in Italy April 20th. 1822
aged five years and three months. –
'I shall go to her, but she shall not return to me.'
2d. Samuel 12. – 23.

Very private it was not to be for unfortunately Allegra's body arrived in Albemarle Street while Murray was holding a gathering of some clerical literary associates. These were probably the same ones that Byron referred to the year before, when he had complained of mistakes in the printing of the Cantos from *Don Juan* which he had attributed to Murray's qualms on publishing the controversial verses: 'I have read over the poem carefully – and I tell you *it is poetry*. – Your little envious knot of parson-poets may say what they please – time will show that I am not in this instance mistaken.' Although Murray tried to be discreet, he was unable to keep knowledge of the strange looking package requiring excise formalities from those present, but he pledged them all to strict secrecy.

At that time Frances Trollope, mother of the novelist Anthony Trollope, was a resident of Harrow. She was a cheerful warm-hearted woman with a strong character who drew round her many well-known and interesting people and her drawing-room had become the centre of Harrow social life. She tried to integrate the two factions that existed there, one led by John Cunningham, the vicar of Harrow who had been made a governor of Harrow school in 1818, and the other led by Henry Drury, the son of the headmaster in Byron's time. She wrote a 500-line satire entitled 'Lines written by a Celebrated Authoress on the Burial of the Daughter of a Celebrated Author', and in this Allegra's arrival at John Murray's establishment is vividly described:

> It was this sad deposit Murray knew
> was now in act to enter his back shop:
> Greatly perplexed he knew not what to do
> It was too late to tell the man to stop:
> And well he guessed how eagerly the crew
> Would catch at every word he might let drop.
> He gladly would have formed some specious lie,
> But feared he might offend his friends thereby.
>
> A letter too was very plainly seen
> Which in a hurried way he opened straight.
> A poet, a smart prebend, and a dean
> Over his shoulder squinted at the date.
> Doubtless these gentlemen could never mean
> To read the letter – but now 'twas too late
> To lie – so Murray said it was a daughter
> Lord B had sent to him across the water.

After the group had assimilated the implication of this unexpected interruption to their meeting they exhanged such comments as 'Depraved', 'Profane', 'Adulterous', 'Vile', 'Accursed' and then departed:

> So forth they passed – each eager to reveal
> To his own clever circle of dear friends
> All they had promised Murray to conceal,
> And not a few that evening were the pens
> That hastily dispatched a glorious meal
> Of what the city to the country lends –
> New spite – new gossip – and a few new lies
> To cheer their country neighbours' hearts and eyes.

A few months later Byron was astonished and angry to learn from the papers that Lady Byron's pew in Harrow church was opposite to the site he had chosen for Allegra, making it appear that this was the reason for his choice. On 21 December he wrote to

Murray blaming him for the 'calumnies you have allowed to circulate in the papers of the subject of the funeral of Allegra. – You *knew* and *know* how desirous I was that the funeral might be private ... I had not the most distant idea that Lady B was a frequenter of Harrow Church ...'.

The funeral had taken place on 10 September 1822. Henry Drury, with whom Byron was on friendly terms, conducted the service, but there were difficulties over the tablet. The vicar, John Cunningham, had received from John Murray through Henry Drury, details of Byron's wishes for Allegra's burial and had replied in a reasonable manner:

Sir.

Mr Henry Drury was so good as to communicate to me a request conveyed to you by Lord Byron respecting the burial of a child in this church. Mr H. Drury will probably have also stated to you my willingness to comply with the wish of Lord Byron. Will you forgive me, however, for so far trespassing upon you (though a stranger) as to suggest an enquiry whether it might not be practicable and desirable to fulfil for the *present* only a *part* of his lordship's wish – by burying the child, and putting up a tablet with simply its name upon the tablet; and thus leaving Lord B. more leisure to reflect upon the character of the inscription he may wish to be added. It does seem to me that whatever he may wish in the moment of his distress about the loss of this child, he will afterwards regret that he should have taken pains to proclaim to the world what he will not, I am sure, consider as honourable to his name. And if this be probable, then it appears to me the office of a true friend not to suffer him to commit himself but to allow his mind an opportunity of calm deliberation. I feel constrained to say that the inscription he proposed will be felt by every man of refined taste, to say nothing of sound morals, to be an offence against taste and propriety. My correspondence with his Lordship has been so small that I can scarcely venture myself to urge these objections. You perhaps will feel no such scruple. I have seen no person who did not concur in the propriety of stating them. I would entreat, however, that should you think it right to introduce my name into any statement made to Lord Byron, you will not do it without assuring him of my unwillingness to oppose the smallest obstacle to his wishes, or give the slightest pain to his mind. The injury which, in my judgement, he is from day to day inflicting upon society is no justification for measures of retaliation and unkindness.

Your obedient and faithful Servant,
J.W. Cunningham

The correspondence referred to concerned a poem Cunningham had written called 'De Rancé' which was published in 1815 and was generally thought to portray Byron, but Cunningham wrote to him denying that any reference to him was intended, and this Byron had acknowledged.

Soon after the despatch of Cunningham's letter to Murray there was a meeting of the vicar, churchwardens, all the reverend masters of Harrow school and many leading parishioners which resulted in a 'Prohibition' being produced and signed by the senior churchwarden dated 17 September: 'Honoured Sir, I object on behalf of the parish to admit the tablet of Lord Byron's child into the church. James Winkley, *Churchwarden.*' Cunningham was therefore compelled to write to Murray more forcefully:

> The churchwardens have been urged to issue their prohibition by several leading and influencial persons, laymen, in the parish. You are aware that as to ex-parishioners the consent of the churchwardens is no less necessary than my own; and that therefore the enclosed prohibition is decisive as to the putting up of the monument. You will oblige me by making known to Lord Byron the precise circumstances of the case.

During the meeting in which this was decided Mr Cunningham had observed, and Mrs Trollope noted:

> But yet I should by no means think it right
> This great man's talents to deny,
> Indeed I own I was delighted quite,
> When Cain that great performance met my eye:
> And should you Mr Drury, chance to write
> To your accomplished friend, I wish that my
> Great admiration of the genius shewn
> In that performance should to him be known.

Henry Drury's reply was succinct: 'Do you indeed – I think it the most blasphemous production that ever came from the press.' Sometimes members of the cliques changed roles rather than be seen to be of the same mind.

The place of Allegra's burial remains unknown. It is thought by some to be in the vestibule of the church, and by André Maurois to be in the turf near Peachey's tomb to which Byron referred to his correspondence with Murray: 'where I used to sit for hours &

hours when a boy – this was my favourite spot'. As the churchwardens' reluctance was directed at the inscription rather than Allegra's body, which had already been buried when they met, it is possible that she lies where Byron wished, and overlooked by the pew that Lady Byron used. There was no memorial stone placed until a plaque was unveiled on the outside of the church in 1980 which reads:

In Memory of
ALLEGRA
daughter of LORD BYRON
and CLAIRE CLAIRMONT
born in Bath 13.1.1817
died Bagnacavallo 20.4.1822
buried nearby
Erected by the Byron Society
19.4.1980

In December Byron wrote to Augusta: 'The story of this Child's burial is the epitome of my life …'. Only Byron's enemies would agree with him for surely Allegra's short life was an ignoble episode, emphasized by the events after her death. He did not see the hypocrisy and cant that he professed to abominate, in claiming for the daughter he had shamefully neglected, all the trappings of the church that he had profaned so often and so loudly in his writing. Neither had he seen that he was diminished by the lack of integrity in telling his agents they had a free hand in arranging the embalming of Allegra and refusing to pay the resulting cost, and further diminished by his dispute with the nuns over extra fees for her illness. He kept himself aloof from all these matters, which were not settled until after his death. They caused trouble and vexation to his banker Ghigi and his steward Zambelli, which led to a bitter end to the warm friendship and trust that had previously existed between them, and anger from the unpaid surgeon who had carried out the embalming.

Hobhouse declared no man had better friends than Byron, but it is noticeable that it was to his publisher, probably in the social climate of that time considered to be not quite a 'gentleman', and with whom his relationship was strained that year, that Byron turned with this very personal affair. He had told Annabella when they first met that he had not a friend in the world. Perhaps she was the only person who would have understood his impulsive desire to have Allegra buried in holy ground, where once he had found a measure of peace, and thus assuage a little his awful sense of remorse and guilt. 'Why not tell me what were or are the objections to the inscription over poor little Allegra? Was there anything wrong in it?' he pathetically asked Murray. It was rumoured then, as it is still stated by Byron scholars today, that Lady Byron was influential in the decision regarding Allegra and Harrow church. Lady Byron has been dead one hundred and thirty years. Why then, was a plaque not erected before 1980, and then with only a simple inscription as was advised by Cunningham, omitting Byron's chosen words, and placed outside the church as distinct from the area inside which Byron had indicated with such precision? The reason at the time for not allowing Byron's wishes to be carried out are explained in Mrs Trollope's words:

> It is indeed a very shocking thing,
> That one who is so very great a man
> Should such disgrace upon our parish fling:
> To send the infant hither was a plan
> Which could not fail much injury to bring,
> But by my preaching I'll do all I can
> To counteract the influence of the bones
> Unhappily now laid beneath our stones.

> But this is done so no more can be said.
> What now demands your most mature advice
> Is, whether o'er the ashes of the dead
> I should consent to place at any price
> A stone on which the child's name may be read.
> *May it not lead the school boys into vice?*
> This is a question that concerns us all,
> And the importance of it is not small.

> 'Indeed Sir you have harped my fears aright,'
> Observed the Doctor with a flattering bow,
> 'I see the thing exactly in this light,
> That I must feel most anxious, you'll allow
> The eternal interest of my pupils might
> be hazarded – were we not steady now.
> I must in short insist on it that here
> No tablet so disgraceful should appear.'

Perhaps the fear expressed prevails today. But let it not be blamed on Lady Byron. Had she been able to influence the churchwardens and others for or against Byron's wishes it would have been most discreditable to them, since she did not belong to that parish. Her friend John Cunningham, the vicar of Harrow church, whom Leslie Stephen described as 'distinguished for courtesy and kindness of heart' became a widower in 1821 and later it was mistakenly rumoured that Lady Byron was engaged to him. The Allegra affair must have been discussed between them and she may have helped Cunningham with his first letter to Murray expressing the desire to avoid remarks that could 'give the slightest pain to his mind', for it is a little reminiscent of the advice she gave Augusta when Byron's return seemed imminent: 'I am very far from wishing to detach you from him in any way by which he could be injured.'

The story of Allegra's burial could indeed by the epitome of Lady Byron's life. It discloses many instances of hypocrisy, but not one can be attributed to Lady Byron. 'They have distorted this as they do everything into some story about Lady B.' Byron wrote resentfully. He might have added, had he lived long enough, that it is typical of what has been said about Lady Byron in that it is inaccurate and unfair, as have been many of the statements made about Byron himself.

12 Following Byron's Death

On receiving the tragic news of Byron's death on 14 May 1824 Kinnaird immediately sent a note to Hobhouse and with it the letters Fletcher had written to Augusta, Lady Byron and George Byron, now the seventh lord. Hobhouse went down to see Augusta who had previously been informed by Sir Francis Burdett. Fletcher's simple words and artless expressions made what he had to say poignantly sad, and Augusta and Hobhouse were overcome with grief. George Byron travelled to Beckenham to break the news to Lady Byron, and on his return he told Augusta and Hobhouse that her distress had been painful to witness. Curiously, one biographer has written that Byron's death came less as a shock to Annabella than as a blow to her self-esteem.

Fletcher came to England in July and met Lady Byron. He told later how distracted she had been, imploring him to remember the words uttered so earnestly but almost unintelligibly by Byron on his deathbed. Fletcher could only tell her that Byron had talked falteringly of Ada, Augusta and her children, and then – 'you will go to Lady Byron and say – Tell her everything; you are friends with her'. With these words Byron was overcome and his voice failed him, and for nearly twenty minutes he tried to talk but Fletcher could not understand a word. Was Byron trying to say that he now recognized that Annabella was ever the true friend to him she had wanted to be, or was he reminding her, commanding her once again to be kind to Augusta? She would never know.

Her sorrow made her ill. Who can know what part remorse – that most bitter of griefs to bear – took in retarding her recovery, but no indication of her feelings was left for the prying eyes of posterity, and the enigma of Byron's last message, which prompted her to write a poem, was to haunt her to the end of her life:

In a far land did he breathe forth that soul
Which had reign'd like a God, and had own'd no control
And no lov'd ones were near him to bless and be blessed.
Or to read ere it faded each wish not expressed! –

But far from the scenes of his birth and his youth,
that breath of sweet song died away in the south.
And silent and lone was the vale of the graves
There were none to divine the last tokens he gave! –

The dying desire that he long'd to impress,
The one truth then reveal'd, that might save and might bless, –
That hallowed last link 'twixt, the living and dead. –
' 'Twas all speechless and void; – and that word was not said.

The effort was made, but all, all, was in vain,
And dark is that page which he sought to explain.
For the voice tho' it strove, it could bring forth no sound,
And the heart tho' it heav'd, had no rhythm nor bound.

That eye which had gleam'd as in flashes from Heav'n, –
Whose glances by angels and demons seem'd given. –
It anxiously gaz'd, but its language and lights
As they faded were seal'd from mortality's sights.

In a letter to Mrs Villiers, Annabella said that Ada had cried when she was told of her father's death, adding: '… it is a great comfort to me that I have never had to give her a painful impression of her father'. Of this period she was to write:

Whoever has once seen in life a *desert* spread before him will recognize the feeling in another mind. It may be lived through, but how much more of faith is required! and we seldom take the right way. It is not as far as my experience goes, by seeking to turn the whole soul to God … but by devoting ourselves to help and comfort all who need what we can give them.

Hobhouse, in spite of his distress on hearing of Byron's death, immediately became obsessed with the need to destroy his memoirs. 'I have written my Memoirs' Byron had told Lady Blessington 'to save the necessity of their being written by a friend or friends, and have only to hope they will not add notes.' The first part had been completed by 1819 and dealt with the poet's early life, and then gave a long and detailed account of his relationship with Lady Byron, and his version of the causes for the separation. He had written to her in December 1819 offering them for her perusal and comments: 'The truth I have always stated – but there are two ways of looking at it – and your way may be not mine ...', and he promised that '*your mark* shall not be erased'. But she had declined to see them, surprised that he should wish to reopen and make public matters that she thought should remain private. Her decision was most unfortunate in view of their fate, for had she read them, undoubtedly some record of the contents would now exist.

As far back as 1821 there had been trouble with Hobhouse, who resented not having seen the memoirs or having been consulted about them, and Byron, exasperated by Hobhouse's attitude, wrote an angry letter to Murray on 24 November: 'Does Mr. Hobhouse dispute my right to leave the Memoirs of myself for posthumous publication?' Byron had alluded to these memoirs many times to his friends, explaining 'It will be a kind of Guide post in case of death – and prevent some of the lies which would otherwise be told ...'. He was very anxious that they should be accurate, writing to Moore to whom he had given them '... and *above all, contradict* anything if I have *mis*-stated: for my first object is the truth, even at my expense'. He had told Moore that he could show them to anybody he thought suitable and Byron himself suggested that Moore should raise money on them before he died, because he would rather they helped him than his grandchildren. This Moore did and obtained an advance of 2,000 guineas from John Murray. However in 1822 Byron told Hobhouse he was considering whether he should regain control of his memoirs, for since the death of Lady Noel, whom he had always believed was hostile towards him, he had felt there was a possibility of reunion with his wife.

Hobhouse had never been able to fully appreciate his friend's genius and had advised that much of Byron's masterpiece 'Don Juan' should be suppressed, as well as referring to Byron's letters in his journal as 'sad trash'. He decided the manuscript should go to Byron's family, by which he meant Augusta, and he told her firmly it was in her brother's interest to destroy his memoirs. Augusta, who knew nothing about them and without guidance was unlikely to have wanted such a drastic step to be taken without due premeditation and advice, was nevertheless quite pleased to have the decision made by Byron's best friend and executor. She had long been embarrassed by her brother's constant references to her in terms of love in his poetry, and she was fearful of what new peril might emerge.

Fletcher had revealed in his letter to her that Byron had taken to reading his bible since his illness in February which pleased Augusta because she had given this bible to him when they parted, and she considered she had herself been redeemed. However Hobhouse thought it 'might be mistaken for cowardice or hypocrisy' and made Augusta promise not to disclose Fletcher's remarks about the bible to anyone. She wrote to Hodgson:

> ... Fletcher says that for the last year his mind and feelings appeared to be changed much for the better ... you see, dear Mr. Hodgson, that Mr. Hobhouse and a certain set imagine that it might be said by his enemies, and those who have no religion at all, that he had turned Methodist ... But let them say what they will, it must be the first of consolations to us that he did so.

It is a pity that Hobhouse did not reflect that Byron did not then, and never would, require lies to be told, or any other kind of 'protection' from his lesser friends. It is surprising, considering how many people had seen the memoirs and that a copy had been made, that so little of what was written could afterwards be remembered. The most quoted part seems to be that on their wedding-day 'Byron had Lady Byron on the sofa before dinner'.

They were accordingly burnt in Murray's parlour in Albemarle Street on 17 May, Annabella's birthday, three days after it was learned that Byron was dead. Of the seven people present, one being John Murray's 16-year-old son, only two, Moore and his friend Luttrell, had actually read them and these two thought and said that it was wrong to destroy them. Moore was of the opinion they should be sealed up and deposited for safe-keeping, at least for a specified period, or that the manuscript should be read and suitable extracts published. Hobhouse was motivated most by the desire to oppose Moore, and Murray, anxious to do the right thing, supported Hobhouse. Wilmot Horton represented Augusta, but was unaware of the pressure put on her by Hobhouse. Doyle was only at the meeting by chance but was known to be a friend of Lady

Byron, and he assumed she would have no objection to the destruction. Byron's reputation suffered grave injury since the public supposed the memoirs were too indecent to be kept under any circumstances.

The controversy over the memoirs dragged on for many months. There was the question of compensation; who should pay Murray, who in fact owned them at the time of their destruction; as well as disagreement on the validity of the action. On 26 November Hobhouse was still trying to calm Augusta: 'For heaven's sake see Lord Lansdowne or anybody in the world – if he can make you think better of anyone so much the better – but it ought not to be – if possible at the expense of others – I never will hear Murray run down in my presence ...'

Robert Wilmot Horton seemed to think that Lady Byron had been involved, for there were rumours to this effect, but Colonel Doyle wrote to him on 18 May 1825:

> ... I regarded myself only as a witness and not as a party to the proceeding. Lady Byron certainly gave no consent to the *destruction* of the manuscript either directly or indirectly – she could never have known that it was intended to destroy it, because I believe that intention was communicated for the first time at the meeting in question. The point at issue before us was not whether the manuscript should be destroyed but whether it should be suppressed – or partially published. ...

Lady Byron wrote to Augusta on 1 June 1825:

> The fact is that I do concur *now* in the expediency and propriety of the destruction, but had the question been *then* submitted to me, they certainly would not have been consumed by *my* decision. It is therefore perhaps well it was not, and of this I feel sure, that you did what you believed consistent with my wishes, tho' of course it was not from consideration for me, but for your Brother's memory, that you were primarily influenced. Such being the case, why am I to sanction this *falsehood?*

On 6 June Augusta replied:

> *To be read at leisure*
> You really and perfectly *astound* me by saying that W[ilmot] throws all the responsibility of the *destruction* on you! How can it be

possible after all that passed on the subject between us – when in consequence of his coming and proposing the direct reverse of what Mr. Hobhouse had the day before – the most extraordinary plans, such as locking up the manuscript at *his* [Wilmot's] Bankers!!! publishing the *un*exceptional parts and so on – I declared I would have *nothing* to do with the thing. He said 'You *must, Moore will not give them up to anybody else.*' I answered '*if I do accept them they shall be destroyed*', that answer closed the whole business! It is really almost incredible that after *that*, he can say you did it ... & I feel so strongly that it was *my sole act & deed* that nothing but absolute inability to pay all should induce me to hear of your paying one farthing – & I must say it has vexed me & does vex me more than I can describe to think that you are to be so taxed for any act of mine. ...

The letter continued at length and there can be no doubt about Augusta's genuine astonishment that it could be thought Lady Byron was implicated in any way. Furthermore in Hobhouse's account of the destruction of the memoirs he says that on the day before they were burned he was told by Murray that Mr Horton would accompany Colonel Doyle '... an intimate friend of Lady Byron who it was thought might as well be represented by some person on the occasion of the destruction of the Memoirs'. In his diary on 24 May 1824 Hobhouse wrote: 'Nothing but Murray's decisive conduct, backed by my own representations procured the destruction of the MSS.'

In *The Journal of Thomas Moore* under 17 May 1824, a summary is given of the events of that day by Lord John Russell who edited Moore's papers after his death. Russell recorded that '... I have omitted details which recall a painful scene ...'. Russell stated that he had seen Hobhouse's account and that the leading facts related by him agree with those given by Moore. Russell had read Byron's memoirs and his opinion was '... on the whole, the world is no loser by sacrifice made of the Memoirs of this great poet'.

If Moore remembered Byron's urgent appeal to him to see that the truth was told after he was dead, he was powerless to achieve it at this, the first hurdle, and he would have been most surprised to have read forty-five years later, in the *Daily News* for 4 September 1869, the letter from William Howitt, a well known Quaker, poet and author of 50 books: 'I knew Lord Byron for some years. ... No sooner was Byron dead having left a carefully written memoir in his own justification, than Lady Byron sought to buy this up. She in fact never ceased her exertions till she had procured the destruction of her husband's own carefully prepared defence ...'. These shameless attacks on Lady Byron could be made with impunity after her death, for there were few alive who could refute them.

Among The Lovelace Papers is an undated note written by Lady Byron: 'Murray is much wronged by popular opinion. The merits of that business have never been properly acknowledged by any party' and in November 1825 she wrote to Joanna Baillie from Brighton:

I am privately mediating some handsome and ostensible acknowledgement to Murray, for the sacrifice he made of his pecuniary interests in surrendering the property of the Memoirs for the very inadequate compensation of the purchase-money, at a time when their value was at least quadrupled by the power of immediate publication. I am thoroughly acquainted with the documents which prove Murray's honourable and faithful conduct in this business, and the less it is appreciated in the world owing to Moore's having gained the popular opinion, the more do I wish to furnish Murray with some memorial of *my* estimation. What occurs to you for this purpose – a present of plate? or a marble bust of Lord Byron? a picture? I wish it were something that would tell its own story, or at least imply it.

Another matter that was to cause trouble and confusion was Byron's will. It caused resentment to his heir because George Byron did not know beforehand he had been disinherited, and he had no money of his own to uphold the title. Byron had left all his effects to Augusta and her children for her own exclusive benefit free from her husband's control, and this was done soon after his marriage in 1815 with Lady Byron's knowledge.

It was while they were still on honeymoon at Halnaby, where Annabella was distressed by Byron's strange and unhappy behaviour. Every day she was hopeful that there would be a change, perhaps through the influence of his sister, about whom he was always talking, and whom she had yet to meet. It did not seem the occasion to annoy Byron by adverse comments about his will, when he asked her to write to the family solicitor Hoar, and also to inform Augusta. This at the time seemed to be the least of her worries, especially as neither she nor Byron at that period had any money. Hoar had declared that he should see Byron before he took

action, but when Annabella insisted that she considered it right
and urged the execution of the will he reluctantly agreed to her
request.

In contrast when Lord Wentworth died later in the same year it
had been omitted to secure his property for Lady Byron's sole and
separate use, the will making her his heir after her mother died
having been drawn up before her marriage. This effectively made
the rights of the property wholly in Byron's name when Annabella
succeeded. On Lady Noel's death in 1822, Byron reluctantly
agreed to arbitration and the inheritance was divided equally
between him and Annabella. The amount Byron left for Augusta
was around £100,000. In addition there would be the rents from
the Wentworth estate as well as the sale of copyrights from Byron's
works less, of course, the payment of outstanding debts and the
security of Annabella's jointure.

Annabella immediately made over her jointure of £2,000 a year
from the marriage settlement to George Byron, and even this
would have gone to Augusta had Annabella died first. Wilmot
Horton wrote of it to Annabella: '... I consider that proposal as one
of the most liberal and magnanimous ... that *ever was made* by Man
or Woman – & yet I think it quite that sort of proposal which
anyone who knows you, or rather *of you*, as much as I do, might
expect you to make ...'. Yet even this was criticized. Byron's will had
been published in the newspapers as had Annabella's gesture over
the money for George Byron, *The Times* remarking it was 'proof at
least' of her approval of her late husband's disposition of the
Wentworth money.

Whenever Augusta felt threatened by critics suggesting that she
had been substituted for the rightful heirs she produced the
friendly letter that Annabella had written to her at Byron's request
in 1815, as if Annabella had possessed a dispensing power to
sanction the disinheritance of their daughter and George Byron.
Annabella loyally wrote to Augusta during the controversy
confirming she had supported Byron in his belief that it was his
duty to provide for Augusta, but how *exclusively* she was relieved
not to have had to consider. Nobody had known whether Byron
had made another will in view of the change in his fortune, or made
any additions, least of all Lady Byron who is blamed for not
informing his heir of Byron's neglect.

Nor apparently, had she seen the book published in 1825 in
which Byron is quoted as saying: 'No man on earth respects a

virtuous woman more than I do, and the prospect of retirement in England with my wife and Ada, gives me an idea of happiness I have never experienced before. Retirement will be everything to me, for heretofore my life has been like the ocean in a storm.' The writer was William Parry, who visited Augusta nine or ten months after Byron's death. She had written to Annabella on 2 March 1825:

> A Mr Parry who was in Greece called here the other day – & not knowing the *sort* of *animal* he was I saw him – *much* to my annoyance he is among the Biographers I fear – a most *vulgar* rough *Bearish* person – he desired me to say if you had any *wish* to see him he wd go to you – I did not encourage him to expect you *wd* wish it & I sd advise you not from what I felt myself.

Parry, during his visit, must have told Augusta what he had recorded in his book, that Byron had spoken warmly of his wife to him many times. He mentioned one day to Byron that he had supposed a difference of religious sentiments between him and Lady Byron had caused the public breach. 'No Parry,' was the reply, 'Lady Byron has a liberal mind, particularly as to religious opinions; and I wish, when I married her, that I had possessed the same command over myself that I now do. Had I possessed a little more wisdom and more forbearance, we might have been happy.' When Byron spoke so wistfully of his wife to Parry, perhaps he was then remembering Annabella as he saw her when they first met, and as he portrayed her in the exquisite verses describing Aurora Raby in 'Don Juan':

> There was
> Indeed a certain fair and fairy one,
> Of the best class, and better than her class, –
> Aurora Raby, a young star who shone
> O'er life, too sweet an image for such glass;
> A lovely being scarcely formed or moulded;
> A rose with all its sweetest leaves yet folded.
>
> He gained esteem where it was worth the most;
> And certainly Aurora had renewed
> In him some feelings he had lately lost
> Or hardened, – feelings which, perhaps ideal,
> Are so divine that I must deem them real: –

His first impressions of Annabella are preserved not only in verse but in the second letter he wrote to her on 26 September 1814: 'There was a simplicity – an – innocence – a beauty in your deportment & appearance which although you hardly spoke – told me I was in company with no common being.'

Parry's words would have been of much comfort to Annabella and she was less sensitive to plebeian mortals than Augusta, but the prospects Byron dreamed about in the last few weeks of his life remained unknown to the one to whom they would have given great solace. William Parry was the artillery man and mechanic sent out to Missolonghi while Byron was there to take charge of the arsenal. Because of his common sense, his straightforward honesty and robust sense of humour Byron came to rely on and trust him and Parry became Byron's favourite and constant companion. It was Parry who, when Byron was dying, had the sense to loosen the bandage round his head to relieve the agonizing pain while the doctors stood around uselessly wringing their hands.

Parry quotes Byron as saying:

> I have lately read of an institution lately established in London for the instruction of mechanics. I highly approve of this, and intend to subscribe £50 to it; but I shall at the same time write and give my opinion on the subject ... Poverty is wretchedness, but it is perhaps to be preferred to the heartless unmeaning dissipation of the higher orders. I am thankful that I am now entirely clear of this, and my resolution to remain clear of it for the rest of my life is immutable.

(When Lady Byron was residing at 6 Pavilion Buildings, Brighton in the 1850s, it is recorded in Brighton annals that she lent the ground floor of her house to the Mechanics Institute for educational purposes such as elocution and French classes.)

Doris Langley Moore in *The Late Lord Byron* gives an incomparable description and analysis of the response that Parry's book received:

> At the time when William Parry paid this unwelcome visit, [to Augusta] he was writing *The Last Days of Lord Byron*, the best, most vigorous, most convincing account by any eye witness of Byron's final struggles in Greece, his personality in sickness and despair, and the personality of his plausible adversary, Col the Hon Leicester Stanhope. There was no man more deserving the kindness of Byron's friends, and no man who received less of it.

It was Parry's misfortune not to be a gentleman – very obviously not a gentleman; and, it seemed outrageous to friends and critics alike that a peer and a peer's son should be written about by a common fellow who had been a firemaster in the Navy. The book was scornfully handled by most reviewers and its author rejected everywhere.

It was rejected because Parry told the truth. In his preface to the book he wrote:

The only object I have in view, in sitting down to write a Preface is to tell the reader why I have written a book … Lord Byron's conduct in Greece has been attacked … also to vindicate his memory from some unjust aspersions. During the last two months of his existence, there was no person in whom he placed more confidence than in me … I aim at nothing but accuracy; and I expect praise for no other quality.

The quality of truth is unmistakable on every page, and quite apart from the references to herself Annabella must have been enthralled had she read it.

On his death, having previously been considered mad, bad and someone who caused ladies to swoon at the sight of him, Byron became a national and international hero. Everyone who had ever had the smallest contact with him rushed into print and almost immediately Medwin, Leigh Hunt and Dallas had their books ready and published, however inaccurate their contents. Augusta, as befitted his beloved sister, became a minor celebrity and enjoyed sharing his posthumous fame. His widow, however, was criticized and disparaged. She was continually harassed and referred to on various matters which resulted in her becoming seriously ill. In 1825, as well as the trouble over the memoirs, the will, and Augusta's problems, her father died at her home in Hampstead at the age of seventy-eight. This must have been a very traumatic time for her as he had been ailing and dependent for some time, and even in 1815, in a letter to Byron (an unlikely confidant it might be thought), Ralph Milbanke had said how much he hated old age.

Did the loss of her father bring back to Annabella wistful memories of long ago, days of another peaceful and happy life, when she had loving parents, and was spoken of with respect and affection? Did she regret striving for a dream which was attained for so short a time, and at such great cost? She had become a wan, dispirited shadow of her former self, her confidence shaken, always on the defensive against constant criticism made through prejudice, lies and ignorance and often afflicted by ill-health. Many doctors are of the opinion that illness, other than that with such causes as infection injury and congenital defects, is psychosomatic in origin, and doubtless much of Annabella's was. But that is not to say that she did not suffer dreadfully and credit should be given for her determination in resisting total collapse.

She found her health was much improved at sea, and in her 'elegant pleasure yacht' the *Prince Leopold*, according to *The Times* in 1825, Lady Byron would cruise between the shores of England and France, or along the south coast from Dover to Poole, sometimes stopping at towns and villages along the way. She was accompanied by friends and family, and Ada was described as a most interesting child 'possessing the same noble and open countenance' as her father. This account of Lady Byron's affinity with the sea sounds more interesting than the one given in a contemporary biography which says that Lady Byron was wont to 'eat heavily ... and then hire a boat so that she could unload her stomach a short distance out at sea'. This image would have surprised Byron, who noted and approved his wife's fastidiousness.

Early in 1826 Augusta wrote to Annabella asking her to lend her money for a settlement for Georgiana, her eldest child, now seventeen years old and engaged to Henry Trevanion, a distant relation. Augusta expressed her gratitude to Annabella for the loan saying: '... we have heard from the *higher powers* consenting to the immediate conclusion, as I (*entre nous* you) have provided the needful'. In spite of both fathers' disapproval the marriage took place on 4 February 1826 at St James's Church, Piccadilly and although George Leigh's name is on the marriage certificate as giving his consent, Georgiana was given away by Augusta's friend Colonel Henry Wyndham and the only members of the family present were Augusta and her daughter Medora.

The next problem in 1826 concerned blackmail. A man called Wilmington Fleming had somehow got involved with Caroline Lamb who had apparently given him her private journal and confessions, and these he threatened to publish unless he was given money. He had already approached Hobhouse but was ignored, and he then appealed to Augusta. Annabella knew, by the last interview she had had with Caroline Lamb, that Byron had told her of his relationship with Augusta and of other crimes he said he had committed. This made her anxious on Augusta's behalf, and she therefore postponed her proposed visit abroad to help her if the need arose. She wrote to Mrs Villiers: 'I think I cannot go abroad and leave her to such impending danger, if my presence can protect her. ... A promise of kindness sealed by death must ever bind me'. However, Augusta asked Hanson to see Fleming and nothing more seems to have been heard of the matter. The question does arise, in view of Augusta's perpetual abject poverty, yet relatively modest style of living, whether she was, and to what extent, in thrall to blackmailers for the rest of her life.

At last Annabella left England and travelled extensively in Europe with her friend Louise Chaloner and Ada, who was accompanied by her governess, returning in December 1828. During her travels Annabella visited Genoa and Ada, who was nearly eleven, had drawing lessons from a Signor Isola 'much employed by Lord Byron in this place, and of course feels a great interest in Ada'. This seems to indicate that Lady Byron encouraged her daughter to be interested in people connected with her father. They went to Switzerland, which reminded Annabella of Scaham. Here, she visited Hofwyl where Emanuel de Fellenberg, the Swiss educational reformer, had started his famous school. She had long been interested in his unorthodox methods which sought to allow cach child to discover and develop the skills to which he was suited, as well as being able to acquire further interests as he progressed. She put her beliefs into action by sending two of her second cousins to the school at Hofwyl.

While she was away she had been in communication with Augusta who had many troubles concerning her husband, who had threatened to leave her, and her children, with whom there were always problems. Augusta's feelings over the will were by no means settled and she had been hurt, as it seemed to her that Annabella had suggested it was an act of '*injustice to his own Child*' – but Annabella replied that if she would only reread her letter she would see that she had said no such thing. A little later Augusta asked Annabella to lend her money again; first she asked for one or two hundred pounds, and shortly afterwards for a thousand pounds. Annabella could see from her demanding attitude and contorted excuses that Augusta's financial state was out of control, and this time she did not comply with the request, although she agreed to hear Augusta's explanations through Mrs Villiers, which Augusta declined to make.

In 1829 Douglas Kinnaird, who had been a friend of Byron and also his banker, business representative and trustee of Augusta's inheritance from Byron, resigned this position. This was due to ill-health as well as the appalling difficulties caused by Augusta's continual interference, muddleheadedness and obstinacy. 'I think she is half-witted,' he told Hobhouse. The trust contained Byron's share of Annabella's inheritance when Lady Noel died. Augusta had no rights in the new nomination but wanted a representative of her choice and proposed Colonel D'Aguilar, a friend and thought to be her lover. He had managed her financial affairs for some time with singularly little success and supported her attitude. Annabella, knowing Augusta's hopeless lack of money sense, was loath to have anyone associated with her appointed. She wrote what she hoped was a tactful letter to Augusta on 26 November: 'Dearest A – I am happy to say that Dr Lushington is likely to accept the office of trustee …'. She went on to say that he was in agreement with Colonel D'Aguilar's suggestions and that his (Colonel D'Aguilar's) conduct had been that of a gentleman. But Augusta was not to be appeased.

Annabella thereupon consulted Dr Lushington who said: 'Frankly speaking, no one but the most ignorant, or the most selfish, of our species could entertain such feelings – and to this is to be added the base ingratitude to yourself, who have shown every disposition to aid and assist her wishes.' He went on to explain that a trustee of Augusta's choice could injure Annabella and Ada to her advantage, whereas Augusta's interests could not be affected by someone of Annabella's choice. It is said that Annabella always acted with a lawyer by her side. It would seem in financial and other matters that she would have been wiser to have taken greater heed of judicial advice. In this case she was confirming that she was legally in the right as well as not being unfair to Augusta, who complained that Lushington had contrived with Kinnaird to obtain the nomination. Annabella explained to her that she had arranged for the solicitor Mr Wharton, with whom Augusta was on good terms, to look after her transactions.

Augusta eventually told Annabella that nothing could make up for the misery and vexation she had suffered but that she would forgive her. Annabella however, who had tried to accommodate Augusta's wishes and resented the implication of injury to her, decided, like Kinnaird, that she had had enough. She had always felt it a duty to ensure that the inheritance now in her care was used wisely and realized it would not benefit anyone for long if Augusta was able to get through the trust money in the same way as her father, Captain Byron, had done by squandering the fortunes of his two wives, yet ending up in the gutter at the age of thirty-five. Others also found Augusta impossible to deal with in financial matters and in 1846 even John Hobhouse, a trustee of Byron's will, was to file a Bill for Chancery to administer the estate, 'for the numerous deeds executed by Mrs Leigh had created so many claimants that he wished to be relieved from responsibility'. The costs thus involved seriously reduced the fund.

Later in the year a request for help came from an unexpected quarter. After their marriage Georgiana and Henry Trevanion had no settled home, very little money and proceeded to have three children in three years. During this time Lady Byron lent them Bifrons, her large house near Canterbury. At the end of 1829 the Reverend William Eden was alerted by neighbours to the prevailing gossip about the Trevanions, which when he visited them he discovered to be true. Medora Leigh, Augusta's daughter whom Byron had looked on so fondly, had come earlier in the year to live with her sister and Henry, and was now pregnant by Henry with his wife's collusion.

William Eden hastily consulted George Byron, the seventh Lord and Mary his wife, and they informed Annabella. She gave financial assistance and they helped the Trevanions and Medora to go to France. Medora, who had been known as Do when a baby, and is variously referred to as Elizabeth and Libby, gave birth to a baby boy in February 1830, who died shortly afterwards. Augusta knew nothing of this, and there was no communication between her and Annabella or the Byrons, presumably at the Trevanions' request.

In spite of her exasperation over the nomination of the trustee, and telling Mr Wilmot Horton that she felt she could have no 'personal intercourse with Mrs Leigh after such a wilful misunderstanding' Annabella, remembering her promise to Byron, called on Augusta several times at her apartment in St James's Palace, but was discourteously kept waiting and Augusta would not receive her. Annabella wrote to Mrs Villiers, who was also ignored: 'You and I have *served her purposes*, and are to be discarded it seems!'

The sisterhood was indeed over. It was very sad that, having withstood the traumas, the suspicions, the striving to be a friend, the gratitude that each had had reason to feel to the other, the bond that had been forged because of Byron was now shattered, and it would seem so needlessly. Annabella had become a kind of surrogate mother to Augusta, and far from having an unwanted interference in Augusta's affairs, she was consulted on each of her many crises and was kept informed of the daily details of her life, as well as receiving reports on new books and items of interest from the court circles in which Augusta moved. Augusta needed the steadying influence of someone whose opinions she trusted, to confide in and keep her on course, and to give her the stability of thought that she lacked. This Byron must have recognized, prompting him to make his appeal to Annabella: 'Be kind to Augusta.' Annabella almost certainly derived satisfaction from this relationship, for she had always enjoyed 'giving out' as she called it and was sympathetic and practical when giving advice.

Augusta had known, as no one else could ever know, how deeply Annabella had suffered at Piccadilly Terrace. They had been drawn together by their mutual anxiety, confidences, and concern for Byron. Many minor discomforts can attend a first pregnancy as well as some trepidation and Annabella was alone except for Augusta, who through her own experience was an immeasurable source of comfort and support. Annabella had loved her deeply, and it was very painful that Augusta had not trusted her.

Augusta now seemed to lose control of her life, and she became increasingly lacking in moral and financial judgement which was to have tragic consequences. The saddest part was, she had abandoned the one person who could have been the trustworthy friend that Byron had foreseen she would need and had hoped that his wife would be.

13   The School at Ealing Grove

With Byron, and then Augusta it seemed, out of her life Annabella found the enthusiasm to channel her energy into a wider field of philanthropic works, the foremost of which at that time was the new and exciting concept of the Cooperative Movement. In 1829 she had had an interview with Robert Owen, generally regarded as being the founder of this movement, but does not seem to have been very impressed – 'Vanity and presumption appeared to me strongly to characterize him.'

Nevertheless she was swept into the wave of idealism surrounding Owen's doctrines for she was deeply aware that the conditions then prevalent for the poor had to be changed. Slavery was an abomination, but she believed that the lower orders in Britain, though possessing freedom, were slaves of a kind, and the slums that Dickens was to describe so graphically a few years later were only too real. Her ideas on socialism were embodied in a letter to her friend Dr King, physician at Brighton Hospital: 'For myself instead of dreading the change of property, I only wish there were a greater probability of it – but I should not the less disapprove a rapacious or a avaricious feeling amongst those who deserve to be benefited. I would rather they should take 3/4 of my property in the right *spirit* than 1/4 in the *wrong*.'

Robert Owen was born in 1771 in North Wales where his father had a saddler and ironmongering business. His education ceased when he was nine, but by the time he was nineteen he was managing very successfully a cotton mill in Manchester. In 1800 he became manager and part owner of the New Lanark mills near Glasgow where conditions for the workers, as in most contemporary mills and factories, were very unsatisfactory. He set about improving housing, and by his personal exertion and influence trained his employees to habits of order, cleanliness and thrift, while the sale of drink was strictly supervised. He devoted special attention to education for the children, and was the founder of infant schools in Great Britain. Although the mills were a commercial success, not all his partners were in agreement with the expense incurred in making these reforms. In 1813 Owen formed a new company that included Jeremy Bentham and William Allen, who would be content with a 5% return on capital. New Lanark was frequently visited by social reformers and statesmen not only from Great Britain, but also continental Europe and all were impressed with the good conditions and the atmosphere of the cooperative enterprise embodied in the motto: 'Each for all, and all for each.'

In 1817 Owen became greatly involved in the concept of community living to solve the problems of widespread poverty caused by the ending of the Napoleonic wars, and the struggle between human labour and the introduction of machinery. His plans interested many prominent people, one of his most dependable friends being the Duke of Kent, the father of Queen Victoria. Unfortunately during meetings he made bitter attacks on all accepted religions and the ensuing adverse publicity brought discredit to his theories. He made some attempts at community living in Orbiston near Glasgow, and New Harmony, Indiana, USA but these were unsuccessful. This was because his followers held divergent views, and due to their impatience, the communes were founded prematurely with inadequate capital. His connections with New Lanark came to an end after many years through differences with his partners over his rigid judgements. However he was highly esteemed for the pioneer social reform he carried out, even if Lady Byron's first impressions were, it seems, correct. The public enthusiasm with cooperative schemes reached its peak between 1828 and 1834, and then faded and the movement collapsed.

As with all her philanthropic work, Annabella did not just send money, she always tried to investigate, understand the problems, sympathize with them and then endeavour to give practical assistance. This committed response and eagerness to help, characterized all the activites in which she became involved. It embraced emotional causes, as it had when she was seeking to rehabilitate Augusta, as well as those concerning the poor, prison reform, slavery and many small unrecorded acts of kindness that only come to light in biographies or sources unconnected with Byron. Many of these people looked on her almost as a saint, which she found discomforting. Soon after the separation she wrote to her father complaining that Lord Gosford, who she did not like because of his rude behaviour to his wife (M.G.), was very active spiritually; 'Because I go to church very regularly and sometimes talk pye-house [pious] Lord G takes to himself the merit of having converted me.'

In Brighton, where she often stayed, Annabella gave keen support to the Cooperative Society and was one of the pioneer members in starting the branch at Hastings, in which she unsuccessfully attempted to involve William Frend. She gave money and land, and constantly tried to attract the interest of prominent people like Dr Lushington, Dr King, the novelist Maria Edgeworth and William Mulready, the painter who had earlier illustrated William Godwin's books. But after one meeting in London in October 1829 she reported to Dr King that 'Goodwill to men was far from being the prevailing spirit. Even *personal* animosity was encouraged' and she, like others, began to be disillusioned.

Lady Byron returned to her interest in education after her disenchantment with the Cooperative Movement. The schools then in existence for the poor were generally called Charity or Dame schools, and these usually only gave tuition in reading, writing and religious instruction and did not prepare the pupils to earn their living. Education was not compulsory until 1876 and then only for children under thirteen, and did not become free until 1891. It is against this background of very limited education for the poor and appalling slum conditions that the value of the work done by Lady Byron and others like her can be appreciated.

Although Annabella had been active in planning village schools for some time, and seems to have started one at Seaham under the guidance of William Frend in 1818, her ambition was to start a school with new ideas which she considered essentially addressed the problem of educating the labouring classes. She much approved of what she had learned of the progressive educational methods developed by Emanuel de Fellenberg at his school in Hofwyl in Switzerland, which she visited during her European tour in 1828. He had successfully developed the ideals and teaching concepts of Johann Heinrich Pestalozzi, which became so well thought of and widely acclaimed that similar industrial schools, as they were to be called, were set up not only in Switzerland but in other countries.

The following abridgement is taken from the account that Lady Byron wrote on the history of how these schools started. This explains their purpose and describes the very different approach to teaching from any previously practised. It also explains the careful choice of tutor or governess to suit a particular pupil in various stages of his development, because a suitable choice at one stage might not be right for the next:

Switzerland, a prosperous country, was invaded by France with whom they had been nominally at peace, on some flimsy pretext in 1798. The object was to quarter and occupy the considerable Napoleonic forces made idle following the recent peace with Italy. The people in the cantons resisted energetically, which infuriated the invading troops who then ravaged the country with fire and sword. Those inhabitants who were not killed fled into the mountains and only the children were spared, and these roamed the ruined countryside where their homes had been. There was compassion throughout Switzerland for these homeless orphans, but the first to take some positive action was Pestalozzi. He had completed his studies to go into the church, but had completely broken down in his probationary sermon thus ruining his future prospects.

He decided to convert his theological teaching into practical Christianity. He sold his property and set off for Unterwalden, one of the worst affected areas. Helped by friends he provided a shelter amid the ruins of the nearby village of Stanz where he fed and clothed the children who were rough, demoralized and diseased. There were frequent new arrivals as word was spread around about this haven. Order and discipline were obtained by selecting from the children the most intelligent and those most likely to be able to control and guide the others. These were taught to assist him in giving lessons as well as the other necessary work like preparing food, collecting wood, mending and repairing etc. He acquired a plot of land and the principles of agricultural cultivation were taught and practised. However Pestalozzi's funds were running out and the school had to be dispersed in 1799.

He had become famous not only for this school but for his writing, his best known book being *Leonard and Gertrude* in which he described his ideal of what the governor of such a school should be, and outlined his philosophy in teaching. He called it the training of the whole man: the education of the head, the heart and the hands, together with the development of the powers of observation; he deeply believed in the enormous benefit of sympathetic application of teacher to pupil. His aim was to develop the children's own faculties and 'not train them as one would a dog'. It was therefore most important to train teachers who fully understood and sympathized with this different and potentially controversial concept.

After leaving Stanz, Pestalozzi established a school at Burgdorf. Here his school soon flourished attracting many pupils from rich and influential families whose fees helped to finance the poor pupils. It also excited the interest of many teachers, most of whom were motivated by the profit to be gained by a new and fashionable system without understanding the underlying principles, and the importance of making labour, especially agricultural labour, a principal means of educating the young.

Providentially he became acquainted with M. de Fellenberg who studied law in Germany with a view to a career in politics. Fellenberg's mother had implanted in him the dictum: 'the rich have helpers enough, help thou the poor', and he became convinced his future role should be in educating the deprived. With this object in mind his father bought him an estate at Hofwyl a few miles from Burgdorf and here he was able to study Pestalozzi's methods in detail. In 1806 he opened a course of instruction for thirty teachers which quickly increased to eighty. Work was varied in different ways such as when a drainage system was needed, introducing one with practical side benefits like allowing the watering of low meadow lands.

One of Fellenberg's trainee teachers was called Wehrli whose enthusiasm for the methods taught led to his son Jacob applying for training at Hofwyl. This young man so impressed Fellenberg that he was soon judged ready to start putting the theory into practice. When a beggar boy arrived and was put under Jacob's tuition the boy at first responded well to the kind treatment and good food, but after a time became idle for which he was sent to bed without food. This caused him to resent the discipline and abscond. The next pupil to arrive was willing and anxious to learn, but he was weakly and spoilt by his mother, seeming hardly suitable for field labour. While he was being encouraged, the beggar boy returned and the two boys competed with each other, the beggar boy showing more aptitude which made the weakling try harder. In consequence of this modest success a third and then a fourth pupil was admitted and so began the Agricultural School for the poor at Hofwyl.

The requirements of the farm led to the employment and tuition of carpenters, blacksmiths, mechanics, shoemakers etc thus rescuing many juvenile offenders from the path of ruin. As other industrial schools were established it was found by experience that it was important to have a gradual extension from a small nucleus. Lady Byron emphasized that it had always been shown that 'It is not the *system* that imparts life but the spirit, the fortitude, the love and faith of the founder.'

In 1809 the school at Hofwyl was enlarged to include the many children of the upper classes who desired to attend. These formed a separate part, since these boys did not have to support themselves by manual labour, but they were taught agricultural management so that they could understand that it was 'incumbent on them to educate the working classes and elevate them morally in the same degree as they avail themselves of their labour to increase their own property'. Often these boys were sent to the labouring school for a time if they needed physically strengthening. In this way the wealthy learned to respect labour, and the poor learned to view their richer companions not as enemies but as sympathizing friends.

Fellenberg died in 1844, but the system which developed from Pestalozzi's vision lives on. There is today a Pestalozzi village near Battle in Sussex where pupils from underdeveloped countries receive education based on his principles, some achieving entrance to university; all benefit from agricultural and self-sufficiency instruction so that they may return to their own countries, where possible, and train others, especially in rural areas.

In 1832 Annabella and Ada moved from Hanger Hill in Ealing where they had been living for three years, to Fordhook House nearby. Lady Byron's name is connected with this house in a map of Ealing which was revised in 1822, so it would seem she had made the decision to live here some years earlier. Fordhook was to be her home for nearly ten years. In 1833, after much careful planning, she established Ealing Grove School a short distance from Fordhook, and she proposed to put into practice as much as possible Fellenberg's principles which she had seen in operation at Hofwyl. However it was not without its teething problems. Not long after the school opened she wrote to Mr Craig, the master in charge who had an Owenite background, as follows:

When you recollect that your qualifications for conducting a Fellenbergian institute is partly derived from your visit to Hofwyl, (which you stated to have been a great advantage to you) you could hardly consider yourself justified in withdrawing at so early a period from this situation for which that visit was intended to qualify you, and I do not think it strictly honourable in any gentleman to have offered you the temptation to do so – In consequence however, of circumstances relating to the pecuniary arrangements, I was not unwilling to release you by next Xmas – and I inform you of this as soon as possible, that you may be enabled to make the arrangements which you consider more for your advantage.

In Doris Langley Moore's biography of Ada the version of this incident is that 'Lady Byron had taken a turn against her chosen headmaster and dismissed him in a very summary fashion'. Lady Byron had sent him to Hofwyl to study the methods of one of the foremost pioneers in eduction at her own expense, and sympathy for Mr Craig is therefore misplaced. In his place Lady Byron appointed Charles Nelson Atlee. When Mr and Mrs Craig handed over to him Mrs Craig would not stay to 'number' the sheets, saying 'Here take the inventory I withdraw', while Mr Craig was both insolent and very abusive to Atlee who kept his temper. Atlee turned out to be so satisfactory that many years later, in 1848, Lady Byron showed her 'appreciation and gratitude' by making over the whole school to him.

Boys at the school worked on the allotments provided in the grounds and each worker was paid for the produce from his labour. Instruction was given in mechanics and masonry, wages being paid where appropriate, and all workers were taught to keep their own accounts, which Lady Byron often supervised. The garden work which was so important a part of the system had its problems with the younger boys. She wrote in 1834: 'no sooner are they left together, without a superintendent, than they begin to fight. They are little better than brutes.' However she thought it was an improvement on the life led by the pupils at Harrow, for she continued in the same letter:

… I will give you some facts, which have been ascertained with respect to Harrow … The elder boys resort habitually to the Red Lion public House – drink to intoxication – have dice and gambling of various kinds, with other vicious indulgences. It is not uncommon for the elder boys to insist upon 2 younger ones being stripped to fight for the amusement of the Spectators, like cocks! … It is the law of the school that if an elder boy is convicted of getting drunk he shall be expelled. In consequence the Masters never see that he is so, unless as happened not long ago, a boy dropped from the bench in church in that state. But the outcry against these evils is beginning.

Presumably she had first-hand knowledge of Harrow school through her friendship with the Revd John Cunningham, and her description appears to be confirmed by two recent writers, for Harrow evidently was not the only public school of ill repute at this time. Mr Burnett, in his book *The Rise and Fall of a Regency Dandy* gives an account of public school life describing how 'Eton in common with most other educational establishments, had sunk to its nadir'. He maintained that it was the conditions that Byron's friend Scrope Davies experienced at Eton, that were responsible for his becoming 'a gambler, a drunkard, and a spendthrift who ended his days in ruin'. In this book the situation at Eton at that time is described as appalling, brutal, filthy, and corrupt, with rats prevailing everywhere.

Peter Quennell, in a contemporary review of a book concerning public schools between 1800 and 1864 quotes an account of Harrow in 1844:

> By 1844 the year he [Charles Vaughan] reached Harrow, the school housed a mere 69 boys; and those were so savagely ill-behaved that he was advised to sack them and begin again.
>
> Their favourite sport, he heard, was throwing stones, preferably at living creatures. Every dog had deserted Harrow Hill, and tradesmen were afraid to approach the buildings lest their horses should be maimed or blinded ...

There would appear to be cause other than fear of homosexuality for Lady Byron's much ridiculed distrust of a public school education being suitable for Ada's sensitive son Ralph, who was saddened '... by some cruel men shooting a squirrel on a tree close to the churchyard. The poor little thing fell whining piteously ...'.

Gradually the difficulties were resolved at Ealing Grove and the number of pupils steadily increased. Ada helped out by giving lessons and she recorded some of her trials in a letter to Dr King:

> ...we came to see our friend Lady Gosford who is here for her health. ... her daughters are doing me great good ... I am trying to excite them to various objects of study & interest ... I teach three fourths of the day at least, and find that I myself gain more perhaps

than they do. I am endeavouring to induce one of them to take up mathematics, but I have rather a difficult task there; however I do not despair.

Lady Byron always maintained it was important to engage teachers of the right calibre, who were sympathetic with the methods followed. She was in regular correspondence with Arabella Lawrence who was a Unitarian, an educationalist and a superintendent of a school in Liverpool. She wrote to Miss Lawrence in 1839: 'If you can find me good and intelligent men desirous of being trained in the agricultural school system. I will give the training gratuitously and they will be sure of situations.'

It would seem that friends may have assisted on occasion for in 1836 Lady Byron told Ada that she had begged her friend Miss Duppa of Hollingbourne House near Maidstone to help her with school concerns. In the late 1960s some books were found in an old attic in Ealing relating to the school. A notebook, in Lady Byron's neat handwriting, records the requirements for the pupils' work; another book lists the names of the boys boarding; another gives the names of the boys who had been disciplined, together with their crime and the punishment. A boy called Franck asked to be removed because he said he was ill-treated. There is a book with the boys' accounts (each set of items has her initials), and another one for their pocket-money with the amount given.

By 1836 the school had a good reputation and had many prominent visitors. Among these was Joanna Baillie, the poet and playwright, who was much admired by Sir Walter Scott and other influential writers as well as by Lady Byron, who had wanted Byron to meet her. Joanna Baillie's house in Hampstead became the centre of a brilliant literary society. Ada's daughter, Annabella King, recorded in her diary that she and her brother Ralph had been taken by their grandmother when she was seven to visit Miss Baillie, who had been 'very kind' to them. Joanna Baillie gives an account of the visit she made to the school in the following extract from a letter to a friend:

Ten days ago I went to see what gave me great satisfaction, Lady Byron's school in Ealing, on the plan of Fellenberg, but only for boys of the common ranks. There were sixty of them, who after doing their lessons of writing, etc got up at the sound of a little bell, and ran eagerly each to his spade or mattock, and worked away at levelling ground and other country work as sturdily, and, in proportion, as effectively as men, but far happier. They work as carpenters too, and keep all the premises in order, and mend their own shoes and clothes. It seems to me an education well qualified to make them industrious and happy, and ready to turn their hands to anything – boys especially qualified for new settlers in our colonies; and the carpenters and gardeners of Acton and Ealing are mighty glad to have them for apprentices, a very good proof of the good effects of their schooling. I saw there likewise many things too tedious to mention, which I greatly approved of – nothing too refined or fantastical. I think you would have been much interested in it had you been with me.

After the school was handed over to Mr Atlee, it was carried on by him and his son until it was closed in 1852 due to the expiry of the lease. Atlee then opened Byron House School in 1859, and when he died in 1866 it passed to his son Charles. In 1886 it was acquired by Dr B. Bruce-Smith who renamed it Ealing Grammar School which closed in 1917. Nothing now remains of these schools but some continuity is retained by a large modern school for higher education, built in the grounds where they once stood. Ealing is a place where Lady Byron's memory was hallowed, and it is a fact that for generations after she died there were many people who were descendants of her contemporaries who would never hear a word said against her. There may be some still.

In the grounds of Lady Byron's school there are today two blocks of flats called Byron House and Noel House. Byron Road runs through what used to be the grounds of Fordhook. In each case, just for once, it is not Lord Byron the poet, but Lady Byron his wife who is commemorated by these names.

14   The 1830s

Early in 1830 Annabella was again distressed owing to the publication of the first volume of Moore's *Life of Byron*. It included many of Byron's letters, some of which related to the separation. One of these was Moore's letter of sympathy to him saying 'after all, your *choice* was the misfortune ...'. Byron had replied on 8 March 1816 with a long letter giving what he apparently believed was the main cause for the separation, namely pressure brought to bear on his wife from her parents. He continued:

> ... I must set you right in one point however. The fault was *not* ... my 'choice' ... for I do not believe – and I must say it, in the very dregs of all this bitter business – that there ever was a better or even brighter, a kinder, or a more amiable and agreeable being than Lady B. I never had, nor can have, any reproach to make her, while with me ....

The letter went on to say her nearest relatives were a 'xxxx', and to imply that had it not been for them all might have gone on 'fairly' if he had had a reasonable chance. He finished up: 'My child is very well and flourishing, I hear; but I must see also. I feel no disposition to resign it to the contagion of its grandmother's society, though I am unwilling to take it from the mother. It is weaned, however, and something about it must be decided.'

Blaming her parents would have made a convenient cover for Annabella as well as for Byron, but she was incensed at the public slight to her parents, particularly as she had always been encouraged to be independent in her thoughts and actions. She wrote to Mrs Villiers: 'You know my mother enough I believe to do

197

justice to her honourable principles. I cannot endure that she and my father should be placed in such a point of view ...'. This accusation had been made at the time of the separation, instancing as proof her two letters 'full of play and affection' as Moore describes them, written on the way and when she arrived at Kirkby, thinking her husband might be mentally ill and needing sympathy and care. The assumption that she had been persuaded against her will, when she remembered how kindly disposed her parents had been towards Byron, infuriated her by its dishonesty, and she decided to write a defence of them and an explanation. Her friends, including Colonel Doyle and Dr Lushington advised her against it, because of reawakening the old controversy and accusations which could only be upsetting for her. She wrote to the latter saying that if he could convince her that she would have to disclose anything against a living person she would sacrifice the memory of her parents, but otherwise 'I ought not to be silent'.

Her *Remarks on Mr Moore's Life of Lord Byron* were included in the second volume after a few copies were printed and privately circulated. They begin:

> I have disregarded various publications in which facts within my own knowledge have been grossly misrepresented; but I am called upon to notice some of the numerous statements proceeding from one who claims to be considered as Lord Byron's confidential and authorized friend. Domestic details ought not to be intruded on the public; if however, they *are* so intruded, the persons affected by them have a right to refute injurious charges ....

She goes on to explain the letters, her concern over Byron's state of mind, and how anxious her parents had been to promote his restoration. She included a statement from Dr Lushington, who was universally respected for his integrity, affirming that when Lady Noel came to see him there was no exaggeration of the facts nor apparent any determination to prevent a return to Lord Byron which Dr Lushington then thought possible. Annabella continued:

> They neither originated, instigated, nor advised that separation; and they cannot be condemned for having afforded to their daughter the assistance and protection which she claimed. There is no other relative to vindicate their memory from insult. I am therefore compelled to break the silence which I had hoped always to observe,

and to solicit from the readers of *Lord Byron's Life* an impartial consideration of the testimony extorted from me.

A.I. Noel Byron

Hanger Hill, Feb 19th, 1830

The *Remarks* seem innocuous enough, but as predicted, they created an outcry. Her words were twisted, and her motives considered spiteful, due to pique at being described ill-suited as a wife for Byron. The fact that Lady Noel made the journey to London on behalf of her daughter, because of Annabella's recent confinement, was disregarded and attributed to interference. No sympathy was forthcoming from her traducers for the long and uncomfortable journey to Kirkby while feeding her child and still suffering from the after-effects of childbirth. It was unappreciated by them that no woman at that time would choose to leave her home so soon in these circumstances unless forced to, or because the alternative was too alarming. She surely must have wished that she could have had the warm comfort of Augusta's support in confirming the truth of her account, but sadly they remained irrevocably estranged.

Thomas Campbell, a poet of note at that time, reviewed Moore's book in the *New Monthly* magazine and wrote a strong defence of Lady Byron. He had written to her beforehand for an 'estimate as to the correctness of Moore's statements', and she had replied 'for your private information' that in order to expose the falsehood of Moore's views, she would have to detail matters which her principles and feelings forbade her to disclose. It was not true for instance that pecuniary embarrassments were the cause of the disturbed state of Lord Byron's mind, but it would be unreasonable to expect this to be believed unless the real cause was revealed.

In his review Campbell wrote:

I have found my right to speak on this painful subject, on its now irrevocable publicity brought up afresh as it has been by Mr Moore, to be the theme of discourse to millions, and if I err not much, the cause of misconceptions to innumerable minds. I claim to speak of Lady Byron in the right of a man and of a friend to the rights of a woman, and to liberty, and to natural religion. I claim a right more especially, as one of the many friends of Lady Byron who, one and all, feel aggrieved by this production ... I write not at Lady Byron's bidding. I have never humiliated either her, or myself, by asking *if* I should write or what I should write ....

He reproved Moore for his injustice to Mrs Clermont, whom Byron had called a spy, and denied that Miss Milbanke invited Byron to correspond with her after she had refused him. He continued:

About that time I occasionally saw Lord Byron and though I knew less of him than Mr Moore, yet I suspect I knew as much of him as Miss Milbanke then knew. At that time he was so pleasing that if I had had a daughter with ample fortune and beauty, I should have trusted her in marriage with Lord Byron ... The almost universal impression produced by his book is that Lady Byron must be a precise and a wan, unwarming spirit, a blue stocking of chilblained learning, a piece of insensitive goodness .... let me tell you Mr Moore, that neither your poetry, nor Lord Byron's, nor all our poetry put together, ever delineated a more interesting being than the woman whom you have so coldly treated.

Campbell submitted the article to Lady Byron on the eve of its publication. She must have disapproved the ill-written exaggerated florid style and the unnecessary attacks on Moore, but she was most alarmed by seeing her letter to him included, which suggested collusion. She wrote at once begging that it be omitted, but he replied that the impression was already issued. She then wrote to Lord Melbourne expressing her regret at Campbell's 'injudiciousness' though she was convinced he meant it good-naturedly, and this letter was shown to Moore. Everyone condemned Campbell's piece and Lady Byron was blamed for appearing to have confided in him. Campbell was a weak character of little calibre and finding his sentiments for Lady Byron were unpopular soon changed his tune. In her book *Three Score Years and Ten* Sophia de Morgan reports that some years later when Campbell was asked why he published a letter from Lady Byron when he knew it was written in strict confidence, he cried like a child.

Annabella's fortieth birthday in 1832 was marked with some retrospective self-examination, which she duly recorded:

My imagination has ascribed to the actions of others motives of a loftier or less worldly nature than really existed. I might have found the springs of action nearer the surface, but I supposed them to be in the mine below. A conduct on my part in conformity with this error, must often have been incomprehensible to others, whilst it seemed to me the straight-forward course. ... *Not to see things as they are* is then my great intellectual defect, and so far from feeling myself wilfully deceived by others in whose characters I have been mistaken, I believe they have often been ignorant of the extent to which they were imposing upon me.

When Byron wrote of Annabella as his Princess of Parallelograms to Lady Melbourne he was showing perception, for Annabella had a logical mind and to her there was right and there was wrong, and nothing in between – no excuses and no fudging. Wrong could be forgiven however great, if there was repentance or at least recognition, and the sinner fully aware of his crime and its consequences. Once that was established, forgiveness would be given, she was certain by God, and she hoped by herself. Not for Annabella the customary platitudes with perfunctory pardon or embellished phraseology. When she told Byron on 3 September 1813 for instance: ' ... it is my happiness to feel that in some degree I live for others' that was the literal truth, as she might have said 'I live for my garden'. She did not feel that she would or should deserve praise. She wrote in a letter to Ada: 'It is not so much *the expressed* as the *distressed* which tends to alienate. When the worst is known there is an end to it! – Amen' and the greatest tragedy of her life was to be because the worst was not made known to her. A part of Byron had approved and yearned for her kind of truth, but the other larger and louder part had rebelled and made him revengeful towards her.

Following the interest shown in Moore's book, Murray proposed to publish a complete annotation of Byron's works embellished with portraits of various women who had played a part in Byron's life. He approached Lady Byron, who did not like sitting for her portrait, and she firmly refused his request. However, unbeknown to her Murray arranged for an artist to go to Ealing and sketch her as she sat in church. On the third visit the artist was observed by her and later questioned, with the result that she consented to sit for a professional portrait by W.J. Newton in 1832.

It was evident from an early age that Ada was exceptionally intelligent, Mrs George Lamb had written to a friend in 1819: '... I never saw so clever a child as little Ada Lord Byron's child. She is full of fun, but very good-tempered and good ...'. She was also highly-strung and Annabella wisely gave much care and attention to finding suitable nurses, governesses and tutors to teach her and she often supervised Ada's lessons herself. Her methods were successful, for not only did Ada enjoy her lessons, requesting her mother when away to obtain for her various books and teaching aids, but as she matured she became interested in teaching others. Moreover, she grew up to be kind in addition to being accomplished. She loved dancing and music, learning to play the harp at which she excelled, as well as showing a pronounced aptitude for mathematics. She also enjoyed riding, and she was encouraged by her mother in all her interests and pursuits.

Annabella was surprised and disappointed that although all Byron's poems were on the bookshelves, Ada took little interest in them or any other poetry. If Teresa Guiccioli thought that Ada had never heard of her father's poems, and that they had been kept from her at home, she must have thought Ada was half-witted. Even should Lady Byron have wished to suppress knowledge of her father, it would have been impossible to keep enlightenment of Byron's works from an intelligent and well-educated girl who bore his name. Ada often met literary and cultured people with her mother, who could have been questioned if she were curious, for she was always outspoken. Moreover she was from an early age an object of curiosity through being the daughter of the celebrated poet and there were regular reports such as 'Lady Byron (widow of the late Lord Byron) and her daughter being on a tour of the coast, have arrived at the Royal Hotel, and will remain at Plymouth a few days to enjoy the beautiful scenery of this neighbourhood' in the newspaper, which she would have seen. She was well aware of the interest shown in her and it is impossible to believe that she did not know why. The reason for Ada's indifference was simple – she was like her father who had written: 'I hate *reading* verse – and always did.'

When Ada was fifteen Annabella recorded in her diary: 'Read to Ada the beautiful lines on Greece in "The Giaour", the "Fare Thee Well" and the "Satire". With the first she was highly pleased from its effusion-of-feeling character; the second she thought laboured and inferior in pathos; the third very amusing though very unlike the person.' It must have been painful for Annabella to have such poignant memories evoked by these poems, and to have them dismissed so lightly. There are no grounds to suppose that she ever spoke disparagingly of Byron to her daughter. It is sheer fiction, which some biographers use as their privilege, to say that Ada was taught to hate her father, and no evidence can be found for such statements, except his own poignant words in 'Childe Harold', possibly born from a desire to encourage sympathy for himself and because they sounded well. It would be curious to deliberately read to a girl of an impressionable age highly emotive poems, in which her mother was depicted as unforgiving, if animosity was felt or directed towards the charismatic and famous man who wrote them.

At the time of her interest in the Cooperative Movement, Lady Byron became anxious over Ada's health. A few months after their return from the Continent in 1828, Ada had an attack of measles, followed by complications leaving her unable to walk or stand, as well as 'too rapid growth'. She was then thirteen years old. Lady Byron would have had the benefit of the best medical opinions available, but such has been the advance in medicine during the last century and a half, that treatment then prescribed now seems primitive and ineffective. The London Phrenological Society was established in 1824 and, as phrenology became recognized by the medical profession and practised by doctors, it rapidly became respected and fashionable. Lady Byron, a staunch advocate, persuaded Ada to make the journey to London, and have an analysis made from an examination of the shape of her skull. Ada, although sceptical, continued to make visits, even after she was married, but the pronouncements made seem mainly that she experienced '*pain* and mortification at the slightest disparagement', whereas her mother was 'morbidly sensitive'. It is customary to ridicule such practices today but by the middle of the nineteenth century phrenology had an impressive list of writers and well-known people among its adherents, including all Queen Victoria's children. Even Byron had been interested, for in a letter to Annabella dated 26 September 1814 he described the examination by Johann Spurzheim, the German phrenologist, of his 'faculties and dispositions' which were found to be strongly marked and antithetical 'so that to believe him my good & evil are at perpetual war – pray heaven the last don't come off victorious'.

Despite Ada's uncertain health Annabella considered she was ready for the London season in 1833, and she was duly presented at court to William IV and Queen Adelaide. Annabella wrote to Mrs King, the wife of Dr King who had taught Ada for a time and was very religious, describing the event on 13 May, adding that Ada was looking forward to the court ball on the 17th. It would not be like Annabella to miss adding a little sermon: 'You would have been amused had you seen me throwing my mind into balldresses! ... However I cannot help wishing *the season* over. May we have as little 'respect of persons' at the end as at the beginning of it – and be as worthy of your kind interest!'

Ada quite enjoyed participating in the round of parties, and in particular the one where she met Charles Babbage, already famous for the calculating machine he had invented. He was then forty-two, a widower, an entertaining raconteur and much in demand by hostesses. Ada was immediately impressed by him. She was shy and a little awkward in manner, and not yet as beautiful as she was later to become; but she had charm through her straightforward outspoken approach, and seemed unaware of the attention she knew she attracted because she was Byron's daughter. She and her mother were invited to see Babbage's machine which they both found of great interest, and he was gratified to show it to individuals who understood something of its construction and complex mechanism, and could ask intelligent questions.

Later on that year Lady Byron and Ada met the king and queen again at the Pavilion in Brighton, an event Ada described at length to her friend Fanny Smith. Fanny was the illegitimate daughter of General Carlo Doyle, the brother of Annabella's friend Colonel Francis Doyle, and was brought up by their sister Selina Doyle. She was friendly with and frequently visited Lady Byron and Ada. Typical of her unselfconscious style with its underlying humour Ada gives an affectionate and detailed picture of her mother, enclosing a sketch to show where the chosen few, including Annabella, sat with Her Majesty:

My Dear Fanny,
    You will like to have an account of Mama's grand exploit on Friday night, the 8th of Nov. 1833. In the first place she looked *very pretty indeed*. She had a white blonde hat and feathers on her head; her gown was a figured satin of a most beautiful colour something between crimson and brown. It was made low like anybody's gown, and had a peak in front (a shape which by the bye becomes Mama particularly), and long sleeves. Her neck was completely covered up to the throat by means of white satin and blonde, beneath which she had her flannels as usual ....
    We staid till near 12, and could not have got away sooner, as we were by desire sitting in the Queen's private circle ... A large black

spot ... marks the spot where sat my illustrious parent, and where the King was for some time, talking to her ....

By the time Ada was attending her second season in 1834, she knew beyond a doubt that the most important object of her life was the study of science and mathematics. Her mother gave her every encouragement, appreciating her daughter's talent because of her own interest and aptitude in this field. Ada was excited and stimulated by Mrs Somerville's new book *The Connection of the Physical Sciences* and they became acquainted. Mrs Somerville was fifty-four years old when Ada met her, and highly acclaimed in the scientific world, being especially distinguished for clarity of expression and lucid discourse in her writings. She had had to conduct her early studies in Euclid and algebra furtively, for her father actively discouraged her pursuit of knowledge in mathematics. This made her helpful and supportive to her young enthusiastic disciple who showed such extraordinary potential, and she became Ada's friend and mentor.

Mrs Somerville also greatly admired and liked Lady Byron of whom she wrote: 'The more I know of her the higher she rises in my estimation, and the more do I regret that the world in general are little aware of her superior talents: her excellence everyone appreciates. I told Mr Babbage that nothing I had seen could be compared with her critique of his book.' Mrs Somerville herself received many honours, including the prestigious commission of a portrait bust of her by Chantrey for the Royal Society.

When the 1834 season was over Lady Byron took Ada on a tour of England to show her another kind of life, during which they visited many different kind of factories to learn something of industrial enterprise and the conditions experienced by the people who worked in them. They also attended such social events as the races at Doncaster. Lady Byron did not approve of racing: '... the desperate gambling among the spectators – the futility of the object – press upon my mind ...'. If only the futility could have been pressed permanently on Ada's mind, it would have saved much anguish in the future. Surprisingly perhaps, Lady Byron thought dancing was 'a valuable accessory in moulding character' and possibly her own delight and ability in this pastime led her to the belief that 'They who dance with temperance will be likely to pray with pleasure.' She approved of archery and planned to have a target at Fordhook. They visited the grounds of Halnaby and

Annabella showed Ada where she had ridden her pony when she was a child, but she kept to herself the painful memories of her honeymoon that this visit so vividly evoked.

After their return Ada was introduced to Lord King by his friend Woronzow Greig, Mrs Somerville's son by her first marriage. Lord King and Ada soon fell in love and seemed well suited. He was ten years older than her and had been in the diplomatic service until his career was ended by his succession to his father's title in 1833. He was widely travelled and was experienced in world affairs and had been employed as secretary to the High Commissioner of the Ionian Islands, thus having a slight link with Ada's father who stayed at Cephalonia before going to Missolonghi. The family seat was at Ockham in Surrey and he had a small estate at Porlock near Minehead. When Ada was about seventeen she had attempted to run away with one of her tutors, a young man who lived near Fordhook. The circumstances were sufficiently serious for Lady Byron, who believed that marriage should be founded on a basis of trust, to confide what had happened to Lord King. It made no difference to his feelings for Ada and the marriage took place in the drawing-room at Fordhook on 8 July 1835, a month after their engagement. The next day Lady Byron gave a party for all the servants and their friends, which was a very happy occasion for everyone but especially so for Lady Byron, who must have been thankful and relieved that Ada had made what seemed to be a loving and suitable marriage.

She abandoned her plan to go abroad for the winter when she learned that she was to become a grandmother. 'Had I gone abroad,' she wrote to Ada on 1 October 1835 'I could not have returned without risk in time for the introduction of the young gentleman or lady into the Family circle. How charming he will be thought by all the admirers of his Papa and Mamma. You see I have settled that I shall have a grand*son*. 'Byron' perhaps – as the name could not otherwise be preserved.' This gentle suggestion, almost a request, to honour her husband's name, surely indicates that she harboured no resentment towards him, but only held sad memories of wasted lives and thoughts of what might have been. She gave Ada the customarily sensible motherly advice telling her that she might be uncomfortable or depressed for the first few weeks, and to take care of her back, and to remember 'the less it is known the better till it cannot be concealed' – a timely warning, since first pregnancies tend to be announced with alacrity and therefore seem tediously long.

It was the beginning of a happy time for Annabella. It had not been easy bringing up Ada alone and there had been many worrying periods. It was a source of great comfort to her that Ada was married to a man who loved her and who was sufficiently mature to perceive that she would need to be handled like 'a wild mountain colt', as Mr Drury had described Byron when he first saw him at Harrow. An added bonus was that she and Ada's husband got on well together. They called each other by nicknames, Annabella was the Hen, Ada the Thrush or Avis and Lord King the Crow: these gave a happy tone of informality to their letters. Lord King did not have a good relationship with his own mother, and soon Annabella regarded him as a well-beloved son and he looked on her as a mother. He appreciated her guidance on starting a school at Ockham which was to be run on the same principles as her school at Ealing and she admired his efficient and caring method of estate management, learning new ideas: 'he shows me what a landowner may do in these respects & *I* have *not* done' she told Joanna Baillie.

She settled down into a pleasant routine, when she did not have visitors, staying in her own room until 12 o'clock reading, or studying Greek. After lunch she wrote letters, followed by a drive in the evening. When she returned she usually found a letter from Ada among those waiting for her, which she kept to the last: 'It is an odd habit – partly from self-control – & partly from nervousness that it is impossible for me to open the most interesting letter first.' Her letters to Ada are interesting and describe incidents in her life and her opinions on various subjects, although often she would see her the next day. She had taken Bowling Green Cottage at Southampton for a change, which was on the water's edge, and only 100 yards from the end of the high street. It had one drawback, but not to her as she 'liked watching sports' – the front lawn was a bowling green. She had formed an attachment which she believed to be reciprocal – 'he is the comfort of my life' – a Belgian waiter named Bernard Henkels. Ada is told: 'My book on de Fellenberg is out ... – price 4d.' This was a period of good health: ' ... the effect [of sailing] upon me is like magic & belongs only to a sailing vessel'. She had heard that Sophia Halliday, her second cousin, had fallen into a sad state of health and she had written to ask if she could take care of her, adding that it 'will be more agreeable now that she does not feel dependent' – the Noels were characterized by their morbid sensitivity, and Sophia was now married.

Among the visits she made in this period was one to her friend the

Hon Mrs George Lamb. Far from liking to be with people inferior to herself as some writers have believed, she sometimes found it irksome, as her letter to Ada on 20 August 1836 reveals:

My dearest Ada.
 Here I am under the roof of her who is more my cousin than any cousin by blood except one. She gratifies my *taste*, and though I have not allowed it to be the director of my friendships I must own I am happier in the society of those who do not offend it. The objects in which I am engaged often made it necessary for me to sacrifice such considerations for not only are philanthropists in general ugly but often less refined than could be desired. Your memory will furnish the examples.

Ada was well during her pregnancy after the early symptoms had passed and occupied her time in playing the harp, for which she showed considerable aptitude, and studying mathematics which she continued to do until shortly before the baby – Byron – was born on 12 May 1836. She had written in the previous month to Mrs Somerville: 'How much I should like to have a mathematical child, and only think what pleasure I should have in teaching it, and how capable I might hope to be too by the time it was old enough (for I should not begin I think the 1st year).' She adored the baby and took great pleasure in reporting his unremarkable progress in her letters to her mother. Annabella recounted in letters to friends how Byron had bellowed all through his christening, completely drowning the voice of the reader, and did not cease even though she had been given him to hold, until the service was over. In a letter from Dover she told Ada, like a typical grandmother, that she would keep Byron's mark so that she could compare it later with his signature. Ada constantly asked her mother for guidance and Annabella gave good common sense advice: 'I will not suspect my grandson of such want of taste as not to *look* at you with more satisfaction than at Green [his nurse] – I think I shall be able to suggest to you some means of amusing him that will be peculiar to yourself.'
 The second baby, a daughter named Annabella, was born in September 1837, and soon afterwards Ada had a long and serious illness. All through her life Ada had suffered periods of ill health, which largely remain undiagnosed and include, apart from severe headaches affecting her sight when she was seven and the paralysis

of her legs when she was thirteen, asthma, hayfever, gastro-
enteritis, palpitations, and swelling of her face and throat strongly
suggestive of angioneurotic oedema. She also experienced at times
extreme changes in mood from elated overactivity to deep
depression and had fears, as her father had had, of becoming mad.
In view of the nature of Ada's disorders it will be seen that Lady
Byron's sympathetic handling of her daughter, and her careful
selecting of suitable nurses and governesses was discerning and
successful. She had encouraged young friends, like Fanny Smith
and Lady Gosford's daughters, to visit as much as possible,
although the employment of the young tutor had proved
unfortunate. Without her foresight Ada could well have developed
a psychotic personality instead of becoming the charming, sensible
girl who attracted the highly-eligible Lord King.

Since refusing to see Annabella after the disagreement over the
trustees, Augusta was wont to speak maliciously of her, as when
she wrote to Hodgson after the *Remarks* in Moore's book were
published, at the height of the Trevanion scandal, and said,
speaking of Annabella: '… I do think nothing were it ever so bad,
could justify anyone in defaming the dead'. Augusta knew that
neither then, nor at any time, had Annabella ever defamed Byron.
Augusta, who would very much have liked to have been on intimate
terms with Ada, but had been discouraged by Annabella, also told
Hodgson: 'I would not for worlds stand in the way of that dear
child [Ada] seeing one so devotedly attached to her father. The very
atmosphere she breathed would be better and purer for *your*
presence.' In the same year Hobhouse expressed his opinion of
Hodgson: 'This Hodgson was, on the whole, the most dissipated of
the set; … a man always borrowing money of Byron …', the return
of which was neither punctual nor certain.

Augusta's unfriendly feelings did not inhibit her approaching
Annabella for money when it was needed. In 1835 she wrote
despairing letters asking for an interview, which Annabella
declined suggesting that her communications could be made
through Mrs Villiers. On 15 July Augusta replied that 'If I could
say what I wish, to you, by letter – or through a third person, I
would not have asked (at any rate *twice*) for an interview. Under
these circumstances will you have the goodness to tell me
definitely, whether you will see me or not – and an early answer will
oblige.' But Lushington warned Annabella '… I really can see no
reaon why you are to be annoyed by personal interviews with Mrs

L. nor what sort of right or pretence of right she has to demand them'. However, desperate as she sounded, in the midst of all the disasters, threatened and impending, Augusta wrote to Hodgson with typical insouciance in 1836:

> On Saturday I was persuaded to accompany a friend to dine ten miles out of town. Of course I became very unwell with a cold, and only the fear of disappointing my friend and upsetting her arrangements induced me to exert myself sufficiently to go. To crown all, it was to a Lion and Lioness Hunter's mansion – Shirley Park; great friends of Miss Jane Porter (the authoress); and *our* object was to see *her*. ... This was the cream of the party; and *I* was to be gazed at as the sister of Lord Byron! I wished so *you* could have heard all the tributes of every sort of *his* memory, at which it was impossible not to be gratified. ... I met the other evening, at a very tiny party at Montalemberts, a Mrs Somerville ... the intimate friend of Ada, to whom Mme de M. presented me and said, 'you know Mrs L that your neice [sic] has called her son Byron?' ... I exclaimed 'I am very glad to hear that!' ... and again we steered clear of Milady B.

In 1838 Annabella departed on her delayed expedition abroad. She wrote to Sophia Frend on 14 September from Rouen: '... you know Rouen, and how much occupation it affords to a curious traveller. Besides the ancient buildings I mean to see the prison and the Maison des Aliénes, both said to be well conducted.' The travels were not uneventful. In a letter to her friend Amelia Murray on 27 September Annabella describes the crossing:

> It was not a pleasurable voyage: first, an engine-man had his leg horribly torn and broken; next, a violent storm at night; and thirdly, an adverse wind, with a very heavy swell all the way; so that the voyage took twelve hours more than usual ... I must go to bed: very tired still. I had seven sick – indefatigably sick – ladies to attend to in my cabin! In these foreign boats there are no proper arrangements for attendance. My maid and I waited on them all, as we were the only sound ones; and Smart gave up for the last twelve hours. It was, indeed, a swell to try the strongest; and a courier who was on board has been in such a state of terror every since, that he cannot be left alone ....

She wrote to Ada on 3 October from Dieppe, telling her how the huge Norman horse began to plunge and the postillion fell under him and at the next stage the same scene was on the point of being repeated. She continued:

I am reading a book which would charm you – Arago's essay on thunder – I think your fears in a thunderstorm would be diminished by studying the subject scientifically – Had I known the fact that vessels are less likely to be struck on the open sea than near land, it would have reduced my ideas of danger during the storm on the 5th Sept when I was in the *middle* of the channel. Did you see the statement, which appeared to Mrs Somerville sufficiently authentic, of the two gentlemen in Yorkshire, who were riding together during the same storm, & whose horses were struck dead, whilst they themselves remained unhurt?

It is possible that this tale did not diminish Ada's fear of thunder as much as her mother had hoped.

That year there were events to remind Annabella vividly of the past. She had had two letters informing her that Byron's faithful servant Fletcher had not been receiving the allowance that Augusta had undertaken to pay after Byron's death, and was nearly destitute. Byron had made full provision for Fletcher of £50 per annum in his will of 1811 but he inexplicably neglected to mention Fletcher in his last will apparently made in 1822. When he became ill Byron told Colonel Stanhope, the special emissary of the Greek Committee in Missolonghi, to state his wishes to Hobhouse and Mrs Leigh that Fletcher should be looked after if anything happened to him. Hobhouse gave Fletcher a small annuity which he used to help start a macaroni factory that failed through no fault of his own and Augusta did her best to assist him but could not keep up her payments. In a letter of 21 April 1838 to Ada, Annabella proposed a fund should be raised to provide an annuity to which she would contribute £100 anonymously, 'and as much as might appear desirable' after application to Byron's friends such as Hobhouse, Harness, and Hodgson. With her usual enthusiasm she considered how best Fletcher could be helped. She thought the annuity should be placed in the hands of trustees – perhaps Lord Byron and Sir Robert Horton – so that it could not be pledged from folly or extravagance. She suggested the wording of the request could be that he was 'deprived by circumstance (for the truth of which the promoters of this appeal can vouch) of the means to which he had looked for support', thereby avoiding implicating Augusta, 'one whose interest I must always wish to consider, as far as justice to others will allow'. A few days later Fletcher turned up at Lady Byron's house. She reported to Ada:

'To my surprise, Fletcher appeared here yesterday, in the character of a Bookseller's Agent. ... You may conceive that I cannot see this man without agitation. No one so forcibly brings your father before me.' He told her that to all his applications in person and by letter to Sir John Hobhouse, who was an executor of Byron's will and had himself been left £1,000, there had been no answer. Fletcher had told Hobhouse that Byron, 'my ever to be lamented Lord ... would Bless you if you will but place me in either a Door keeper's place at either Houses of Parliament or even as a Porter or any trifling thing in the India House ...'. It seems as if the plan for Byron's friends to assist Fletcher did not materialize, which must reflect discreditably on all those who should have been concerned for he was confined to prison for debt in the same year, his release apparently being due to Augusta. André Maurois states that Fletcher 'was helped like everybody, by Lady Byron, and in his last years became the beadle of Golden Square in Soho'.

The second event happened while Annabella resided for a time at Windsor with friends around her like Fanny Smith and Olivia Acheson, who had been one of Ada's 'scholars'. Lord Melbourne, who had captivated the young Queen Victoria, and was her Prime Minister and friend, paid his cousin Annabella a visit. Sad memories were revived: 'his resemblance to my father made it almost a revelation' Annabella told her son-in-law, and both Annabella and Melbourne were emotionally affected. They had each been hurt through Byron and each of them reproached – Annabella for being unforgiving and implacable and William, Caroline Lamb's husband, for neglecting his young wife's need for constant attention and demonstrative affection. Through Lord Melbourne, the Queen had expressed a wish to meet his cousin, but perhaps because of their age difference, for the Queen had not been born until three years after the separation, Annabella had no wish to start an acquaintance which she might find tiring and of little interest, and excuses were made for not attending. Lord King was made the Earl of Lovelace later in the year, doubtless in recognition of his previous diplomatic work in the Middle East and Greece, expedited perhaps as a consequence of this meeting.

In July 1839 Ralph, Ada's third and last child, was born. Feeling she had sufficiently achieved her function as a mother Ada now craved access to the world of mathematical science, and she was given full support towards this goal by her husband and mother.

She wrote to Babbage asking for advice and explaining that she felt she had the ability for understanding and advancing the boundaries of scientific knowledge. At first he was non-committal in his replies, but she persisted until he was finally persuaded to stay with Ada and her husband at Ockham, and the visit began Ada's long-desired association with the pioneer of computers.

The 1830s had been a decade of achievement and contentment for Annabella. Her school at Ealing was satisfactorily founded and doing well. Ada was happily married. She might give prison reform and the abolition of slavery a rest for a while and try something a little more frivolous – after all she had been 'quite the fashion' in the year 1812. She would go to Paris.

15 Medora

The visit to France turned out to be different from anything Annabella could have conceived for in July 1840 she was unexpectedly thrown once again into the Byron orbit, from which it seemed she had escaped. She received a letter from a solicitor, Sir George Stephen, informing her that Elizabeth Medora Leigh had written to him from Pontivy in France. He enclosed her letter appealing for help, in which she made known that she was ill and destitute and had a child to support. Since her involvement in the scandal at Bifrons in 1830, reports had reached Annabella from various sources of the irregular behaviour on the part of the Trevanions. Lushington had always strongly advised against any renewal of her association with Augusta or any of her children, and had even warned Lord King before his marriage to Ada that 'he must not know Mrs Leigh'.

Had Annabella been the cold calculating woman she is depicted, or even been moderately prudent, she would have asked Lushington to deal with the matter, advanced a sum of money perhaps and not become involved. Instead she wrote a kind letter asking Medora, whom she always called Elizabeth, to meet her in Tours, thus activating another period of torment, frustration and criticism. Ever since she had seen a gentler Byron than she would ever know, looking at Augusta's child at Six Mile Bottom, Medora had held a strange fascination for Annabella. Byron's tender expression when he played with Medora had also been remarked on by Hobhouse, for there is an entry in his journal for 1 July 1831: 'I have been listening to a sad story from Colonel Leigh and his wife ...' and he relates the Trevanion scandal at Bifrons, ending with: 'The young girl was Lord Byron's favourite niece. I recollect her a little blue eyed chubby creature whom he used to fondle, what a fate ...'.

When Annabella met Medora in Tours she heard of all that had happened to her in the ten years following the birth of her first child. In May 1830, Medora had returned from France to England with the Trevanions having arranged for the baby, which was born prematurely, to be looked after in Calais. She heard later that he had died. She stayed with her mother in the apartment at St James's Palace, and the Trevanions lodged with a relative nearby in Cadogan Square. Augusta had not seen her daughter for over a year and was apparently unaware of what had happened. She went out most evenings and returned late at night, having encouraged Trevanion to visit her apartment, and he was therefore alone with Medora for much of the time.

Trevanion received a letter from a friend in Calais in July telling him that a man claiming to act for the seventh Lord Byron had been making enquiries at the place where the Trevanions had stayed. He had offered twelve hundred pounds for the child that had been born, but was told the baby had died of convulsions when he was about two months old. This information must have been very upsetting for Medora who seems to have had a strong maternal instinct especially as, if true, she could still have been in France when the baby died. Since Annabella and Lord Byron had helped the Trevanions and Medora to leave Bifrons, it is credible that they tried to find Medora's child. Medora wrote in her autobiography that all letters relating to this episode were amongst her papers in her strong-box, her most valued possession, and perhaps it was this that helped to influence the final fate of the box.

In January 1831 Medora found that she was again pregnant by Trevanion. He wrote a distracted and confused letter to Augusta referring to his last wild note, to the taking of laudanum and to the secret of his misery, but Augusta made no comment or enquiry and passed it to Medora. This letter was followed by one composed by Trevanion and Medora disclosing what had happened previously, as well as the fact that Medora was again pregnant, for all of which Augusta was bitterly blamed. Augusta immediately wrote a muddled bewildered letter to Trevanion, the drift of which was to reassure him of her love:

Show me only how I can comfort and support you – confide in me dearest – ... I am convinced, dearest, that as I have opened my heart and feelings to you, you will comfort me! I need not point out to you the means! Your own heart will dictate them – and as you are dear! MOST dear! *much* MUCH is in your power! Heaven bless, comfort and guide you!

A strange letter from a mother to the man who has ruined the lives of two of her daughters, and stranger still that it was not destroyed.

Trevanion immediately replied to Augusta's letter with an angry and accusing note. She had at first taken the revelations calmly, but grew increasingly agitated as she became aware that her husband, George Leigh, would have to be told. She wrote again to Trevanion, a long letter of comfort and loving sympathy: 'Do not accuse yourself dearest, and make yourself out what you are NOT. Remember I *do* '*depend* on your love' – and oh! how I have *loved* you! – How I will always love you and God bless you! dearest.'

Augusta then wrote to Medora but with much less tenderness, describing her own distress, entreating her daughter to resist temptation and reminding her that she had committed deadly crimes. She expressed her great disappointment that it would be hopeless now she supposed for Medora to be confirmed at Easter, for which Augusta herself had intended to prepare her. Medora later said that her mother had tried to make her 'employ means to destroy my child'.

Medora went with the Trevanions to Bath where relations lent them a house, and Augusta continued to write to Trevanion in affectionate and seemingly untroubled terms. It was not a happy household and there were many angry and violent scenes between the three of them during which Medora was told that her birth was 'the result of adultery and incest' and that her mother during her love affair with Trevanion had promised him each of her daughters in turn. Georgiana was five when Byron's relationship with Augusta began, and she may well have recalled incidents at home and during the times that Byron and Augusta had stayed at Hastings and Newstead Abbey with the children, for Byron was never discreet.

There must be some explanation for Augusta's extraordinary behaviour in writing loving and explicit letters to Trevanion, and her apparent indifference to her daughter's second pregnancy by him. Trevanion certainly did not repay Augusta's devotion to him with money, for he even took the little that she had managed to settle on Georgiana for his own use, and later tried to tamper with his wife's marriage settlement from the money Byron had left in trust, causing Hanson to tell his fellow executor Hobhouse: 'I really think poor Mrs Leigh and all connected with her are mad.' It would seem more than likely true that by an understanding between them regarding her daughters, Trevanion was rewarded for gratifying Augusta's abnormal passions. These may also explain her attraction to Byron as he had told Lady Melbourne: 'I never got the sort I preferred before ....' referring to his liaison with Augusta.

Teresa Guiccioli is sometimes compared with Augusta and it may be that they had more in common than an ability to amuse Byron, for Henry Edward Fox, Lady Holland's son, became Teresa's lover after Byron's death. In his journal is the entry: 'I was not prepared for the extreme facility of the conquest, which (such is the perverseness of one's nature) scarcely gave me pleasure. She is too gross and too carnal ... it is alarming when she talks and expects a constancy of five years ...'. The affair was passionate and angry and at last, because Teresa was 'jealous' and 'troublesome', Fox broke it off with the comment: 'Poor Lord Byron! I do not wonder at his going to Greece!'

Augusta was shattered when Georgiana told her she could not endure Trevanion's cruelty any longer and she realized her daughter, with her three small children, would be returning to her, and that her husband could no longer remain unaware of all that had happened. On being informed Colonel Leigh was horrified and went at once to Bath, collected Medora, took her to London and put her in a home for pregnant girls, where he visited her regularly until she asked him not to come. He wanted to prosecute Trevanion for abduction but Augusta opposed him. The child was stillborn. Trevanion helped Medora escape and together they travelled to France where they lived in Normandy for two years as M. and Mme Aubin.

At the end of the first year, in December 1831, Medora became a Roman Catholic and presumably because of this grew increasingly depressed by her unsatisfactory life and frequent miscarriages. After months of deliberation she decided to enter a convent, against the wishes of Trevanion. She wrote to her mother telling her of this decision, saying she was ill and penitent and needed money to keep her in the convent, but before a reply came she had to leave because she discovered she was again pregnant. She returned to Trevanion and they moved to Morlaix in Brittany where they lived as brother and sister.

In May 1834 a daughter, baptised Anne Violet Leigh but always known as Marie, was born to Medora. They lived in acute poverty and because she refused to renew her former relationship with him, Trevanion ill-treated her, and made her work as a servant to him and to the mistress he eventually installed. She became so ill that even Trevanion was alarmed, and in 1838 he called in M. Carrel, a medical man, as doctors were then called. M. Carrel befriended Medora and with his good treatment she gradually recovered, but she remained very weak. She confided all her circumstances to him and, acting on his advice, she wrote to Lady Chichester, her mother's half-sister, giving an account of her sufferings over the last few years. Lady Chichester sent five pounds and Medora was able to leave Trevanion with M. Carrel's help and move with Marie to Pontivy a few miles south of Morlaix. Trevanion thereupon informed Georgiana that M. Carrel was pursuing Medora for the money which he was trying to obtain for her. Medora had implored Lady Chichester to intercede with Augusta for forgiveness, and believing Medora's death to be imminent, Augusta executed a deed for £3,000 in 1839 so that Marie could be provided for when that happened, and Medora was given a copy. Because of her acute poverty and ill-health she was advised by her solicitor to sell her reversionary interest in the deed which would raise a few hundred pounds for immediate necessities, and to do this she unsuccessfully applied to Augusta for possession of the deed.

It was at this point that Lady Byron received the letter from Sir George Stephen. On meeting Medora at Tours in August 1840 she was so shocked and moved by Medora's appearance that she was overcome with pity and instead of arranging quiet lodgings nearby, as she had planned, she decided to take Medora and Marie, now six years old, to Paris, Medora travelling as Mme Aubin.

Augusta, hearing from M. Carrel that Medora was in Lady Byron's care, wrote humbly to her asking for information. When Annabella had been told of the Trevanion scandal in 1832 she had commented to Mrs Villiers: 'I own that I consider the conduct of that Mother *towards her children* as evincing a state of the utmost depravity – and one that would suffice to estrange me from the nearest Relative *in blood*.' Medora's vivid account of her mother's neglect, and the suffering she had been through did nothing to change Annabella's belief that everything Augusta had anything to do with was doomed. She therefore felt it necessary to write a sufficiently blunt letter to deter Augusta's fatal interference.

Paris. January 20th 1841
... could I have believed that you had a Mother's affection for her, you would not have had to ask for information concerning your child ... you left her unprotected and destitute ... Her malady, the effect of physical and mental suffering combined, can be retarded ... I would save you, if it be not too late, from adding the guilt of her death to that of her birth. Leave her in peace!

Although she was convinced she had to write in these terms, it upset her and she had 'bad headaches' for days afterwards.

There was another factor besides compassion in Annabella's resolution to help Medora. Her critics say it was to punish Augusta but it was deeper and more subtle than that. It comprised the love she would always feel for Byron, that made it impossible for her to love other men, although there were many from whom she might have chosen a husband. This kind of emptiness that could never be filled was common to women who had loved Byron, whether they were aristocratic, intellectual or proletarian. It was mixed up with another emotion she probably never recognized; there are people who, while leading a pure life themselves, are nevertheless fascinated by sin. Medora, conceived in sin, was loved by and was a part of Byron. Annabella, by loving her and encouraging her to use the pet name Pip that Byron had called her, allowed feelings that had long been buried to return which might be sublimated by her special feeling for Byron's child. Furthermore by saving Medora, with whom she had had an immediate empathy, she could achieve something towards fulfilling her promise to Byron, which had been checked by what she considered as Augusta's foolish intransigence.

Although Augusta and Mrs Villiers had been estranged for ten years because Mrs Villiers disapproved of Augusta's irresponsible obstinacy and distrust over the trusteeship, Augusta appealed to her in her distress at receiving Annabella's unequivocal letter. Mrs Villiers advised Augusta to make a 'perfectly correct' statement of affairs between her and Medora since she had left England with Trevanion, and ask her half-sister Lady Chichester and her son the Earl of Chichester, to whom she had shown all correspondence, to endorse what she said. This was carried out and the packet received by Annabella in Paris, but she returned it unopened to Augusta's solicitors with a note on the outside saying that she had considered the correspondence closed by her reply to Augusta's enquiry about Medora. Resulting from this Mrs Villiers wrote to Annabella on 19 February 1841 saying that she felt Annabella had been misinformed on certain points and had consequently misjudged Augusta. She explained she was writing because 'she [Augusta] was in the deepest distress, and implored my advice – and whatever might have been my previous determination, *that* was not the moment when I could refuse any aid that it might be in my power to afford …'. She told Annabella about the advice she had given Augusta and that when the packet was returned:

> I went to her – and then offered to write myself … I can assure you that nothing but the strong feeling I have that it is a duty to help any fellow creature in distress, and more especially one in whose fate I have been interested from her childhood – would have induced me to trouble you on a subject which for so many reasons must be a very painful one ….

Annabella replied that the character of Mrs Leigh's former correspondence had decided her not to engage in any more, but she would willingly attend to any *facts* in Augusta's favour. As to her distress, she did not understand why she was so much to be pitied now that her daughter was to be protected, where she had before been destitute.

Thus started a series of twenty letters between the two women, which surely no one, unless biased, could read in their entirety, and not feel the honesty and integrity of both. Mrs Villiers, elderly and ailing, endeavoured to be entirely correct in every statement to Lady Byron, whom she much respected, and she was determined not to omit any circumstance that could ameliorate Augusta's conduct. Annabella, prejudiced by past disillusionment with Augusta's misrepresentations and evasions, and seeing Medora only as a loving child who had been grievously wronged, was nevertheless anxious to be just, and to withhold blame until the grey area where truth becomes buried had been, if possible, uncovered and explored. The main points from their letters are summarized in the following extracts.

Mrs Villiers could hardly believe that the writer of the letter of

December 1838: 'My own dearest kindest Mamma, your dear kind letter has made me *so* happy' and ending 'we *have* been CRUELLY deceived towards each other!!!' could now be engaged in a lawsuit against her mother because she *could not* do what she only promised to do *if she could*. Mrs Villiers explained that Augusta had signed and executed a deed for one specific purpose, and found it was to be appropriated for another which would make it difficult to resist the claims of the other children; – that Augusta had been advised to keep the legal document, and Mrs Villiers added that she herself would also have advised this had she been consulted; – she knew, she said, that Annabella had had nothing to do with the circumstances in which mother and daughter each accused the other of fraud, or the instigation of the present proceedings to obtain the deed because this had all started before she and Medora had met; – she claimed that Medora had threatened to take a bottle of laudanum had she not been allowed to go to Bath with the Trevanions which was when Augusta first learned of the criminality; – although Augusta had erred no one can tell until they are tried how they would act through *intense fear* as Augusta had of her husband; – Augusta had not known of the whereabouts of Medora from July 1831 to June 1833 and thus could not write to her; – she had promised money that she could not send because of the expense of maintaining Georgiana out of her already over burdened income, made worse by paying high rates of interest on loans; – she had received most unfriendly letters from Medora which she later discovered were dictated by Trevanion; – she had wanted to go to France to look after Medora and bring her home but had been told by M. Carrel that it would make Medora's serious condition worse; – she had appointed and kept the deed as security for Marie because Medora had said the knowledge of this deed would soften her dying moments; – Augusta had been rude to Sir George Stephen because of Medora's averred distrust and aversion to him; – the claims of Georgiana's children, deserted by their father, must surely have greater claims on Augusta than the child of that daughter who caused the desertion.

In her replies Annabella made the following comments: although Mrs Villiers gave her no reason to regret or repudiate the letter (20 January 1841) she had sent, Augusta could rest assured that she would never give her own views to anyone unaccompanied by Augusta's statement with its attestation by Lord and Lady

Chichester – if it were impossible for Augusta to send a remittance for the food, fire and clothing which M. Carrel had confirmed to Augusta were so vital for Medora's recovery, why was she denied the only resource available, i.e. the sale of the reversion?; – she assured Mrs Villiers that Medora would always be left free to act towards her mother as she might think best but that she would not '*promote* the renewal of their intercourse convinced as I am most fully that after the birth of E's [Medora's] first child when she returned to her mother's protection, Mrs L. was accessory to the continued criminality. You *ought not* to believe this on my assertion, but you ought to believe and I feel assured you will – from what you have formerly known of me, that I have come to this horrible conclusion *most reluctantly*'; – she could not reconcile Augusta's fear of Colonel Leigh on certain occasions with her resolute opposition on others, – such as Georgiana's marriage, and added that Augusta often felt obliged to act in a manner which seemed like timidity; – that Georgiana's situation was the same as it had been before Augusta had promised Medora £120 a year which did not materialize; – that if Medora threatened to take laudanum then all the more reason for her not to be left out of Augusta's sight; – the loving letter from Medora to her mother in 1838 seeming to clear Augusta of complicity in the Trevanion affair was an answer to a letter skilfully adapted to elicit expressions of confidence and tenderness and that in Annabella's opinion Medora's affection for her mother had never been eradicated, although Medora had been most indignant at the charges made of fraud; if the deed was left in the hands of the person who executed it – a married woman and in debt – there could be no security from it, therefore why was not the deed surrendered, now that the apprehension for its being rashly disposed of had been removed?

It is hardly surprising that Mrs Villiers's efforts to defend Augusta were unavailing. The correspondence between Annabella and Mrs Villiers continued over five months until July and then there was nothing else to say. Both women were mentally and emotionally exhausted and must have questioned during the following years whether the subjects of their letters had been worthy of the time and dedication they had been given, but there was no open estrangement, just silence. Annabella was sorry that Mrs Villiers would have disapproved of her not opening the package giving Augusta's statements, but in accepting it, she could have been drawn into correspondence with the Chichesters which might reveal to them Augusta's reckless and immoral conduct. Although she herself could no longer trust Augusta, she would never say or do anything to harm her, preferring that Lady Chichester was allowed to consider her cold and unfeeling than to be inadvertently enlightened.

At first all had gone well between Medora and her protectress in Paris. Annabella wrote to her daughter frankly acquainting her with Medora's paternity. Ada replied:

St James Sq. February 27th 1841

Dearest Mama,
     I am not in the least *astonished*. In fact you merely *confirm* what I have for *years and years* felt scarcely a doubt about, but I should have considered it most improper for me to hint to you that I in any way suspected. ... I fear she is *more inherently* wicked than *he* ever was.

Annabella replied:

... it is indeed consolatory to me that I can make you the friend of my past as well as of my present life, *without reserve*. ... Strange to say I have been led to acquit *him* of some portion of the guilt by recent disclosures respecting her conduct to her child – for one who could, *as she clearly did*, connive at the ruin of a daughter, must be capable of injuring a brother in the same way. I had believed her to have been wholly a victim ....

In April 1841 Ada and her husband came to Paris for a few weeks to meet Medora. Before they came Annabella wrote to Lovelace telling him the substance of her correspondence with Mrs Villiers, 'an able straightforward woman, who uses no détours, and will do justice, I believe, when the rights of the case are shown'. The letter ends: '... as it is impossible to say how this may end, I wish you to have the means of knowing how far I am right or wrong – and I shall only esteem you the more for convincing me of being in error, if you can'.

Ada was a year and a half younger than Medora and at once showed kindness and friendship to her. On their return to England Lady Byron established herself at Moore Place in Esher together with a house next door to accommodate her visitors, a custom she adopted wherever possible. She was to stay there ten years. The Lovelaces lived a few miles away at Ockham Park and Lady Byron, with Medora and sometimes Marie, often visited them. The two young women were musical. Ada playing the violin competently while Medora was accomplished at singing and accompanying herself on the piano. Lady Byron was often away leaving her close friend Mrs Jameson, the authoress and art critic, in charge. To begin with Anna Jameson and Medora got on well together: '… it is impossible to know her without loving her', Anna wrote, although some people did for Mrs de Morgan, who saw Medora daily before she joined Annabella at Esher wrote of her: '… she spoke falsely of my husband and myself, and in short contrived many temporary estrangements and did as much mischief as any human could do, before Lady B's intense love for her husband's child would allow her to see clearly. The little girl was as wicked as the mother'. And Anna Jameson, whom Medora called Aunt Twaddle, revised her first impression after closer acquaintance. 'The mind is all wrong', she wrote, 'unless the current be turned I anticipate nothing but mischief & misery'.

Medora grew bored with the life that had seemed like a dream when she had first met Annabella. Now she felt restricted and complained she had not enough money; and even worse, there was a lack of men for her to charm. She slandered her solicitor Sir George Stephen, by saying he was the lover of his wife's sister, a respectable headmistress of a girls' finishing school at Brighton, and this mischievous accusation caused a lot of worry and upset. Stephen felt it necessary to write an explanation to Mrs Villiers as well as Medora from whom he wished to receive a letter of rebuttal. '… I have I believe, seen her [his wife's sister] but four times within the last twelve years … That she is, and always had been most warmly attached to me is true enough: it would be disgraceful to her were she not – after all the exertions I made for her family at a time that I could ill afford it …'. This letter to Medora got lost – her letters to him were delayed – Mrs Villiers was angry – Annabella maintained it was not Medora's fault. In spite of all this annoyance Sir George Stephen remained Medora's most steadfast advocate.

There were many distressing 'scenes of fury' when it seemed as if Medora must be insane. She knew that as a daughter of Byron she became an object of interest, and liked to encourage this belief, especially as she became aware of its value as a weapon to use against her mother, her relations, and the woman who had done so much to protect Augusta from knowledge of her relationship with Byron becoming generally known. Annabella wrote a memorandum 'Remarks on E' which she put in a sealed envelope, marked 'not to be opened without my leave', noting that 'There have been in unguarded moments slight allusions to means of working on her mother for future advantages. ... In consequence I must, without disclosing my reasons protect the Mother by my future arrangements.'

On 31 May 1842, the day the Chancery suit was to be heard, Augusta's counsel surrendered the deed. However Medora was far from satisfied. She wrote in her autobiography:

> In May 1842 my long anxiety in the matter of the Chancery suit was ended. The suit was concluded in a way, without consultation with me, that showed me, that all that had been promised me, unsolicited and unsought, was not sincere, and that I had been in a manner, sacrificed in my mother's interest. I openly expressed to Lady Byron all I felt, and my determination of leaving England immediately, and solicited from her [Lady Byron] the means to do so.

The 'scenes of fury' before she left were terrible:

> I had *never* seen anything like it [Annabella wrote to Selina Doyle] She has told me that I was her bitterest enemy and threatened every kind of revenge ... but I never forgot I was her only friend. – You can witness how careful I have been not to imply (when I was half-distracted) anything that could injure her. She obliged me to quit my house some weeks before she left England, by rendering it intolerable to me – but I loved her still – One chapter more in the self-incurred sorrows of your friend.

A maid called Nathalie Beaurepaire had been engaged for Medora while they were in Paris before coming to England and it was agreed that Nathalie would accompany Medora to Hyères, a small town patronized by the English on the French Riviera. Annabella had always paid Nathalie's wages and would continue to do so, but now it was contrived that Nathalie's husband Victor would also join them as protector and a sort of courier, though the Beaurepaires considered themselves more companions than servants.

Annabella had consulted Medora over how money was to be transferred to her. Gently and tactfully she wrote on 17 July 1842:

There is a difficulty to be obviated about the name – your drafts and receipts must be in the name given in you passport ... Mr Wharton and I had some conversation on the subject, and he suggested as the only safe course, that any person who could be trusted to deliver the money to you should be the medium of its transmission. Do you trust Nathalie sufficiently – I shall of course have your own assurance privately of the remittance having been paid you.

Medora had arranged to leave her precious strong-box with all her important papers with Annabella at Moore Place, but she decided just before leaving that the deed was to be deposited with Lovelace.

Their farewells were fond. Annabella wrote: 'We *have* parted. For my life's sake I dare not encounter the agitation of saying farewell – but you are nearer to my heart than ever ...' and Medora wrote:

If climate does not do me good & I never come back you will find all my letters & papers in order & I feel that all I have done will satisfy you & not make me a less dear child to you. Dearest Pip, I have come up to-day early on purpose to get you a Daguerotype done of me – I have heard you say it would please you to have one – but the sun is clouded over but you shall have one, & as little ugly as possible. ... I no more wish a farewell than you – we have parted – if we meet not again here we shall only meet in happiness hereafter ....

Ada's farewell at Moore Place was less friendly. She wrote to her mother on 23 July 1842: 'The last half-hour I was there I was compelled to hear a discourse on the bitterness of dependence and threats of throwing herself down the throat of the first man she could get hold of to marry ... "at least I should not depend on *charity*".' This was probably the main cause of Medora's intransigence. She was proud, and she chafed at restrictions. She was twenty-eight years old and desperately wanted the security of a husband. But in the circle that she moved in under Lady Byron's protection and as Ada's friend, it was unlikely to be easy to find an acceptable suitor. Ada continued: '... Mrs J [Jameson] is the black sheep at this moment. She [Medora] says that it was *she* who used to look grave over innocent fun and jokes; and who wanted to separate you and her, while *pretending* the reverse; in the most artful manner'.

Medora did not stay at Hyères long. Although Annabella had sent books, and extra money for carriage drives and tuition for Marie, the letters from Medora became increasingly carping and dissatisfied, and little attempt was made to live within her allowance although she and the Beaurepaires moved to a cheaper house outside Toulon. They all hated it and longed for Paris, and in March 1843 they decided to leave the south of France, Victor paying for the journey out of his own money.

This move to Paris was contrary to Lady Byron's conditions, which had been agreed to, but they nevertheless stayed in a hotel using her name as security. Selina Doyle and her sister Adelaide were staying in Paris at the same time and were approached by Medora who told Adelaide that Annabella had been cruel and mean, and had abandoned her to the mercy of servants. This resulted in Adelaide, who did not know any of the real circumstances, paying the hotel bill. Medora was also confiding the secret of her birth to various people, including the Doyles and the Beaurepaires. She also told it to a prominent lawyer Antoine Berryer, and persuaded him to write to Annabella who was already being inundated with letters from the Doyles, the Beaurepaires and Medora.

Annabella now thought Medora might be insane and she asked her friend Dr King, who was proprietor of a lunatic asylum, to go without delay to Paris, writing to him on 27 April 1843: 'The suffering has been great to me of expressing myself harshly towards one who has been the object of such tender interest – one whose cradle I had watched with peculiar feelings ...'. Dr King, although a very old friend, did not know about Medora's birth, though in a letter a few days later she forewarned him: 'I have felt that there is a process going on for the disclosure of some truths long hidden, which it may not be in the power of any of us to prevent or retard. You will say why attempt to suppress the truth? ... But there would be affliction to some, and ruin to others in the publication.' She authorized him to double Medora's allowance to £300 if she agreed to resign control of herself and her child to her. This Medora refused, and as Dr King considered her of sound mind, Annabella terminated all communications and the annuity of £150 but she would pay the same sum to trustees, unbeknown to Medora, provided the deed was retained and Medora lived a decent and respectable life.

On hearing of Medora's bitter narration to M. Berryer

Annabella wrote to Olivia Acheson: ' ...she has gone so far that I can never hold intercourse with her again. I think of having a seal with a large *Gull* engraved on it – can you give me a motto?' She was soon to learn that Medora, accompanied by Captain Barrallier, a friend who had followed her to Paris from Hyères, had returned to England preceded by the Beaurepaires. The Beaurepaires had been busy trying to extract money from Lady Byron and then began blackmailing her, as well as the Lovelaces, asserting 'loss of character' because they had been engaged in the belief that their mistress was a respectable widow named Mme Aubin. They maintained that the stigma of the truth on their name meant that they could not now be employed. Victor threatened to knock Lovelace down in the street, so that he could be arrested, gain publicity and tell a fearful story to the world. In the end, on Lovelace's advice, the Beaurepaires were reluctantly bought off by Lady Byron to save the publicity of a scandal and were never heard of again.

Captain Barrallier advised Medora to try and placate Lady Byron which Medora refused to do, and realizing nothing was being achieved, called for advice on a firm of solicitors called Banon and Smith with whom he had formerly dealt. He saw Thomas Smith who, it transpired, had met Byron briefly in Greece twenty years before and had never forgotten the magnetism of his personality. A meeting was arranged between Mr Smith and Medora who brought Marie with her, and being favourably impressed by them both, he decided to try to help them.

He suggested that Medora should write an account of her life so that he could study it and see what course of action seemed most appropriate. This was done and after reading her autobiography he attempted to communicate with Lady Byron through Lushington to try and improve relations between her and Medora. Since Lady Byron had been consistently misrepresented by Medora and everything that she had tried to do for her had failed, she felt she could no longer assume the role of her protectress. Even her commitment to protect Augusta from disgrace all those years ago was in peril through Medora's indiscreet divulgences. Medora would have to find out for herself that there is a code in every walk of life to which those who refuse to conform must pay the price. If she insisted on returning to a life of immorality, as now seemed likely, Annabella was not going to subsidize it. However she was prepared to give some financial assistance if Medora agreed to surrender the deed to trustees 'as a sacred provision for her child', give a written expression of contrition and return to seclusion in France. But Medora would not surrender the deed which was now in her possession.

Medora then desperately wrote to all the relations she could think of as well as people who had been her father's friends. Hobhouse noted in his journal that he had had a communication from 'Elizabeth Medora Leigh stating herself to be a *child* of Lord Byron and starving – some impostor I *hope*', but he made no enquiries. The only reply came from the Duke of Leeds, son of Augusta's half-brother, who sent ten pounds. In Medora's letter thanking him she unwisely whined about her cruel treatment from Lady Byron, which Barrallier and Smith, who were given a copy, deeply deplored and she heard no more from the Duke of Leeds. During months of patient mediation Smith had to admit defeat except for having obtained the return of the deed and the strong-box to Medora.

Her last hope was to see her mother and on 12 August she called at St James's Palace and left her card, but the servant returned with the reply 'Not at home'. Not one person wanted to or would help her. Among her many troubles Augusta was now on extremely bad terms with Georgiana, one of her sons was gambling and not only heavily in debt but threatened with dishonourable discharge from the navy. Her husband had been in a prison for debtors and she was seriously ill with dropsy. Medora wrote to her:

August 13th 1843
8 Church Row,
St Pancras

My Mother
   The motive that led me last night to ask what I have long since hoped to be spared, to meet once more, you, I so tenderly loved, was not as you have given me the right to do, to accuse and reproach you, nor yet to seek to awaken your pity for the misery I owe alone to you –. … I have expected and sought nothing from you – but now compelled to seek aid and protection from all who will give it. … could I have felt I was writing to a *Mother*, I would have said much, now I can only beg you, by the memory of my father … no longer to forget and neglect what you still owe.

Your child
Elizabeth Medora Leigh

In October Medora moved to cheaper lodgings in St Pancras. She changed her solicitor again to Sir John Hughes who advised her to contact Trevanion, the father of her child. This idea was most distasteful to her pride and she refused, but on Christmas Day she wrote to Hughes authorizing him to write to Trevanion. He had already done so and had received no reply, but he wrote again enclosing Medora's letter. In January 1844 this was returned with a letter from Trevanion in which he declared: '... it is entirely out of my power at the moment to contribute to the education of the young girl who was the subject of your letter ...'. He now had an income from his father's estate and property in Brittany but he callously avoided alluding to the paternity of his child.

Hughes approached the trustees to ascertain the conditions under which Medora could receive the annuity. She could keep the deed which had meant so much to her, for Marie; she must live in seclusion in France; and her cherished strong-box in which were papers pertaining to her life, had to be left in Hughes's care. She left a new will with her solicitor leaving everything to Marie. On 27 May 1844 Medora borrowed five hundred pounds with the deed as security, paid her debts and left England for ever.

She took lodgings in a *pension* in St Germain-en-Laye, but she got increasingly into debt so that by the end of 1845 it was clear that in time her troubles would be as desperate as before she left England. Perhaps the memory of that long wait for replies to her pleading letters which never came – save one, and the lonely bleak Christmas Day of 1843 caused her to undergo a complete change of character. She placed Marie in the Convent of the Nativity in St Germain and she persuaded the owner of the *pension* to employ her as a servant. She was now thirty-one years old.

One of the lodgers was Colonel de Grammont who came with his orderly Jean-Louis Taillefer. The soldier soon fell passionately in love with Medora and for the first time she knew what it was to be truly loved by a devoted and sincere man. In May 1846 she discovered she was pregnant and in November, when she could no longer work, Taillefer took her and Marie to St Affrique in the south of France where he had arranged for them to stay. He could not marry until he had finished his military service but she had no doubts that he would keep his word to make her his wife and to adopt Marie. On 27 January 1847 their son Jean-Louis Elie was born. Taillefer arrived the same day and as soon as possible took them to his native village, Lapeyre, a few miles away. He then had to return to his regiment and Medora was left with the children to make her home.

She had always been a good mother to Marie and now, although she was very poor as were all the inhabitants, she was accepted by them, possibly because Taillefer was well-liked, and they found her agreeable and unaffected. She had cut herself off completely from her previous existence with no regrets, adjusting to a new simple life in which she worked hard and was at peace. The only thing she missed from the past was a piano and after a time she was able to obtain one. She sang and accompanied herself and others; she was independent for the first time; and she was free from the constraints of a society to which she could not belong.

Taillefer duly came back, and on 23 August 1848 they were married amidst joyful celebrations in which the whole village joined. They had almost one year together and then Medora caught smallpox. She made a new will leaving everything including 'the Deed of Appointment under the will of the late Lord Byron' to her husband and their children which she signed on 23 August 1849 – her first wedding anniversary. She entreated Marie not to forsake Taillefer and to look after Elie. She forgave her mother and those 'who have so cruelly persecuted me, as I myself hope to be forgiven' and she asked her solicitor Hughes, who had arranged her legal matters before she left England, to send her the precious box with her papers. On 29 August she died.

Hughes however found the will unacceptable for probate. There was no legal representative; he could not read the names of the witnesses; why was it signed E.M. Leigh if she were married; why did the death certificate refer to Mme Aubin. All the villagers were simple country people and Taillefer was distraught with grief. Medora had been near death when she wrote it. There was no money for legal advice and Marie, then fifteen years old, did her best but mistakes were made through ignorance. It would appear that Hughes was totally uncooperative, influenced perhaps by others, or because it was evident that there would be little money available to pay him. The strong-box remained in his care and the will was not submitted for probate. He sent Marie's communication to Lord Chichester with whom he had had previous correspondence, and the bare facts of Medora's death became known to Augusta, Lady Wilmot-Horton and Lady Byron. Marie made no attempt to write to any of them.

So matters rested until a M. de Waroquier arrived in his native town of St Affrique for a holiday in 1852 and heard the sad story of the Taillefers in Lapeyre. He got in touch with his old friend

Colonel de Grammont who spoke most highly of Taillefer and his wife, who he remembered from his stay at St Germain-en-Laye. M. de Waroquier decided to offer assistance, but he had no more success with Hughes than Marie had had, which convinced him that injustice had been done and he determined to enquire further. Through Lord Brougham, whom Medora had known at Hyères and who now lived at Cannes, he appealed to a former grand chancellor of the French Embassy in London. He also appealed to M. Roux, a friend of his from the French Embassy, and he wrote to Lord Melbourne.

However it was not until 19 May 1863 that the box was finally opened in Hughes's office in the presence of the chancellor of the French Embassy, M. Roux, Hughes and a legal colleague of Hughes. The contents were more than enough to prove that Elizabeth Medora Leigh was indeed the child of Lord Byron as she had claimed. It was no victory however, for Hughes and his legal colleague insisted it was the custom in England to burn all papers such as this, which showed immorality. Roux strongly objected but was overruled, and as with Byron's memoirs, everything was burnt except the letter to Hughes from Medora affirming that he could write to Trevanion, and Trevanion's shameful reply. The deed which had caused so much heartache and distress had been of no benefit to Medora or her heirs except as security for the five hundred pounds she had borrowed to pay her debts in England.

De Waroquier proved a loyal friend. While Marie was still in charge at home Taillefer injured his foot making farm work difficult, and in 1855 de Waroquier arranged for Taillefer to work for his son as a coachman. At the same time he undertook the education of and responsibility for Elie, thus allowing Marie to take up her religious vocation in the Convent of the Nativity in St Germain. 'I am a little puzzled how to dispose of this new production' Byron had written to Augusta in 1817, speaking of Allegra, 'but shall probably send for & place it in a Venetian convent, – to become a good Catholic – & (it may be) a *nun* – being a character somewhat wanted in our family.' But it was Marie not Allegra who fulfilled Byron's prescient aspirations, and she used to speak of him affectionately: 'Poor Byron, I am very fond of him.' After taking her final vows she became Sister Saint-Hilaire and died in 1873.

The truth in accounts of Medora's sad story is often distorted. It has been said that if Annabella had been more like her friend, the worldly and experienced Anna Jameson, she might have been better able to curb Medora, ignoring the fact that Anna Jameson was in charge for much of the time at Moore Place. Had Medora shown an affinity with anybody else Annabella would have been very relieved, but Medora had quarrelled with most people, sooner or later, until she finally settled down with Jean Taillefer.

Annabella made it a condition of her protection that it would be withdrawn if Medora accepted money from elsewhere. It would not have been appropriate to give her reasons precisely but it was hardly to discourage regular family contributions for these were not offered. Medora was captivating to men and would have had no difficulty in attracting lovers, but Annabella had made it clear from the beginning that her guiding principle was to free Medora from a life of vice.

Some people maintain that Annabella told Medora the secret of her birth, but not only did Medora already know it but she herself had the confirmation in her strong-box. Annabella merely corroborated what could not be denied and which explained her concern for Medora as Byron's daughter. 'She was unfortunately in possession of that fact before she was connected with me, and after much embarrassment from her allusions to it, I determined on admitting it' she wrote to Selina Doyle in 1843.

There were others with better claims to protect Medora. Byron's friends for example: '... no man ever lived who had such devoted friends ...' Hobhouse wrote in his journal. He enlarged on this belief to Ada, the daughter all London wanted to meet: '... I ventured to tell her what I knew to be true – that I was the best friend her father ever had'. He was then a wealthy man. Yet when Medora wrote to him in dire distress he did not answer, although he knew of the Trevanion scandal in 1831. Had the position been reversed it is impossible to believe that there would have been no response from Byron.

There were the Chichesters and the Leeds, who as relatives could have insisted on their prerogative to act. 'When I was a happy child, you used to be kind and good natured to me' she had written to her Leeds cousin in her letter of appeal. The Chichesters were well aware of the circumstances that had led to Medora's desperate situation when she first approached Lady Byron.

It is not befitting for others to say, then or now, that those who could have given help, or more help, *should* have done so. But it *should* be remembered that only Lady Byron responded, not just with money, but with love, a warm welcome to her home and an introduction as a member of the family to her daughter and son-in-law. It seems strange that she alone among the many people who knew Medora receives censure.

16   The 1840s

Despite her personal tribulations and disappointments Annabella was becoming widely known and respected as a highly intelligent woman committed to benevolent humanitarianism. In sources unrelated to Byron a different Annabella emerges from the unsympathetic portrayal familiar to readers of Byron's biographies. In the latter she is rarely appreciated for her enthusiasm, keen intellect and outstanding organizing ability. Lady Byron is referred to in many letters of the period, for she made a habit of introducing men and women of similar interests to each other, as well as to influential people who could help in their particular province. The importance of her contribution to philanthropic work was recognized much later in the century, not only in Britain, as the following extract makes clear. The article was called 'The Princess of Parallelograms or The Case of Lady Byron', written by Myra Stark for the Keats-Shelley Association of America in 1982.

> In fact, Lady Byron belongs with the first wave of women to emerge in the 1840's and 1850's out of the confines of the Victorian home into the first work permitted them. ... She belongs with Louisa Twining, Mary Carpenter, Octavia Hill and Florence Nightingale in this regard; and every writer on the feminist movement in England from Ray Strachey in *The Cause* (1928) to Josephine Kamm in *Rapiers and Battleaxes* (1966) has placed Lady Byron among them stressing the importance of these pioneers in taking the first step for women out of the home.

She knew many of those who were prominent in the advancement of rights for women, but she was by no means a radical feminist. In a letter to a correspondent she explained where she disagreed with her friend, the sociologist Harriet Martineau:

> ... I lament some of her [Harriet Martineau's] theories, and none more than her female emancipation tenets. I consider them injurious to those she desires to befriend for these reasons.
> 1. That they lead women to undervalue the *privilege* of being exempted from political responsibility.
> 2. That by stimulating them to a degree of exertion, intellectually, for which their frames are not calculated, the ability to perform private duties is impaired – Mind is transferred from its legitimate objects.
> 3. That by mixing imaginary with real grievances, the redress of the latter is retarded. –
> I would however allow that some women, like Miss M herself, may be fitted for a wider sphere of action and influence, and her career shews that it may be obtained by them. If she cannot speak in the Senate, she no doubt influences Senators by her works. If she cannot vote, she effects more by instructing others in the duties of the elective franchise.

Annabella was tolerant of opposing viewpoints, telling Edward Noel that: 'I take in newspapers of all kinds ... living as much retired as I do this is the more necessary – I must read all sides, if I cannot hear them. At 5 o'clock every afternoon I have *The Times* for an hour and read anti-Poor Law, anti-educational, anti-temperance articles.'

Her cousin Robert Noel had introduced Lady Byron to Anna Jameson in 1834. The impression made by Annabella is recorded by Mrs Jameson's niece and biographer Gerardine Macpherson as being 'at first more in accordance with the opinion entertained by the friends of the poet-husband', that is to say implacable. Anna Jameson had written several books before *Characteristics of Women*, a psychological study of Shakespeare's heroines which appeared in 1832, firmly established her in Europe as a scholar of repute. In one of her letters to Robert Noel, she wrote: '... outwardly, I stand in the world an enviable being, so at least every one tells me; inwardly, it is a hard struggle. Of how many women might the history be comprised in those few words – "She lived, suffered, and was buried!" '. She determined that she would not be one of them.

Anna Jameson soon changed her first impressions, and referring to the success of her book *Winter Studies and Summer Rambles* she wrote: 'One of the most beautiful letters I have received is from

Lady Byron.' There are many references to Lady Byron in Gerardine Macpherson's biography of her aunt, mostly in letters from Anna Jameson to Robert Noel, and the following excerpts are typical:

'My American friend, Miss Sedgwick has been in England and has made a most favourable impression. Lady Byron in particular was very kind to her.'

'... Lady Byron, whose fine and truly noble character improves and opens upon me ...'.

'... the more I know her the more I admire her, and would, I think love her much, for she has a rare heart and mind ... I dined with her on Friday to meet Dr Lushington, a man I have long wished to know ...'.

'... I am very much struck by the singular powers of her mind and her very uncommon character. I begin to understand her, and there is scarcely any subject on which I would not speak to her openly ...'.

In 1840 Lady Byron attended the Convention of British and Foreign Anti-Slavery Society which was held in London on 12 June. In Benjamin Haydon's painting of the event she is seen sitting with Mrs Opie, wife of John Opie the artist. Her friend and lawyer Dr Stephen Lushington was among the many notable people present and, in his capacity as a Member of Parliament, he gave warm support to Thomas Buxton and others throughout the anti-slavery struggle. Benjamin Haydon noted in his diary his reaction to Lady Byron which seems reflected in his painting of her head:

July 3rd. ... Put in the negro's head, and the head of the delegate from Hayti. Sketched Lady Byron and Lucretia Mott. With Lady Byron I was deeply interested. There is a lambent sorrow about her, bland and touching, but she was no more fit for him than a dove for a volcano. Poor Lady Byron! She looks as if she *saw* an inward sorrow. Perhaps his sublime head is always haunting her imagination like the '*dira facies*' in Virgil.

During the six years since they had met. Anna Jameson and Annabella had become closely attached to each other and the intensity of the kind of love Anna Jameson gave Annabella was to make Anna feel 'almost one being'. They shared their most intimate thoughts and helped each other through many vicissitudes. Annabella was always especially appreciative of Mrs Jameson's support and advice through the difficult period with Medora. She was inspired to write some verses in 1841 which were called 'On a Portrait of Mrs Jameson by her Father':

> *In those young eyes, so keenly, bravely bent*
> *To search the mysteries of the future hour,*
> *There shines the will to conquer, and the pow'r*
> *Which makes that conquest sure, a gift heav'n sent.*

It may be this poem to which Joanna Baillie referred in a letter to Anna Jameson: '… the verses [by Lady Byron] you have been kind enough to transcribe for me are beautiful and were they found among any new version of Wordsworth's poems, they would be much admired … yet I have verses of hers that I like still better'. Anna Jameson however, was critical and more discerning when she wrote to Annabella: 'The thought in your verses is very beautiful and poetical, but as usual you almost strangle it in the expression. I think it is part of your character … that you shrink from making *words* the vehicle of feeling …'. Byron had told Medwin: 'Lady Byron had good ideas, but could never express them; wrote poetry too, but it was only good by accident.'

When Anna Jameson's father died she wrote: '… my principal comfort through all the misery of the last six months has been in the constant kindness and affection of Lady Byron.' This depiction of kindness is repeated by many of the people who knew Annabella, and Mrs De Morgan, who knew her very well said: 'Her nature was extremely affectionate. She threw herself into the feelings of those she loved, and sometimes was disappointed by finding that she had herself suffered more from her sympathy than had the object of it.' She also remembered that friends had told her that Annabella had been a cheerful little girl who always liked to make people happy.

In 1842 Anna Jameson undertook to go to Seaham and visit the only place that Annabella was ever to think of as home. Just the name evoked floods of memories, of her happy and innocent childhood, and then more vividly and painfully, of Byron. Byron playing on the rocks laughing, and as she had supposed, loving her; Byron listening patiently to her beloved father's stories, sometimes repeated and often long; Byron, making such a good impression on everyone that they missed him dreadfully when she had to send him away on account of his passion which she had thought was solely for her. She was to be haunted until she died by these memories of him which returned too often unbidden, undesired.

Mrs Jameson reported that the house was now uninhabited but that Annabella's family was spoken of with respect. One of the trees in the garden was known as 'Byron's Hawthorn', and she was shown the room where, not Miss Milbanke, but Lady Byron was married. In that year the song that was sung and whistled from the Strand in London to the banks of the Ohio was 'Home Sweet Home' and when Annabella heard it sung not long after this visit, in the beautiful, clear, wistful voice of the German soprano Henriette Sontag, it brought back the past so agonizingly that she 'rained tears', as she had on her visit to Seaham with Sarah Carr twenty-five years earlier. That year Annabella wrote to Lovelace: 'I have worked very hard in arranging papers & other valuables. I have found in the course of my search, a portrait of Lord Byron which I valued perhaps more than any other possession & believed to have been stolen. It was done at seventeen – and has nothing of the misanthropic expression of all the later pictures.'

Annabella continued with her charitable work, but her first enthusiasm had waned, for the people she met were often hypocritical, tiresomely self-opinionated and tediously boring. However, the work was vital, her name stimulated interest and many were the unassuming practical suggestions that accompanied a financial contribution. The following letter is an example:

10 St James' Sq. London
Aug 10, 1842

Sir,
I have much pleasure in acknowledging your letter of the 9th conveying a kind, and I trust not undeserved expression of confidence, on the part of the Working Class members, in my zeal for their welfare.

It has always been repugnant to my feelings to publish my *private* attempts to acquit myself to the duties I owe to my fellow creatures, & I must therefore decline the insertion of my last letter in the newspapers – But I have no objection to you making that use of my present communication if the following suggestion be deemed likely to promote the objects of the committee.

It appears to me, and to a land-owner whose opinion is entitled to greater weight both from his knowledge of these subjects, &

extensive possessions, that as no *immediate* profit can be derived
from an allotment, it would be advisable (when the land is given for
the alleviation of distress) to remit the *first* quarter's or half year's
rent – the nature of the soil and other circumstances would
determine the extent of that indulgence in each case.
      I am sir
                              Your obt servt.
                              A.I. Noel Byron.
Mr James Thompson
Chronicle Office
Leicester

Although Ada's children were said to speak with a 'vulgar' tone,
and with a vocabulary acquired through the eldest child, Byron,
having shown at an early age a predilection to join the estate
workmen and copy their habits and accent, Lady Byron was very
proud of her grandchildren. On 20 November 1842 she wrote to
Ada that Mrs King, who had spent three nights with her while
Byron and Ralph were staying, was deeply interested in them as
had been Mrs Barwell who was also there. They were amazed 'to
see the children so good and tractable and happy – you are indeed
in great danger of being considered the best of Mamas!' and two
days later she wrote: 'I am alone with little Ralph, whose improved
health & spirits give me great pleasure.' Byron departed with a
glowing testimonial. 'He had no lessons but he was never idle,
never tiresome, never ennuyé – on the contrary full of glee and
ready to do everything that was desired by others – He showed
remarkable good sense in one or two practical matters – the visit
was very agreeable to him and yet he was happy to return to
Annobellow, as he calls her.'
      In January 1843 Mrs Jameson wrote to Robert Noel: '… I think
her [Lady Byron] greatest care is Lady Lovelace's health. She is far
from well or strong. They are very happy together'. Lady Byron
was indeed becoming increasingly concerned over her daughter's
health. Ada was expected to carry out her role as the wife of the
Earl of Lovelace, who also held the prestigious office of Lord
Lieutenant of the County of Surrey, on the comparatively small
allowance of £300 a year. She was encouraged by Lovelace to
have no lady's maid, even though this lack of what was considered
a normal and necessary requisite for a woman of Ada's social
status, was questioned by her mother. Annabella was appealed to

for help and advice on every facet of their lives which cannot have been easy or always welcome to her, for she had never shown much enthusiasm for domesticity, and even as a child had not played very much with dolls. As an example of her casual attention to home matters, in a letter to her friend Caroline Bathurst there are apologies for having forgotten to give her any lunch. But because of her own talent that had been wasted, she understood Ada's desperate yearning to prove herself, and made every effort to give her daughter – Byron's daughter – the chance she believed she should have.

Since Annabella had wide experience in the area of education it seemed advantageous to enlist her assistance in introducing possible candidates for the post of tutor, but she insisted that the final choice must be made by the parents. However, Lovelace, who spent a lot of time at Ashley Combe, his estate near Minehead, supervising the building of sea-bathing facilities, told Ada that whatever course they took regarding a new tutor, they must be entirely guided by her mother. He did not wish to see a potential applicant 'without being fully in possession of what she [Lady Byron] thinks ought to be said, & the tone I ought to take with him'. Like many outwardly successful and autocratic men, he often needed to be praised and reassured. Ada and William did not have the youngest child, Ralph, baptised, and since they were Unitarians, the non-acceptance of the Holy Trinity made a choice of schools difficult in an age where religious doctrines were outwardly important and unorthodox beliefs could frustrate entry to schools, prevent academic advancement, and as Ralph was to find, cause problems at university.

Ada was now not interested in the children: '... unfortunately *every* year adds to my *want* of pleasure in my children. They are to me irksome *duties* & nothing more' she wrote to Woronzow Greig. She was becoming increasingly restless, feeling she would never reach the fulfilment of doing what she really wanted to do, which was to study advanced mathematics without being perpetually interrupted. In July 1843 she wrote to Babbage:

> ... I am reflecting much on the work & duties for you & the engine which are to occupy me for the next two or three years I suppose, & I have some excellent ideas on the subject. ... One first & main point, *whenever* & *wherever* I introduce the subject, will be to *define* & to *classify* all that is to be legitimately included under the term

discovery. Here will be a fine field for my *clear, logical & accurate,* mind, to work its powers upon; & to develop its *metaphysical* genius ....

In this confident self-appraisal Ada differed from Mrs Somerville, who was aware that although she had a faculty for explaining abstruse scientific problems with clarity she had never made a discovery herself and had 'no originality'. Ada's conviction that she had exceptional powers was shared by her tutor, the distinguished Augustus De Morgan who was the first Professor of Mathematics at the University of London, and had instructed her over a long period. He was the author of many books on mathematics and logic, and unrivalled as a teacher, many of his pupils becoming themselves distinguished.

Ada was not Annabella's only worry that year, for Anna Jameson wrote to Robert Noel on 21 October that Annabella's friend, Mrs Henry Siddons, daughter-in-law of the famous actress Sarah Siddons, had had an operation for dropsy: 'Lady Byron was with her during the operation, supported her through it, and has ever since been on hand. I am in a manner with both, for Lady B. requires almost as much watching as her friend; and what will be the issue of so much emotion and fatigue, and the horrible London atmosphere I dread to think.' Mrs Siddons died about a week later.

This was the year when the Medora episode had become most distressing. The Beaurepaires were suing Annabella, and the penniless Medora refused to accept any conditions for help. Annabella must have often felt despondent but those who knew her sympathized and admired her fortitude. Joanna Baillie wrote to Anna Jameson: '... I heartily agree with all your good wishes for her [Lady Byron]. She is a most respectable as well as agreeable woman, and has conducted herself through a life of many cares and troubles in a very exemplary manner ...'.

It would seem that Annabella's health was invigorated in spite of the traumas or perhaps due to them for Anna Jameson reported that '... on my return to London a fortnight ago, I found Lady Byron looking rather better than usual, and her mind principally occupied by cares for her grandchildren whom she has taken on her hands till Christmas I believe ...'. The Lovelaces were therefore able to consider without distractions the matter of Ada's studies in consultation with Augustus De Morgan.

Annabella believed that owing to Ada's fluctuating moods and tendency to dramatize, which was widely observed because she was always an object of interest, she appeared to others more disturbed than she in fact was, although she was prone to gastric disorders. Judging by Ada's ability to express herself exceptionally well in letters, and markedly better than her mother, this seems a reasonable judgement. Annabella wrote to De Morgan:

> I find both from your letter to Lady Lovelace & from Mrs De M's today, that you are most likely anxious to prevent Lady L, from injuring herself by mathematical study. But I feel apprehensive that this caution may be carried too far – I have at all times observed that she was the better for pursuits of that description – & if she would but attend to her stomach, her brain would be capable even of more than she has ever impressed on it ... After the few weeks which I passed with her at Bristol it is impossible for me to share in the extent of apprehension entertained by some friends who judge from report instead of observation. The consciousness of making progress in science seems to me an essential element in her happiness, & appears not less desirable to Lord Lovelace than to myself.

Three days earlier she had written to Ada:

> You are right, I believe, in your construction of the Professor's very kind letter, and I only hope you will see him and 'do justice to yourself', by not appearing less right and reasonable than you are *au fond* – & by not reflecting any of the various diseases which may have been imported to you – No one who saw you as you are could fancy a *discontinuance* of Mathematics necessary.

The reply from De Morgan is of value in assessing the truth of opinions expressed today by less qualified judges, which depreciate Ada's ability in the field of scientific mathematics:

> My Dear Lady Byron
> I have received your note and should have answered no further than that I was very glad to find my apprehension (of being a party to doing mischief if I assisted Lady Lovelace's studies without any caution) is unfounded in the opinion of yourself and Lord Lovelace, who *must* be better judges than I am, on every point of the case but one, and *may* be that one. But at the same time it is very necessary that the one point should be properly stated.
> I have never expressed to Lady Lovelace my opinion of her as a

student of these matters: I always feared that it might promote an application to them which might be injurious to a person whose bodily health is not strong. I have therefore contented myself with very good, quite right and so on. But I feel bound to tell you that the power of thinking on those matters Lady L has always shown from the beginning of my correspondence with her, has been something so utterly out of the common way for any beginner, man or woman, that this power must be duly considered by her friends, with reference to the question whether they should urge or check her obvious determination to try not only to reach but to get beyond, the present bounds of knowledge. ... Lady L. has unquestionably as much power as would require all the strength of man's construction to bear the fatigue of thought to which it will unquestionably lead her ... Perhaps you will think that Lady L. will like Mrs Somerville go on in a cause of regulated study, duly mixed with the enjoyment of society, the ordinary cares of life, & c & c. But Mrs Somerville's mind never led her into other than the *Details* of mathematical *work;* Lady L. will take quite a different route ...

Having now I think quite explained that you must consider Lady L's case as a peculiar one I will leave it to your better judgement, supplied with facts, only begging that this note may be confidential. All here pretty well. I hope your house is free from illness and remain

Dear Lady Byron
Your very truly
De Morgan

Jan 21st 1844

Annabella spent most of 1844 travelling, sometimes accompanied by Ada, in the hope that her health would improve. Ada was showing signs of mental strain and the problems of the children's education and her own ambitions remained unresolved. Her mother continued to try and encourage and reassure her: 'Dr King says he has had patients whose faces & hands swelled like yours & has always considered it a good thing as the fulness is distributed more safely.' Lovelace had become a member of the Royal Society, where women were not admitted, as an 'Aristocrataic amateur' as Babbage disparaged it, in the hope that Ada might creep in on the pretext of working for him but that had not been possible. She appealed to Greig, Mrs Somerville's son, in December 1844: '... could you ask the secretary if I might go in now & then (of a *morning* of course) to hunt out the things I require ... I want to get entrée to their library in a quiet & unobtrusive manner … Perhaps early in the morning …'. However, like his mother, Ada was not admitted, but Mrs Somerville at least had had her bust accepted and remains the only woman so honoured in the hall of the Royal Institution.

Anna Jameson reported in 1845 that after her return from a visit to Edinburgh she 'spent three short happy days at Kirkby with Lady Byron who was busy with tenants' schools, game laws, and manifold projects for the benefit and happiness of others'. However, later she described how she had found Annabella trying to recover from one of her terrible fits of illness: '… of all human beings she is the one most necessary to my heart and to my mental and moral well-being; the only one, I might say, uniting in her most extraordinary character and peculiar destiny all I most love, with all I most reverence …'.

Bertel Thorwaldsen, the celebrated Danish sculptor, had made a bust of Byron in Rome in 1817 which was widely acclaimed. In 1826 Hobhouse, who had instigated the arrangements for the bust, formed a committee to commission a statue of Byron with the intention of placing it in Westminster Abbey, even though some two years earlier the proposal for the interment of Byron in the Abbey had been rejected. The statue, sculptured by Thorwaldsen using the head cast made in 1817, arrived in England after some delay but was refused admission to the Abbey by two successive deans and remained in the Custom House cellar for five years. After the second dean's death in 1844, Hobhouse wrote a pamphlet with the object of impressing the new dean with a testimonial justifying a permanent memorial to Byron in the Abbey. It was a rambling, sentimental, irrelevant and unsuccessful plea. Referring to Byron's friends he said: 'They were not blind to the defects of his character, nor of his writings, but they knew that some of the gravest accusations levelled against him had no foundation in fact; and perhaps the time may come when justice may be done to the dead without injury to the feelings of the living …'. Annabella also considered that Byron should have been commemorated in Westminster Abbey and wrote some verses reflecting her views which she had sent to Augusta when the matter was first discussed:

> *Think ye to tear the laurel from his brow;*
> *To him ye had not dared the thought avow,*
> *To Byron's name a cenotaph refuse,*
> *Reserve it for the sager laureat Muse;*
> *Your pious zeal should decimate the crowd*

To whom immortal honours are allowed.
In Milton mark the regicidal stain
And banish Dryden, profligate, profane ...

O could I bring to light the unconfest,
The deep dread secrets of the human breast,
How many hearts a kindred pang must own
And who would feel in grief, in guilt, alone!
Judge not but weep for one who never knew
The blessings that descend on some like dew:
Stern o'er his childhood Calvin's spirit lowered,
And every hope of mercy overpowered

She knew better than anyone that, notwithstanding Byron's treatment of her, there was deeply enshrouded in the turmoil of his spirit, a stern Calvinistic vein that would never fade. While her words may not be universally acclaimed, they surely do not suggest that the sentiments expressed were written in bitterness, considering that any influence her name might have could only be favourable to Byron.

An intimation had been made that the statue would be welcomed by Trinity College, Cambridge, but Hobhouse was annoyed by the attitude taken at Westminster Abbey. As might be expected from the man who had undervalued Byron's genius when alive, allowed his memoirs to be burned after his death and suppressed Fletcher's disclosure that he had read Augusta's bible, he was incapable of addressing himself to the problem of reconciling Byron's taunting the Christian faith in his works and life, with the acceptance of his statue into its most sacred shrine. Hobhouse was oblivious to the fact that it was immaterial that 'in mixed society Lord Byron was not talkative', as he had written to the dean in his letter but he seemed to be satisfied with his effort and sent a copy to Ada. Meanwhile the statue was exhibited in the studio of Sir Richard Westmacott, the sculptor, whose figures representing the progress of civilization stand over the portico of the British Museum.

Ada had seen the statue of her father and told Hobhouse when he was dining with them in St James's Square that she did not like it. Annabella had also been to see it with Anna Jameson, who reported that there were tears in Annabella's eyes when she said: 'It is very beautiful but not half beautiful enough for my dear

Byron!' When Hobhouse returned the Lovelaces' hospitality he
showed them the bust of Byron which had been done for him by
Thorwaldsen and Ada appeared interested and affected by it.
Since the well-known paintings of Byron which she would have
seen are described by people who knew him well, such as Teresa
Guiccioli and Sir Walter Scott, as not being at all like, she probably
felt something of her father's charisma and personality for the first
time.

The statue finally went to Trinity College, and was placed in the
beautiful Wren library. It was inspected and approved by
Hobhouse: 'It is a beautiful work of art and is in an admirable
position. Little did he or I think ... that he would have a statue, and
the only statue, in that splendid building'. Periodically the question
of its being moved to Westminster Abbey recurs for review. In
1924 the dean explained in a letter to *The Times* his reasons for
declining a memorial to Byron in the Abbey, namely that space was
limited, especially in Poet's Corner, and that the Abbey was not a
literary Valhalla but primarily stands to witness for Jesus Christ.
Moreover, he continued, Byron had by his dissolute life and
licentious verse earned a worldwide reputation for immorality, and
a more suitable place should be chosen to honour his poetical
genius such as a square or university. In 1941 there were again
letters in *The Times* on this subject, which caused the Master of
Trinity College, G.M. Trevelyan the historian, to reply that should
a request for the statue ever be made '... it would be much worse
than useless. It is in an excellent position and we are very proud of
it'. It seems eminently suitable, as well as dignified, to have this
impressive sculpture in such a beautiful setting.

Anna Jameson continued to give news of Annabella to Robert
Noel: 'Of Lady Byron I can only tell you that she seems to have set
up a foundling hospital. She has her grandchildren and little
Montgomery all on her hands; but her last letter to me was
cheerful, and without complaint of her health.' It was about this
time that Ralph looked at her steadily saying: 'How much older
Byron will think you when he returns.' Like other grandmothers
she had learned to take such observations with fortitude and
humour.

Mrs George Bancroft, the wife of the United States Minister to
Great Britain, called on Lady Byron at Esher in May 1847. Her
husband, when a young man, had visited Byron at Leghorn in May
1822 and pleased him by reporting that his work, particularly 'Don

Juan', was much admired in Germany where Bancroft had been studying. In her *Letters from England* Mrs Bancroft describes the visit:

> Lady Byron is now about fifty-five and with the remains of an attractive, if not brilliant beauty. She has extremely delicate features, and a very pale and finely delicate skin. A tone of voice and manner of the most trembling refinement with a culture and strong intellect, almost masculine, but which betrays itself under such a sweet and gentle and unobtrusive form that one is led only to perceive it by slow degrees. She is the most modest and unostentatious person one can well conceive.
>
> She lives simply, and the chief of her large income (you know she was the rich Miss Milbanke) she devotes to others.
>
> After lunch she wished me to see a little of the country round Esher and ordered her ponies and small carriage for herself and me, while Mr Bancroft and Miss Murray walked.
>
> We went first to the royal seat, Claremont where the Princess Charlotte lived so happily with Leopold, and where she died. Its park adjoins Lady Byron's, and the queen allows her a private key that she may enjoy its exquisite grounds. Here we left the pedestrians while Lady Byron took me a more extensive drive, as she wished to show me some of the heaths in the neighbourhood which are covered with furze, now one mass of bloom.
>
> Lady Byron took me to the estate of an neighbouring gentleman to show me a fine tower, covered with ivy, where Wolsey took refuge from his persecutors, with his faithful follower Cromwell ... I could not help thinking as I walked up and down the beautiful paths of Claremont Park, with its fresh spring air blowing about me, the primroses, daisies and wild bluebells under my feet and Lady Byron at my side, that it was more like a page out of a poem than a reality.

Annabella was introduced to the Reverend Frederick Robertson by Robert Noel in 1848, for which she was always grateful. He had become the vicar of Holy Trinity Church in Brighton in 1847 and through him it became famous all over the world. His eloquence and compassion attracted thousands of people from every class of society to hear him, and when he preached queues formed early to get into the church. Books of his sermons were eagerly sought, and his readers included the four ex-prime ministers Lord Rosebery, Lord Balfour, Lord Oxford and Mr Lloyd George, as well as Queen Victoria and Prince Albert, Lord Tennyson, Dean Stanley and many other well-known people. When he died at the age of thirty-seven he had become a man of international stature, even more famous in America than in Great Britain. he was a radical and original thinker and a brilliant conversationalist, with the ability to mix with working-class people as an equal. Crabb Robinson the celebrated diarist and special foreign correspondent of *The Times*, wrote of Robertson: 'Take him for all in all, the best preacher I ever saw in a pulpit; that is, uniting the greatest number of excellences, originality, piety, freedom of thought and warmth of love. His style colloquial and very scriptural.'

There was an immediate rapport between Annabella and Robertson, possibly because of his great regard for Byron's poetry. They soon developed a mutual sympathy and understanding, as well as a strong personal attraction, although she was more than twenty years older than him. His good looks, vibrant personality, unorthodox saintliness and their mutual esteem made him an interesting and agreeable friend. They confided in each other, and gradually she revealed some aspects of her marriage to him. Robertson told Crabb Robinson that Lady Byron was one of the noblest and purest women he had ever met: 'Her calm subdued character, warm sympathy and manifold wisdom have been one of my greatest privileges here.' Stopford Brooke, his biographer, recounts how Robertson often sought her counsel and kind, encouraging support, which he always received. Her friendship gave him new life and supplied him with the strength to conquer his trials, of which at this period he had many.

In 1849 Annabella was very pleased to receive a letter again from Mrs Villiers. She replied from Brighton on 18 February 1849:

Dear Mrs Villiers,
    Your open-hearted and very gratifying letter has been returned from Hastings. Let me recall to your recollection that our correspondence ended by a proof of my attention to your wishes in a trifling manner – I have therefore always felt that it rested with *you* to resume or drop the intercourse.
    Not having that sort of Self-importance which imagines hostility from no notice, and trusting that I could not have left on your mind any impression of personal unfriendliness, I had only to acquiesce, – little anticipating that I should ever have to read expressions as kind as those you now use and for which I feel grateful.
    Since you have alluded to *that* unhappy business, I will just say that I regret having yielded to legal advice in avoiding to discuss it viva voce. Had we conversed upon it, I am persuaded that some

mutual misapprehension would have been prevented. I am still ignorant in what respect I was *really* deceived, tho' I might appear to be so, from that feeling of honor [sic] which forbade me to admit unnecessarily anything to the disadvantage of the person who had placed herself under my protection, until she had recovered the means of existence independently of me.

Dismissing all that intervened, believe me most willing to join the end with the beginning, and if life be granted us, to become again, dear Mrs Villiers,

Yours Affectionately
A.I. Noel Byron

Due to Ada's increasing interest in mathematics and her disinterest in her children Lady Byron had had her grandchild Annabella fully in her care since 1847. It is not surprising in view of her experience with the education of children that she believed firmly in the careful selection of a governess in whom she had perfect trust and in this Lovelace fully supported her. However as she approached the age of sixty she felt that she was no longer able to supervise Annabella's upbringing adequately. On 3 May 1849 she wrote to 'Dearest Lovelace' that she felt the time had come to resign her management of his daughter because as her powers expanded, her own were becoming more and more limited physically. 'The recollection of the confidence reposed in me & which has made my task so pleasant will always be gratifying to your affectionate mother.' So warm and close was their relationship that at times they were 'mother' and 'son' in letters.

During this period Lady Byron often visited Anna Jameson and her sister in Bruton Street. Their niece reported that Lady Byron was: '… always an interesting figure in any society; and the quiet drawing room became the scene of many a lively talk and animated discussion' on such topics as art, literature and social progress.

Elizabeth Blackwell, the first woman doctor, obtained her MD at Geneva, New York State in January 1849, and came to England a few months later. Through Lady Byron and others she met many influential people, such as Michael Faraday and John Herschel. She was a highly intelligent woman of vision who immediately recognized in Lady Byron a kindred spirit. Their correspondence, which continued until Lady Byron's death, covered various topics, often of a technical nature. For instance a letter Lady Byron wrote on 9 December 1851 gave Elizabeth Blackwell detailed information concerning magnetic influence and enclosed a pamphlet on the subject. Florence Nightingale helped Elizabeth Blackwell gain entry into St Bartholomew's Hospital where she was admitted by the dean to various departments to broaden and develop her work. She recorded in her autobiography a visit to Annabella at her home in Brighton where she met authors and artists and particularly remembered Fanny Kemble, who swept through the door in rustling rose-coloured silk declaiming Shakespeare. It was Elizabeth Blackwell who inspired Elizabeth Garrett Anderson, the first woman doctor in Britain, to take up medicine, thus causing her mother, it is said, to have a breakdown crying '... the disgrace will kill me'. Dr Blackwell returned to America and opened a hospital entirely staffed by women, but found that there were no 'equivalents for Bessie Raynor Parkes, Lady Byron or Barbara Leigh Smith'. She became the first woman to be placed on the British Medical Register in 1859 and returned to England writing: 'I am convinced that England is the place where we should work to best advantage. Lady Byron, Mrs Bracebridge, the Peter Taylors, Miss Goldsmith ... each the centre of a large and very different set of people are each of them sure we should have a large and valuable practice'. She had a practice in London until 1879, when for health reasons she moved to Hastings where she lived and practiced at Rock House. She died in her ninetieth year.

At the end of 1849 Annabella became very ill. She wrote to Robert and Louisa Noel from Southampton on 14 December.

I take a better day to write to you. Which I have long intended to do – but for a person as ill as I am, every day brings too much to do. Happy as the greater part of my occupations are – I came here for the sake of a Medical Man – the only one I know who does not see facts through hypothesis, & possesses great knowledge & abilities Dr Bullar – ... I have begun with Self, knowing your anxiety from Mrs Jameson, & also wishing to explain that my health must be paramount in all my plans. I cannot therefore say to you, as I have before done & should rejoice to do again – 'Come to me & be assured of a home in England from which you can make excursions' – I dare not & must not receive my dearest friends, as they will testify, except for very short visits & with long intervals, of solitude & *silence* the latter being of great consequence to my Chest – My voice is quite changed, & soon fails – I could not *now* talk to you. If you do come in the Spring, I will live in hopes of exchanging a few thoughts & feelings viva voce – What arrangements have you thought of as the most economical? for in our Railroad world, Travelling is no cheaper I think, taking all things into account, than in Family Coach times.

She was as usual optimistic, and learning that they were anxious, explained briefly the nature of her ailment. She was concerned that Robert and Louisa, to whom she was devoted, would not be offended because they had not been invited to stay with her. The rest of the letter contains news of the Mairs and their family, Mrs Mairs being a granddaughter of Sarah Siddons who had stayed at Halnaby so many years ago; her thought on politics: 'The change of opinion about your political views is a curious proof how much less reason than self-interest there is in most people's profession', and Louis Napoleon's appeal to France in his last speech, ending with: 'Lovelace well & in a castle he has formed out of his new Mansion in Surrey'.

At that time illness was far more widespread than in modern times and an up-to-date progress report on the sender's health and anxious enquiries regarding that of the recipient are common in letters of this period. Yet often Lady Byron's granddaughter Annabella King would start letters to her: 'Thank you very much for your letter but you hardly ever mention how you are.' Her life and work continued in spite of her chronic bad health, due entirely it would seem to her keen enquiring interest in people and all that was going on in the outside world. Nothing was too small in consequence for her undivided attention, or too complex for her to apply her mind to learn and understand.

In spite of her distressing attacks of illness and the nuisance of not knowing when they would recur, these last few years were probably one of the happiest and most satisfying periods of Annabella's life. It was not to last.

17   The Years of Grief

Ada and her husband toured parts of the Midlands and the north country in 1850, going to the Doncaster races and making their first visit to Newstead Abbey. Newstead had a strange and powerful effect on Ada, which she described to her mother: '... I feel as if, however, it ought to belong to *me* ... I seem to be in the Mausoleum of my race ...' and this feeling gradually grew into a great affection. She wrote again a few days later: 'Altogether it is an *epoch* in my life, my visit there. I have lost my *monumental* and *desolate* feeling respecting it. – It seemed like descending into the *grave*, but I have had a *resurrection*. – I do love the venerable old place and all my *wicked forefathers!*' She felt profoundly that she had returned home. They walked in the woods, and went to Hucknall church where many of the Byron family were buried. Ada saw the tablet commemorating Byron given by Augusta and was very conscious of the closeness of her father lying in the vault beneath her. It was then that she conceived the idea of being laid close to him when she died, and during the visit she secretly spoke of her wish to Colonel Wildman.

Thomas Wildman was the owner of Newstead Abbey at that time and had bought it from Byron who had been a friend of his at Harrow. He had spent a considerable sum of money restoring with taste and feeling the beautiful buildings redolent of past religious history and the relics of monks and Byrons who had lived there long ago. Ever sensitive of being called cold and unforgiving by Byron's friends, and cast as such in his poetry, Annabella reacted immediately to Ada's letters by writing a self-defensive one. She reminded her: 'If the mythic idea generally entertained of your father, affords you satisfaction, do not forget dearest Ada, how much of it is owing to my own line of conduct ... *You* must not be infected in an error resulting from *their* ignorance ...'. She proceeds to stress that whatever Ada and Lovelace might hear from the 'partizans of Byron', she had always been his best friend, not only in feeling but in fact. What was really worrying to her was that they could be given an untrue or distorted account of the separation, and in view of the close relationship she had with her grandchildren '... it would be better for them not to have known me, – if they are allowed to adopt the unfounded popular notion of my having abandoned my husband from want of devotedness & entire sympathy ...'.

The dilemma was that since she had never discussed or given a reason for the separation, they could well believe one given them by people they liked, and who were Byron's friends. Ralph, their younger son who was brought up by his grandmother from the age of nine, wrote many years later: 'I never heard her [Lady Byron] say she had been injured by Lord Byron, or that the separation had been a willing act of hers or anyone else's. I grew up in the belief that it had been an event like illness, loss of fortune, exile, captivity, shipwreck or death, a catastrophe forced by some powerful though hidden cause.' There is no reason to suppose that Ada was given any other explanation. Even to Robertson, to whom Annabella revealed the whole truth of her marriage, she said that Augusta was only part of the cause for the separation, and at no time did she blame Byron, but was only sadly aware she 'could do him no good'. Yet had Byron not met Augusta, not known obsessive love or consuming guilt, at least she would have had a fair chance. She wrote in an unfinished narrative about 1854: 'I might have had duties, however steeped in sorrow, more congenial with my nature than those I was compelled to adopt. Then my life would not have been the concealment of a Truth, whilst my conduct was in harmony with it.' However she did not say this to Ada or Lovelace, or to others, and she tried to ignore the false assumptions which were made in error and published as the truth.

Ada's letters describing her deep affinity for Newstead revived many sensations for Annabella, who as she grew older was increasingly sensitive to criticism that she had been unforgiving. She was also susceptible to impotent resentment, that she herself had fuelled censure by her silence through the years, which many people had regarded as a vindication of Byron. She told Ada that: '... in early & indeed middle age I could resist emotions which now overpower me'. Convinced that her conduct had been in Byron's best interests she had always been able to ignore what was said. But now she felt vulnerable in respect of her grandchildren, and not so sure that she *ought* to have borne the burden of silence. Both Lovelace and Ada wrote back reassuringly, and Ada's letter was particularly perceptive:

> Nothing passed while I was there which could, directly or indirectly, bear the slightest relations to his *matrimonial* history, or to any of the *indefensible* points of his life. I am persuaded that there is nothing of the *Partisan* about Col. Wildman; and if *all* my father's friends had been of W's sort, it would have been well for him. But after schooldays they lost sight of each other. ...

The Lovelaces continued their tour of Yorkshire, and Ada seemed to enjoy every moment, making it the most successful holiday she could remember. She felt well, and found exploring mountainous country even in bad weather exciting and stimulating. Lovelace, who was always interested in buildings, left Ada with their friends Lord and Lady Zetland so that he could visit castles and cathedrals, and rejoined them on the third day of the Doncaster races. He told Annabella proudly that Ada had distinguished herself by her judgement of horses while they were being paraded before the race. He reported that he had had his pocket picked, that the servant John had lost eighteen shillings and that the maid had won 'something', but of Ada's racing bets he said nothing, only that: 'I fear this visit will force me to become a breeder of racers. I am threatened by an eager ardent avis, that *this* business is profitable.'

Annabella, very conscious that she herself now had no roots, was not surprised at Ada's reaction to Newstead Abbey. It was and is a beautiful place, with a mystic aura evoking sensations of another age, spirits at every turn, sadness and tragedy, yet enfolded in a solitary and peaceful enchantment. She conceived the idea of buying the estate and wrote to Ada with this proposition. It was considered carefully by Lovelace, who confessed that 'Nothing that I have seen has interested me half so much as Newstead', but even if the owners had been persuaded to sell at a special price to Byron's family, he considered the financial commitment too great and the idea had to be abandoned.

In talking over memories of her life with Byron to Robertson,

Annabella came to reflect more and more on the continued hatred towards her that Byron had revealed in his letters to Augusta. Had she not seen these letters, there was no way she would have known of his bitterness, nor even of his continuing love for Augusta, for to other people he spoke often of his wife and usually with regret for the continuation of the separation, the reason for which he always maintained his ignorance. Therefore when he made his several apparently sincere attempts at a reconciliation, it could well be that but for these letters she might have agreed to live with him again.

Augusta had found it quite possible to avoid seeing people when it suited her, as when Annabella was seeking a reconciliation over the trustee affair and when Medora had desperately tried to see her, by simply being 'not at home', so that she could just as easily have contrived a means of avoiding the revelation of all Byron's letters to her, and still accepted Annabella's highly valued friendship. Thus Augusta had showed Byron's love-letters to Annabella either because she regarded this as part and a sign of her redemption or because she knew they would cause distress and make a reconciliation impossible, which with her own reputation restored could only be advantageous to her. It may have afforded her as well an exquisite opportunity to relish giving Byron's wife and her own confessor the evidence of Byron's enduring bitterness, which contrasted so sharply with his warm and tender avowals of love for herself. To Annabella, who in spite of their differences still loved the woman she had called sister, and believed her nearly redeemed, this aspect of their correspondence did not occur.

Annabella told Robertson that she had come to believe: 'It is not possible, if I have read human nature rightly, for anyone to keep up such bitter resentment without believing in some cause for it ... He *must* have come, had he lived, to the belief that *from first to last* I had been his only truly devoted friend – it was not permitted!' Augusta had intimated, on the occasions when she had tried to obtain money from Annabella, that she had something of consequence to communicate. Perhaps, Annabella thought, kind references to her in letters had been omitted or distorted, perhaps she had even been maligned to him. This idea became obsessive, as did her longing to see Augusta again. If Augusta were to confide in her, and her suspicions were true, there could be tears of regret and forgiveness, and a state of peace would come to her and, she hoped, to Augusta, and even perhaps to Byron. The unforgiving ghost that had haunted her for so many years could at last be laid to rest. They might be friends again as they had once been, and she could be 'kind to Augusta' and keep the promise she had made and found impossible to fulfil.

She talked about it to Robertson and suggested that he accompany her, trusting implicitly in his power to heal intransigent wounds. After some delay, for both women were old and ill, a meeting was arranged for 8 April 1851. Augusta came by train, and alone, which engenders a sympathy possibly undeserved, since her daughter Emily with whom she lived could doubtlessly have accompanied her. As might have been foreseen the meeting was a disastrous failure. Annabella was almost incoherent with painful emotion, and indignant that Augusta seemed to regard it as a chat for old times sake, and an opportunity to give her side of the Medora episode with no apparent contrition. Perhaps Augusta hoped for Annabella's counsel and influence, on which she had leaned so gratefully in the old days, to guide her through the present state of hatred and estrangement between herself and her daughter Georgiana. When Annabella endeavoured to bring Augusta to the answers she wished so much to have, Augusta lightly pushed her questions aside by saying Hobhouse had even commented on her loyalty to Annabella, claiming that she had risked Byron's affection because of it, and the reunion was instantly doomed to fail. It was too much to expect of human nature that one last meeting could dissolve the mistrust and misery that each had endured for so many years because of their ill-fated relationship through Byron.

They both wrote afterwards and Augusta, who had not beforehand liked the idea of a third party, now wanted to see Robertson again, but Annabella, remembering Augusta's insidious guile, discouraged the proposal. She wrote an account of the meeting and the narrative ends: 'My calm conclusion is that the state of her mind was absolutely unimpressible by any representations of mine, which is some consolation for my own deficiencies or want of judgement in any respect, overcome as I was by feelings that have not yet been brought under perfect subjection.'

Aware by the signs on her face that death was beckoning Augusta, did Annabella feel pity and compassion, or bitterness and jealousy towards her? Did Augusta every consider how much suffering she had been the means of generating for Annabella, and when she repeated Hobhouse's remark was it in innocence or to exult? Whatever their real feelings were, the truth went with each to the grave.

A few months later Annabella received word that Augusta was dying. She wrote, called and offered assistance which was thankfully accepted. Then she asked Emily to whisper two words of affection not used for many years – *Dearest Augusta* – and was told that 'tears long dry had flowed again, and that those words were her greatest consolation'. Augusta tried to send her a message, but it could not be understood, and a few days later on 12 October 1851 Augusta was dead. Another link had gone, another message missed.

Twenty-six moneylenders presented their claims after Augusta's death. Both her parents had brought disgrace to her mother's family, and she must have early developed a sense of obligation and learned that it was judicious to make herself pleasant and conceal her errors. She had the ability to make people laugh with her inconsequential chatter, and had a kind and good-natured manner while never attempting to question the results of her actions – a kind of 'Moral Idiotcy' [sic] Annabella had called it. Annabella perhaps felt regret that she had left those pitiful requests for money unanswered, for remorse comes freely in the wake of death. But she had always regarded herself as a trustee of the money she had fortuitously inherited and spent it sparingly on herself and carefully on behalf of others, believing it was incumbent on her to use it wisely where there was injustice, oppression and no other source of hope. She had little sympathy with rank stupidity, constant wickedness and flagrant dishonesty. Giving money to Augusta was the equivalent of throwing it into a bottomless pit due to her total lack of financial judgement, the constant demands on her to keep her dissolute sons from disgrace, and the necessity of maintaining Georgiana and her children, as well as the possibility of blackmail.

When her friend 'M.G.' died in 1841 Annabella became a second mother to her four daughters all of whom, like his wife, had been terrorized by the evangelical zeal of Lord Gosford and his sister. Annabella's favourite was Olivia, who had long yearned to be a Catholic and join a convent. Annabella's humanitarian ideas on religion were viewed with mistrust by Lord Gosford and his sister, causing her to be ostracized from the family. Four years before Olivia at last became a postulant in 1850, Annabella had written:

Even in illness the thought of you is more happiness than pain to me
– the thought of a spirit which always seems to me to shed its light
through an alabaster vase – so softly, so tenderly, that the weak may
look upon it without pain, and the hardened find it has power to
melt –. Only one severe *personal* grief remains to me – the loss of
you.

In 1851, when she was a dying woman, Olivia told Annabella
that 'I could not help thinking this morning how happy it would
make me to see you a Catholic before I die!' Ada told Annabella: 'If
I had a little less brains I should & would be a good Catholic, &
cling to that certainty which I do long for ... but brains interfere
with blind faith'. Annabella perhaps knew this dilemma.

Olivia died on 28 March 1852. In her grief, Annabella reacted
bitterly against the Catholic religion and wrote to Olivia's sister
Millicent on 5 April:

There is another point of view, dearest Millicent, in which I look at
her death; & perhaps *you* will take the same view of it. It has
emancipated her from the tyrannical Church under which she
suffered such thraldom. ... *Lone* as you are, Millicent, in every *other*
respect. [All her sisters had now died] you must almost feel a
Stranger upon Earth. Believe there is one who feels for that
loneliness.

Her resentment was caused by believing that Olivia's life was
shortened by the austere regime, but it did not last. She had met
Cardinal Newman at the convent and told Caroline Bathurst: 'He
is no Hypocrite – but a man in whom the elements are discordantly
combined ...'.

If Annabella felt any qualms of conscience after Augusta's death
concerning her promise to Byron to be kind to her, there was soon
to be a cruel form of nemesis, the manner of which could not have
been foreseen during the previous happy years. The awful
disclosure relating to Ada's double life only gradually became
known. She had started getting into debt in 1847 or 1848 and by
1850 had become heavily involved in a gambling syndicate with
racing men of the lowest standing. Annabella was appealed to, and
had, as she believed, cleared all debts under a strict promise of
secrecy. Ada's health, never robust, was giving cause for concern
and further medical advice was sought.

On Derby Day, 21 May 1851, Ada lost £3,200 over and above

her other debts. Lovelace was distraught and apparently witless, for in June he rushed off with no warning to consult Annabella at Leamington, where she was undergoing treatment for her health and already very worried on account of her ill friend Miss Doyle, who indeed died the next day. He arrived unexpectedly at eleven o'clock at night and proceeded to unburden himself of all his anxieties including the disquiet now being felt over Ada's health. As Ada had suffered regularly from menstrual problems all through her life, the symptoms which would have been arresting in another woman, namely haemorrhages, perhaps did not seem as serious at that time of night as in fact they were. Annabella had always found that Ada's health fluctuated wildly: 'I wish Ada was less hopeful when better, & less depressed when worse – for there is reason to fear that her state will always be liable to these alternations' and therefore she tended to react calmly to all Ada's states, as when she had encouraged her not to abandon her scientific work which meant so much to her. Also Annabella may have thought Lovelace was using Ada to gain sympathy for himself, when he saw how annoyed she was by his extraordinary behaviour and lack of consideration. He always maintained afterwards that Lady Byron had not been greatly concerned about Ada's health, although what he expected her to do at that time of night is not clear. What Lady Byron wanted to do was to see Ada to find out exactly what had happened and how matters now stood and rectify things where possible, but Lovelace refused to allow it saying that Ada did not feel up to being questioned. This was probably true as, apart from her health problems, Ada had much more reason than Lovelace knew for not wishing to be interrogated.

Annabella was appalled and furious with Lovelace. She accused him of deserting Ada in circumstances of temptation and allowing her to be exposed to low and unprincipled associates. As an older and experienced man of the world he should have understood that genius was always 'a child', and that Ada had invariably been easily excited and overconfident of her powers. If only she had been advised to confide in her mother she could have had thousands of pounds where she had had hundreds. She wrote to Ada and her words, for once simply expressed, convey her grief and deep distress, for she knew with dread foreboding that her secure, happy world of trust, that she had valued so highly and which had been lovingly built up over the years had suddenly crumbled and could never return. In her worst hour, with so much at stake, she was honest with Ada. Many would have kept silent over her altered feelings for Lovelace, which might have been wiser, but it was not in her nature to dissemble or compromise, for she could only be, as Byron had said, 'Truth Itself':

Brighton
July 3rd 1851

I suffered so much from the proximity at Ockham under circumstances which prevented me going to E. Horsley that the question of future intercourse must be settled at once. I cannot endure such a position & should take means to prevent its recurrence.

As to any apprehension on your part of what might be too exciting in your present state of health, I trust that, – as you once told me I had never in your life uttered a word which wounded you, – you would be able to say so still, after we had met. Besides, you know that I always look *forward*, & with more hope than you do –

I must however own, with the greatest pain, that there is one difficulty in respect to our intercourse. Of this I must make you the Judge, because it concerns your nearest & dearest feelings – I cannot – will not – be on the same terms as before, with your husband. I had adopted him with all a Parent's affection, & he was fully aware of it, for on last Dec 10th he expressed his sense of it in words engraven on my memory. I do not quote them because it would now be ungenerous. Nothing will ever induce me to enter with you upon the subject of my altered feelings towards him – such as they are they are not likely to change – but they do not exclude the kindest wishes for his welfare –

As I pass thro' London tomorrow I shall send to your house for a reply. Whatever it may be – it will make no change in that which *has* undergone no change & never *will* – O Ada had you but known what a word from *you* could have done.

Yours
A.I. Noel Byron

But Ada was now beyond all human endeavour to be helped, medically or otherwise, and her mother's entreaty was ignored.

Apart from an occasional unsatisfactory meeting in Brighton, there followed a period of estrangement between the Lovelaces and Annabella lasting nearly a year. In March 1852 Annabella asked Lushington to visit Ada to clear all her debts. Although he understood he had done so it was later discovered that this was far from the case. He found her health had deteriorated seriously and visibly although hopeful medical reports were still being given in spite of the pain she was suffering. She wrote to her mother: 'I have a great desire to see you; & yet a *great dread*. I fear yr not being fully aware of the *extremely* delicate condition I am in ...'. The truth was that poor Ada was terrified that her mother, if she looked into the debts, was much too intelligent not to become aware of her secret scandalous life, and once aware, would wish to inaugurate her redemption, for which in Annabella's faith there was no sin too great. but Ada was not yet ready to repent.

By June mother and daughter were united and in August, at the Lovelaces' request, Annabella assumed control of their home at 6 Great Cumberland Place in London. The depth of the calamity now began to be apparent. Ada was being blackmailed. The servants were suspected of chicanery, and a woman called Wilson had been transferred from Babbage's employment to act as a kind of lady's-maid but was in fact a betting go-between. The Lovelace jewels were pawned and redeemed twice by Annabella, who was on oath not to tell Lovelace.

The quarrel between Lovelace and Annabella was never healed in spite of his entreaties. She blamed him bitterly when she knew he had given Ada a note authorizing her betting on the Derby Day of 1851, and for his own involvement in gambling which had not at first been disclosed. Lovelace refused to withdraw his hurtful accusation that Annabella had spoken 'slightingly' of Ada's illness at their meeting in Leamington, although he knew that cancer was not definitely diagnosed until her examination in July 1852, over a year later. He wrote to Annabella in August 1851 soon after the beginning of the estrangement:

My sorrow is increased by the absolute impossibility in which I am of understanding what it has been on my part that occasions your change of feeling, – or where my conduct, as regards yourself, ought to have been different in the events that have preceded this ... If there is any further explanation I can yet give and that you wish for, I will give it – but I do not feel that your condemnation of me without any definite cause being assigned is in accordance with justice.

But Annabella now regarded Lovelace in a completely different light from formerly and realized the signs had always been there, but she had, perhaps expediently, chosen not to see them. There was no attempt by him to take some of the blame for Ada's actions, and it could be seen now that he had always been dictatorial and mean. He had been harsh too, especially to his son Byron, frightening him with a squib in his face when he was a small boy scared of bangs, threatening him with blinkers 'from a nasty dirty horse' when his eyes strayed during lessons and punishing him for tearing his cape when he was thrown from his horse into a bush. When he taught the children after a tutor was sacked Ada wrote: '... I do not think W – has a particularly enlightened or skilled method of instruction; and besides that ... I don't think he is over patient ...'. At one point Annabella bluntly told them: 'I think both you and L – exact manners from Byron which it has not been possible for him to acquire at his early years & under the circumstances & if his attention be too much turned upon himself by reproach he will be shy & awkward for life.' Letters from the child to his father at the age of ten were criticized by him for being too informal. It is likely that this continual friction with Lovelace was what made Ada insist on her first and favourite child going to sea at the age of thirteen, in the hope that by being removed from his father's constant correction, Byron would become happier and more amenable to behaving in the manner expected of the Viscount Ockham, the title by which he was known.

Letters from Ada written in previous years to her mother indicate that Lovelace had been scarcely less patient with her than he was with his children. 'He is a good crow, (tho' he *does* try to murder his thrush now & then). The attempts on my life & limbs are very droll (in retrospect)' and a year or so later she wrote: 'The Corvus has at times behaved so *very* ill, before the P[earce]s ... you will be amazed to hear that he seems to have made all kinds of blundering awkward apologies to the P's (at Minehead) *after I was gone* ...'. It is apparent in this letter that Lovelace feared she would not return to him.

In 1845 Ada had revealed to Greig, Mrs Somerville's son, in whom she confided more than anyone else, that '... *my* existence is one continuous and unbroken series of small disappointments – & has long been so ... it is not *his* fault that to *me* he is *nothing* whatsoever ... He is a *son* to me ...', which in view of her declared indifference to children was ominous. In 1852 Ada wrote to her mother respecting Lovelace's prospects of becoming Lord of the Admiralty: 'I believe L– has the reputation of being *crotchetty* [sic] & *impracticable*, – & one who would not work well with others.'

Another matter that had been rankling with Ada over the years was money. She told Greig in 1848 that she had borrowed £500 because the small sum that had been settled on her – £300 per annum – was inadequate to meet the expenses arising from her position as Lord Lieutenant's wife, such as various contributions to worthy causes. For example Ada was remembered very gratefully many years later by a Welsh boy, whose great talent as a harpist was recognized by her, and through whose patronage money was raised to send him to the Royal Academy of Music. 'Very heavy expenses which are at this moment entailed on Lord L by his Buildings & by some other circumstances have made me feel that I should be wrong if I adopted your suggestion of applying to *him* (at present).' She did ask Lovelace for an increase of £200 per year, but he declined to 'bind' himself. Ada felt guilty about the debt of £500 and only told her mother that '*books* and *music* are THE two things which have made me *overflow* at times'.

Lovelace could spend vast sums of money on unnecessary building at Ashley Combe and East Horsley Towers but would not install a bathroom at either place to enable Ada to have the frequent hot baths recommended by her doctor for her health, and neither was it arranged for her to try a change of air in a warm country which might, her doctors thought, prove beneficial. Instead, most rooms were fireless and carpetless, and there was constant noise from the continual building which everyone was always being called upon to admire. Ada never complained, perhaps unwisely, and merely observed to Greig in 1848: '… I do *really acquit* him of all *intentional* wrong; & think that ignorance has been the cause of the discomfort & difficulties I have been allowed to experience …'. She knew that following her mother's death, which sometimes seemed imminent, Lovelace would get £7,000 per annum and she would still only have for her own use what he chose to give her. Many years later he was to oppose the marriage of their daughter Anne, because the inheritance through Lady Byron's will, instead of passing to the son of his second marriage, would go to her future husband and their sons. Ada also must have felt a little hurt that her father, with whom she felt a strong affinity, had not remembered her in his will, even by a message or a poem dedicated to her. Her nearest and dearest relations seemed to have acquired a lot of money, but she did not appear to be entitled to any of it. It does seem an extraordinary situation, and it is hardly surprising that Ada attempted to use her 'metaphysical genius' to remedy the state of her finances.

All these incidents, revealing that Lovelace was a difficult man to live with and to work with, could be regarded as the rough and tumble that many marriages go through and survive. What Annabella would never forgive Lovelace for was the typically thoughtless visit to Leamington which had provoked the quarrel, his astonishing irresponsibility and deceit over the betting, and the fact that he had been the means of preventing her seeing and helping her dying daughter for nearly a year. Ada had always been pliable and Annabella believed she could have been persuaded to see her mother if it had been put to her that in the circumstances she should do so, because, like her father, she had a strong but unconventional religious faith. Ada was much comforted by Annabella's presence, when her mother was at last admitted to the Lovelaces' house, and she also gained courage and consolation from the visits of the Revd Frederick Robertson who was already afflicted with the brain tumour which would kill him within a year.

Ada's suffering became intense, and there were many times when it was supposed death was near, but it was not until 21 September that she made her last and most painful confession to Lovelace concerning her relationship with John Crosse. The two families had known each other for years through his father Andrew Crosse owning an estate at Broomhill in Somerset, near Ashley Combe, and Ada had visited the Crosse household in November 1844. Since Crosse was one of the disreputable racing associates, he, like the others, was not given permission to visit Ada until she begged her doctor to intervene, and he then wrote to Lovelace as tactfully as possible:

> ... I know that for several years Lady Lovelace has had a great friendship for two or three gentleman – I allude especially to Mr Crosse and Mr Babbage ... I beg particularly to urge your Lordship not to heedlessly disturb Lady L. by depriving her of so much of Mr Crosse's society as she wishes or has strength to bear ... I think in her present deplorable state it would be both cruel and mischievous to debar her from what has been such a source of comfort & happiness. ...

It must have been a bitter blow to Lovelace's pride and his anger was apparent during and after Ada's hesitant confession to him. He went away for a short break and left a note dated 7 October 1852: 'During my absence of a few days from home it is my wish that

Lady Byron should be considered in every respect as the mistress of my home and family and to possess all the authority of Lady Lovelace and myself.'

While Lady Byron wrote to her intimate friend Emily Fitzhugh, and sat by Ada listening to her agonizing groans, mingling with 'the little Bullfinch singing carelessly his wonted airs' she must have wondered, as others have done at times of deep sorrow, how unimportant marks of ordinary life can continue and be noticed. There was no respite for Ada from torturing pain. When Lady Byron could see that death was near, she spoke gently to her daughter of God and peace and her words calmed Ada and brought tears to the eyes of the nurse and doctor. The biographer Doris Langley Moore, with amazing insight, states that 'she was well satisfied with her performance'. But her son-in-law whom she could not forgive was kinder: '... but for her I know not how I could have stood the aggravation of distress ...' he wrote to Charles Noel. Mary Lovelace, the future wife of Ada's son Ralph, wrote in the epilogue to Ethel Mayne's biography of Lady Byron: 'Ada, in the midst of her suffering, was most pitiable in her self-reproach and Lady Byron alone, with her steadfast faith in a merciful God and in a life to come, could bring light and hope into the death-chamber. She had the supreme comfort of being able to give comfort.'

Ada died on the evening of 27 November 1852, aged thirty-six, the same age as her father had been when he died. Her coffin was placed beside his in the vault of the village church of Hucknall Torkard as she had requested. In 1853 a memorial to her was erected by her mother in the churchyard at Kirkby Mallory on which are the words:

Inscribed by the express direction of
Ada Augusta Lovelace. Born Dec. 10th 1816 died Nov. 27th 1852.
To recall her memory
Erected by her mother A.I. Noel Byron. MDCCCLIII

The inevitable difficulties of clearing up Ada's muddled affairs with unscrupulous associates and suspect servants was made much worse by the animosity between Lady Byron and Lovelace. He beseeched her for forgiveness: – 'Do not treat lightly a request which is so important for the recovery of my peace of mind' – but finding she could not or would not soften her attitude towards him, he became embittered, writing of 'the tortures your daughter's misconduct had inflicted' on him and accusing Lady Byron to others of being hostile and severe and of wishing a fatal illness, presumably as a retribution, on her daughter.

Ada had told her mother she desired Wilson, the go-between, to be given £100 but Babbage, who had employed her previously, wrote to the solicitors saying this should be the first payment of an annuity to her. Greig managed to ensure that all Ada's letters to Crosse were burned, and he was required to sign to that effect, and that there were no copies. There was dispute over Ada's books, and evidence of much disreputable double-dealing, fraud and robbery. To what extent Babbage was implicated in Ada's disaster is unclear but what is certain is that she could not have got into that situation alone. The 'book' referred to in their letters, which appear to be in code, such as 'Don't forget the *new cover* you promised to bring for *the book*. The poor book is very shabby & wants one. There is a great deal I want to explain to you *which can't be by letter* ...' is still unexplained. One suspects Lady Byron discovered more than she was prepared to divulge. Among Ada's lists and fragments of letters she found a note dated September 1852: 'To my mother "Malgré Tout" PS: 17 – V8.' Verse 8 from Psalm 17 reads: 'Keep me as the apple of the eye, hide me under the shadow of thy wings.'

There was another bitter quarrel resulting from Ada's financial troubles. Anna Jameson revealed to Annabella following Ada's death that she had been approached by Ada for money in the past which she had lent, saying she had 'shielded the memory of Lady Lovelace from the Cruel World', and that she had been under an oath of secrecy. Annabella, at the lowest point of her life, was bitterly hurt and upset and never forgave Mrs Jameson. She felt that had Anna Jameson persuaded Ada to confide in her mother it was possible that much of the debâcle that followed could have been avoided. If she had failed in persuading her, a person of integrity would have alerted Annabella herself – with whom she had felt 'almost one being' – and if the promise was too sacred to break, for ever remained silent. The *Encyclopaedia Britannica* gives this information in Anna Jameson's entry: 'Her friendship with Lady Byron dates from about this time [1845] and lasted for some seven years; it was brought to an end apparently through Lady Byron's unreasonable temper, ... she went to Italy with her niece ... Geraldine Bate'. In fact, Lady Byron and Mrs Jameson met in

1834 and the niece was called Gerardine (she married Robert Macpherson). Disregarding these errors it is typical of the self-perpetuation of biographies as well of reference books that, although no reason is given, or probably known for the quarrel, there is no hesitation in blaming Lady Byron.

Annabella was not the only one to suffer from Anna Jameson's duplicity. Robertson wrote in his diary that in a conversation in the past with Anna Jameson she had asked his opinion on the theology of virgin worship 'which I gave to her, and which I perfectly remember seemed new to her'. Three years later her book *Legends of the Madonna* was published with no acknowledgement to Robertson and the *Edinburgh Review* gave her much credit for her originality of thought. 'It would be awkward' Robertson wrote after he had read the publication 'if I were inclined to publish these sermons, for it would be hard to prove that plagiarism was not on my part, and it would seem ungenerous to charge it upon her'.

Lady Byron wrote to Lovelace on 4 January 1853: 'To you, Lovelace, I have been the most faithful of friends, & at no time more actively & self-sacrificingly than in the last year & a half' and he replied on 6 January:

> And yet with all your severity and coldness, which drives me into these indignant remonstrances with you, the last page of your letter is too true for me not to re-echo and confirm it. You have been too noble and generous (in some things), self-denying in all, for me not to bear ready testimony to it. In most fine qualities you have not your equal on earth, and my love for you is as ardent as ever, however you may repel it. ...

Mary Lovelace, his daughter-in-law, wrote many years later: 'She had lost a son, and he had lost the best and most inspiring influence of his life.' It is customary to blame only Lady Byron for being unforgiving in this quarrel but it must be remembered that before his marriage to Ada he had not got on with his mother or brother, and for years after Lady Byron's death there was hostility in the Lovelace family in spite of the efforts of his second wife and his daughter to improve matters, for instance in a letter from Lovelace's wife to his daughter Annabella dated 22 May 1875:

> 9 St George's Place, S.W.
> Dear Annabella,
>   I was dreadfully troubled & distressed when I heard the result of

W's [Annabella's husband Wilfrid Scawen Blunt] visit the other day ... Lord L. came in at 7.30 he was late, tired, & a little worried with other matters – he was not as patient as he might & I really think would have been at another moment – we all know how much sometimes hinges on a favourable moment. – Constant estrangement is very sad & therefore I hope you will try to do all you can to aid me in trying to end it.

It is likely that it was through Annabella's support that there had been harmony in the days of the Thrush, the Hen and the Crow. In a letter to Robert Noel, Hester King, Lovelace's sister, wrote of Lady Byron: '... her influence has upon them [the Lovelaces] as well as everybody she is much with, a most beneficial influence ...'. Two of those to whom she had been closest were devastated when Annabella ceased to be their friend, which seems to indicate that she had exceptional steadying qualities not commonly acknowledged. For from the time of the quarrel with Lady Byron, Anna Jameson never knew good health or happiness again. Of this her biographer and niece, Gerardine MacPherson, wrote: 'I have too good reason to know that the wound was one from which Mrs Jameson never recovered.' She was unable to concentrate or write with her former vitality, and was enfeebled in body. She destroyed all her letters from Lady Byron for she could not bear to be reminded of her, all that is except for two written early in 1854 which reflect Annabella's unswerving commitment to her pole star of truth:

Would you have me say I think these right when I do not? – would you have me concur in them when put into practice by you? Would such a course be more faithful to friendship than the Truth?

and shortly after this the second letter:

You say 'I never believed your feelings alienated from me, TILL you told me they were'.

Now, on the contrary, in the close of the year 1852, when my whole being was so absorbed that I could not have borne any added excitement or agitation, & whilst you were accusing me of being false to friendship, I maintained that I was 'as ever your friend' ...

The year following, in Dover St, you drove me, by your persevering attacks to say something about 'alienation' – but if you would look to *facts*, my subsequent intercourse with you, my visits in your society, would shew how far that *word* was from being verified.

'Yours has been a bitter connection to me in every sense' wrote Byron to his wife in 1821, the year before he inherited a considerable fortune from her mother's death. Perhaps she remembered in the following years the irony of his words, for apart from the curious quarrel with Edward Noel, the instances of being hurt and injured by the disloyalty of people she had loved and befriended came about in one way or another through her connection with Byron. In 1857 she wrote to Mrs Mair, the daughter of Mrs Henry Siddons:

> It seems to me as if I were only of some value to those who have no personal connection with me. I accept gratefully the lot of serving *strangers*, and it really comes upon me as a surprise when I myself am the object of deep interest – so many ties have been broken that I say 'what next?' … I am not often so communicative.

Mrs Mair had visited Seaham when a child with her mother in 1818 when Annabella was staying there after her visit to Newstead. Many years later she recalled:

> She was in great grief and suffering, and she has often told me that the interest she felt for me – the occupation of teaching, playing with, and loving me – brought her more cheerfulness and comfort than anything could have done. – She has been thought cold by those who do not know her, but I often think of those soft almond-shaped blue eyes, which never looked on me but tenderly, and wish that she could have been known more truly as she was, and less as a somewhat reserved, shy manner caused her to appear.

One person who always highly valued Annabella's friendship was the Revd Frederick Robertson, especially during the last years of his life when he was almost worn out with strain and torturing pain. It felt 'as if an eagle was rending there with its talons' in the back of his head and neck, caused by the tumour in his brain. Although his mental powers were in decline, he was still able to give some of the most striking sermons he ever preached. His visits to Annabella in Esher brought him peace and comfort for he had many trials in the parish, made worse by difficulties with a senior churchman in Brighton. 'I write in torture …' were the last words he wrote. He died on 15 August 1853 aged thirty-seven. It was said of him by a fellow pastor: 'He was the truest, purest, and most gifted man I have ever seen.' This kind of acclaim was made many times by all classes of people who heard him, including Henry Crabb Robinson who was always impressed by his profound wisdom, writing in his diary that Robertson had the brain of a lawyer and could unravel the most complex problems.

Rarely, if ever, has Brighton seen such a moving funeral procession as that which followed the body of Robertson. All shops from Montpelier Road on one side of the town to the Extramural Cemetery on the other were closed. The principal townsmen assumed mourning and pavements and balconies were crowded with hundreds of grieving spectators. Lady Byron left her sick-bed to follow in the procession on foot. She was not worthy, she said, even to walk behind the hearse. A large impressive monument marks his grave, on which the inscription includes 'Honoured as a minister, Beloved as a man, He awakened the holiest feelings in poor and rich, in ignorant and learned'. On another side is the inscription by the working men of Brighton: 'In grateful remembrance of his sympathy and in deep sorrow for their loss the members of the Mechanics' Institution and the working men of Brighton have placed this medallion on their benefactor's tomb'. People of all ranks and classes from the working-class, tradesmen and the rank and wealth of Brighton mixed with the representatives of every denomination and sect including Jews, Unitarians, Quakers and Roman Catholics to gather together round the tomb, merging their differences in one deep feeling of love and sorrow. It was a touching and unaffected tribute to the reality of his work. Seventy odd years later, on the centenary celebration marking the consecration of Holy Trinity Church, the Archbishop of Canterbury wrote of Robertson:

> His story is unique. It is absolutely without precedent that a man who held no conspicuous public office, who bore no part in public affairs, who was in no sense a leader of any party in the church or state, and who died at the age of thirty-seven, should some seventy years after his death, be commemorated on this scale, solely because of the sermons and addresses he delivered in his own chapel in Brighton during six short years of pastoral ministry.

Robertson's widow wrote to Annabella expressing her debt of deep gratitude and affection which would take a lifetime to repay for the 'gentle kindness' and efforts to guard his memory 'with a sensitive delicacy peculiarly your own'. His mother also wrote to 'My dear dear Lady Byron' telling of the deep gratitude she felt for all that Annabella had done. She 'soothed his worn heart by your calm judgement … and jealously guarded his dear memory from a shadow of reproach' – for there were those who were ready to condemn his outspoken, restless, speculative spirit, and were envious of his fame.

Lovelace became resentful over Annabella's unrelenting withdrawal from his company. True forgiveness however does not lie in the will but in the heart, and she had now no allegiance and no respect for him, so that renewal of their relationship could only have been a travesty of their former mutual trust and affectionate esteem.

The last two years had been like a horrendous nightmare from which she would never wake. She had lost in death her daughter and three people to whom she had been deeply attached, and in conflict Anna Jameson and Lovelace, whom she had believed were her greatest friends. Apart from her grandchildren, everything that had meant most to her, that had given meaning to her life, had been destroyed.

Lady Byron wrote to her grandchild Annabella King on 19 February 1853, three months after Ada's death:

> If I mistake not this is your Father's Birthday, & I think I cannot do anything more appropriate to it than to tell you what I should have wished to show you (had it been in my power) in your Mama's handwriting, her injunction to you to 'make your Father your first object'. I am sure your own feelings would suggest that course, – at the same time the knowledge of your fulfilling a duty to *both* Parents at once, cannot but afford you satisfaction – for in that letter of hers addressed to me, there are also wishes concerning you & myself which I do not think it necessary to mention at present.

(These were that she should be sole female protector and responsible for Annabella's upbringing.)

By contrast Lovelace's bitterness grew with the passing years until his malice was vented on Lady Byron after her death by the infamous public disclosure of some very private and personal letters, for the purpose of destroying her reputation, although he knew the interpretation ascribed to them was false. His victory was complete for on her death he succeeded to the Wentworth estates and fortune which he enjoyed for thirty-three years.

18   The Noels

After her father's death in 1825, although there was no obligation to do so, Annabella assumed responsibility for educating and settling 'these children of mine' as she called the four Noel brothers, which was to demand much of her time, money and attention and be the cause of worry and pain. They were the sons of the Reverend Thomas Noel who, as Byron expressed it, 'had his father observed the rights of the Church' would have inherited the Wentworth title and estates from his father the 2nd Viscount Wentworth instead of Judith and her daughter. As it was, Thomas and his sister Anna Catherine were illegitimate.

Some biographers say that Judith had deliberately discouraged her brother from marrying his mistress Catherine Vanloo who had borne his children, but it was far more likely that he could not marry her because she was a Roman Catholic – a greater obstacle to marriage with a peer at that time than lack of rank or pressure from relations. It was also said that Judith prevented her brother from marrying Lady Anne Lindsay after Catherine Vanloo's death in September 1781, but in a letter to Judith on 25 May 1782 Lord Wentworth made it clear that it was Lady Anne Lindsay who was less than enthusiastic about marrying him because she had not forgiven him for his former preference for Vanloo: '... it would now not be *my* fault if I did not make her your Sister ...'. In 1788 he married Lady Mary Ligonier, and Judith wrote to her aunt: 'You & I have so longed wished to see him a *Married Man*, & so long almost *dispaired* [sic] of its ever happening, that the unexpectedness of the event adds to the pleasure of it.'

When Catherine Vanloo died, Lord Wentworth wrote to his aunt Mary Noel, who had brought up himself and his three sisters:

'My chief anxiety is about the poor children … it never was or is my intention to do for them in such a manner as more legal heirs to my estate … can grumble at. The boy I shall educate well, & inculcate into him that his future livelihood must depend on some profession he may chuse [sic].' Anna Catherine was adopted by Mary Noel and married Vincent Hilton Biscoe in 1790. Thomas was educated at Rugby and Christchurch, Oxford, took holy orders and was generally considered at this time good-looking with a pleasant personality.

To provide for his children Lord Wentworth stipulated in his will that his Gloucestershire estates were to be sold for payment of his debts and the legacies, but in 1815, when the Byrons, Milbankes and many others were suffering financially the value of land had slumped so steeply that the trustees were reluctant to sell. Thomas Noel and his sister sued the trustees and later Ralph and Judith, and this suit dragged on from 1816 until after Judith's death in 1822. Lord Wentworth had presented Thomas with the livings of Elmsthorpe and Kirkby, but Thomas employed a curate, and in order to secure the living for one of his sons if required, he applied to Byron in 1822 thinking Annabella likely to be unsympathetic to him in view of the legal action he had taken, but she willingly agreed to the request. He had met Byron as he had asked Annabella if he could officiate at her marriage, to which she assented, although the vicar of Seaham, Richard Wallace, was present and witness to the ceremony. Thomas Noel was charmed with Byron, who had taken a ring from his finger and given it to Thomas as a souvenir of the occasion, but his daughter wrote to a friend that 'Papa expects something more *substantial* for the service he has rendered Lord Byron'. The Noels were to prove difficult to please.

The Revd Thomas Noel had become very bitter with his lot in life and regularly through the years pursued Annabella and others for money. He wrote to her from Calais on 15 March 1828:

Madam,
    You are no doubt aware that I for some years since, by a suit in the Court of Exchequer recovered a farm in Kirkby Mallory (the property of a person named Lee) the titles of that farm together with the arrears & the costs of suit. That investigation at the same time as it awarded me the property I demanded proved to me that I had a similar claim upon the Kirkby estate. I was in some degree aware of

this during the life time of my Father, but as the living was his gift I refrained from insisting on my dues. The case being now different, I think it right to inform you of my claims. In the Spring of 1824, I wrote to your solicitors Wharton & Ford upon the subject whether they informed you or not of my application I am ignorant. ... However I feel confident that I am making an appeal to your justice & wisdom & that you could not in conjunction with the sentiments of religion you profess wish or attempt to retain what is strictly & legally mine. Awaiting your speedy answer as my solicitor has else immediate orders to proceed ...'

(Following this letter in the Lovelace papers is a pamphlet giving particulars for application of free passages to Sydney NSW.)

The next year in a letter dated 21 October 1829 to the Revd Thomas Noel's eldest son, also called Thomas, Annabella informed him that his father was to be released in Calais:

If he knew how very glad I feel to think of his liberation, his malice towards me would surely be softened! It *is* not – for his last letter to Mr Wharton contained such an insinuation against me as determined me to return it to him – I have entrusted the £200 to Mr Pilcher, who was going to Calais, and will transact the business in a kind and considerate manner.

However, far from his malice being softened, in 1834 Noel wrote to Hobhouse from Calais, reminding him of their previous acquaintance at Byron's wedding and begging for 'a trifle' to assist his wife and daughter to join him 'as I am banished here by my first cousin the present Lady Byron'.

By 1846 his bitterness and rancour seemed to have become pathological:

5 Belle Vue Place, Plymouth
Feb 10th 1846

Madam

A stranger has afforded me the assistance of the loan of £60 which your silence or contempt on my application denied me, & which from the *Consanguity betwixt us* and your ample means derived from my late Father you could so readily afford to his *Publickly acknowledged* son. Much of his property you are now enjoying had he not been so suddenly seized with paralysis he meant to leave to me & my sister, as *He stated* to me previous to his leaving Kirkby for London for the purpose of altering his will.

Thomas Noel

He had married Catherine Smith in 1796 whom Judith described as 'a poor timid low-spirited creature', and they had six children, one dying in infancy. The last was Sophia who married and had two children, the remaining four were the sons, Thomas, Robert, Charles and Edward.

On 21 May 1825 Annabella wrote to Robert: 'Deprived as you know I am of the power to assist your mother, I have had some comfort in thinking of an experiment which may still enable me to be a friend to her younger children – but this must depend upon your willingness to accept the office of their Trustee ...'.

Thomas was born in 1799 and had always been difficult due to his 'nerves', his bad temper, his choice of unsuitable company when young and his poetical sensitive temperament. He also seemed not to like work: 'If by my own exertions I could supply you with *work*, I believe I should labour indefatigably all day long' Annabella told him.

However she was kind and sympathetic to Thomas, providing in 1830 an allowance of £500 per annum which allowed him to marry Emily Halliday. Annabella encouraged him by transcribing his poems and offering very gently an occasional suggestion: '... I am flattered by your sending & happy to think that I am even slightly serviceable to you, "macte tuâ vistule" – which means, being interpreted, go on with your sonnets' she wrote in 1836. To his poem 'On the view of Hanwell Lunatic Asylum' she put forward a tentative change, ending: 'I can find no further fault. It is a very good one.' After transcribing another poem 'To the follower of Church authority', she went on: 'I know not that I have anything adapted to be set to music. If there is anything I have ever sent you which you think would do – pray give it to the setter. Would this little thing I made last night do?'

The Invalid's Invocation to Spring

O come, and on my sick-room smile
sweet spring, once more:–
I've look'd for thee a weary while

With longing sore:–
O spread upon the balmy gale
　　Thy healing wing,
And softly fan this cheek so pale,
　　Spring, sweet Spring!

I've watched the blue breaks in the sky,
　　And thought at last,
That thou in sunny robes wert nigh,
　　but soon they pass'd –
Cold grew my heart and at its core
　　Hope ceas'd to cling; –
O come and warm that heart once more,
　　Spring, sweet Spring!

I long to see the earth again
　　Look gay & glad,
And those who wear diseases' chain
　　Less wan & sad. –
Where yonder sable yew tree waves,
　　Thy sun-light fling –
O brighten that cold field of graves
　　Spring, sweet Spring!

She continued: 'Milton good reading – will return it soon & look out for a song. Lovely morning this – 22nd April. May it do you good. If you can improve the above invocation pray do. Alter epithets or whatever else you like.' She genuinely admired his poetry, which she likened to that of William Cowper. A slim book of his poems was published in 1841 under the title 'Rhymes and Roundelays', the best known being 'The Pauper's Drive' of which the first and last verses are given below:

> *There's a grim one horse hearse in a jolly round trot;*
> *To the churchyard a Pauper is going, I wot;*
> *The road it is rough, and the hearse has no springs,*
> *And hark to the dirge that the sad driver sings: –*
> *'Rattle his bones over the stones:*
> *He's only a Pauper, whom nobody owns!'*
>
> *But a truce to this strain, – for my soul it is sad,*
> *To think that a heart in humanity clad,*
> *Should make, like the brutes, such a desolate end*

And depart from the light without leaving a friend!
Bear softly his bones over the stones;
Though a Pauper, he's one whom his Maker *yet owns!*

Thomas lived at Boyne Cottage in Maidenhead, tended his garden and wrote poetry. His happiness, he said, was contemplating on a large scale the boundless beauties and wonders of Creation, but his radical beliefs pained him and he was hypersensitive. He thought workhouses were an abomination by separating man and wife and that 'the facts mentioned by Lord Brougham in his speech on the slave trade made one blush to be a man and almost doubt a providence who permits we creatures to be guilty of such execrable (no word is sufficiently strong) cruelties towards one another'. He became secretary of the local book club and seemed less than pleased with Lady Byron's gifts to the management committee:

The second parcel of books came safe last week, the greater part of which I can offer at the next meeting, but Dr Channing's works wd not be accepted, if I know anything of sectarian nature. Besides the book is all to pieces & contains your marginal comments. I cd have Napoleon & Milton taken out & bound up, & these wd be acceptable but his Unitarian arguments wd not relish with our orthodox members – there's no Unitarianism in Maidenhead that I ever heard of – The two vols of '*Lives of Eminent Missionaries*' have Miss Montgomery's name in them. Perhaps they have been sent by mistake – Some odd volumes of '*The Fainly Library*' have been sent, but the Society has lately bought the whole, so these I shall keep back. I will let you know what I have retained & you may tell me what to do with them.

Annabella was off her guard in one letter to him for he replied: 'there is a passage in your letter received today 'Poor Charles has three to one against his side of the argument in his own family'. The epithet 'poor' would appear to express pity as if he had not fair play among us three'. He continues about Charles liking farming and planting and not gardening, adding he knows that he is 'a non-earner of the staff of life'. Evidently intercourse was maintained with Annabella for his wife Emily wrote sadly to her from Brighton:

2 Clifton Road, Brighton
Jan 11th 1859

My dear Lady Byron
My darling boy breathed his last 10 o'clock this morning.
He is in good and merciful hands – we should not weep for
him. –
I thank you for your last kind acts towards him – and trusting you
are pretty well – believe me always
Yours gratefully
Emily Noel

The second son Robert was born in 1803 and has left a pleasing
account of playing billiards with Annabella at Kirkby not long after
the separation: 'She so frequently smiled and indulged in little jests
when Ada and I amused ourselves that if she was sad at heart that
state of mind was not apparent to me. The impressions stamped on
my mind were of soft kind manners, and a playful cheerfulness.'
He joined the Leicester Militia in 1821 reaching the rank of major
with the reputation of being a particularly efficient officer. He then
became interested in medicine and registered as a medical student
in Edinburgh, where he was introduced by Annabella to her friend
Mrs Henry Siddons, whom he grew to love and respect.
However he decided to abandon medicine, which he later
regretted, to enter the church. Annabella supported Robert with
sympathy and a 'handsome' allowance for the extra tuition
necessary to study theology at Cambridge. She wrote from
Hastings on 23 March 1826: 'I hope you will never again hesitate
to ask me any question relative to your interests, which I feel very
anxious to promote by any means in my power ...'. His education
he said had been 'sadly defective' and he went back to Edinburgh
to be coached in mathematics and the classics, under the
protection of Mrs Siddons. He then joined Annabella in Milan in
1826 and travelled with her to Genoa where she was to spend the
winter. He recorded in *A Fragment of Autobiography*: 'I passed about
three months with her, she assisting me every day with my
mathematics and Latin exercises. I went through the first five
books of Euclid again with her and we read the whole of Virgil's
Aeneid together ... Through Lady Byron's introduction I made
several interesting and pleasant acquaintances in Genoa belonging
to the aristocratic and cultured classes ...'.
After his entry to Cambridge the following year he was to

discover that he could not accept the thirty-nine articles of religion and therefore had to relinquish his clerical vocation. Probably because he was introduced to George Coombe, the founder of the Phrenological Society and a friend of the Siddons family, he became interested in phrenology. He took plaster casts of the heads of many different kinds of people, such as mechanics, writers, imbeciles, criminals, and those of the professional classes so that a comparison could be made of their skulls which would add practical experience to the study of behaviour patterns. He became president of the Dresden Phrenology Society, and among other works wrote a history of phrenology in German. He lived in Austria and Bavaria for many years, mixing with interesting and celebrated people. One of these was Anna Jameson, the writer and art critic, whose books he much admired, and a warm friendship developed between them.

In 1838 he married Louisa von Hennigen, a German girl of aristocratic parentage who was much loved by all the family, including Lady Byron. During their honeymoon at Wiesbaden Annabella joined their party and described an amusing episode to Ada:

> A droll incident has occurred at the Table d'Hôte, where I was with the rest of the party. Next to me sat an English Miss, and opposite to her a young man, of the demi-gentleman cast. He observed that Lady Byron had arrived here yesterday. She replied 'Oh, what I would give to see her!' 'You would be very much disappointed if you did' said he 'she is very short, of a swarthy complexion and looks as if she would never smile.' He went on to say that he had seen me five years ago with you, and then you came in for your share – as being 'very fond of accounts. What a thing for a Poet's daughter!' Still my fair neighbour persisted in wishing to see me & asked where she could meet with me – 'Oh, you will be sure to see her at Church, she is very *pious*!' I thought it honourable to hear as little of the conversation as possible, but it was loud enough to compel me to do so ... Do you remember that Forester, in Miss Edgeworth's story *made believe* to die, in order to hear what would be said of him? He had better gone to the Table d'Hôte! Dr Wilson had told R Noel before that he heard great curiosity expressed on the day of my arrival, to see me. I thought this gone by; but as it is not, I shall get some rouge and a brown wig & make myself captivating. I ought to get stilts, too, it seems. ...

The years went by and it is clear from the letter Robert wrote to her on 8 February 1847, that Annabella had kindled in him a deep sense of friendship:

I feel such a strong desire to have a little chat with you – my now – remaining earliest & best friend – that I cannot resist it. Perhaps I am doing wrong to take up your time, even for a quarter of an hour, but if you knew how often I converse with you in thought, how often my mind reverts to the days that are passed, & with what feelings I review the proofs of untiring kindness you have shown me, and perceive how much I owe to you with encouragement & example you would understand at least that I often find it a hard matter to resist the longing to commune fully with one, with whom so much that works within me is appreciated.

In the following eight pages he discusses many subjects including death, the fear of being an invalid and his hopes: '... however, that with such poor health as I possess I must live for 200 years to come to accomplish all I wish. I must be satisfied to add my mite to the cause of truth ...'.

Annabella was devoted to Robert and particularly Louisa. On 8 August 1854 she wrote to her from Southampton:

I wish you to have the pleasure of telling Robert of what concerns the interests of himself & his family ... I find I may contribute more than I had hoped towards the comfort of those whose marriages could scarcely have taken place without my aid – and I feel therefore that under any contingencies, I should prevent the later years of those marriages from being *less* well provided. ...

Apart from short visits it was not until 1863 that Robert and Louisa became resident in England at 10 Neville Street, London where Robert died in 1883. He bequeathed his head casts to Ralph Lovelace who had become Lord Wentworth, and they stayed at Wentworth House in Chelsea until they were given to the Francis Galton Eugenics Laboratory. They are now housed at the Slade School of Art in London University and it is hoped they will eventually be exhibited with Robert Noel's original notes.

In October 1831 Lady Byron wrote to Charles Noel, the third son, born in 1805: 'I hope you like the prospect which I told Robert to disclose to you of being the resident agent at Kirkby. You would have £100 per annum with lodging ...'.

Arrangements were made for Charles to undertake management of all the affairs of the estate with the help of Mr Harding, already employed as an overseer. Charles was to be given a much wider role and Lady Byron told him that his convenience was the 'only

point in choice of habitation'. The relationship between them was a
happy one, and in her letters to him she expressed herself more
naturally than in her often 'strangulated' style. Her chief concern
being education, a Captain Bromley had planned a school for her
to set up and in a letter to him dated 30 October 1830 she wrote
that she had decided that the building proposed was too large and
suggested only half to be built with a temporary division to separate
the boys from the girls and if the school increased the other half
could be added. She thought there should be two rooms over the
schoolroom, which could be used as sickrooms as Florence
Nightingale had advised her, a kitchen and a small washhouse. She
wished the children to be taught, baking, cooking and washing to
prepare them for domestic service.

The following extracts from some of her letters to Charles
written over the next few years, many of which are undated,
indicate that she was caring and compassionate over affairs of the
estate, as well as being a good organizer. She stated her views and
suggestions clearly giving her reasons and she never dictated to
him but asked him 'tell me what you think best'. She also included
bits of news from time to time about his brothers and his sister
Sophia, intimating that she maintained a friendly interest in them
all:

December 23rd [probably 1831]
This only to inform you that I sent a parcel yesterday by Pickford's
van ... flannel jackets for the Poor and some spelling papers to be
pasted on boards for the children. Robert sends his love. I wish I
could get Capt Bromley's writing apparatus. ...

... Bricklayers and carpenters to be paid monthly as you suggest ...
Best plan for teaching she thinks is to select two or three of the most
promising boys, and to prepare them for teaching the others. Young
Thomas [Miss Montgomery's nephew] may be useful to you. She is
also anxious that you should perfect yourself in land surveying or
measuring and will send you any books and instruments you want, if
you will let her know what they are. [Written for Annabella by her
friend Mary Montgomery.]

I have been thinking more about the Co-operative Society at Kirkby
and would not discourage the wish entertained by the labourers –
only there is one condition I would make – that is – to give *another*
name to the association because of the mistakes or mischievous

designs of many who call themselves co-operators, therefore prejudice is immediately excited ... I think it more prudent to say nothing but call the Society by some plain English name like 'Work-owners Benefit Society'. ...

The demoralized state of Kirkby of which you complain is unhappily irremedial till the minister there should attend his duties in a spirit more consistent with the principles of Christianity. I should wish to see the plans of cottages and the estimates before they are commenced. I have got a 'Farmer's Journal' book for you here and some other agricultural works. Young Thompson is learning surveying and may be able to teach you.

Tell Shilton people their claim shall be looked into immediately – consult Mr Miles of Leicester by letter or in person. I think the charge for the schooling of Peckleton families should be paid up by me to this time and henceforward a certain sum should be paid by the Parents according to their circumstances.

I will subscribe to the Female Club at Shilton. I do not like the idea of lessening Pegg's means of subsistence now that he is old and infirm ...

In one letter she told Charles that if he catalogued the books then he had to make a charge to her for this extra work:

'I will write to you today dear Charles, not because I have any business to communicate but because you say you are low, and you may therefore like a little *friendly chat* ...'. She goes on to tell him about Dr King's writings '... which appear to me to be the best exposition of Christianity ever yet presented ...'. She outlines one of Dr King's principles to him and ends up by telling him 'in confidence' that a young man follows Ada around.

'On full consideration of the advantage which I derive from the faithful and friendly manner in which you fulfil the duties of the agencies, I feel it not less [word illegible] to you than agreeable for me to add fifty pounds p.a.'

On 24 March 1837 she wrote to him that she knew a woman who might suit him as a mistress for the school but she had to bring her four small children. Would this be a burden? – adding 'she has the requisite capabilities'.

I am happy that you see your way about the Shilton Poor, and you may be assured the funds shall not be wanting to render the experiment effectual and permanent. I would give up half my own dinner rather than fail to help my fellow Creatures at this crisis. Pray express my sentiments strongly on this point at the meeting as it may stimulate others.

Yours Ever
A.I. Noel Byron

The great thing is not to delay as the people are starving.

I find on enquiry that *one kind* of Draining only, comes under the class of permanent improvement which are chargeable on the Estates – I believe Surface Draining is NOT.

I saw poor Edward one day looking much worn. The child was lost, I believe, through ignorance.

Dear Charles – I have been reflecting on the evils of the Public House at Kirkby and wish to know what you think of a plan I have for preventing them – it is – *to be the Public-house keeper myself* not to let it but to place a person at the head of it whom I would pay a fixed salary so that he could have no interest in encouraging drunkenness and might be dismissed for any misconduct like others receiving a salary. 'I suppose the licence might be taken out in your name ...

In another letter Charles is advised 'there is a possible mistress for the school' – this time with five children. Many and varied were the young sent to Charles for instruction in land management and general help when they found difficulty in settling. Ada's son Byron was one, and it was Charles that Lord Lovelace asked to find Byron when he disappeared following the death of his mother in 1852.

Through the years Charles continued to be a tower of strength and a staunch friend to Annabella. Many and diverse were the matters to be considered so that they were always in constant correspondence. The cutting down and planting of trees; the affair of Lady de Clifford, the tenant of Kirkby Mallory Hall and the rabbits which were rampant and damaging, even in the kitchen; would Lady Byron provide a pew for a Miss Scudamore?; the children at school had improved but it was now barely large enough; bibles had been bought; an allowance of £115 had been made to Mr Hancock as he was in trouble and his was the worst farm; Sophie was expected with Lionel and the children and would stay for some time; Sophie was not coming but was going to Bath instead. There were vexations and the problem over the rabbits was serious: '... but in consequence of the impertinent language of Lady de Clifford's gamekeeper I must beg of you to take notice of the man's conduct before the proper authority ...' Charles informed Annabella. However the issue was eventually resolved after Annabella's conciliation and 'Ldy de Clifford expressed much regret for the damage done' by the rabbits and was thoroughly reconciled with Charles, Annabella reported to Ada.

Edward, the youngest son of the Revd Thomas Noel, was born in 1806. He was charming and an idealist, but disinclined to work and very sensitive about his social status. He had enjoyed Hofwyl where he had stayed five years when he and his brother Charles were sent there by Annabella for their education, and it had the effect of giving him vague but noble ideas, which Annabella fostered by helping to establish him on the Greek island of Euboea in 1831. In 1836 she told Ada in a letter that: 'at one time the family considered me to have ruined both his health and fortune by having promoted his "Wild Scheme",' for Edward was often ill from malaria and dysentery. He and Frederick Fellenberg, son of the director of Hofwyl, who accompanied him, hoped to put into practice the principles learned at Hofwyl, helped by the encouragement given from the Greek scheme to foster foreign interest in developing the land.

In 1837, while on a visit from Euboea, Edward fell in love with Fanny Smith who was staying with Annabella at Fordhook. Their courtship was not without problems and it was to Annabella that Fanny turned for counsel:

My dearest Fanny – In addition to what I suggested for your comfort in a conversation at Fordhook, let me add one more reason to make you thankful that you are thus united to one for whom you would think no sacrifice too great – Nothing can be more injurious to a man than ungratified love – it wastes and destroys the constitution. I look to future days of tranquil enjoyment to [word illegible] our dear Edward – your *smiles* will be his best medicine – but I know you cannot call them forth at will, and I wish to give you cause for them, in making you feel that you are to be the instrument of good to him as I am convinced that he will be to you – yes after *that* moon, so foolishly called Honeymoon, your happiness will only increase –

I think Saline Draughts of 200gms. Potash & Soda mixed in a dessert spoonful of lemon might help you to sleep, if you are feverish – I will enclose two papers of Potash & Soda, for that purpose – you may bestow the other one on Neddy with some Heat? – Do not let yourself feel cold. A fire would lessen your nervousness. I shall hope to get to you tomorrow but Ada may not be able to see me – At any rate let me find food if I present myself at one –

Your ever attached
AINB

7 o'clock St James – very tired after my Party.

I have not added to my letter to your aunt [Miss Doyle] that you came here, lest it should annoy her – but perhaps you may feel it best to tell her – I shall of course not speak of it to anyone.

After their marriage Edward and Fanny Noel returned to Euboea and for about three years there was a friendly, warm and intimate correspondence between them and Annabella. Annabella made a purse for Fanny and told her she hoped the holes were not too big. More news of Ada was requested but Annabella did not wish to say more for fear of 'being misunderstood' but she ended the letter 'O let me still be the friend to whom all may be told.' Edward apparently was not yet ready to work and Annabella asked 'Why do you speak as if there was nothing for you to do?' Edward was worried that a man who held the position of a land agent would not be regarded as a gentleman but was told that Lord Lovelace said that he had been to houses where such a position would be considered an acquisition and the question of being a gentleman was decided by education. She told him of the professor who went to a friend of hers in distress, uncertain whether his status entitled him, after a challenge, to be shot. She assured Edward 'It seems that you would not lose that privilege.'

Possibly because she had the impression that Edward's letters were less cordial than hitherto, Annabella, who was always uneasily aware that she sometimes spoke and wrote in a pompous and didactic style when she did not mean to do so, wrote to Edward: 'I have great reason to suspect myself of a dogmatic way of writing of late, not certainly from dogmatical feelings, but from the necessity of saying my say in the shortest manner owing to physical pressures. I really never write with perfect ease – I mention this in order to prevent you from imparting to my feeling the brusqueness of my style.'

She hoped to encourage Edward to improve his own small estate, in which, after his household, he could exercise his Christian duties. It would improve his own mind she said, to understand the physical and moral wants of the people as well as the practical care of the land and houses. He did have some successes and in a letter to a friend Annabella describes how Edward had established a 'System of Confidence' by which he lent the villagers money – to which she had contributed a loan of £1,000 – to buy oxen or to build stone cottages for about 5% or 6% return. He had repaired the church and was preparing to build a school and she had sent Edward and young Fellenberg to Greece to see if there were any new ideas which would benefit the country and themselves. In one letter she seems less optimistic and she told him: '... if there were not an insuperable bar to your taking orders, I could place you now in a most delightful Rectory – at my beloved Seaham –'. It cannot be said that Annabella did not try to find satisfactory vocations for her 'children'.

Perhaps the course of true love was not always smooth on Euboea. She wrote to Fanny: 'I am glad to find you are aware of one weakness in your character *too much dependence upon kindness* ... it is happier for both parties when there is not too exquisite a sensibility to every passing cloud on each other's brow ...'. By the early 1840s it was apparent that Fanny was prone to sensitive misgivings, and Edward worried constantly about her health for she was losing rather than gaining strength. Miss Doyle, Fanny's aunt, came to stay for about six months and evidently this proved a trial. She was aggrieved at being second to Fanny in Edward's affections, Hester King (Lovelace's sister) reported to Robert Noel, and they did not like her meddling and reproaches.

Then there came a bitter and mysterious estrangement. It seems to have started in 1842. In a letter to Ada, Annabella refers to religious differences and she finds it odd that they are vexed with her not feeling altogether as they do. Annabella wrote to Ada on 29 October 1843:

What do you think of Ed's having been in London the other day without coming to see me, & coolly letting me know it? – What can he mean by so extraordinary a change? – I have continued to write to them on the same friendly terms as ever – & they have been living in fact on the £200 which I excused his repaying till his father's death – At the beginning of this year I expressed a wish that they would accommodate their plans a little more to mine than they have done, with the hope of our meeting – How truly Noel this is! The more they are obliged the more anxious they are to show independence or what they conceive to be such. ...

On 28 November of the same year Annabella wrote a long letter from Esher:

> Dearest Ada,
>   I told Lovelace that I had asked Edward to specify what employment he desired. He can imagine nothing that would suit him except the occupation of 'Lecturer' – 'Author' or perhaps Superintendent of an Educational Establishment *with leisure to follow his studies*. ...

She continued by telling Ada that she would have to let him go his own way unassisted for Edward thought he *ought* to develop the powers and abilities that he was conscious of possessing. She had written to Fanny with her usual affection but had received no answer until eventually a letter came, but not in Fanny's usual 'simple natural Style'. She decided not to reply to Fanny to avoid making any unfriendly remarks about Edward, or on the other hand seeming to ignore him.

By 14 December the situation had worsened: 'Edward has positively refused to acknowledge the receipt of money from me – was ever anything so strange?' She sent a packet of his letters to Ada asking her to give her opinion about them, asking what she could do to put matters on the right footing because she did not want to 'treat' with them in a way that would make it difficult to befriend them if they were in distress. She was annoyed that Edward seemed to think he could effect a reconciliation without first giving '*an unqualified acknowledgement*' that they had done her an injustice, which of course she would accept, if he made that clear, for he had a habit of writing words that on the second careful reading had a different sense, she told Ada.

She had bought two of Edward's paintings from the shop in Leamington where they were sold, as it was as an artist that he now maintained his family. They had positively refused the opportunity of explaining or trying to re-establish friendly relations between them. Annabella had written kindly to Fanny in her need. (This must have been caused by the death of their baby after only a few days illness which had been attributed to teething, and had devastated Edward and Fanny.)

The quarrel went on and in 1844 Annabella told Ada that Edward's account of it differed from her own. He accused her of breach of promise to others and himself in regard to pecuniary affairs. He told her she was devoid of heart and incapable of friendship: '(things which might have been said in a passion & as such I was willing to forget) I repeated that accusation on paper sometime after without any expression of regret ... But I have explained why I was willing to allow him the utmost latitude for repentance short of indulgence as would make me appear to acquiesce in his charges ...'. Annabella was obviously extremely upset for she had been very attached to them both and very kind. There was never to be a reconciliation, and it was a very great sadness to her.

The clue to the heart of the matter may lie in a letter Annabella wrote to Ada in 1852: 'Think of Edward Noel's taking huff after consenting to sell his drawings, at the money being sent direct to him! – It seems there was to have been make-believe that he did not know where it came from, though he was to pocket it. But the Ellisons sent it direct.' The same pride that would not acknowledge receipt for money, or allow evidence of labour was still alive. Inherited resentment unhelped by Fanny's emotional insecurity may have made their arrogance beyond Annabella's powers of persuasion to assuage. Annabella directed on her death-bed that all her correspondence from Robert and Edward should be burned.

The bitterness of the quarrel is revealed in a letter written many years later in 1922 by Edward's daughter Alice to Mary Lovelace in which, although she had given intimate details of her mother's life, she would only say of the break: 'The sequel to the great friendship between Lady Byron and my parents was a very painful one – I cannot write about that.' It is ironic that Annabella is so often accused of being implacable, and yet in this instance it was to her that, in spite of her efforts, forgiveness was denied. She was apparently unaware of having acted in any way that could cause mortal offence to two people of whom she was so very fond, and in whose affection she had felt secure.

In August 1853 the Revd Thomas Noel died. Charles had been cut out of his will, possibly because he worked for, and got on well with Lady Byron, but there had been an agreement made between the four brothers years before in Calais, that they would share equally between themselves what property their father left, regardless of what he decreed.

Charles wrote to Annabella:

Peckleton Sept 1st 1853
My Dear Lady Byron
    Before I get any letters from my wife or Friends relating to the will of my late Father I wish to place on record my earnest desire in relation to that document. First I freely forgive the dead. Next I wish to prove to the widow that I cannot in hope of a future world before my eyes use the same weapons in defence. I therefore desire that no steps on my account may be taken to resist the will as it is, and I trust that I may be enabled to live and die without receiving in any way benefit from my Father's property. ...

His wife wrote to Annabella at about the same time from 6 Pavilion Buildings, Brighton which Lady Byron had lent her for a short holiday:

6. Pavilion Buildings
Dear Lady Byron
    Thanks, grateful thanks, for your very kind & sympathetic note rest assured that no exertions shall be spared on my part to try to tranquilize Charles' mind – were everyone as unselfish as yourself dear Lady Byron how much more happiness would there be in our intercourse with others – but alas when money is the theme how few are willing to part with that but I do trust that the Brothers will see the necessity of acting up to what they before bound themselves to do to share & share alike – I do not mind so much for myself women can bear privations better than men – but I endeavour to look at the bright side and trust that all may end well – my purpose in now troubling you with these few lines is to ask you to do me a favour *for* Charles – when I left home – he had been amusing himself by endeavouring to polish stones in a rude way and he wished me to enquire of a lapidary here the price of a machine for polishing stones – and I ventured to *order* one as I felt sure it would amuse him – it was to be 3£ – and now he writes that he thinks he ought not to have it – would you oblige me by letting it be a present *from* you to *him* – you see I am already, acting up to the kind wish expressed in your note today – Do not distress yourself about the piano I ventured to engage one for a week for 7 shillings as Mrs

Bond said it was very necessary that Mary should practice often in the day – With best wishes, believe me, dear Lady Byron
Yours gratefully
Mary Anne Noel
I hope Charles will take advantage of your kind invite – he told me with tears in his eyes when he came home from visiting you the last time, that you could not act more kind to him, if he really was your son –

Sadly Charles and his wife Mary Anne died of smallpox in 1857 and they are commemorated in the Unitarian church at Hinckley:

This tablet was erected by the admirers of
Charles Noel Esq
who departed this life May 7th 1857
and Mary Anne his wife April 21st 1857
as a tribute to their memory and an expression
of regret at their loss to the cause of temperance
and social reform in this neighbourhood
Their epitaph is written

Robert wrote to Annabella from Geneva on 2 September:

The news contained in your lines of last Tuesday has caused me a considerable shock indeed I am almost surprised at my painful sensations. I cannot help feeling that, however bad a father ours was, still I may have been the negligent son … you sign yourself Dearest friend 'yours gratefully' Though I have no claim to any thanks yet if you are satisfied with Ralph's [2 words illegible] & our endeavours to meet your wishes I can assure you I feel a peculiar pleasure. I owe you a large debt of gratitude & it harmonizes with my affections, can I but pay off a little interest now & then. …
Believe me as always most truly and gratefully yours R.R. Noel.
Louisa sends her warm love.

Thomas wrote to her from Boyne Cottage, Maidenhead on 6 September:

I have heard from Bob
and written to him
Dear Lady Byron,
Do not fear that I, for one, could for a moment wish to take advantage of Charles' present self-sacrificing mood of mind. In

reply to two letters, urging us to disregard him, and take and divide what we can get by the will as it stands, I have told him that it cannot be:– that we are all bound in honour, if not in law, to share alike in the paternal property, having been consenting parties to the appointments made at Calais. ...

I see no reason to fear that we shall quarrel amongst ourselves. I wish for nothing but what is equitable, and doubt not but that the rest desire the same.

This exclusion, I fear, has given Charles a terrible shake. It is the reflection upon his character that it implies which hurts his feelings, – not the supposed loss of money. He shall lose none of it if I can help it.

Ever yours most sincerely
T. Noel.

Out of the four brothers, three were appreciative, even thankful, for her exertions on their behalf. It was not a bad score considering the difficulties, and the fact that she was only seven years older than the eldest and as a woman had limited powers and status. It was just that the one who had opted out so unexpectedly from her sphere, who was so defiantly proud and acutely sensitive, was the one she had loved most – for his idealism, his poetry and his painting. His delicate, easily upset wife was the girl she had lovingly helped to bring up, who had called her home Ford-happy-Hook, and with whom she had had such fun in the days when they played at being troubadours and she had felt carefree for a while. It hurt terribly that her friends – the same ones who had warned her that Byron only wanted her money when he asked for her likeness and said he wanted to live with her again – were now comforting Edward and his children. They never seemed to have tried to calm the overemotional, soothe hostile feelings or attempt to heal the rift even after Fanny died of consumption in 1845. Sometimes money appeared to be the ultimate cause of most of her pain however prudently and wisely she tried to administer it. How could she know if that, not her, was all that they really cared about? She became very ill for a time.

19   The Last Years

Harriet Beecher Stowe (1811–1896), the celebrated American writer and philanthropist, came to England in April 1853 with her husband Dr Calvin Stowe, a Congregational minister. She is best known for her book *Uncle Tom's Cabin*, which brought her widespread acclaim, and her work for the abolition of slavery. She had first-hand experience of this cause as she had lived for eighteen years in Cincinnati, with only a river separating the Beecher household from a slave-holding community, and she and others of the intellectual circle in which her family moved continually harboured slaves and helped them escape to Canada. Motivated and inspired by her religious beliefs, she took an active part in the political, economic and moral problems relating to slavery as well as being involved in other fields of philanthropic work. She had many famous friends, among whom was Oliver Wendell Holmes, the distinguished American physician and man of letters, and she was considered by such eminent twentieth-century scholars as Professor Denis Brogan to be one of the most important women of modern times.

One of the purposes of her visit was to form a liaison between English and American women on what had become the foremost issue of the day – the emancipation of slaves. It was at a lunch party where there were many notable people present, that Mrs Stowe first met Lady Byron who immediately interested her. She wrote down her impressions:

> ... she still had, to a remarkable degree, that personal attraction which is commonly considered to belong only to youth and beauty. Her form was slight, giving an impression of fragility; her motions

were both graceful and decided; her eyes bright and full of interest and quick observation. Her silvery-white hair seemed to lend a grace to the transparent purity of her complexion, and her small hands had a pearly whiteness. I recollect she wore a plain widow's cap of a transparent material and was dressed in some delicate shade of lavender which harmonized well with her complexion. ... calm, selfpossessed, and thoughtful, she seemed to me rather to resemble an interested spectator of the world's affairs, than an actor involved in its trials, yet the sweetness of her smile, and a certain very delicate sense of humour in her remarks, made the way of acquaintance easy. Her first remarks were a little playful; but in a few moments we were speaking on what every one in those days was talking to me about – the slavery question in America.

Mrs Stowe's description of Annabella is remarkably reminiscent of Byron's, which he wrote down in his journal after Annabella's first refusal of him forty years earlier:

She is a very superior woman, and very little spoiled, which is strange in an heiress – a girl of twenty – a peeress that is to be, in her own right – an only child, and a *savante*, who has always had her own way. She is a poetess – a mathematician, and yet, withal, very kind, generous, and gentle, with very little pretension. Any other head would be turned with half her acquisitions, and a tenth of her advantages.

Mrs Stowe immediately noticed the originality and 'peculiar incisive quality' of Lady Byron's remarks, and how very informed she was on all American topics. 'Her morality on the slave question, too, impressed me as something far higher and deeper than the common sentimentalism of the day. Many of her words surprised me greatly, and gave me new material for thought.' They discussed books and Mrs Stowe found that Lady Byron had read widely and extensively revealing 'habits of clear, searching analysis, her thoughtfulness, and, above all, that peculiar reverence for *truth* and sincerity which was a leading characteristic of her moral nature'.

In May Mrs Stowe held an assembly of twenty to thirty well-known people. Henry Crabb Robinson was one of them and recorded in his diary that Mrs Stowe was agreeable and quite unpretending, but 'a far more interesting person was Lady Byron to whom Mrs Jameson introduced me'. He and Lady Byron were soon on visiting terms and she discussed with him the feasibility of writing a narrative which would do justice to the memory of Robertson, whom Crabb Robinson had much admired. In their correspondence they discussed many matters, especially concerning literature and in writing of Lord Byron she said: 'It is enough for me to remember, that he who thinks his transgressions beyond *forgiveness* (and such was his own deepest feeling) *has* righteousness beyond that of the self-satisfied sinner ...'. She often remembered the words of Robertson who had thought highly of Byron's poetry: 'Religious people, as usual, never penetrate below the surface.' When Mrs Stowe returned to America she felt that in meeting Lady Byron: 'I had found one more pearl of great price on the shore of life.'

During the last few years Annabella had become interested in the work of her friend Mary Carpenter of Bristol. Mary Carpenter was one of the most remarkable women of the nineteenth century, and had previously set up a ragged school in 1846, a reformatory school for boys and girls in 1852, and was active in getting the Reformatory Schools Act passed by Parliament. She soon realized that a separate school for girls was needed and in 1854 Lady Byron made possible the purchase of Red Lodge and another house now demolished. The importance at that time of Mary Carpenter's work in Bristol, now so nearly forgotten, is made clear by the account in Jo Manton's book *Mary Carpenter and the Children of the Street.* She described the plight of the child orphaned in tragic circumstances, who was refused admission to a church orphanage through lack of proof that she was born in wedlock, but accepted unreservedly into Mary Carpenter's school. The reformatory was closed in 1919 and today is a museum and art gallery. In it there is a plaque over a fireplace with the inscription:

SACRED
To the memory of
ANNE ISABELLA NOEL, DOWAGER LADY BYRON,
who, ever devoting the many talents entrusted to her
to the service of her Master,
purchased these premises, September 1854,
for the purpose of rescuing young girls
from sin and misery,
and bringing them back to the paths of holiness.

She was born May 17th, 1792,
and departed this life May 16th 1860.

Faithful until Death.

Annabella paid a visit to Dover in 1855. On 2 September she wrote to Ralph telling him that Dr and Mrs King had enjoyed his visit to them in Brighton so much that they wished it had been longer and they hoped that he would visit them again soon. She suggested that he gave his sister elementary mathematical instruction, and that he got his violin overhauled for better practice. She finished by saying: 'I can't tell you how pleased I am to find you so welcome a visitor to my estimable friends – Ever dear Ralph your affectionate GM.' But in her next letter to him on 7 September she was depressed. Her health was worse, and her eyes painfully inflamed:

> ... I came here for two or three reasons – one of them good medical advice – another sailing – but the weather has been too strong for this – & I have been for a fortnight past almost alone with my illness – without interesting books & going out only under physical pain – the wish to be giving out to some human beings could not be gratified. I mention it as a curious instance of the isolation which sometimes attends a social position like mine. The services which I am so willing to render are not asked because not expected from me! A Right Honourable wall is around me! ... All my Grandn doing well ... Ockham came down here to spend 6 hours with his Granny! ...

Perhaps the few weeks of holiday were beneficial for in an undated note, probably of this period, to Mrs De Morgan she wrote: 'Do you not think that changes of air might again do you good? I wish I had a country house to offer you, but perhaps I could extemporize one, if it would be acceptable – A Kirkby Pheasant herewith. I am not knocked down yet – too much fire & fury in my const^n the reverse of yours it seems.'

Annabella met George MacDonald in 1855. He was then thirty-one, married with children, very good-looking, a novelist and poet, an idealist, and a thinker who was to be rated with Trollope and Carlisle. He had been a Congregational minister with unorthodox views, such as believing that redemption can be attained even in hell. He had been discouraged by his superiors for his unconventional ideas which led to his resignation as a pastor. He endeavoured to earn a precarious living by giving lectures at Manchester University where Professor A.J. Scott was principal.

Lady Byron wrote to MacDonald after she read his recently

published narrative poem 'Within and Without' which had received considerable acclaim. It had affected her deeply by its relevance to her own experience. In it, the couple after much suffering are united in death and possibly the words:

Pray God, beloved, for thee and me,
That our souls – may be wed eternally

expressed her abiding belief that Byron's spirit would come to her in peace hereafter.

Professor Scott was a friend of hers and when she learned through him in 1856 that MacDonald had little money and was in ill-health, she paid the travelling expenses for him and his wife Louisa to visit Algiers and arranged accommodation for them. She also wrote to her friend Mr Leigh Smith, who was wintering in Algiers with his three daughters, asking him to call on the MacDonalds. The Leigh Smiths were well-read, cosmopolitan and freethinking, and through them, MacDonald was later to meet many influential people who helped him in his career as a lecturer. From time to time Annabella discreetly gave MacDonald small sums of money, always very tactfully for he was a Scot and very proud: 'I hope it is no disgrace to me to be rich as it is none to you to be poor' she said '... if I can do anything for you, you must understand Mr MacDonald, it is rather for the public than yourself'. He appreciated her direct way of speaking which made it easier for him to accept her gifts without embarrassment.

They became firm friends, and he gave her his manuscripts for her opinion, which he did not always like. She invited him to her home: 'You shall be treated most inhospitably – put into a room apart with a private entrance ... No note will be taken of your goings out and comings in. When socially disposed, you will *invite yourself*. My house has often been called Liberty Hall.' It is to be hoped that she remembered to offer him what she had been known to forget, something to eat.

From the time of the separation Annabella had found it difficult to settle in one place and call it home. It was the only outward sign of her inner desolation that she, who could give peace to others, could never find it for herself. It seems the effect of the spell cast upon her was too deep to be broken even by a Princess of Parallelograms, for after Ada's death, when she had no further necessity for a permanent home, she could neither put down roots nor welcome solitude:

> *Though thy slumber may be deep,*
> *Yet thy spirit shall not sleep;*
> *There are shades which will not vanish,*
> *There are thoughts thou canst not banish;*
> *By a power to thee unknown,*
> *Thou canst never be alone;*
> *Thou are Wrapt as with a shroud,*
> *Thou are gathered in a cloud;*
> *And for ever shalt thou dwell*
> *In the spirit of this spell*
>
> ['Manfred', 1816]

She seemed to plan a different abode for each season, and to move even more frequently during the last years of her life, often renting a house for only a month or two. Because she found it mentally stimulating she liked Brighton more than anywhere else, and one of her more permanent homes was 6 & 7 Pavilion Buildings. According to the *Brighton Herald* dated 27 March 1852: 'This fine range of buildings sweeping round from Castle Square to the entrance of the Pavilion is now in a state of great forwardness. ...The new houses are the admiration of everyone'. Later she moved to Junction House where she nursed Ralph when he had scarlet fever, keeping him in her own room while he was ill. Both these houses were near the Chain Pier, which was opposite the building where Byron in 1808 had stayed with a young woman who went about with him dressed as his 'brother'. Perhaps Annabella felt his spirit, then guiltless, still lingered. She had a summer residence at Ham Common near Richmond in Surrey, where her friend Emily Fitzhugh lived at Rose Cottage, and Miss Montgomery was nearby at 1 Park Villas, Richmond. She had also had a house on the Tackleway at Hastings. George MacDonald came to live in Hastings although she had told him 'there is no life of mind in the place'. She also occupied The Limes at 123 Mortlake High Street SW14 for a time, and her correspondence shows her London addresses were many. Her final move was to 11 and 12 St George's Terrace, Primrose Hill in 1857.

In 1856 she was reminded of the unhappy past by letters from Lady Wilmot Horton and Augusta's half-sister, Lady Chichester:

7 Grafton Street, May 8th [1856]
Many thanks dear Lady Noel Byron for your note and enclosure. I had been rather surprised at not hearing from Emily Leigh ...

She had written to me saying that her Brother Frederick was in an almost *hopeless state* in the Isle of Man – Dropsy, &c. &c. – but that he had met with a very kind friend in a Clergyman there – who had taken great interest in him, and that he was *very penitent* and resigned! ...

Mrs Trevanion is now what they call '*independent*' since her Husband's death ...

Ever yours affectionately
A.B.W. Horton.

Grosvenor Place, May 25th 1856
My Dear Lady Byron
I received your letter on the subject of poor Emily Leigh's affairs late on Saturday – it gave me additional cause to lament the loss of our much loved friend Mrs Villiers, to whose clear and superior judgement I should have referred the question contained in it – As it is, I can only state my opinion that the Addition you kindly propose to make of £10 Annually ('during pleasure') to her present allowance will be most welcome, especially as that income had lately diminished by £10 in consequence of a change of circumstances in one of the contributors. ... I am on the verge of 80, but should it please God to spare me another Winter to go to Brighton I shall be much gratified if we could meet once more in this world, that I might have an opportunity of assuring you of ye grateful sense I have *ever* entertained of your kindness to my late sister and to several Members of her unfortunate family.
I am with great regard,
Yours faithfully
M. Chichester.

This letter must have pleased Annabella since she had been sorry to keep aloof from a woman she both respected and liked. 'I preferred being misconstrued to the alternative of giving so much pain to so good and kind a heart as the Sister's' she had written to Mrs Villiers on 19 November 1851.

Another unexpected and appreciative letter dated 24 November 1856 was from Richard Realf, one of the many individuals, seldom heard of, to whom Annabella had been kind. Richard was born in 1834 and when he was seventeen he had some poems published, but because his life was unsettled and far from satisfactory Robertson introduced him to Annabella for guidance. After a period with Charles Noel at Kirkby Mallory, which seems to have been standard treatment for confused adolescents, he went to the United States to live with the Revd Mr Pease of the Five Points House of Industry in New York. He had seen in the *New York Times* a mention of a donation of £6,500 'to the sufferers of this territory' from Lady Byron and wrote to tell of his gratitude for the 'facilities in advancement' she had given him five years ago, but he had 'failed in these things'. She heard from him again in 1858:

> May God bless you forever ... In all my life there will be a thought of pain – in all remembrances a touch of self-accusing bitterness – but for you dear Madam – and for yours, there will be only gratitude and blessing in the heart of Richard Realf.

Mrs Stowe returned to England in 1856 even more famous and applauded than before and was accompanied by her sister, husband and children. One of her 'brightest anticipations' was to see Annabella again, who at the time was confined to bed. In the book she later wrote about Lady Byron she described her visit:

> I found Lady Byron in her sick-room, – that place which she made so different from the chamber of ordinary invalids. ...
>   By her bedside stood a table covered with books, pamphlets, and files of letters all arranged with exquisite order, and each expressing some of her varied interests. From that sick-bed she still directed, with systematic care, her various works of benevolence, and watched with intelligent attention the course of science, literature and religion; and the versatility and activity of her mind, the flow of brilliant and penetrating thought on all topics of the day gave to the conversations of her retired room a peculiar charm. You forgot that she was an invalid; for she rarely had a word of her own personalities, and the charm of her conversation carried you invariably from herself to the subjects of which she was thinking. All the new books, the literature of the hour, were lighted up by her keen, searching, yet always kindly criticism.

This visit to England was mainly for the publication of her latest novel, *Dred*, a copy of which she sent Lady Byron who in thanking her said: 'If there is truth in what I heard Lord Byron say, that works of fiction live only by the amount of *truth* which they contain, your story is sure of a long life.' Mrs Stowe told her that she had since childhood been powerfully influenced by Byron because, surprisingly for a minister in his environment, her father had had his works in his library and a sermon he had preached about Byron had left a deep and lasting impression on her. When the awful news came that he was dead she had gone to a lonely hillside to think about him and pray. Lady Byron already knew about her regard for the poet through a mutual friend and told her: 'It was one of the things that had made me wish to know you. I think *you* could understand him.'

She invited Mrs Stowe and her family to lunch with her, and talked with each child separately so that they soon felt at ease. She advised them as to what they should see and study in London and they were never to forget the interest and charm of her conversation. Soon after this Mrs Stowe with her husband and son Henry spent the evening with Lady Byron and others whom she had invited including her grandson Viscount Ockham. Mrs Stowe commented to Lady Byron on Ockham's muscular strength, comparing him with the Farnese Hercules. Lady Byron replied that that of itself would account for many of Ockham's eccentricities, for his body required a more vigorous life than his rank called for, but that he had noble traits and she felt sure that his present experience of employment among workmen, with the interest in their families which she was trying to encourage would yet fit him to do great good when he became a peer. Mrs Stowe said this benevolent attitude of hopefulness was strongly characteristic of Lady Byron, who always remained loyal to her wayward grandson.

Since the death of Augusta in 1851 and Ada the following year, Lady Byron had been giving consideration as to whether she ought now to make public the facts relating to her separation from Byron, and if she were to, the manner in which it should be done. With her deep sense of truth, she had a strong feeling that Byron, who had always abominated cant, would not be at peace while a lie was being preserved and the truth had not been told. Certain friends that had been confided in under a pledge of secrecy that was always kept, had died or where now old, and she herself suffered from increasing ill-health. She had discussed with Robertson the possibility that after her death he would publish her memoirs and letters and she had started writing up episodes in her life which could be used to form the basis of a future narrative. With his premature death the matter remained unresolved. In a sketch for the preface she wrote:

Yet when I look at the accumulation of difficulties in my way, I feel that the truths I may bring forward will but partially dispel these illusions, so long accepted as realities, – Apart however, from any view, to benefit the unknown Reader who may have little disposition to attend to me, I naturally desire to leave a few counter statements for the information of my grandchildren, for I own that on that point the opinion formed of me does touch me.

When it was known that a cheap edition of the works of Byron was to be published in 1856 accompanied by an account of his life, Lady Byron's friends urged her to seriously reconsider whether she had not a duty to reveal what had really happened. There had been many rumours before her marriage as well as afterwards which had been quelled but had not been forgotten, and there was Byron's poetry, in which he had been recklessly outspoken but which he had never wanted suppressed. She decided to ask Mrs Stowe for her opinion. Mrs Stowe was a woman of recognized integrity with considerable experience of the world, who came from a different environment, as well as having been an admirer of Byron since childhood. She seemed the ideal person to give an unbiased judgement. Lady Byron arranged for Mrs Stowe to visit her when they would be undisturbed and acquainted her with the whole story of her marriage.

She told how she first met Byron, her doubts when he first proposed as to whether she could make a good wife for him, her joy when she received his very beautiful letter offering himself again and her reply telling him all she felt – all that was in her heart, his strange behaviour at Seaham, her offer to release him from the engagement but remain his friend, her deep sympathy for him because of the constant remorse and anguish from which he seemed to be suffering, until finally she told how she found Augusta and Byron in compromising circumstances which could scarcely be mistaken and she was ordered to her room where she fell sobbing to her knees, wondering what on earth she should do. Later he had told her that what had happened in the past would continue and that she must submit because he craved the stimulus of vice. Even after Augusta confessed their relationship in her confused and disorientated way, Annabella sometimes could hardly believe what she had been told. Surely Byron was simply trying to shock her, or perhaps he was mentally ill as Augusta insisted he was, and his rages were a symptom of the 'malady' as

Augusta called it; maybe in her overwrought state she had
misconstrued Augusta's muddled account – except that Augusta
had seemed to promise that it would never happen again – indeed
it had not happened since their marriage, and she expressed such
desperate sorrow and regret that both of them had wept, and
through their shared secret became emotionally very close.

Mrs Stowe was amazed and shocked at what she had been told
but agreed to give the matter careful consideration. Her first
reaction had been that a full disclosure should be made
immediately, but after nearly two weeks deliberation she wrote on
17 December 1856:

> On *that subject* on which you spoke to me the last time we were
> together. I have thought often and deeply.
>   I have changed my mind somewhat. Considering the peculiar
> circumstances of the case, I could wish that the sacred veil, so
> bravely thrown over the past, should never be withdrawn during the
> time that you remain with us.
>   I would say, then, Leave all with some discreet friends, who, after
> *both* have passed from earth, shall say what was due to *justice*.
>   I am led to think this by seeing how low, how unjust, how
> unworthy, the judgements of this world are; and I would not that
> what I so much respect, love, and revere should be placed within
> reach of its harpy claw, which pollutes what it touches. ...
>   Such, my dear friend, are my thoughts; different from what they
> were since first I heard that strange, sad history. Meanwhile, I love
> you ever, whether we meet again on earth or not.

It seemed an appropriate solution to Lady Byron, as in this way
an impartial decision could be made about access to her papers if it
was thought necessary, and her grandchildren, who were her sole
concern, could not be charged with acting in a biased spirit
through their loyalty to her. She made arrangements that all her
papers were to be left to three trustees with precise instructions
which were set forth in her will. These are repeated in the following
extract so that the frequently made statement that she spent the
remainder of her life after the separation collecting evidence for
writing her case against Byron may be properly assessed:

> ... I give to Henry Allen Bathurst of Doctors Commons London
> Miss Francis Carr of Ockham Park Surrey and Miss Mary Carpenter
> of Great George Street Bristol all written papers in my possession

whether they be manuscripts of my own or letters addressed to me or documents of any other kind of a private nature Upon Trust that they will forthwith deposit the cases containing them (which cases I direct them or one of them to seal immediately upon my decease and my Executors are to allow them to do so) at some Bankers to be agreed upon by them or any two of them and to be opened from time to time and resealed only by them or one of them with the knowledge of the other two and I direct that no one else however nearly concerned with me shall upon any plea whatsoever be allowed to have access to or inspect such manuscripts or documents ... I wish that the three above named trustees or the survivors or survivors of them or the trustee or trustees to be appointed as next hereinafter mentioned shall exercise their discretion in dealing with them according to what they consider would be my wishes in regard to the ultimate disposal there of and having especial regard to the welfare of my grandchildren. ...

The Stowes returned to America in 1857 but were shortly afterwards struck by tragedy. Henry, who had accompanied them to England and was his mother's favourite child, was drowned in the Connecticut river while a freshman at Dartmouth College. Mrs Stowe said she received more comfort from Lady Byron's letter of sympathy than from any other source.

Annabella had been feeling the strains and stresses of old age for some time, and at the end of the fifties her poor health was increasingly troublesome. 'Tho' nobody came to know how I am I will write a line to say I am still tight rope dancing but hope not to slip ...' she wrote to Robert Noel's wife Louisa. She suffered with 'noises in the head', presumably what is now called tinnitus, and also 'displaced viscera' which was probably a prolapse of the uterus which apparently followed Ada's birth. 'I receive visits from everybody who chooses to see me now as I begin to want relief from solitude my eyes not being fit for much employment' she had written to Lovelace in 1852 and now her interesting visitors were fewer although they still came. Crabb Robinson wrote in his diary for 16 April 1859: 'Called on Lady Byron, and found with her a very interesting man, a Mr MacDonald ... the talk was altogether interesting.' There were frequent invitations from her to the MacDonalds to 'share our tea, dinner at 6 o'clock' and the carriage would take them home at eight or later.

Annabella was still concerned with everyday happenings, literature, science and world affairs, and especially with the activities and happiness of her grandchildren.

Ockham, her eldest grandchild, who had declared he would never take up his peerage, did not grow out of his naturally rebellious and shy character. Lady Byron always gave him sympathy, understanding and encouragement, especially when he most needed it after he finally left the navy in 1853, for which his father never forgave him. She obtained what she hoped would be a suitable companion and tutor for him in the son of Dr Arnold, the famous headmaster of Rugby, but Ockham ran away and became a dockyard labourer known as John Okey. Little is known of Ockham's short and it would seem unhappy life except that he was a 'common sailor', returned from sea to Hull destitute and ill, and was looked after by some friends of Lady Byron. Apparently he was staying with Lady Byron when he was introduced to Mrs Stowe at the lunch party in 1856. In the same year she wrote to Robert and Louisa telling them that he was returning to England, and being still a minor she regarded this period as most important for him. She followed this up with a proposal on 23 June 1856:

I wish to submit to yours & Louisa's consideration an alternative of your returning abroad this year.

It is to inhabit a house not far from the River but in some healthy spot, such as St George St West where you could give poor Ockham a home when he came to London – This last year of his minority is of such importance to him that I should think no expense too great to secure to him during that time the best social influences, & to counteract more lowering associations. He has every disposition to cultivate your intimacy – you stand well with his Father – In short I do not believe there is any person who could do so much towards his own welfare & that of the many with whom he is Connected – But should such an arrangement appear to you practicable, or worth trying for 2 or 3 months it must be an absolute secret that I have originated it. You must act as from your own inclination, which I trust you could do honestly, towards him. I should secure you from economical anxieties.

After the 24th direct to me
No 1 Cambridge Terrace
Regents Park
Yours most truly A.I. Noel Byron.

In her next letter to them Annabella wrote: '… I had been afraid to express all the importance I attach to your being in England on Ockham's account less Louisa should sacrifice her Family feelings

& other objects. ... I feel sure you can make him – not the Peer, which he will never be, nor the men Workman which he would be – but the Man'. She told them that Ockham had studied welfare for the working-class, and that he would be far better than most to express a view on this because of his independence and habit of intercourse with all ranks of society. Unfortunately this plan apparently did not materialize but she still did not give up hope and in 1857 she told Robert and Louisa she had not heard from Ockham, though she had discussed him with De Morgan who had had much experience with the aberrations of youths of that age. De Morgan found that often there was an extraordinary change between twenty-one and twenty-five. 'He liked O's having a single attachment & would not object to a Working woman as his wife, if of another vocation.'

On 23 November 1859 Crabb Robinson recorded in his diary that Ockham was expected in England and Lady Byron was hoping he would stay with her. 'He is an ultra-radical!' she had said but she was planning to encourage him to take an interest in engineering and to perhaps obtain a partnership for him in a suitable firm. He had had dreams of travelling round the world with a friend in their own steamboat, but this was not to be, for he died in 1862 of consumption. He was nursed in his last illness by his sister Annabella. From his few short letters he seems a likeable individual who could not adapt to the period or position into which he had been born.

Ralph, the younger of the grandsons, who had been in Lady Byron's care with tutors since he was nine, and had told her when he was about eleven: 'When I see a cow licking her calf I always think it is so like you Granma.' It was not always easy having 'under no control but mine, which is legally none' an adolescent who had very decided opinions of his own. When Ralph was just eighteen there was a difference of opinion between him and his grandmother. He wanted to travel to Scotland alone and unknown wherever his fancy might lead him. She felt someone should 'direct his course and the duration of his wanderings'. She consulted her old friends the Mairs of Edinburgh, with it would seem a satisfactory outcome. 'I am glad to say that Ralph does not seem as averse as I feared he would be to spending 2 or 3 days with you – if they should be extended I should think it very good for him ...' she wrote and continued 'you will "pity the sorrows of a poor old" – Granny when you think of my having, *unaided by any human being,* to manage such a big thing as he is! – and will not wonder at my wishing to take Mr Mair into partnership and to make you Vice Grandmama'.

It had always been her practice to encourage Ralph to think for himself in religious matters. In 1859 he consulted her over a problem during his first year at Oxford:

> Univ. Col. Oxford. Nov 20th 1859
>
> Dear G.M.
>
> ... Next Sunday there is to be a communion which all members of the college who were not present at the last communion are expected to attend.
>
> As you know, I should not in any case wish to join in one, besides which I neither have been nor wish to be confirmed, and I believe no one whom has not been confirmed can take the communion. (I might go back a step further, and say I never was baptized in what would be called a valid form of baptism, without which one cannot be confirmed). What do you think I had better do? Simply not to go, or to say beforehand that I cannot? After hearing what you think I had perhaps better also ask Mr. Donkin, as he knows the ways of the place. ...

Ralph goes on to outline his beliefs on university reform, hypocrisy in religion and the effects of a classical education that 'seems to be chaining the living to the dead'. In later years he came to wish he had had a less inhibited upbringing. He wrote to his sister Annabella in 1868:

> I should not have lamented any loss if I could have been entirely formed & instructed by her [Lady Byron] ... I certainly now think that some of the greatest mistakes made in my management were in accordance rather with my mother's desire than my grandmother's – I was supposed to possess such a vigorous genius as to need a very solitary & depressing education – I had not as it turned out sufficient mental & moral vitality to thrive under such restrictions.

Anne Isabella King had always adored her grandmother. She told Agnes, Woronzow Greig's wife, in 1867 that Lady Byron 'was really like a guardian angel & I owe almost all the good I have learnt in some way or other to her'. Lady Byron wrote to Mrs Stowe on 3 May 1859 from St George's Terrace:

> ... I am in London now to be of a little use to A [her grand-

daughter] –; not ostensibly for I can neither go out, nor give parties; but I am the confidential friend to whom she likes to bring her social gatherings, as she can see something of the world with others. Age and infirmity seem to be overlooked in what she calls the harmony between us, – not perfect agreement of opinion (which I should regret, with almost fifty years of difference), but the spirit-union can you say what it is?

They were both reading Mrs Stowe's latest novel *The Minister's Wooing* and she continues the letter by reporting their opinions about it:

... I have an intense interest in your new novel. More power in these few numbers than in any of your former writings, relating, at least, to my own mind. It would amuse you to hear my granddaughter and myself attempting to foresee the future of the love-story; being, for the moment, quite persuaded that James is at sea, and the minister about to ruin himself. We think that Mary will labour to be in love with the self-devoted man, under her mother's influence, and from that hyper-conscientiousness so common with good girls; but we don't wish her to succeed. Then what is to become of her older lover? Time will show.

This letter was to be the last she wrote to her friend for shortly after it was received Mrs Stowe returned to England. On her first visit to Lady Byron she found her in one of her bad periods of health:

When I called on her at this time, she could not see me at first: and when, at last, she came, it was evident that she was in a state of utter prostration. Her hands were like ice; her face was deadly pale; and she conversed with a restraint and difficulty which showed what exertion it was for her to keep up at all.

These attacks, to which she had long been subject, had become worse and more frequent with age. They have been variously described as hypochondria, menopausal problems and moods caused by bad temper. However they are the classic symptoms of a congestive heart condition which is both painful and debilitating.

Another visit was arranged, and Mrs Stowe's account continues:

That interview was my last on earth with her, and is still beautiful in memory. It was a long still summer afternoon, spent alone with her in a garden, where we walked together. She was enjoying one of those bright intervals of freedom from pain and languor, in which her spirits always rose so buoyant and youthful; and her eye brightened, and her step became elastic.

One last little incident is cherished as most expressive of her. When it became time for me to leave she took me in her carriage to the station. As we were almost there, I missed my gloves, and said, 'I must have left them; but there is not time to go back'.

With one of those quick, impulsive motions which were so natural to her in doing a kindness, she drew off her own and said, 'Take mine if they will serve you'.

I hesitated a moment, and then the thought, that I might never see her again, came over me, and I said, 'Oh, yes! thanks'.

After Mrs Stowe died in 1896 these gloves were found in a drawer carefully folded and wrapped with a rosebud and a card on which was written: 'Lady Byron's gloves'.

From the beginning of 1860 Annabella became markedly more frail and the worries she had had for the last few years that she would become bedridden or of unsound mind grew more persistent. Perhaps she now regretted that she had not become the Catholic her beloved Olivia had so desired for her because she was alone. In the spring death drew near and as responses to outer stimuli ceased, her last thoughts while life ebbed away were surely with her dearest Byron, the only man she had ever loved.

> *Pray God, beloved, for thee and me,*
> *That our souls – may be wed eternally.*

On 16 May 1860, the day before her sixty-eighth birthday, Annabella Byron died at St George's Terrace. Her death certificate records the cause of death as: 'Bronchitis 21 days Pleurisy 10 days'. Her granddaughter and her friend Mrs Barwell were with her. Mrs Barwell wrote to Dr Bence-Jones: 'About four o'clock she passed from sleep without a pang or struggle.' Dr Bence-Jones was the son-in-law of Annabella's great friend Lady Gosford, the 'M.G.' of her youthful confidences. Annabella King wrote to Mrs George Lamb: 'My darling suffered very much, except the few hours before the end. The end was in sleep, which passed into the sleep of death – gently and calmly.' Soon afterwards Ockham and Ralph came. It would have pleased her to have had all her beloved grandchildren with her again for the last time.

The next day Thomas Woolner RA, sculptor and poet, wrote to his friend Mrs Tennyson, wife of the poet laureate Alfred Tennyson:

> Yesterday I had to go and see a cast taken of the left hand of Lady Noel Byron, wife of the poet. The summons said it was essential that an honourable man should do it, or I should not have been troubled. I do not much like taking casts of anyone dead, but could not refuse in this case, as I know so many of their friends. But I am glad I did go, for a nobler sight I never saw – she looked as if she were living, and had just dropped to sleep, and as proud as a queen in her splendour, I think there never was anything finer than her brow and nose. ... She seemed to have been almost adored by those about her.

Annabella was buried in Kensal Green Cemetery in London next to Mary, Amelia and Sophia Lushington, the sisters of her friend and solicitor, who it was rumoured had been in love with her. On her tomb is a simple inscription:

Ann Isabella Noel Byron
Born at Seaham
In the County of Durham,
17th May 1792
died
16th May 1860

Near her lie Anna Jameson who had died two months previously, Hobhouse, Augusta and her husband, John Murray, Byron's publisher, and Giovanni Battista Falcieri, 'Tita', Byron's faithful servant, who was with him when he died.

They did not spell her name correctly. Like the false conceptions made while she lived it was not amended and has endured ever since. Byron would surely wish her to have, what he had sought in vain for himself, a fair hearing and 'Truth Itself' be told.

Perhaps she is best summed up through the words of Judith, Lady Wentworth, Ada's granddaughter: 'My mother said Lady Byron was the sweetest and gentlest person she ever knew, and *very amusing.*'

Epilogue

The MacDonalds

The MacDonalds were in particularly difficult financial circumstances in 1860 just after their seventh child was born, and Louisa had the terrible misfortune to lose her purse containing all their money. Lady Byron was by then dead and there was no one now they could go to. George and Louisa stood hand in hand in silent despair in their small drawing-room in Albert Street, Regent's Park. Then the postman came up the steps with a cheque for £300, the legacy that Lady Byron had left them and which in coming at this time of privation seemed sent from heaven.

George MacDonald wrote over twenty novels. He dedicated his first, *David Elginbrod* (1863), to Annabella: 'There are a few rich who ... enter into the Kingdom of Heaven in spite of their riches. She to whom this book is dedicated is – I will not say was – one of the noblest of such'. In *The Vicar's Daughter* he drew her as Lady Bernard: 'She was like a fountain of living water ... I believe no one knew half the munificent things she did'. To a friend he wrote: 'I counted her one of the noblest as well as one of the ablest of women; and that so far from being cold hearted, I believe she loved her husband to the last, whatever the *last* may be interpreted as being.'

Obituary

Harriet Martineau was a writer of repute, famed for her rational judgement and often painful honesty. It was because Anna

Jameson had been 'the subject of various depreciatory animadversions' by her that Anna's niece Gerardine Macpherson felt obliged to write her aunt's biography after her death: '... all or almost all, of Harriet Martineau's friends fared just as badly in her hands ... I state this with frankness as one of my strongest motives for the work I have undertaken ...'. However the biographical sketch that Miss Martineau wrote for Lady Byron's obituary in the *Atlantic Monthly* and *Macmillan's Magazine*, expresses only admiration and praise. She gives instances of how Lady Byron helped people anonymously, and in cases of poverty would pay a sum of money into a bank for administration by an intermediary. She describes some of the philanthropic works in which Lady Byron took part, especially her great interest and achievement in education. Landowners and other wealthy people visited the schools that she opened on her Leicestershire and Warwickshire estates, and returned to their homes to set up similar establishments. She continued:

Her mind was of the large and clear quality which could comprehend remote interests in their true proportions and achieve each aim as perfectly as if it were the only one. Her agents used to say that it was impossible to mistake her directions, and thus her business was usually well done.

Her taste did not lie in the 'Charity Ball' direction; her funds were not lavished in encouraging hypocrisy and improvidence among the idle and worthless; and the quality of her charity was, in fact, as admirable as its quantity. Her chief aim was the extension and improvement of popular education; but there was no kind of misery that she heard of that she did not palliate to the utmost, and no kind of solace that her quick imagination and sympathy could devise that she did not administer.

... Years ago it was said far and wide that Lady Byron was doing more good than anyone else in England; and it was difficult to imagine how anybody could do more.

She has sent out tribes of boys and girls into life fit to do their part there with skill and credit and comfort. Perhaps it is a still more important consideration that scores of teachers and trainers have been lead into their vocation, and duly prepared for it, by what they saw and learned in her schools.

... Her mind was as liberal as her heart and hand. No diversity of opinion troubled her; she was respectful to every sort of individuality, and indulgent to all constitutional peculiarities. It must have puzzled those who kept up the notion of her being 'straight-laced' to see how indulgent she was even to Epicurean tendencies, – the remotest of all from her own.

... All that could be done in the way of personal love and honour was done while she lived; it only remains now to see that her name and fame are permitted to shine forth at last in their proper light.

Memoir of a Friend

These observations recall to my mind one whose friendship was the chief blessing of my earlier years, and whose loss can never be replaced – Lady Noel Byron: she who was traduced and misunderstood; one of those pure spirits little valued by the world, though worshipped by those who knew her well. Some others besides myself, still on this side of the grave, can bear witness to her excellence.

I think I may consider that I am justified now in printing some extracts from her letters, and some verses of her writing; she cannot speak for herself now – she never did speak for herself when she *could* have done so; but for the sake of truth, for the sake of some who, I think, would not intentionally be unjust, for the sake of the gratitude and the love I bore her, and for the sake of her blessed example, I cannot write of past years and write nothing about her. In one of her beautiful letters, she says:

'I hope to leave this world without having said a word that could damage anybody, and so I must let people say what they will of me. Yet there is one thing that does sometimes surprise me: some of those I have been most kind to have construed it as unkindness; but persons of experience tell me this is no uncommon circumstance; still, any kind things one has done will always be pleasant to remember, and the kindness one has received will never be forgotten; so the inner peace, more precious still than the outer, will not be disturbed.

My term is not likely to measure yours, so you may possibly hear what is said of me when I can give no more offence'.

The above is taken from *Recollections* by Amelia Matilda Murray, writer, botanist and artist and maid of honour to Queen Victoria, published in 1868.

Mrs Stowe's Book

Death did not bring seclusions or peace to the memory of Lady

Byron. Teresa Guiccioli, who in 1847 had married the Marquis de Boissy, wrote a book about Byron when she was approaching her seventieth year called *Lord Byron jugé par les témoins de sa vie*. When it first appeared in France anonymously in 1868, it was considered badly written, a very boring mixture of anecdotes from all the other not very good or accurate accounts which had been published concerning Byron since his death, and remarkable only for the extraordinary venom with which Lady Byron was attacked. When it was translated into English by Hubert Jerningham and published a few months later in England, it was known to be by the Countess Guiccioli and aroused wider interest.

She had written to Lady Blessington in 1832 to complain that in the *Journal of Conversations with Lord Byron* Lady Blessington had been far too lenient in her references to Lady Byron. Teresa had always been aware that most people associated with Byron would have known that their affair had cooled on his side long before he went to Greece, and that communications to her after that had been few and perfunctory and mainly through her brother Pietro Gamba, who had accompanied Byron. It was the woman who bore his name and gave birth to his child of whom he spoke on his death-bed, while she herself had not been mentioned, perhaps not even remembered. It is likely too, that Teresa had sometimes had to endure Byron meditating aloud about his wife as he was inclined to do, often with regret and sadness, and pent-up hatred and jealousy was poured into her book. Byron had called his wife his moral Clytemnestra in his poetry but Teresa Guiccioli alleged that Lady Byron was worse than Clytemnestra because the guilty one of antiquity only killed her lord:

… Lady Byron left her husband at the very moment that she saw him struggling amid a thousand shoals in the stormy sea of embarrassments created by his marriage … in vain did he, feeling his conscience at ease, implore some enquiry and examination. She refused; and the only favour she granted was to send him one fine day, two persons to see whether he were not mad … because she could not understand the possibility of tastes and habits different to those of ordinary routine, or of her own starched life … she was perhaps the only woman in the world so strangely organized, – the only one perhaps capable of not feeling happy and proud of belonging to a man superior to the rest of humanity; … An absolute moral monstrosity, an anomaly in the history of types of female hideousness, had succeeded in showing itself in the light of magnanimity. But false as was the high quality in Lady Byron, so did it shine out in him true and admirable. ...

The book consisted of 912 pages of which fifty-seven were concerned with Byron's marriage, so that Teresa's resentment against Lady Byron might have been understood and overlooked had not the reviews of the book reactivated the acrimonious controversy which lay just below the surface whenever the Byron separation was broached. It seemed as if the public suspected there was something they did not know and until they were enlightened, each side must be goaded and made to suffer abuse, which was now however directed mainly against Lady Byron. John Paget, a barrister, reviewed the book in the celebrated *Blackwood's* magazine. He began:

One of the most beautiful songs of Béranger is that addressed to his Lisette, in which he pictures her, in old age, narrating to a younger generation the loves of their youth; ... This charming picture has been realized in the case of a poet greater than Béranger, and by a mistress more famous than Lisette. The Countess Guiccioli has at length given to the world her *Recollections of Lord Byron* ... There is something inexpressibly touching in the picture of the old lady calling up the phantoms of half a century ago; not faded and stricken by the hand of time, but brilliant and gorgeous as they were when Byron, in his manly prime of genius and beauty, first flashed upon her enraptured sight. ...

The article closed by comparing Lady Byron with a murderer who uses subtle poisons to escape conviction, while expressing pity for her victim:

Lady Byron has been called 'The Moral Clytemnestra of her Lord'. 'The Moral Brinvilliers' would have been a truer designation. The conclusion at which we arrive is, that there is no proof whatever that Lord Byron was guilty of any act that need have caused a separation, or prevented a reunion, and that the imputations upon him rest on the vaguest conjecture; that whatever real or fancied wrongs Lady Byron may have endured are shrouded in an impenetrable mist of her own creation, – a poisonous miasma in which she enveloped the character of her husband, raised by her breath, and which her breath only could have dispersed.
'She dies and makes no sign, O God! forgive her.'

There were few words of defence for Lady Byron in England or America. Not all her friends were dead, but those that were left who knew the truth were silent, for they felt that they had been confided in and if she, who had been cruelly attacked during her life, had not spoken, then they should not speak now. One of the journalists who staunchly supported Lady Byron was Mrs Norton, granddaughter of the playwright Sheridan, herself one of the 'sick and hunted of the herd' as she described women who were separated from their husbands, and possibly she was influenced by her friend Lord Melbourne, Annabella's uncle. Ralph Lovelace reported Mrs Norton's commentary in *The Times* of 13 February 1869 to his sister: 'I send you *The Times* review of the Guiccioli Compilation – it is perhaps the ablest – it is too hostile to B. for my taste, although not so violent as the abuse of A.I.N.B. in the work itself.' Mrs Norton said that Mme de Boissy's book was a disappointment and only a mosaic of tessellated scraps from previous biographies and notices of Byron's life. She continued: 'Miss Chaworth is almost cursed in the violent blame expended upon her; her alienation of intellect and melancholy being openly indicated as a just judgement of Providence for having disappointed the passion of the lad of fifteen. ... Lady Byron is maligned with a persistent rancour so excessive, that astonishment almost supersedes indignation as we read.'

Harriet Beecher Stowe has been universally condemned because she felt compelled to write an article called 'The True Story of Lady Byron's Life' which was published simultaneously in the *Atlantic Monthly* and *Macmillan's Magazine*. Mrs Stowe remembered that Lady Byron had often spoken of Byron in their conversations and always with kindness and gentleness. It took a great deal of courage to speak up for Lady Byron at that time and Mrs Stowe, who was advised by her husband and son against getting involved, knew that by doing so she was jeopardizing her own reputation and literary fame. She had made no promise not to reveal the matters that had been deliberately divulged to her, and had she then advocated immediate disclosure, she felt sure her advice would have been considered. In any case she herself intended to have always remained silent but after Teresa Guiccioli's book appeared, she gave the matter much thought and concluded it was her duty to make known what she had been told in the interests of truth and justice.

The repercussions from her article were devastating, for not only were Lady Byron's enemies encouraged to fantasize and invent, but her friends and family were appalled and horrified at the revelation. Even in the contemporary relaxed climate of moral opinion, incest is not something that most people would wish to see made public and it was felt to be an unpardonable intrusion into family privacy. The only protest was a letter from Wharton & Ford, the solicitors, asserting that the slanders of a mistress against a wife should be treated with silent contempt, but the substance of the article was not denied.

Mrs Stowe was astounded at the public reaction against her and decided she must now write a book to explain in depth the 'simple story' that she had told in her article. The book was called *Lady Byron Vindicated. A History of the Byron Controversy* and was published in 1870. She was ill, it had to be dictated, and it was composed in a hurry, but the very artlessness of its bad construction and florid language seems to point to a sincere if misguided belief in her task. She was convinced that the endorsement of slanders and lies, which she believed them to be, by a reputable and long established periodical like *Blackwood's Magazine* should be confronted and challenged. If she who knew the truth kept silent now, how would future generations have the means of judging Lady Byron fairly? Many people believed Byron's repeated claim that he had not known what he was accused of when his wife refused to return, regardless of there being nothing to prevent his going to court to find out and, if he chose, to apply for restitution of conjugal rights. The law at that time was lenient to men in matrimonial disputes, and women had no rights even concerning their own children. Therefore it would have to be a very serious reason for condoning a wife who had left her husband, yet Byron dared not legally contest his wife's action, content to profess his ignorance of the charge against him by word of mouth.

Mrs Stowe said she had known nothing about Lady Byron's trustees until she was approached by them for letters concerning a proposed memoir of her friend which was later abandoned; nor did she know of the whereabouts of friends or family still alive, since it was ten years since she had had connections with England. She had hoped someone would come forward and refute the cruel accusations, or that extracts from Lady Byron's letters and papers would be published. 'Had this been done' she wrote 'I had been most happy to have remained silent. I have been astonished that anyone should have supposed this speaking on my part to be anything less than it is, – the severest act of self-sacrifice that one friend can perform for another, and the most solemn and difficult tribute to justice that a human being can be called upon to render.' In America, far from attempting to give Lady Byron a fair trial, the later editions of Thomas Moore's *Life of Byron* quietly omitted to include the 'Remarks' she had written in defence of her parents in 1830 although they were still included in the standard work published by John Murray in England.

It was Mrs Stowe's deeply held opinion that: 'Lord Byron belongs not properly to the Byrons or the Wentworths. He is not one of their family jewels to be locked up in their cases. He belongs to the world for which he wrote, to which he appealed, and before which he dragged his reluctant, delicate wife to a publicity equal with his own,' and therefore she had a right to be heard in challenging the publicly expressed calumnies of Byron's mistress against Lady Byron which were reinforced by hostile reviews.

In England the storm of abuse grew, some of it turning against Byron with the result that while some people refused to believe Mrs Stowe's allegation concerning Augusta and himself, they accused him of other crimes, for which there was no evidence, and which did him much greater and lasting harm. One delicate journalist wrote in *The Times* that he almost felt he would never open Byron's works again.

Abraham Hayward, a well-known journalist and lawyer of dubious repute, was retained by the *Quarterly Review* to protect the reputation of the Leigh family. He argued that Augusta must have been innocent of the charges made by Mrs Stowe because she was too old (she was twenty-nine in 1813) and too ugly, and her love for Byron was therefore of the maternal kind. Since Augusta, from most accounts, was a charming and attractive woman at that time, always preoccupied with 'Gauzes & Satinns', it is likely she would have been less then pleased with this theory.

Lord Lovelace committed the ultimate betrayal by offering Abraham Hayward perusal of some of Lady Byron's letters to Augusta from November 1815 to early 1816 which had unaccountably been left in his care. Phrases like 'It is my great comfort that you are in Piccadilly', 'You have been ever since I knew you, my best comforter' and 'though Heaven knows you have considered me more than a thousand would have done – more than anything but my affection for B., one most dear to you, could deserve' reveal the affectionate nature of the letters that Annabella was writing at the time to Augusta. The letters were generally assumed to have come from the Leigh family, and it was stated in the magazine that they were from 'legitimate sources' authenticated by the Earl of Chichester, Lord William Godolphin Osborne, and Mr George Leigh, Augusta's only surviving son. Lovelace also gave Hayward a malicious account of Lady Byron's conduct not only regarding the separation, about which his knowledge was scanty, but of her involvement with Medora in which he had taken a leading role, where every detail was discussed with him, his advice constantly sought and his safe used for Medora's precious papers. It is clear that the bitterness Lovelace had felt after losing Annabella's friendship still festered all these years afterwards. It is hardly surprising that in his letter to Abraham Hayward accompanying the papers he insisted on 'complete silence to every person, even those nearest to me, as to the source of this information'. Ralph's wife, Mary Lovelace, revealed in the book *Ralph Earl of Lovelace* which she wrote about her husband only that 'It suffices to say here that in 1893 a box containing extremely important papers ...' was found to have been in possession of William, Earl of Lovelace.

The Lord Chief Justice, Sir Alexander Cockburn, joined in the general disparagement of Lady Byron by writing to Hayward on 7 November 1869 expressing the view that she had had 'an ill-conditioned mind preying on itself till morbid delusion was the result; or that she was an accomplished hypocrite, regardless of truth, and to whose statements no credit whatever ought to be attached'. Curiously most of those attacking Lady Byron declared she had hallucinations and not that she was untruthful, possibly because it was more difficult to refute since, such was her reputation for integrity, few people would believe that she had lied.

Alfred Austin, a future poet laureate, whom Browning called 'a filthy little snob' wrote *A Vindication of Lord Byron* which was published in 1869. His defence of Byron rested on the presumption that it was quite impossible for Lady Byron to have acted towards Augusta in the way she did, had Augusta been guilty, which in any case would be difficult to prove; that when Byron had showed acute remorse, and told his wife he had a dreadful secret she had neither fled nor exposed him; that Augusta was given a presentation copy of 'Childe Harold' with the dedication 'To my dearest sister and my best friend, who has loved me much better than I deserved, this volume is presented by her father's son, and most affectionate brother'; that Augusta must have had a high standard of principles for she had objected on moral grounds to the publication of 'Don Juan'; that Lady Byron had allowed Augusta to live with money anxieties, quoting as evidence a letter from Augusta apologizing humbly and gracefully to the recipient for not paying her debt. Regrettably the writing of such letters had become for Augusta an art in which she excelled.

William Howitt, referred to by Austin as 'an impartial hand' not only wrote to the *Daily News* falsely declaring that Lady Byron was responsible for the destruction of Byron's memoirs, but he also subscribed an article to Austin's book describing the 'peculiar condition' of her nerves:

> I knew her for some years, and visited at her house in town, at her summer residence at Richmond, at Esher, and met her at the house of her son-in-law, Lord Lovelace, at Ockham. She also visited us at Esher and Highgate ... I have seen her of an evening in the most amiable, cordial, and sunny humour, full of interest and sympathy; and I have seen her the next morning come down as if she had lain all night not on a feather-bed, but on a glacier.

It would seem that Lady Byron had thought he was a friend. It obviously did not occur to the 'impartial hand' that she was prone to these upsetting attacks caused by a chronic illness.

In *Blackwood's* magazine John Paget criticized from a different angle, comparing Lady Byron with the most degraded of street-walkers in the Haymarket, giving preference to the latter, if she had known of Augusta's guilt and had remained publicly as well as privately friendly with her. When the sentiments of Paget and others are considered, the value of Lady Byron's silence is apparent and the disbelief with which Mrs Stowe's revelations were met showed that her silence had been virtually total. Augusta remained in court circles untouched by scandal and Byron, had he wished, could have returned to England at any time and taken a distinguished place in society. The letters published in the *Quarterly* convinced readers that Lady Byron could not have believed the allegations and yet have befriended Augusta so warmly and so openly. But if Augusta *had* been guilty, they said, then it had been Lady Byron's duty to have spoken out at the time of the separation, and thereby gained the respect of all in rendering a service for the good of mankind. They did not expound on the sacrifice of her own reputation that she had made, or the consequences for Byron and Augusta had she 'gained the respect of all'.

Mrs Minns, the maid who attended Annabella during her honeymoon and was now a spry old lady in her eighties, was located and interviewed by a correspondent from the *Newcastle Daily Chronicle*. She was born near Seaham, had known Annabella since her childhood, and had been her personal maid for ten years. She had left service to get married, and had given birth to a baby shortly before Annabella asked her if she would return after her marriage for the first few weeks of her honeymoon. Mrs Minns was her constant companion and confidante but because of a solemn promise to her mistress that she would never disclose any details of Byron's conduct, all that she would ever say was that 'it occasioned her the greatest distress'. Mrs Minns had advised Annabella to confide in her father and take his advice, but although this was considered, Annabella and her husband left for London and her parents remained unaware of the situation. Mrs Minns said: 'Lady Byron was by no means of a cold temperament but that the affectionate impulses of her nature were checked by the unkind treatment she experienced from her husband.'

There was one letter of support for Mrs Stowe which is given in full since it is seldom quoted:

To the Editor of *Macmillan's Magazine*

From the son of an employee of Sir Ralph Milbanke.

Sir, – I trust that you will hold me from any desire to be troublesome, or to rush into print. Both these things are far from my wish. But the publication of a book having for its object the vindication of Lord Byron's character, and the subsequent appearance in your magazine of Mrs Stowe's article in defence of Lady Byron having led to so much controversy in the various newspapers of the day, I feel constrained to put in a few words among the rest.

My father was intimately connected with Lady Byron's family for many years both before and after her marriage; being, in fact, steward to Sir Ralph Milbanke at Seaham, where the Marriage took place, and, from all my recollections of what he told me of the affair (and he used often to talk of it, up to the time of his death, eight years ago), I fully agree with Mrs Stowe's views of the case, and desire to add my humble testimony to the truth of what she has stated.

Whilst Byron was staying at Seaham previous to his marriage he spent most of his time pistol-shooting in the plantations adjoining the hall, often making use of his glove as a mark; his servant being with him to mark for him. When all was in readiness for the wedding ceremony (which took place in the drawing room of the hall) Byron had to be sought for in the grounds, where he was walking in his usual surly mood.

After the marriage, they posted to Halnaby Lodge in Yorkshire, a distance of about forty miles, to which place my father accompanied them and he always spoke strongly of Lady Byron's apparent distress during and at the end of the journey.

The insulting words mentioned by Mrs Stowe were spoken by Byron before leaving the park at Seaham; after which he appeared to sit in moody silence, reading a book, for the rest of the journey. At Halnaby, a number of persons, tenants and others, were met to cheer them on their arrival. Of these he took not the slightest notice, but jumped out of the carriage, and walked away, leaving his bride to alight by herself. She shook hands with my father, and begged that he would see that some refreshment was supplied to those who had thus come to welcome them.

I have in my possession several letters (which I should be glad to show to anyone interested in the matter) both from Lady Byron, and her mother, Lady Milbanke, to my father, all showing the deep and kind interest in the welfare of all connected with them, and directing the distribution of various charities, etc. Pensions were allowed both to the old servants of the Milbankes and to several poor persons in the village and neighbourhood for the rest of their lives; and Lady Byron never ceased to take a lively interest in all that concerned them.

I desire to tender my humble thanks to Mrs Stowe for having come forward in defence of one whose character has been much misrepresented and to you, sir, for having published the same in your pages.

I have the honour to be, Sir, your obediently, G.H. Aird.
Daourty, Northamptonshire
Sept. 29th, 1869.

Another man who knew that Mrs Stowe had written the truth was Thomas Smith, the solicitor who, twenty-six years before, in vainly trying to help Medora had asked her to write down an account of her life. He had carefully kept her autobriography and papers and in the interest of justice now gave it to Charles Mackay, editor of the *Illustrated London News*, who arranged for limited publication in 1869.

Astarte

Ralph Lovelace, Ada's son, had never been given any information concerning family secrets, nor had he heard any hints or rumours to suggest there were any, but he had become aware of them when he was about twenty-three through reading Byron's 'lines'. There was no means of verifying his suspicions as he did not then have access to Lady Byron's papers. Miss Mary Carpenter, one of the three trustees, the other two being Miss Frances Carr and Henry Allen Bathurst, was desirous of keeping control of the papers herself, visited London to examine them carefully and came to the conclusion that the papers contained a record of evil which should be burned and never disclosed. Ralph wrote a long letter to Mr Bathurst reminding him that they were 'strangers in blood' to Lord and Lady Byron and suggesting that he and his sister should be given more authority, but the trustees had to act in unison and there was a long delay while Miss Carpenter travelled in India.

After Lady Byron's death Ralph had been persuaded to consider writing a record of his grandmother's life, apart from the marriage and separation, by people to whom her memory was held in veneration. They spoke of her intellectual distinction, the rare nobility of her character, her enthusiasm and whole-hearted support of the projects she undertook, her liberal ideas and the magnetism of her personality. It was thought her true character could be shown through her letters and the papers of such well-known people as Harriet Martineau, Florence Nightingale, Henry Crabb Robinson and the many other interesting men and women she had known. But he had first to reconcile their portrayal, and the tender guardian of his youth that he remembered, with the hateful impression left by Byron of his Clytemnestra and unforgiving wife. He had to find out why there was such a wave of dislike towards her after Mrs Stowe's book was published, and why his father, from whom he was estranged, bore her such resentment. Early in 1869 he had been given by Mr Villiers Lister of the Foreign Office some of the letters written by Lady Byron to Mrs Villiers in 1816 as well as some very confidential letters of a later period. 'Which gives precise information on everything' he told his sister (17 March 1869) 'I find that Augusta is not put in too painful a light for publication if it is decided to publish the facts at all – Augusta's character is more sympathetic through what I have read than from what I knew before – but a character not to be trusted'.

It was a difficult period for Ralph. He had married Fanny Heriot in 1869 but the marriage was unsuccessful. He was angry at Mrs Stowe's disclosures, feeling she had had no right to make them. His sister, who was called Anne after her marriage to Wilfrid Scawen Blunt in 1869, and like Ralph had guessed the secret from Byron's poetry, was horrified when 'the odious Stowe pamphlet' was published, because her adored grandmother had it seemed, con-fided the secret of her marriage to such a vulgar woman as she deemed Mrs Stowe to be. However she considered it was best to establish the truth now so that the subject could be laid to rest and a new generation would not inherit the worry and distress that she and her brother had endured. She questioned her father, but he became evasive and pointed out that the only witness to Mrs Stowe's allegations was her grandmother. Her husband wrote to Dr Lush-ington's son Godfrey hoping that through him some facts could be elicited but Godfrey Lushington dare not question his father, who was now an old man and had been deeply grieved at the scurrilous nature of the libels that had been made on Lady Byron's name. Anne herself then wrote to Dr Lushington who did not reply, and for a time she was unhappily swayed by her father against her grand-mother, who, she thought, must have been mistaken in her beliefs and should not have told anyone of them.

Dr Lushington had always had a high regard for Lady Byron which had only increased with time and intimacy. He had written a letter to his sister-in-law a few months before Ada died in 1852 when Annabella was surrounded by difficulties and sorrow:

> If there be a wonderful person in this world it is Lady NB: her energy of mind, her bodily exertions, the strength of her affection, the cool decision of her judgement, all increase instead of diminishing by the continued severity of the trial – I am in boundless admiration of her – of her heart intellect and governed mind – Most brightly she shines in this dark shade of Affliction –.

His inability, despite his widespread fame and exceptional talents, to influence those who misconstrued her unselfish actions, which he had foreseen and warned her against, imbued in him a bitter sense of failure which he would discuss with no one.

In 1872 Ralph was beset by further anxieties. His home was broken up, his wife had incurred serious debts, he failed to get the divorce he desired and he was haunted by the recollection of a scrupulously truthful woman who was being publicly arraigned for propagating the vilest calumnies against her husband, yet he who had lived with her since he was nine had never heard her say one word that could hurt Byron's name. Ralph was by nature deeply reserved. For years he had been drawn to the Catholic religion but had hesitated through reluctance to accept the confessional, and the idea of corroborating an opprobrious statement which he felt was wickedly made even if it were true, was profoundly repugnant. He did not have a free hand, for the trustees and the descendants were divided in opinion on what were the right measures to take, and all were influenced by Dr Lushington whose counsel, as it had been for so many years, was to postpone revelations.

It was Leslie Stephen who precipitated Ralph's decision to start his crusade for justice. Leslie Stephen was made editor in 1882 of the proposed *Dictionary of National Biography*, the first volume of which was published in January 1885. He made many literary contributions himself and had written a long feature on Byron containing the words: 'It can only be surmised that Lady Byron had become jealous of Byron's public and pointed expressions of love for his sister, contrasted so forcibly with his utterances about his wife, and in brooding over her wrongs had developed the hateful suspicions communicated to Mrs Stowe and as it seems to others.'

It was not that this was so dissimilar to the other disparagements of his grandmother, but this time it was made by a man whom Ralph knew to be a man of honour and integrity and who insisted on unbiased fact in the articles submitted to him for inclusion in the Dictionary. Eventually Ralph had gained possession of most of the letters and papers and had begun the task of reading and sorting. He found that 'Lady Byron's veracity was undeviating – And whenever she had to speak of Mrs Leigh she adhered throughout most accurately to such information as she possessed'. When Leslie Stephen was shown these papers he completely changed his views and wrote a statement on 18 December 1887 for Ralph authorizing the rejection of his previous judgement, but he died before a correction could be made in the next edition of the Dictionary. It is possible that his public slur on Lady Byron's character, which he later found was totally mistaken, contributed to the nervous illness which led to a breakdown in 1889. However he helped and advised Ralph in collecting and arranging some of the letters between Lady Byron and Augusta to form the book *Lady Noel Byron and the Leighs*. In 1887 thirty-six copies were printed for distribution solely to members of the family. Ralph wrote at the end: 'The only object has been to put on record some part of the truth of the relations between Lady Byron and her sister-in-law – and this being done, the subject is best left "homily undelivered".' But he knew he had not done enough.

Two years after the death of his first wife in 1878, Ralph married Mary Caroline Stuart-Wortley. She described in the memoir she wrote of her husband, the intolerable guilt he had felt at not having discharged 'a sacred obligation' to publish a statement following Mrs Stowe's revelations, which would, he believed, have made impossible the allegations against Lady Byron which had followed. She recalled that he was never to forget the bitter experience of the publicity engendered by Mrs Stowe's book which finally galvanized him into starting his investigations:

> It must have been in the course of the winter of 1899–1900 that a scene took place which remains vividly in my mind [Mary Lovelace wrote] My husband was walking up and down the room, trying to ease the fever of his soul by talking out the everlasting dilemma … how to hide the faults of one ancestor without doing black injustice to another … how to suppress truth without adding to a mountain of lies. I was listening for the hundredth time with indescribable weariness and in secret revolt at the sacrifice of *his* life – he wound up his complaints with: 'Oh! if only I could have peace!'. And I, thinking aloud rather than intending to suggest any definite action exclaimed: 'There will never be peace till the truth has once for all been acknowledged.' He wheeled round in his walk and faced me: 'Ah! you think so, do you?' And I realized that my words had confirmed the thought that was already formed in his own mind.

Ralph now had possession of all the letters and papers that had belonged to Lady Byron including the box of letters that Hayward had seen which had been found in his father's custody after his death in 1893. He also had had access to, and had copied some years before, Byron's letters to Lady Melbourne which were inherited by Hobhouse's daughter Lady Dorchester. She had recommended that these letters were published without the passages referring to Byron's love for Augusta. Further packets of letters from Augusta had also come to light. Although there could no longer be any doubt about his suspicions, a decision about what he should do was not easy, for there were a number of people involved, all with different proposals and opinions.

In 1896 Colonel Murray, the publisher, had asked Ralph to be editor-in-chief of a new edition of Byron's poems and letters. Ralph however became increasingly dissatisfied with the situation owing firstly to the prevailing sense of urgency due to a competitor who had similar designs, and secondly to a misunderstanding with Murray over the permission for copying and printing Ralph's letters, and he therefore resigned from the undertaking. There was further irritation when the third volume of letters and journals edited by Rowland Prothero appeared in July 1899, for in *The Times* review there was a statement to the effect that no evidence existed to prove the precise nature of the charges on which Lady Byron separated from her husband. To Ralph this was an 'amazing statement' and there followed an acrimonious correspondence with Colonel Murray, conducted through his friend and legal advisor Mr Francis Smith.

At last Ralph overcame his reserve and felt able to begin the tragic story of his close ancestors, amply supported by letters and extracts from Annabella's unfinished narrative of her life. Ralph's book was finally completed and published in 1905 with the title *Astarte*. He had intended it to be limited to private circulation only, anxious not to benefit financially from the sad story of his ancestors, but for copyright reasons it was necessary to print two hundred copies. Ralph had been strongly influenced by Leslie Stephen's hope that as few as possible of 'poor Mrs Leigh's very painful letters' should be included, with the result that the evidence did not appear to be as conclusive as the correspondence he possessed proved that it was.

Initially the book was praised and among those who wrote to Ralph were Algenon Swinburne who said that scribbling strangers had made him write it but it was a matter for congratulation that it was admirably discharged; Henry James wrote that it was very good because it did not give special pleading or yield to temptation to dress Lady Byron in any graces in any shape or colour; the Hon. John Fortescue, king's librarian at Windsor Castle wrote: 'Yours should be, and I hope, will be the last word upon the subject.' Lady Ritchie (daughter of W.M. Thackeray) wrote: 'No one will ever misjudge Lady Byron again. Death has come with its oblivion and all is over' and the granddaughter of Mrs Villiers wrote: 'It makes me like & even understand Byron better than I ever did before.' This was what Ralph had intended, was the reason for his writing the book and why he had aimed at telling truthfully what had happened. It was his grandfather as well as his grandmother whom he was writing about. He was concerned only with doing justice to the memory of his ancestors, and attempting to still the venomous tongues of the ignorant, with as little injury as possible to Augusta.

When Ralph died suddenly six months later however, unfavourable criticisms of *Astarte* were made. It created a greater furore than Mrs Stowe's book had done since it was not so easy to dismiss as lies and was by no means welcomed for revealing the truth. Rowland Prothero, later Lord Ernle, author of *Letters and Journals of Lord Byron* and the leading Byronic scholar at that time, who had seen and studied what came to be known as the Lovelace Papers, wrote in a book privately printed by John Murray in 1906:

> Lord Lovelace has industriously raked from the muck heap a number of cases of such an attachment as that which he charges against his grandfather. But he has not done his scavengering fairly. He has suppressed the only case which is really pertinent. Byron was not the man to be outdone by his father. His possession of certain letters, written by his father, Captain Byron, to his own sister and the knowledge of their contents would spur him on to boast ... of a similar vice.

Ralph's hope that his book, revealing the truth of what had happened in the past, would end the distasteful rumours surrounding an episode which had caused great suffering in his family, was misplaced and the denials continued. On 4 December 1911 Marie Belloc noted in her diary, after dining with the Protheros, that not only did Rowland Prothero acknowledge that he had known the truth, but she observed: 'How odd that the Murrays won't admit it, even to this day, and that they persist in publishing books to prove the whole story is untrue.' She might have been even more surprised to read in *Lord Byron Accounts Rendered* by Doris Langley Moore:

> The accusations of incest even Byron's half incest as Lord Lovelace correctly called it – was considered inexpressibly dreadful; if it had to be made at all (and hardly anyone could see why it should) it was

enough that it had been made against the poet and Augusta. The general verdict was that it had been in extremely bad taste for a man to present a case against a distinguished grandfather for the sake of defending a grandmother whom nobody was attacking and that there was no need to multiply such disclosures.

Conceivably Byron, who had written his memoirs and expressed the hope that they would not be added to, so that no lies were told after he was dead, would have despaired of those who professed to be his friends but were afraid to face the truth.

The second edition of *Astarte* was published in 1921, fifteen years after Ralph's death, to which Ralph's wife, Mary, Countess of Lovelace added extra letters in the interest of clarity. She wrote in the introduction: 'Those who know the pain and travail of mind with which it was produced, and how distasteful to the author was the duty of clearing away once for all the cloud of calumnies and injustices which had settled round certain facts, feel that the time has come for defending his memory.'

Ralph Lovelace has not been given the recognition he should have for writing *Astarte* because it is commonly believed that Byron's personality is so blended with his poetry that to seem to dishonour his moral character is to prejudice his literary reputation and judge his genius by principles of behaviour. Lady Byron, who knew his imperfections as a man better than anyone, had consistently recognized Byron's incomparable genius. She gave a copy of 'Childe Harold's Pilgrimage' to Ralph when he was fifteen years old, with the inscription:

To the Grandson of Byron
Glory in the Poetry, study the philosophy, but mistrust
the Personality. Sept 6th 1854.

Ralph made no judgement. He gave every mitigating circumstance and he was scrupulously fair. He would have much preferred to follow his Alpine and scholarly pursuits. Mrs Stowe, then at the height of her literary fame, could have had no possible personal gain from writing scandal, as her book in defence of Lady Byron was deemed, and it lost her many readers. Neither book would have been written had Teresa Guiccioli not attacked Lady Byron so violently in her book. The statement often made that Lady Byron spent her life collecting evidence against Byron can hardly be true. She had, as advised by Mrs Stowe, arranged what seemed an impenetrable safeguard for her papers against intrusion from any source including her own descendants, and this would indeed have never been breached, had the trustee Mary Carpenter had her way. However, many people will argue that to deny this part of Byron, who hated hypocrisy and proclaimed his love for Augusta to the world in his poetry, would be a very great misfortune for his readers.

Had the young Augusta been less well cared for by Mrs Byron she would have undoubtedly died and thus played no part in Byron's life. Annabella might have learned to 'govern' Byron but then, he had said, there would have been no more poetry.

By such threads of chance are destinies woven.

Short Bibliography

Blessington, Countess of, *A Journal of Conversations with Lord Byron*, 1834 (William Veazie, Boston, 1858)

Bos, Charles du, *Byron and the Need of Fatality* (Putnam, London & New York, 1931)

Elwin, Malcolm, *Lord Byron's Wife* (Macdonald & Co, London, 1962, reissued by John Murray, London, 1974)

Elwin, Malcolm, *Lord Byron's Family* (John Murray, London, 1975)

Gunn, Peter, *My Dearest Augusta* (The Bodley Head, London, 1968)

Lovelace, Countess of, *Ralph, Earl of Lovelace, A Memoir* (Christophers, London, 1920)

Marchand, Leslie, A., *Byron: A Portrait* (John Murray, London, 1971)

Marchant, Leslie A., *Byron's Letters and Journals* (John Murray, London, 1973–82)

Maurois, André, *Byron* (Jonathan Cape, London, 1930)

Mayne, Ethel Colburn, *Byron* (Methuen & Co, London, 1912)

Mayne, Ethel Colburn, *The Life and Letters of Anne Isabella, Lady Noel Byron* (Constable & Co, London, 1929)

Moore, Doris Langley, *The Late Lord Byron* (John Murray, London, 1961)

Moore, Doris Langley, *Ada, Countess of Lovelace* (John Murray, London, 1977)

Moore, Thomas, *The Life, Letters and Journals of Lord Byron* (John Murray, London, 1830)

Parry, William, *The Last Days of Lord Byron* (Knight & Lacey, London, 1825)

Stowe, Harriet Beecher, *Lady Byron Vindicated* (Sampson Low & Son, London, 1870)

Turney, Catherine, *Byron's Daughter: A Biography of Elizabeth Medora Leigh* (Peter Davies, London, 1974)

Wentworth, Lord, *Lady Byron and the Leighs* (William Clowes and Sons Ltd, London, 1887)

Wentworth, Lord, *Astarte*. Ed. Mary, Countess of Lovelace (Christophers, London, 1921)

Index

Doyle, Adelaide, 227
Doyle, Colonel Francis, 96, 174–5, 176, 198, 204
Doyle, Selina, 93, 204, 227, 260, 287
Drury, Henry, 165, 166, 167
Duff, Mary, 31–2
Durham, 76

Ealing Grove School, 192–6
Eden, George, Lord Auckland, 22–3, 44, 133
Eden, Revd William, 185
Edleston, John, 34–5, 120
educational reform, 183, 188, 189–96
  in Switzerland, 183, 189–92
Elemore Hall, Durham, 17
Euboea, 285, 286–7

Fellenberg, Emanuel de, 183, 189, 191, 192
Fellenberg, Frederick de, 285
Fenwick, Dr, 51, 68
Fleming, Wilmington, 182
Fletcher (Byron's valet), 39, 89, 171, 174, 211–12
Fordhook House, 192, 196
Foster, Augustus, 26
Fox, Henry Edward, 217
Frend, Sophia, 210
Frend, William, 20, 189

Gamba, Count, 158, 159, 160
Gamba, Pietro, 158, 159, 160, 314
Genoa, 160
Giraud, Nicolo, 39, 120
Glennie, Dr, 29–30
Godwin, Mary, 151
Gosford, Lord, 189, 258
Gosford, Mary, 25, 48, 56, 57, 134, 258
Gosford, Olivia, 258–9
Greece, 163, 285, 286
Greig, Woronzow, 206, 241, 244, 263
Guiccioli, Teresa, 156, 158, 160, 162, 163, 217, 313–15, 329

Halliday, Sophia, 207
Halnaby Hall, Yorks, 18, 76, 205–6
Hanson, John, 29, 33, 40, 66–7, 89, 155
Hanson, Newton, 155
Harrow Church, 164–70
Harrow School, 30–3, 193–4
Hayter, G., 26
Hayward, Abraham, 318
Henkels, Bernard, 207

Hobhouse, John Cam
  accompanies Byron to Europe, 37–8
  visits Seaham with Byron, 75
  attitude to marriage breakdown, 99
  hints at Byron's homosexuality, 119–20
  Annabella's views on, 142
  travels with Byron in exile, 152–3
  attitude to Memoirs, 171–4, 176
  asked to help Fletcher, 211, 212
  fails to help Medora Leigh, 229, 233
  commissions Byron's statue, 245–6
  other mentions, 33, 40, 109, 116, 182, 185, 310
Hodgson, Francis, 34, 35, 99, 113, 209, 211
Hofwyl school, 183, 189–92, 285
Holderness, Lady, 28, 33
Hoppner, Richard, 154, 164
Horton, Robert Wilmot, 174, 175
Howitt, William, 176–7, 320
Hughes, Sir John, 229–30, 231, 232
Hunter, John, 28

Jameson, Anna, 224, 226, 233, 236–9, 245, 250, 267–8, 269, 280, 310
Jocelyn, Lord, 26

King, Annabella (granddaughter of Annabella), 195, 208, 250, 306, 307, 309, 324
King, Dr, 187, 227, 296
King, Lord, see Lovelace, Earl of
Kinnaird, Douglas, 184
Kirkby Mallory Hall, 90, 123, 139, 149, 266, 281–5
Knight, Mrs Gally, 51

Lamb, Lady Caroline, 17, 25, 42, 44–5, 61, 119, 182
Lamb, Mrs George ('Caro George'), 25, 102, 103, 201, 208
Lapeyre, France, 230, 231
Lawrence, Arabella, 195
Le Mann, Dr, 89, 93
Leeds, Duke of, 229, 233
Leigh, Augusta (half-sister of Byron)
  birth, 27–8
  early acquaintance with Byron, 33
  feelings at Byron's marriage, 76
  relations with Byron & Lady Byron during their marriage, 81–91
  relationship with Byron, 101, 105–13, 121
  duplicity, 122, 124–5
  relations with Annabella after separation,